SYSTEMS OF TREATMENT FOR THE MENTALLY ILL

SYSTEMS OF TREATMENT FOR THE MENTALLY ILL
Filling the Gaps

Richard E. Gordon, M.D., Ph.D.
Associate Professor of Psychiatry and Psychology
University of Florida
Gainesville, Florida

Katherine K. Gordon, R.N., M.A.
Project Manager
Career Education for Mental Health Workers Project
Human Resources Institute
University of South Florida
Tampa, Florida

GRUNE & STRATTON
A Subsidiary of Harcourt Brace Jovanovich, Publishers
New York   London   Toronto   Sydney   San Francisco

Library of Congress Cataloging in Publication Data

Gordon, Richard E
    Systems of treatment for the mentally ill.

    Bibliography: p.
    Includes index.
    1. Mental health services—United States. 2. Psy-
chotherapy—United States. I. Gordon, Katherine K.,
joint author. II. Title. [DNLM: 1. Mental disorders—
Therapy. 2. Mental health services—Manpower. WM 400
S995]
RA790.6.G67   362.2'0973   80-27491
ISBN 0-8089-1338-7

Grune & Stratton, Inc.
111 Fifth Avenue
New York, New York 10003

Distributed in the United Kingdom by
Academic Press Inc. (London) Ltd.
24/28 Oval Road, London NW 1

Library of Congress Catalog Number 80-27491
International Standard Book Number 0-8089-1338-7
Printed in the United States of America

Contents

v

    Morton Cohen, Jeffrey R. Bedell, Lawrence Weathers,
    Susan Fertig, Julia Adams, Richard E. Gordon, and
    Katherine K. Gordon   63
    Unit Dose Procedure
    Periodic Review of Medications
    Single Daily Dose Regimen
    Polypharmacy Reduction
    Decreased Use of Concentrates
    Cost Efficiency
    Self-Medication Training
    Implementing Self-Medication Training

5. Measuring Progress in Psychiatric Treatments and Programs
    with Proficiency Gauges and Psychosocial Rating Scales
        Richard E. Gordon, Carolyn J. Hursch, Phillip W. Drash,
        Joseph W. Evans, and Katherine K. Gordon   73
    Psychoeducational Assessment
    Theoretical Framework
    Psychosocial Data Collection
    Developing Proficiency Gauges
    Reliability and Validity of Proficiency Gauges

6. Filling the Gaps in the Treatment of the Individual Patient   93
    Biomedical Model
    Behavioral Model
    Psychosocial Model
    Psychodynamic Model

7. Using Psychotherapeutic Games to Train Patients' Skills
        Lawrence Weathers, Jeffrey R. Bedell, Herbert Marlowe,
        Richard E. Gordon, Julia Adams, Valerie Reed, Jo Palmer,
        and Katherine K. Gordon   109
    Format of Games
    Communication Games
    Problem-Solving Games
    Assertion Games
    Self-Medication Games

                    PART B: IMPROVING MORALE AND
                    PERFORMANCE OF STAFF   125

    Manpower Problems in the Public Mental Health Sector
    Integrating Systems of Management and Education

Contents

vii

Acknowledgments

Many persons have contributed to the ideas and research described herein. Whenever possible, they have been given credit. Collaborating authors have reviewed the chapters in the sections describing their program areas. All deserve credit for the chapters where their names appear. Others whose work is described—students, faculty, and staff who did not participate in the actual writing—are mentioned in the references.

We would like to especially thank a number of persons who participated in the program from the earliest stages. Special credit goes to Dr. Stuart Cahoon, who, as Director of Mental Health in Florida, provided us with the opportunity to perform this work; to five psychologists—Roger Patterson, Director of the Gerontology Program, Phil Drash, Director of the Child-Adolescent Program, Jeffrey R. Bedell, Director of the Adult Program, Henry Bates, Associate Director of the Child-Adolescent Program, and Eileen Edmunson, Director of the Community Network Development; to a social worker—Art Slater, Director of the Career Education for Mental Health Workers Project; to three nurses—Virginia Cuthbert, Maxine Hatcher, and Susan Fertig; to two physicians—Manuel Alvarez and Alvaro Restrepo; to an activities therapist—Judy Quick; to two educators—Shirley Redcay and Herbert Marlowe; to an engineer—David Eberly; to a gerontologist—Michael O'Sullivan; to an occupational therapist—Tamara Harrell; to an administrator—Elnomac Creel; to a pharmacist—Morton Cohen; to a medical records librarian—Carol Foster; and to many office personnel—Lill Barry, Betty Alfonso, Audrey Weislo, Helen Spurgeon, and Martha Miller, in particular. Our thanks go to Sue Kirkpatrick, who typed the final draft of the manuscript, and Lucinda Hagler, who did likewise with the references.

Many others have contributed in various ways. Dean Travis Northcutt of the College of Social and Behavioral Sciences at the University of South Florida provided valuable support and counsel; Drs. Lewis Bowman of the Political Science Department and James Anker of Psychology have helped in many ways, as have President John Lott Brown of the University of South Florida and Dr. Anthony Reading, Chairman of the Department of Psychiatry. We appreciate the help given by staff in Florida's Department of Health and Rehabilitative Services, including in particular that from the following persons: Jamil Amin, Robert Ashburn, John Awad, Bennie Barnes, George Clarke, Robert Constantine, Robert Furlough, Ernie Haar, Peter Ivory, Peter Kreis, David Pingry, Robert Roberts, Alvin Taylor, and Helen Williams. The following staff, students, and others helped carry out and report on the treatment, training and education, research and evaluation, and dissemination services: Julia Adams, Kathy Amuso, Robert Archer, Adlai Boyd, Carla Dee, Lawrence Dupree, Lisa Dworkin, Joseph Evans, Dennis Ford, Robert Friedman, Rick Gordon, David Hung, Gary Jackson, Suzette Lavandera, Mark Lefkowitz, Margaret Malchon, James Messina, Valerie Reed, Katherine Reed, David Sanders, Gail Smith, Edwin Solomon, Beverley Standahl, Lawrence Weathers, and Richard Weinberg. Albert Rust provided statistical analyses and Marilyn Stegner provided illustrations.

We are especially grateful to a number of colleagues who helped make this work possible in a variety of ways: Dr. John E. Adams, Chairman of the Department of Psychiatry at the University of Florida provided Dr. Gordon with leave from his University duties. Drs. Frank Riessman and Alan Gartner of the City University of New York, and Robert Slotnick and Abe Jeger of the New York Institute of Technology have published a number of our papers and monographs. Dr. Jules Masserman, former President of the American Psychiatric Association, requested and published an early work on modular psychiatric treatment in volume 19 of *Current Psychiatric Therapies.* Dr. John Talbott has been an inspiration and a guide. Drs. Gail Barton, George Adams, and Alan Beigel, of the Program Committee of the American Psychiatric Association, requested that we develop and teach a course and symposia on components of the new systems of care at annual meetings of the American Psychiatric Association. Drs. Howard Davis of the National Institute for Mental Health and Harold McPheeters of the Southern Regional Educational Board have continually provided guidance and support, as have Vernon James and Donald Fisher of the National Institute of Mental Health. Dr. McPheeters reviewed an early draft of this book. Dr. Philip Phillips, delegate from the Florida Psychiatric Society to the Assembly of the American Psychiatric Association, has repeatedly offered sound critical advice and encouragement. Drs. McKinley Cheshire, David Cheshire, Ronald Shellow, Lloyd Wilder, Stanley Holzberg, George Metcalf, Betty Metcalf, Virginia Haggerty, Norbert Skoja, and many other psychiatric, psychological, and nursing colleagues offered ideas and support.

In establishing these programs we sought to comply with standards set by the Joint Commission on Accreditation of Hospitals. In particular, we required staff to provide written descriptions of policies, programs, and procedures. Before being implemented, treatment plans, research designs, training manuals, dissemination strategies, and other materials were developed, discussed, and modified internally and by colleagues elsewhere. Outcomes of treatment, research, and training were measured, tested, and evaluated in terms of these predeveloped written procedures. Progress reports, minutes of proceedings, and other manuscripts provide a record of staff activities. Some of these documents are included in the appendix. Wherever possible, the persons responsible for developing the reports, procedures, manuals, or documents are credited by reference or authorship. However, since many of these materials do not bear authors' names or initials, or were written by a variety of individuals over time, some persons who deserve credit may inadvertantly have been overlooked. If so, we regret the omission, and recognize their contribution here.

Slater, Bowman, K. Gordon, Redcay, Bedell, and Marlowe produced course modules and edited monographs and other publications that received widespread dissemination. Examples of these materials appear in the appendix.

In cooperation with staff from Florida's Mental Health Program Office, faculty from the University of South Florida, personnel from Florida's Community College programs, and colleagues from the Florida Mental Health Institute, we wrote Title XX training and NIAAA research grants and obtained funding both for expanding the gerontology program and for statewide training and dissemination of new treatment techniques. Personnel at the state mental hospitals, trained in part under these grants, and in the Career Education for Mental Health Workers Project (Grant Number 5T41MH 14150, National Institute of Mental Health), have successfully implemented many of the innovative treatments described in the following chapters, including the entire gerontology program in two public mental institutions in the state.

Title XX training funds paid for part of the tuition of staff trainees at the state hospitals, for the development of treatment and training manuals (some examples of which are presented in the appendix), and for the support of students and staff, as well as that of visiting faculty from the University of South Florida, including Darrell Bostow, Jerry Koehler, Louis Penner, and Frank Sistrunck. These faculty helped develop training, dissemination, and evaluation materials, and helped analyze the evaluation data reported here. Examples of some of their work performed with Title XX grant funds appear in Chapters 5, 13, and 15. We appreciate their help and that of Joan Piroch and Nancy Goldstein, who also worked under Richard Gordon's direction and on these grants; they upgraded the quality of gerontology training manuals and other reports, and prepared them for public dissemination and use.

Preface

The innovations presented herein are products of a continuing effort since the early 1950s to combine behavioral, social psychological, educational, psychopharmacologic, and psychodynamic therapies, together with evaluative methodologies and new management techniques, in the treatment and prevention of mental disorders. Unlike our previous works, *The Split-Level Trap, The Prevention of Postpartum Emotional Difficulties,* and *The Blight on the Ivy,* which reported results of studies that we carried out personally, the current volume compiles findings from joint efforts conducted with many collaborators.

This volume is for a wide audience: for mental health professional and paraprofessional practitioners, especially those who wish to learn new methods of treating the chronic mental patient; for administrators, public officials, and policy makers who bear the responsibility for planning and financing the care of the mentally ill; for psychoeducators and their students who are preparing to provide combined treatments; for third party payers, accrediting agencies, and others who evaluate the quality and comprehensiveness of treatment programs; for patients and their families who want to know what treatments are available so that they may seek out programs that best suit their needs; for researchers who wish to evaluate the procedures described in their own independent studies; and for the general reader who wishes to learn about the power of modular psychoeducational, behavioral, and peer management and support therapies to correct behavioral abnormalities.

The main themes, as presented in the chapters that follow, but not necessarily in order of their importance, are the following: (1) Current psychiatric treatment of the chronic mental patient is fragmented, and persons and organizations who provide various services in hospitals and communities spend much time guarding their turf and not reaching out to meet the needs of the patient. (2) Patients require more than medications, behavior modification, and dynamic psychotherapy; they need training in techniques of coping, building their psychosocial skills, and obtaining human supports in the community; many need assistance with housing and other help from organizations and agencies; these needs are not provided by many mental health professionals and programs. (3) Paraprofessionals, the patients themselves, and families can be taught to fill many of the gaps in the services that patients require. (4) Programs can be developed that meet the unserved needs of patients with present resources. (5) Psychiatrists and other mental health professionals supervise and monitor combined treatments for hospital inpatients, and provide consultation and professional care when needed in community programs for enhancing outpatient skills and supports. (6) Mental health administrators and policy makers can implement these combined treatment methods in their own mental health systems without major new expenditures of funds. (7) Program directors can establish an atmosphere of high morale, strong motivation, and good cooperation among all levels and disciplines of staff.

The programs described herein train not only patients and their families but also community agency staff, teachers, and managers of foster homes and congregate living facilities. These comprehensive programs of services augment traditional methods in the treatment and rehabilitation of the chronically ill child, adolescent, adult, and elderly mental patient. They combine management of the acute manifestations of mental illness, time-limited hospital treatment to control the early stages of illness, modular psychoeducational and peer management inpatient programs to overcome basic skill deficits as well as effects of repeated institutionalizations, standardized assessments to present patients' skill and support deficits on graphs and to evaluate progress of both individual patients and of programs, training for placement in community living facilities, preparation for participating in community peer-support networks, and development of aftercare programs that maintain and enhance patient gains from residential treatment.

The programs for adult patients provide components for the integrated treatment model presented in Chapter 2 and schematized in Figure 2-1. The children's and elderly patients' projects diverge somewhat from this model: behavior management, formal education, and family and foster parent training are emphasized with young children, rather than peer management and support; projects for elderly patients concentrate on placing them in appropriate community housing after skills training, rather than on teaching them job skills and peer management and support.

All the programs illustrate integrated treatment and training approaches for community personnel, which are conducted by treatment facility staff whose primary job descriptions call for them to provide inpatient services. In addition to performing the latter, these staff, most of whom are paraprofessional mental health workers, reach out from their residential treatment facility and overcome the isolation and fragmentation in mental health and human services. Staff train expatients and community agency and other personnel to conduct an integrated patient-care system. Private practitioners join in these integrated services; they refer their private patients for skills and support training, while they themselves continue to provide medical and insight treatment and other psychiatric care in their own offices.

The programs described here were implemented from 1975 through 1979. During that period Richard Gordon took a leave of absence from the Departments of Psychiatry and Clinical Psychology of the University of Florida in order to serve as Director of the newly established Florida Mental Health Institute, and planned and supervised the development and implementation of the treatment, training, management, evaluation, and dissemination programs described here. Katherine Gordon left the Student Mental Health Services of the University of Florida to serve during this period as Coordinator of the Career Education for Mental Health Workers Project at the University of South Florida, on whose campus the Florida Mental Health Institute is located, and played a major role in designing and establishing the modular training, educational, and dissemination programs described, as well as in originating the graphic methods of presenting standardized guages of patient's proficiency and progress in skill development for inclusion in their clinical charts.

Although we worked in Florida, and many of the descriptions of the fragmented mental health program are taken from a Harvard University study of the state's public service agency, the problems are widespread. We have quoted many authorities who describe a similar atmosphere of chaos in the care of the chronic mental patient throughout much of the nation; our personal observations on visits to many public and private psychiatric facilities in other states, and in attendance at national psychiatric meetings reaffirm their reports. We believe that the descriptions of problems and their solutions apply to many public and private systems of mental health services; we suggest that state and private hospitals can use similar techniques to those developed in Florida for filling gaps in the care they provide. For this reason we do not refer specifically to the Florida Mental Health Institute by name throughout the main body of this book, but speak of programs developed by a research and training (R&T) facility or center that are suitable for wide dissemination.

Systems of Treatment for the Mentally Ill describes how to integrate a number of different treatment approaches into a combined whole. It shows what can be done, presents examples that give the reader an indication of the nature of each new treatment and how it is delivered, and provides data that point to the benefits of the combined approach. This book is not a cookbook, however; it does not purport to teach in fine detail how to conduct each form of treatment. We hope that it will provide an example that will help mental health systems to modify their treatment programs and yet avoid some of the strains and turmoil associated with major change and reorganization. What was done in one system with difficulty can possibly be accomplished in others with less strain and discomfort.

It was the policy of the Florida Mental Health Institute and the Career Education for Mental Health Workers Project at the University of South Florida during our tenures in those organizations that all training and evaluation materials, reports on findings, procedural manuals, and other similar documents receive early publication and wide dissemination for public use. Much of the data summarized here have been published elsewhere in the scientific literature or reported in public presentations. References are provided for those readers who wish to examine the data, methodology, and other issues in greater detail.

The book includes a number of illustrative examples of methods used in treating patients, in coping with psychopolitics, and in administering a research and training facility. As we have done in our previous books to protect individual privacy, we have disguised and fictionalized names, life events, and other identifying characteristics of patients and other persons involved in the incidents used to illustrate the various principles discussed. Most case histories are composites. Any similarity to any persons living or dead is unintentional.

The findings and conclusions reported here are by no means our last word on the subjects. These studies are part of continuing investigations. New results will cause us to modify our views. Because some of the treatment programs described here have been underway for only brief periods, their data are preliminary. Subsequent publication will report new findings. However, there can be little doubt, based upon today's information, that programs that integrate the wide range of treatments, management techniques, evaluative methods, and educational procedures described in this book offer great promise of improving the quality of life of the chronic mental patient.

Contributors

Julia Adams
Robert P. Archer, Ph.D.
Jeffrey R. Bedell, Ph.D.
L. Adlai Boyd, Ed.D.
Morton Cohen
Philip W. Drash, Ph.D.
Eileen D. Edmunson, Ph.D.
Joseph W. Evans, Ph.D.
Susan Fertig, R.N., M.N.
Robert M. Friedman, Ph.D.
Nancy Goldstein
Carolyn J. Hursch, Ph.D.
Margaret Malchon
Herbert Marlowe, Ed.S.
Jo Palmer, M.A.
Shirley Redcay, M.D.
Judith Quick, M.A.
Valerie Reed, M.A.
Arthur Slater, M.S.W.
Edwin Solomon, M.A.
Lawrence Weathers, Ph.D.

Integrating Treatment Systems for the Mentally Ill

1
Introducing Model Treatments

This book presents model systems for treating chronically ill mental patients. Developed over the past four years at a public mental health research and training facility and adjoining university, the entire program is built on new methods of psychoeducational treatment, management, and assessment, with an objective of reducing costs and extending the capabilities and efficiency of professionals to provide improved services. The uses of structured group and class skill-building procedures, peer and natural supports, standardized testing instruments, and paraprofessional assistants have been investigated with patients of every age.

New techniques have either supplanted or supplemented older ones. Using a typical state hospital staff, the new programs combine modularized skill building, behavior management, and patient support network therapies with conventional pharmacologic and psychodynamic treatment methods (see Glossary). These programs provide unique, inexpensive, and successful systems of patient care that fill numerous gaps in current treatment of the chronic mental patient. They integrate former mental patients into mainstream community life. For example, among a group of elderly patients who had formerly resided in a state hospital for two years and who received the treatments, 77.4 percent were remaining in noninstitutional settings a year after moving out into the community, as compared to 25.9 percent of a matched group who received traditional state hospital care.[1] The discharged patients in the new treatment program lived in homes throughout the community and behaved in a normal manner; they, their families, and other persons who knew them well, expressed great satisfaction with their treatment and the quality of life it helped them to attain. Similar results were obtained with younger adults and child and adolescent patients.

There is tremendous need to improve the care and treatment of the chronically ill mental patient. We hope that the findings presented here will contribute information and ideas that will assist those who are shaping mental health programs throughout the field.

The book describes an adventure, the launching of a new research and training facility. Not only does it reveal the discoveries made during four years of research, it portrays the struggles involved in sustaining the operation in its early years when the program seemed on the verge of collapse. Readers who themselves must cope with the confusion and conflict in the public mental health and human service sectors will be able to observe how the staff of one facility succeeded.

The case history of Suella P., a chronic mental patient, provides an example of problems in today's management of patients, and of some of the therapy models and integrative techniques proposed for improving treatment and care.

Illustrative Case History: Suella P.

In the predawn haze, a shrimp boat spotted a body floating with the outbound tide toward the mouth of the bay. The fishermen pulled a nearly nude young woman aboard, limp and exhausted, but still feebly resisting their aid. Pushing away their hands, the woman mumbled incoherently about losing her child and about her being cleansed for her sins. Four hours later she was admitted to the psychiatric unit of a general hospital, from where she was transferred to a state residential psychiatric facility. There she continued withdrawn and resisting help. When questioned, she rambled vaguely about her child and her sinfulness.

So began the fourth residential treatment episode in the life of a chronically ill mental patient, Suella P. But the treatment Suella was to receive was nothing like any she had ever experienced before. It would bridge the gap between institutional care and community follow-up; it would provide her with self-help skills as well as social supports from peers that she could use upon return to the community; it would prepare her to benefit from continuing psychopharmacological, dynamic insight-giving, and behavioral therapies after discharge; and it would link up her self-help, peer-support, and professional care into one unified, unfragmented system. It is no wonder that when Suella left the mental institution nine weeks after admission, she wore a t-shirt with the facility's logo emblazoned on it (see Figure 9-4).

The fact is that most hospitalized chronically ill mental patients like Suella can be treated effectively and returned to a life of high quality in a natural community surrounding—in their own home, a foster home, or a boarding home. They can usually be diverted from long-term and repeated hospitalizations by time-limited interventions. Persons at high risk for mental illness can be aided by primary prevention; however, innovative management and treatment programs are required to prepare mental patients of all ages for independent lives in the community. Organizational structures must be developed to help invent, evaluate, and disseminate successful new treatments, and manpower must be trained to implement successful innovations. This book describes successful treatment and management approaches, organizational structures, manpower training programs, and dissemination strategies for improving the psychiatric care of many of these mental patients. Suella's case history, as well as those of other adult, elderly, and child patients, illustrates the principles discussed.

The plight of the chronic mental patient has been extensively documented: the stigma resulting in neglect and rejection, the lack of adequate financing of care, the roadblocks to obtaining adequate services, the fragmentation and lack of a comprehensive network of community services providing continuity of care, the lack of trained treatment personnel, the disincentives to the provision of quality care, and the paucity of relevant research.[2-6] The shortcomings of contemporary models of mental health treatment are documented by the poor quality of life and the "revolving door" recidivism that is so frequently observed among mental patients.[7-9]

These problems have been compounded by the emergence of a social policy to "deinstitutionalize" chronic mental patients. Unfortunately, the implementation of this policy has often failed;[1, 3,10] thousands of patients have been dumped out of mental hospitals without adequate community alternatives and services. Simply moving the chronic mental patient from a hospital to the so-called "community" fails to solve the problems. Life in third-rate hotels and city slums is no solution for the deinstitutionalized. The increase in numbers of former mental hospital patients reinstitutionalized in nursing homes bears out these observations. If deinstitutionalization is to become a meaningful reality, new and creative models of treatment must be provided.

Slater et al.[7] identified the multiple needs of elderly patients; Talbott[6] stated them as ten commandments that should govern actions toward deinstitutionalization. This book describes integrated systems of treatment programs that fulfill most of these needs and commandments. Here are some of Talbott's commandments that these programs obey:

1. Prepare patients for discharge before they leave the institution.
2. Make sure that their housing needs are met.
3. Help clients surmount the barriers to participation in the health and mental health delivery systems.
4. Offer a range of community services that provide support.

5. Provide continuity of care.
6. Conduct services in small local units, usually in groups of about 25 members.
7. Perform continuing research and evaluation, and also training and education.

Providers of treatment and rehabilitation services cannot themselves fulfill Talbott's commandments related to financial and governmental issues that they do not control, such as funding or conflict of interest in governmental services. But the projects described in the chapters that follow carry out the above functions that treatment facilities can provide without political action. They offer programs of care for chronically ill mental patients that successfully deinstitutionalize many of them and divert others from entering institutions.

DEINSTITUTIONALIZING THE CHRONICALLY ILL MENTAL PATIENT

"Deinstitutionalize" means "remove the character or status of an institution from. . . . " The treatment programs described here are designed not only to discharge patients from institutional status, but also to remove the character of the institution from them and to prepare them for successful lives.[12] The treatment programs are inexpensive to implement, since they are conducted largely by paraprofessional mental health workers, families, and the patients themselves, utilizing written procedures developed by professionals and carried out under their supervision. Nurses, psychiatrists, psychologists, educators, social workers, and paraprofessionals can work harmoniously together, conducting not only treatment and assessment, but also evaluative research and training at little extra cost.

Actively psychotic hospitalized mental patients, either in the acute initial phase of their disorder or in an exacerbation of a chronic illness, initially may require mostly medical and nursing care.[13,14] Like the novice skier who needs an orthopedist to set a broken ankle, or the overweight smoker who requires intensive care in the coronary treatment unit for an infarcted heart, acutely psychotic patients primarily need medications and other medical treatments, and skill in communicating is of minor importance. Their medical care can be conducted by foreign-born physicians whose mastery of the English language is less than their knowledge of medicine. Later, when the patients are ready to begin to learn how to avoid recurrences of their illnesses, the patient with the healed ankle can attend classes for skiers, the one with the heart attack can attend smokers' and weight watchers' classes, and the mental patient can attend psychosocial skills training classes. All these classes require nonmedical teachers whose primary assets are the ability to communicate the specific knowledge in their skills-building area, and to train the patients to master the skills needed to perform effectively.

All three patients, once the medical emergency is under control, can benefit from psychoeducational and peer-support training classes; these reduce the likelihood of their suffering future repetitions of their illness. The chapters that follow will describe an integrated group of programs of effective, inexpensive treatment and prevention for psychiatric patients of all ages that combine medical, behavioral management, psychodynamic, psychoeducational, and social support approaches.

COMBINING BEHAVIORAL, SOCIAL, PHARMACOLOGIC, AND DYNAMIC THERAPIES

For 30 years methods derived from learning theory and experimental work in behavioral and social psychology have been used independently and in combination with psychodynamic and psychoparmacologic approaches to increase the capabilities of therapists in treating individuals and groups of psychiatric patients and their families.[15-17] Since 1953 we have sought to combine behavioral, social psychological, educational, medical, and psychodynamic therapies in the treatment and rehabilitation of mental patients. We collected quantitative data through systematic investigations of new treatment techniques on our own patients and those of colleagues, hospitals, and clinics. Utilizing objective indicators of treatment outcomes—performance at work, earnings, stability of marriage, subsequent physical and mental illness, hospitalization, entanglements with the law, etc.—we have assessed progress and evaluated the effectiveness, productivity, and efficiency of different treatment methods; treatment procedures are modified on the basis of evidence, both the results of our own clinical research and those of others. Follow-up studies, as long as 4–5 years after completion of treatment, have measured the long-term benefits of various procedures. We found that psychodynamically oriented individual and group psychotherapy alone does not offer much to the majority of poorly educated, unemployed, or low-income chronically ill mental patients who so frequently orbit in and out of mental institutions. Continued analysis of the social psychological stresses in patients' lives and their sociodynamics, and evaluation of their response to treatment, has led to continuing modifications in therapy.[16,18] Comparative studies of psychiatric outpatients, inpatients, psychosomatic patients, and normals led to a thesis that many patients were unskilled in coping with stress, and that many were inadequately supported by friends and family.[18-23] Therapeutic innovations, therefore, included greater effort at training patients in coping techniques and in assisting them in building supports. Treatment utilized behavioral techniques such as "sessions for learning, review, rehearsal and practice."[16] Once we began to employ these skills-training, supports-building, and social management techniques in individual and family therapy, we began to succeed in reducing the need for hospitalization and rehospitalization of seriously ill mental patients. Social behavioral techniques were combined with pharmacotherapy and dynamic psychotherapy in the successful treatment of child and adult mental patients of all ages. Results with these treatment approaches are recapitulated in Table 1–1, which incorporates data reported in early papers.[16,18]

This table shows that approximately one-third of each group were severely ill psychiatric patients; 15–16 percent had previously been hospitalized. As each new therapeutic tool—major tranquilizers, behavior management with social skills and supports building, and psychic energizers (in that order)—was added, the patients' need for hospitalization or for ECT (electroconvulsive therapy) decreased. Together, these three treatment innovations reduced the use of the more restrictive or intrusive heroic therapies—hospitalization and ECT—from 30 percent to 7 percent. Further, the addition of skills training in the treatment process, which was called *social psychotherapy,* was the single most important element in cutting down the need to hospitalize and rehospitalize severely ill mental patients. These and other reports indicated that social psychotherapy also helped the less severely ill adult and child patient groups in that it cut down on the average number of treatment sessions they required and increased their acceptance of therapy.[18]

Evaluations showed that psychoeducational approaches to skills and supports building (see Glossary) were also effective in settings such as orientation classes for college students and antenatal classes for expectant mothers. In these, at-risk groups of persons in transition periods of their lives with similar needs and problems were brought together for training and preparation.[23–28] In addition to specific orientation for the new phase of their life, they received systematic classroom instruction and training with discussion and feedback. They learned techniques for asserting, enjoying leisure, avoiding emotional stress, conferring, planning, obtaining advice, practicing good study and health habits, enhancing social and cognitive skills, and solving problems, as well as for building social supports with helpful friends and family. Evaluations have shown the effectiveness of this classroom training with experimental groups as compared to controls in modifying behavior, increasing skills, and improving social supports. These preventive efforts significantly reduced academic failure, emotional disorder, and physical health problems. Findings from these studies have received wide dissemination and use.[28–39]

Since 1970, several studies demonstrated the clinical application of social and daily living skills training procedures with psychiatric patients.[40–45] Token

Table 1-1

Effects of introducing psychotropic medications and behavioral management techniques in reducing patients' need for hospitalization and electroconvulsive therapy

| | | | Type of care required | | | | |
| | | | More intrusive or restrictive care | | Outpatient care | | |
Treatment introduced	Number of patients	Percentage of patients hospitalized previously	Inpatient hospitalization (percent)	Electro-convulsive therapy (percent)	Psychological treatment plus major psychotropics (percent)	Psychological treatment plus minor tranquilizers (percent)	Totals (percent)
(1) Dynamic psychotherapy alone	115	15	22	8	0	70	100
(1) Dynamic psychotherapy (2) Major tranquilizers	246	16	17	2	14	67	100
(1) Dynamic psychotherapy (2) Major tranquilizers (3) Skills and support training	217	16	9	1	20	70	100
(1) Dynamic psychotherapy (2) Major tranquilizers (3) Skills and support training (4) Psychic energizers	232	16	7	0	23	70	100
Totals (mean percent)	810	16		30		70	100

economies have also been used to motivate patients to become actively involved in the treatment program.[46-51]

Psychoeducational treatment approaches that stem from experimental research in social and behavioral psychology, when combined with traditional ones derived from psychodynamic psychiatry, increase the capabilities of mental health professionals who are experienced in their use to manage the treatment of a larger number and variety of difficult patients effectively and inexpensively.[16,52] This book will introduce psychiatrists, nurses, and other mental health professionals, who are not familiar with them, to technologies of behavior management and social psychology as used in administering mental institutions and managing mental patients. It will show how they are integrated with traditional techniques. The book will also go several steps further, and will describe an organizational structure and management approaches that integrate a variety of psychoeducational, psychodynamic, behavioral, pharmacological, and group dynamic procedures in treating psychiatric patients, in evaluating the effectiveness of the treatments, and in training others to use them.

INTEGRATED PROGRAMS

Replacing the "nonsystem" described by Talbott[53] for treating chronic mental patients, the programs here provide structured systems of services along a number of different dimensions. Suella's case history and treatment program and those of other patients will be used to illustrate the principles discussed. The chapters that follow in Part A provide a general overview of a systematic, integrated approach to patient care. Modular skill building, behavior management, and peer management and support are introduced in Chapters 2 and 3. These innovations are designed to upgrade the quality and effectiveness of mental health care in a cost efficient manner. They operate within the constraints of resources of typical public mental hospitals whose manpower consists mostly of paraprofessionals and of physicians whose first language is not English. These innovations augment traditional individual and group psychotherapies and pharmacotherapy.

Chapter 4 presents a novel program that combines unit dose and single daily dose medicating in the hospital with psychoeducational training for self-medication after discharge. The efforts of pharmacists, nurses, patients, psychiatrists, paraprofessionals, and psychoeducators are joined into a single effective program. Together, they prepare patients for taking their medications after discharge, and thus they cut down on recidivism.

The use of standardized assessment instruments for measuring patient progress, as well as for program evaluation, is described in Chapter 5. Both previously developed rating scales and staff-originated proficiency gauges for assessing progress in modular skill training are discussed.

Chapter 6 illustrates how different types of treatment—biomedical, psychoeducational, and social—are combined in the treatment of the chronically ill mental patient.

An innovative method of providing psychoeducation by means of gaming is described in Chapter 7. One paraprofessional staff person can manage the treatment of up to 30 patients at a time in a training session.

Part B describes techniques used for motivating paraprofessionals and counteracting staff "burnout," for harmonizing interprofessional relationships, and for educating and training personnel throughout the entire mental health and human service sectors. Chapters 8–10 show how gaps in the cooperation between professionals and in the training and education of personnel are filled.

The succeeding parts discuss specific programs for psychiatrically ill children and youth, adults, and elderly patients. These programs offer a continuum of services in day hospital and day treatment, residential, community support, and follow-up projects that serve as models for linking hospital and community treatment efforts that often are disconnected and fragmented in other settings. Assessment and evaluation methods are presented. These programs forge links between mental health and other human service agencies that aid mental patients and other clients. Training for personnel in those other agencies to provide mental health care is described. These chapters present a number of inventions.

Part C describes programs for children and adolescents. Chapters 11 and 12 introduce psychoeducational programs for severely disturbed children and adolescents. Chapter 13 offers family therapy programs including psychoeducational family training and the teaching family model.

Part D presents the adult programs. Chapter 14 shows how modular skill building in the residential setting, peer support in the community, and professional and paraprofessional aftercare are combined in the treatment and management of adult patients.

The modular treatment program for elderly patients is described in Part E and Chapter 15.

Concluding remarks are offered in Chapter 16. The potential benefits of modular psychoeducation and support building in schools and other health settings is explored. Integrated systems for deinstitutionalizing chronic patients and for developing mental health manpower are considered.

The Appendix includes a glossary of terms and provides examples that illustrate the modular psychoeducational approaches discussed in the book.

The following pages show how these programs were developed. Sufficient detail is provided in the main text and the appendix for mental health professionals and educators, administrators, government officials, and other interested persons to learn how to establish the treatments and other services elsewhere in private or public facilities. Readers will learn how to create an organizational structure where a small cadre of professionals of different disciplines work together harmoniously; the professionals manage trained paraprofessionals who provide effective, inexpensive treatment of high quality in an atmosphere of high morale and creativity; they also innovate, evaluate, train, and disseminate. The programs are being implemented within current wage guidelines and budgetary constraints; they mostly utilize presently employed personnel in the hospitals and other mental health agencies.

PSYCHOPOLITICS

A number of chapters are peppered with examples of psychopolitical issues. The mental health professional or manager who wishes to work in the current mental health "nonsystem"[53] must not develop any illusions that innovation, training, dissemination, and improving the treatment of the chronically ill mental patient are accomplished in a serene, relaxed atmosphere. The atmosphere in much of the public mental health sector is one of conflict, tension, and adversary relationships.[54] The neophyte who knows what he is getting into, as Cohen showed in training military inductees,[55,56] and we reported for college freshmen and new mothers,[23-28] will adapt better and suffer less stress.

The problem is not with individuals but with the entire nonsystem that promotes separation, fragmentation, and discontinuity—gaps. Our purpose in this book is to describe and disseminate successful systems of service that have been developed and evaluated despite the disincentives to integrating services. Ultimately, the nonsystem must and will be changed. Meanwhile, it needs to be understood so that the job can be done under the present circumstances. A few words are needed, therefore, to explain where problems exist in the public mental health sector today.

McNett[57] quotes Gartner and Riessman, who state that mental health and human service professionals are under attack from a whole range of budget-cutting, tax revolt, antigovernment forces in our society. A large mainstream sector says that mental health professionals are wasting money and patients are not getting better. These forces do not want any more mental health professionals, nor to raise their salaries.

Research and training centers are particularly afflicted. No longer is mental health research an honored activity upon which public largesse is bestowed just for the asking, if it ever was. A mental health research and training facility is expected to prove its worth, and sometimes it is asked to justify its existence in the very first years of its life! And its professionals must do likewise.

Paul[58] has pointed out a number of obstacles in the implementation of effective treatment programs for chronic mental patients:

The data are clear at the federal, state, and institutional levels that neither evaluation criteria nor funding incentives focus upon effective treatment (p. 103).

The bureaucratic, administrative, and political "system" not only frustrates attempts at change but inadvertently discourages effective treatment programs and improvements in methodological-technical procedures (p. 111).

Methods of evaluation encourage paperwork rather than effective treatment (p. 113).

Talbott[59] has written about the problems of the public mental hospitals:

First, the state facility cares for the most difficult patient population—the severely and chronically mentally ill . . . Second, the staff interested and knowledgeable about working with these patients in a rigid governmental setting are few and far between . . . Third, the very nature of governmental services guarantees that it is highly bureaucratic, filled with paperwork, law suits, regulatory minutiae and inconceivable delays and harassment; it is rigid, with more attention given to monitoring, policing, and controlling than to treating, caring, and doing; it is underfunded with high expectation, low support, . . . and becomes a political football for the press, campaigning politicians, disgruntled relatives, and members of the community. Fourth, these hospitals . . . have no lobby for their clientele. Finally, there is the stigma with which mental patients . . . live (p. 70).

During the period when the programs we developed here were being implemented, evaluated, and disseminated around the state, the public human service agency of which the research and training facility was a part was being reorganized. The reorganization decentralized the eight service programs—mental health, retardation, vocational rehabilitation, public health, children's medical services, aging services, social welfare services, and youth services. The state legislature removed control from the central program offices and gave daily operating management to administrators in each of the state's 11 districts. The role of the central program office was reduced to providing programmatic guidance, but no day-to-day operating management. This reorganization attracted considerable interest around the nation because of the possibility that it might improve delivery of treatment and care, especially since it collocated all eight services under one roof in each community. Management in each of the districts was placed in the hands of "generalists," who were chosen not because of their programmatic expertise or scientific training, but because they had ability in public administration.

The Kennedy School of Government at Harvard University conducted a case study of the public agency and assessed its performance after reorganization. Its case report presents a study of the situation that prevailed in the human service agency and in the research and training center prior to implementation of the programs described here. Its report, which we shall call the "Harvard Case Report," serves not only as a study for comparing the effects of the new programs developed, but also for showing where gaps remain in mental health and other human services. We shall present quotations from the Harvard Case Report throughout this book to point out how proposals that emerge from the studies reported here fill gaps in the present system that, we believe, are similar to those in many other states.

Before presenting the descriptions of the programs, let us consider what currently happens to a chronic mental patient in today's public sector through the case history of Suella P., the mental patient whom the fishermen hauled out of the bay and whose fourth hospital admission was described in the opening sentences of this chapter. Her story and others will be followed throughout ensuing chapters and will illustrate the principles discussed.

Illustrative Case History: Suella P. (Continued)

A psychiatric history was obtained initially from Suella's roommate, Marsha, then later from the patient herself when, after receiving psychotropic medications, she began to recover from the acute phase of her psychotic episode. This was the fourth psychiatric hospitalization of Suella P., a 25-year-old separated mother of a three-year-old little girl, Mary Ellen. Suella and her husband, Tom, a tomato farmer, had moved to Florida four years previously from a military base in South Carolina upon Tom's discharge from the Army. Suella, a tall, gangly, plain woman, met Tom when he was serving as an enlisted man at the army base near her birthplace in South Carolina; she had worked as a waitress in a tavern near the base.

Prior to meeting Tom, Suella had been employed in a number of low-paying jobs since the age of 16, mostly as a waitress or salesclerk. She came from a broken home. Her mother had deserted her and her father when Suella was six. Her father, an alcoholic, had sent Suella to live with his mother. When Grandma died two years later, Suella went to live with a series of paternal aunts and uncles, in none of whose homes she stayed long nor felt welcome or secure. She always worked hard doing housework, cooking, serving meals for her aunts and uncles, but tended to let schoolwork slide. No one encouraged Suella to learn or to express her feelings. "Mind your tongue. Keep your place. Do your chores. Don't forget you're an orphan. Be glad you've got a place to live." These were the watchwords of Suella's childhood. She obeyed, kept her feelings to herself, and got out as soon as the law allowed.

Leaving school at age 16, having completed the eighth grade, Suella got her first paying job as a clerk and moved into her own furnished room. At 18, Suella married an attractive newcomer to her hometown; he drifted out of her life a few months later, and she underwent her first mental breakdown. Following a suicide attempt, she was hospitalized for four months in a state mental institution. She divorced her first husband when she was 19.

She next got a job near the military base and began dating soldiers. A series of brief, unsatisfactory sexual encounters ensued, one of which was with Tom's older brother, Erwin. Suella did not care much for sex, but believed it was necessary if she was to keep men interested in her. When Erwin completed service and returned to Florida, Suella began to date Tom, whom she married when she was 20.

Suella remained at her tavern job until Tom's discharge from service and their move to Florida. She found a new job in a bar and grill near Tom's farm. She continued to work until her eighth month of pregnancy. For the next four months she stayed at home.

The year with Tom in South Carolina was idyllic for Suella. For the first time in her life she had a home with someone who cared for her, remained loyal to her, and did not leave her. The move to Florida, however, introduced conflict and stress. The only neighbors nearby were her in-laws, Tom's mother, his brother Erwin, and Erwin's childless wife. Erwin created special problems for Suella.

Behind her back, Erwin bad-mouthed Suella to his mother and wife, calling her a whore, and telling them about her sexual conduct in South Carolina. When with her alone, however, he made sexual remarks and passes, and tried to force her to renew their previous affair. Suella did not tell Tom about Erwin's conduct; she was not one to express her feelings, expecially her fears, and she was afraid to let Tom know about her premarital sexual activity. Even though Erwin's behavior with Suella continued after the birth of the baby, Tom did not learn about it. Tom knew that his mother and sister-in-law ignored his wife, but did nothing to remedy that situation either.

Suella adapted well to pregnancy while she continued to work. But, after the birth of her daughter, her problems began again. Alone in the farmhouse with the baby, lonesome while Tom was in the tomato fields, afraid of his brother, inexperienced in babycare, and with nowhere to turn for advice and support, Suella began to be tormented with anxiety and self-doubt. She began to dwell on thoughts of doing harm to the baby and of her premarital sinfulness, stirred repeatedly by the remarks of her brother-in-law. She began to fear she would again lose her mind. She was haunted by thoughts of being hospitalized again and deserting her baby. Neither Suella nor Tom were churchgoers, but they both had grown up in a fundamentalist tradition which practiced spiritual cleansing in a literal manner, by immersion in water. Awakened one night by the baby's wanting a midnight feeding, Suella felt tired, confused, and angry. Unable to return to sleep, she began to hear whisperings telling her she

*was going to kill the baby. They told her to purify herself with water. Terrified,
she awakened Tom.*

Tom quickly dressed and rushed Suella to the hospital emergency room.
There the physician on call recognized that she was hallucinating and delusional, and admitted her to the psychiatric ward. A few days later she was transferred to the state hospital.

Suella remained at the mental hospital only a month. Her symptoms died
down quickly once she began to receive tranquilizers and got away from Erwin
and her in-laws. Upon returning home, she began outpatient care at a local psychiatric clinic. But things got worse, not better. Tom was now cool toward her.
Why should he stay married to a crazy woman? If she did not pull herself together, he told her, he was going to leave her. His mother and brother agreed
with him, and told him to get out of the marriage. They decided that now was
the time to tell Tom about Suella's premarital sex life. That did it for Tom.
He packed his clothes and moved back with his mother.

Things were also complicated for Suella at the clinic. Her case was used
for teaching student professionals who were learning to conduct counseling and
psychotherapy. Every eight weeks she received a new therapist. Her treatment
was inconsistent. Sometimes the new therapist gave her advice different from
that of the previous one. One told her to give up the baby, get her own apartment, go back to work, forget about Tom; she had her own life to lead. Another
told her that her responsibility was to be a mother; he tried unsuccessfully to
persuade Tom to move back. This conflicting advice confused Suella. She had
not wanted her marriage to break up; she would like Tom to come back. But
she also sensed that she needed to work to maintain her sanity. She also wanted
her baby, whom she hoped to provide with the love and security and feeling of
being wanted that she had missed as a child. On top of all this confusion Suella's voices returned. Her medications were changed but the threats continued.
"You're going to kill the baby. You're going back to the mental hospital. You'll
never get out."

The staff at the clinic began to worry about the possibility of Suella harming her child. Since she would not part with Mary Ellen, they sent her back
to the state hospital. Neither Tom nor anyone else in his family wanted anything to do with Suella or her child, so Mary Ellen was sent to live with foster
parents while her mother was away.

It was during this third hospital admission that Suella met Marsha, another mental patient with whom she became friendly. Also, while Suella was
in the hospital, Tom moved back to his farmhouse, and put Suella's things in
storage. The state hospital staff encouraged Suella and Marsha's friendship.
So, when Suella was ready for discharge, she made plans to move in with Marsha in her apartment. Social service workers at the state hospital arranged for
Mary Ellen to be returned to her mother.

It was a good arrangement for both women and the little girl. Both women *obtained jobs. Suella returned to waitressing, which freed up her mornings and afternoons to look after Mary Ellen. Marsha got home from her office job in the later afternoon and took over the care of the child. The two women were conscientious housekeepers, so they created few problems for each other in running their apartment. But the psychiatric clinic continued to stir doubts in Suella's mind. Now she was assigned to a therapy group run by a therapist who believed in free expression with minimal structure. Some of the group's members, themselves patients, criticized Suella's arrangement with Marsha. "Break up this sick relationship," they said. "It's not healthy for mental patients to be dependent, especially upon each other. Go separate ways."*

Other patients disagreed. They told Suella to trust her own feelings, to make decisions for herself, not to look to the doctors or other patients for direction. Suella felt caught in a bind. She was confused, but said little. Trained to be obedient, she did not know whom to obey. Some said do one thing, others equally confidently told her do the opposite, a third group said make up her own mind. But the problem was that Suella did not have enough information, nor skill in making decisions or solving problems, nor self-confidence to make up her mind. Furthermore, no one did anything about her psychotropic medications. She took them conscientiously when told to do so, even though the pills sometimes made her groggy. But no one now seemed to care whether she used medications or not. When her supply ran out, she did not renew the prescriptions.

Another thing about the group bothered Suella. Despite her promiscuous premarital experience, Suella was a prude. The therapists in the group encouraged the patients to "let it all hang out." They encouraged the use of street language to help desensitize patients about their sex hang-ups. Suella felt that expressions like "Stop fucking your mind" and "Get your shit together" were vulgar. Her aunts and uncles did not talk like that. Even the soldiers who slept with her had not used such words in her presence. Not only was she bothered by people using such language, she was confused about what they meant.

In the group no one asked what Suella and Marsha were gaining from each other. No one took into consideration that the women were benefiting from sharing the rent, or that each had pitched in with 200 dollars so they could buy a beat-up but functional Volkswagen "bug" together, or that they enjoyed raising little Mary Ellen, or that both women had been rejected by their families and were providing each other with companionship and emotional support. Some of the group and the clinic staff worried about the effect the two former mental patients were having on the little girl. They advised Suella to give up her daughter.

But Suella did not want to give up her child or Marsha. Under the combined care of Marsha and Suella, Mary Ellen was thriving. The women dressed her up as they would have loved to have been dressed up when they were little girls. They talked to her, read her stories, played with her, took her to the play-

ground as they would have liked someone to have talked with and played with them when they were children. They went to the zoo, the circus, and Disney World, places that were new experiences for Suella and Marsha, as well as for Mary Ellen. None of the clinic staff knew about how Suella was raising Mary Ellen. Suella did not tell them; they did not ask.

Suella's happiness was not to last. Clinic staff continued to worry about the possibility of Suella harming Mary Ellen. They remembered that her voices had said that she would kill the child.

One afternoon, when Suella was minding Mary Ellen in the apartment, the doorbell rang. A uniformed sheriff's deputy was at the entrance. "Are you Mrs. Suella P.?" He handed her a document. "Sign here." It was a complaint filed by the psychiatric clinic. Suella should show why custody of Mary Ellen should not be taken from her and transferred to the state.

Suella was dumbfounded. The people to whom she turned for help were taking everything away from her. For the next four days she could not sleep well. She tried to get up courage to talk to the people at the clinic, to tell them that she was not harming the child. She and Marsha discussed the dilemma. Neither had a solution. They did not have the money to hire a lawyer. They could not take the child and leave—they had no place to go. They were going to lose Mary Ellen.

Suella obtained an appointment, finally, at the clinic. A social worker talked with her. The therapist was very sympathetic, and tried to show Suella that it was for the best. She had not been able to make up her own mind to give up the child, so now it was being done for her. She did not need to feel guilty; she had done the best she could for the child. The social worker did not mention medications.

Suella was distraught. A few days later, after work she returned to the apartment physically and emotionally exhausted. She had not had a good night's sleep in over a week, ever since she had learned that the authorities were going to take away her child. She climbed into bed, but tossed and turned for hours. Sometime after three in the morning, she got up and walked out of doors, dressed only in her nightgown. Once again the voices returned. "You," they said. "You. You're crazy. You'll never see Mary Ellen again. You're going to the mental hospital forever. Purify yourself."

Suella got into the VW and drove to the nearest beach. After parking the car, she walked out as far as she could into the bay. When the waters reaches her chin, she drew up her feet from the sandy bottom and let herself float. The outgoing tide swept her away. A half hour later the shrimp boat fished her out of the water.

Suella's history illustrates the fragmentation, inconsistency and lack of integration in the care of the chronic mental patient today. The chapters that follow will show how all this changed for Suella, and how her program of treatment taught her how to help herself, and how to utilize the support of patient peers like Marsha and the backing of paraprofessionals and professionals. It provided a consistent theme and continuity of care, and bridged many gaps between hospital and community and between self-help and professional services.

REFERENCES

1. Patterson RL, Jackson GM: Behavior modification with the elderly, in Hersen M, Eisler RM, Miller PM, et al. (Ed.): Progress in Behavior Modification, Vol. 7. New York, Academic Press, 1980, pp 206–239
2. Bachrach L: Deinstitutionalization: An Analytical Review and Sociological Perspective. Washington, D.C., U.S. Government Printing Office, 1976
3. Bassuk EL, Gerson S: Deinstitutionalization and mental health services. Sci Am 238:46–53, 1978
4. Group for the Advancement of Psychiatry: The chronic mental health patient in the community. 10:102, 1978
5. Talbot JA (Ed.): The Chronic Mental Patient. Washington, D.C., The American Psychiatric Association, 1978
6. Talbott JA: Care of the chronically mentally ill—still a national disgrace. Am J Psychiatry 136:623, 1979
7. Slater A, Gordon K, Patterson R, et al.: Deinstitutionalizing the elderly in Florida's state mental hospitals: Assessing the problems. Tampa, University of South Florida, Human Resources Institute, Monograph Series No. 2, 1978
8. Ellsworth RB, Foster L, Childers B, et al.: Hospital and community adjustment as perceived by psychiatric patients, their families and staff. J Consult Clin Psychol 32 (Suppl):1–41, 1968
9. Schooler NR, Goldberg SC, Boothe H, et al.: One year after discharge: Community adjustment of schizophrenic patients. Am J Psychiatry 123:986–995, 1967
10. Hogarty GE, Katz MM: Norms of adjustment and social behavior. Arch Gen Psychiatry 25:470–480, 1971
11. Talbott JA: Deinstitutionalization: Avoiding the disasters of the past. Hosp Community Psychiatry 30:621–624, 1979
12. O'Sullivan M, Patterson R, Eberly D, et al.: Presentation to Mental Health Program Office Advisory Council. Tampa, Florida, 1979
13. Gordon RE: The psychiatric emergency, good intentions vs good sense, Consultant 1:34–38, 1962
14. Anderson WH, Kuehnle JC: Strategies for the treatment of acute psychosis. JAMA 229:1884–1889, 1974
15. Dollard J, Miller NE: Personality and Psychotherapy. New York, McGraw-Hill, 1950
16. Gordon RE: Sociodynamics and psychotherapy. AMA Arch Neurol Psychiatry 81:486–503, 1959
17. Fairweather GW (Ed.): Social psychology in treating mental illness. New York, John Wiley, 1964
18. Gordon RE, Singer M, Gordon KK: Social psychological stress. Arch Gen Psychiatry 4:459, 1961
19. Gordon RE, Gordon KK: Psychiatric problems of a rapidly growing suburb. AMA Arch Neurol Psychiatry 79:543–548, 1958

20. Gordon RE, Gordon KK: Psychosomatic problems of a rapidly growing suburb. JAMA 169:15, 1959

21. Gordon RE, Gordon KK: Social psychiatry of a mobile suburb. Int J Soc Psychiatry 6:90–100, 1960

22. Gordon RE, Gordon KK: Emotional problems of children in a rapidly growing suburb. Int. J Soc Psychiatry 4:85–97, 1958

23. Gordon RE: The Prevention of Postpartum Emotional Disturbance. Ann Arbor, University Microfilms, University of Michigan, 1961

24. Gordon RE, Gordon KK: Prediction and treatment of emotional disorders of pregnancy. Am J Obstet Gynecol 77:1074–1133, 1959

25. Gordo RE, Gordon KK: Social factors in the prevention of postpartum emotional problems. Obstet Gynecol 15:443–448, 1960

26. Gordon RE, Kapostins EE, Gordon KK: Factors in postpartum emotional adjustment. Obstet Gynecol 25:156–166, 1965

27. Gordon RE, Gordon KK: The Blight on the Ivy. Englewood Cliffs, N.J., Prentice-Hall, 1963

28. Gordon RE, Gordon KK, Gunther M: The Split-Level Trap. New York, Bernard Geis Associates, 1961

29. Williams JH: Psychology of Women: Behavior in a Biosocial Context. New York, Norton, 1974, p. 282

30. Grimm E: Women's attitudes and reactions to childbirth, in Goldman GD, Neilman DS (Eds.): Modern Woman: Her Psychology and Sexuality. Springfield, Ill., CC Thomas, 1969 pp. 148–149

31. Brazzell C: Teaching Materials Currently Used in Mental Health Worker Training Programs. Atlanta, Georgia, Southern Regional Education Board, 1974, p. 39

32. Haire D, Haire J: Implementing Family-Centered Maternity Care with a Central Nursery. Hillside, New Jersey, International Childbirth Education Association, 1968, pp. II–15, 16, IV–13

33. Coelho GV, Hamburg DA, Moos R, et al.: Coping and Adaption. Public Service Education No. 2087, Chevy Chase, Md., National Institutes of Mental Health, 1970, p. 61

34. Gordon RE: Stress and your patient—and you. Consultant 1:42–46, 1963

35. Gordon RE: The psychiatric emergency. Child and Family 2:82–85, 1963

36. Gordon RE: Les urgences psychiatriques, bonnes intentions et bons sens. Consultant (Quebec) 1:34–37, 1964

37. Sherman JA: On the psychology of women. Springfield, Ill., Thomas, 1971, pp. 61, 171, 206–208, 210, 213

38. Gordon RE: Questionnaires, in Johnson OG, Bommarito JW: Tests and measurements in child development: A handbook. San Francisco, Jossey-Bass, 1971

39. Gordon RE, Gordon KK: Maladies psycho-somatiques et problemes residentiels. Rev Lyonnaise Med 11:889–894, 1962

40. Eisler RM, Miller PM, Hersen M, et al.: Effects of assertive training on marital interaction. Arch Gen Psychiatry 130:643–649, 1974

41. Eisler RM, Herson M, Miller PM: Shaping components of assertiveness with instructions and feedback. Am J Psychiatry 131:1344–1347, 1974

42. Wallace CJ, Teigen JR, Liberman RP, et al.: Destructive behavior treated by contingency contracts and assertive training. J Behav Ther Exp Psychiatry 4:273–274, 1973

43. Liberman RP, King LW, DeRisi, WJ, et al.: Personal effectiveness: Guiding people to assert themselves and improve their social skills. Champaign, Ill., Research Press, 1975

44. Liberman RP, Ferris C, Salgado P, et al.: Replication of the Achievement place model in California. J Appl Behav Anal 8:287–299, 1975

45. Hersen M: Modification of skill deficits in psychiatric patients, in Bellack AS, Hersen M (Eds.): Research and Pratice in Social Skills Training. New York, Plenum Press, 1979

46. Davion G: Appaisal of behavior modification technique with adults in institutional settings, in Franks CM (Ed.) Behavior Therapy: Appraisal and Status. New York, McGraw-Hill, 1969
47. Gelfand DM, Gelfand S, Dobson W: Unprogrammed reinforcement of patients' behavior in a mental hospital. Behav Res Ther 5:201–207, 1967
48. Kazdin AE: The failure of some patients to respond to token programs. J Behav Ther Exp Psychiatry 4:7–14, 1973
49. Kazdin AE, Bootzin RR: The token economy: An evaluative review. J Appl Behav Anal 5:343–372, 1972
50. Kazdin AE: Behavior Modification in Applied Settings. Homewood, Ill., Dorsey Press, 1975
51. Patterson RL (Ed.): Maintaining Effective Token Economies. Springfield, Ill., Charles C. Thomas, 1976
52. Rusk TN: Future changes in mental health care. Hosp Community Psychiatry 23:7–9, 1972
53. Talbott J: Deinstitutionalization: Avoiding the disasters of the past. Hosp Community Psychiatry 30:621–624, 1979
54. Greenblatt M: Psychopolitics. New York, Grune and Stratton, 1978
55. Cohen RR: Mental hygiene for the trainee. Am J Psychiatry 100:62–71, 1943
56. Cohen RR: Factors in adjustment to army life. War Med 5:83–91, 1944
57. McNett I: Made for each other. APA Monitor 10:1–2, 1979
58. Paul GL: The implementation of treatment programs for chronic mental patients: Obstacles and recommendations, in Talbott JA (Ed.): The Chronic Mental Patient. Washington, D.C., The American Psychiatric Association, 1978
59. Talbott JA: What's wrong with mental hospitals. Hosp Staff Psysician: 68–70, 1979
60. Whitman D: Reorganization of Florida's human service agency. Kennedy School of Government Case Program, C95-80-040. Cambridge, Mass., Harvard University, 1980

2

Building Skills with Modular
Treatment and Training

What would a new car cost if old Henry Ford had required every employee to possess a Ph.D. in mechanical engineering? How many automobiles would be cruising the highways today if he had not developed the production line that employs workers at various levels of training—unskilled, semiskilled, and skilled—to perform many simple tasks that contribute to the creation of a complete automobile? Today's psychiatrists treating thousands of seriously ill patients who orbit in and out of hospitals are faced with an analagous situation. Can they provide quality treatment with staffs of limited training and budgets of modest size? They can, if they consider the finished "product" to be the total behavior pattern that a human being needs to live happily and purposefully in modern industrial society. This total behavior pattern is, of course, a complex of many simple behavioral skills that are learned. Many patients in mental hospitals have never developed adequate skills; others have lost skills while living in an institution where behaviors needed for independent living are not rewarded. A mental health worker or recovered patient with limited formal education can easily be trained to teach a single component or module of a behavioral skill. It is not essential for the teacher to understand the theory behind the teaching method, nor the selection of the target skill, nor the development of the treatment module, in order to teach it effectively.[1]

This modular psychoeducational approach does not focus just on "cur-

Portions of this chapter appeared originally in Gordon R, Patterson R, Eberly D, et al: Modular treatment of psychiatric patients, in Masserman J (Ed.): Current Psychiatric Therapies, vol. 19, New York, Grune and Stratton, 1980, and are reprinted with permission.

ing" maladaptive behavior nor dwell on what is "wrong" with a person; rather, it looks at what is "right," and attempts to increase the number and quality of each patient's adaptive skills. It augments present psychiatric treatment, replacing the frequently dehumanizing atmosphere in many institutions with one of purpose and direction for the patients. Modular psychoeducation provides a new technology for getting patients out of institutions and assisting them in reestablishing themselves in the community, and for diverting other patients from the path of long-term or repeated institutionalization.

MODULAR TREATMENT

Where are the mental patients in a treatment unit of a center utilizing modular treatment? Most hours of the day, when they are not at meals or consulting with their professional therapists in individual, group or family counseling, they are in classes. One group is attending a session on self-assertion, learning to resist pressure in constructive ways and to express feelings clearly, strongly, and tactfully. Another is receiving instruction on how to fill out a job application. Sitting at desks with typed course materials attached to their clipboards, they are taking notes just as if they were attending high school or college classes. On the adolescent unit a group is improving their skill in communicating, learning to listen, to request information from others, and to convey interest through body language. Elderly patients on the gerontology unit are learning to prepare nutritious meals. Nothing is happening haphazardly; the entire curriculum has been designed by the professional staff to fit a sequential program of training which systematically improves patients' skills in areas where assessments have shown they have deficits. Training modules are being developed to enhance skills in most areas where patients show impairments. When the deficits are shared by large numbers of patients, as in the areas of communication, problem solving, and self-assertion, a modular psychoeducational approach to skill enhancement training can be utilized. When the impairment is uncommon, as with head banging or feces smearing, or the patient's cognitive ability is limited, as with senile elderly patients and nonverbal autistic children, the psychological training must proceed in an individualized and sometimes less structured manner.

Treatment and Training Modules

Patients learn new skills in "modules," minicourses designed by the professional staff but taught by paraprofessionals. Bates adapted the modular treatment approach for psychiatric settings from its use in education and industry.[2,3] Bates' proposal to treat chronically ill and other patients in classes using psychoeducational modules provides an important innovation. Here indeed was a next step—a more systematic, structured and measurable step— in the treatment, education, prevention, evaluation, feedback, and therapy modification sequence we had conducted for over twenty years. Modular psychoeducation offered the potential for an easily evaluated treatment technique with assessment built into each module, in which paraprofessionals with limited training could provide hundreds of patients with quality, standardized treatment, and training under the supervision of only a few professionals. Truly, modular treatment could provide the answer to the mental health needs for great numbers of the nation's chronically ill mental patients if such programs could actually be shown to be effective in practice.

A modular psychoeducational treatment program received approval for implementation in 1975, and the first project was launched in December 1975, for 64 elderly patients of both sexes, half in residential and half in day hospital treatment. Each module contained the following elements:

1. A clearly defined psychoeducational goal, a statement of the number of hours required to complete the course, and recommendations regarding optimum numbers of students in a class and their educational prerequisites.
2. A statement of behavioral objectives.
3. A list of materials needed for the course.
4. An instructional design.
5. A standardized pretest that is given before the main content of the course.
6. The main content, which consists of the procedures by which the student can achieve each behavioral objective.
7. Standardized assessments that measure proficiency.
8. A standardized post-test that follows completion of the main content.
9. A final section that provides feedback from the patients to the instructor.

We require that psychoeducational staff, like staffs responsible for other patient services, prepare written treatment plans with manuals for implementing modular treatment. These manuals are also used for training and dissemination in workshops, consultations, mailings, and presentations. Each manual's detailed written plan, stated objectives, and precisely defined step-by-step procedures for achieving the objectives is in striking contrast to many traditional educational and psychological treatments that have ambiguous objectives and eclectic procedures (e.g., much classroom instruction and group therapy). By spelling out the details and assessing performance, professional staff are assured that a quality service is being rendered that can be replicated by other trained MHWs (mental health workers) in different settings and with different patients.

Modules are standardized, evaluated regularly, and revised periodically. Standardization allows procedures to be developed that can be readily understood, implemented, and assessed by minimally trained individuals. Evaluation submits the processes to objective scrutiny to determine if they work, under which conditions they do work, and how effective they are. Practices are not rigid; modules are revised and re-evaluated in the light of feedback, new techniques, experience, theory, and specific treatment needs with different populations.

The package of modules provides a bank of highly specific standard techniques demonstrated to be effective with certain clients in groups; with minor modifications they are suitable for adaptation to a variety of treatment settings.[4] Examples of modules and training manuals are provided in the Appendix. Before describing them in detail, a few words are needed now to provide definitions of terms that will be used in the pages that follow.

Terminology: Patients, Clients, Students, and Members

The first word of the previous section referred to mentally ill persons as "patients." Yet the last paragraph used the term "clients." When does a patient become a client, a member, or a student? Why the confusion in terminology?

Most mental health legislation traditionally referred to the mentally ill as "patients." In recent years, however, in an effort to avoid the stigma with which the expression "psychiatric patient" has become associated, legislators, administrators, nonmedical professionals, and others have increasingly adopted the term "client." But this annoys many psychiatrists and other physicians and nurses who consider that they treat patients. "Lawyers deal with clients," they maintain. To avoid confusion in these pages, as well as to defuse emotional controversy, we propose to use the following definitions, which take physical location and professional discipline into account.

Patients are treated by doctors, nurses, and other mental health professionals in hospitals, clinics, and physicians' private offices. They generally receive examinations, laboratory tests, diagnoses, and medications.

Clients obtain nonmedical counsel and assistance from lawyers, psychologists, social workers and paraprofessionals, usually in community settings.

Members belong to groups or organizations, whether peer management groups in the hospital, or community support programs.

Students meet together in classes conducted by teachers or trainers who also may supervise individual trainees in practical on-the-job or psychoeducational treatment applications or principles being learned.

Patients in the hospital become students or trainees when they attend skills building classes, clients when they are helped to find a home in the community, and members when they are admitted to a peer management group or leave the hospital and are included in a community support group. Every day they reside in the hospital, however, they are full-time patients. In the community, on the other hand, they resume patient status only for a few hours each month when they visit and obtain treatment from a psychiatrist or other physician. The rest of the time they are just like the rest of us—workers, students, members, citizens, and, occasionally, clients and patients. Remember that, at one time or another, each one of us has been a patient, client, member, or student.

In the pages that follow physicians and nurses will generally write about the patients they treat, social workers about the clients they counsel, educators about the students they teach or train, psychologists about the clients they train and counsel, and community network directors about the members of their group. Mentally ill persons, like everyone else, fill different roles when they interact at different times with various professionals, paraprofessionals, and each other.

Behavioral Management Terms

Many behavioral management terms will be used in these pages—prompting, modeling, shaping, and the like. Sometimes they will be defined in the text. Otherwise, the reader who is unfamiliar with the precise meaning of a term should consult the Glossary, where definitions are supplied and examples provided.

Professionals and Paraprofessionals

This book will adhere to tradition in its definition of professionals and paraprofessionals. Professional mental health personnel include psychiatrists, other physicians who work in mental health settings, psychologists, and persons with doctoral degrees in education who work in mental health, nurses, and master's level psychiatric social workers. These individuals may have completed the licensing and certification requirements of their fields.

The term paraprofessional mental health worker (MHW) refers to those individuals who are, or can be, trained to function in mental health service delivery positions that would normally require a baccalaureate degree, equivalent experience, or less, and who are not otherwise included under national classification systems of certification or recognized professional disciplines. Social service workers who hold a bachelor's degree are included under the category of paraprofessionals.

Allied health professionals and persons in professions outside mental health will be referred to by field or discipline—gerontologists, lawyers, occupational therapists, and the like.

PARAPROFESSIONALS (MHWs) AS THERAPISTS

There is a strong precedent[5] for using trained mental health workers as therapists, with professional supervision or consultation. Paraprofessionals are being trained in community college human service programs,[6] in workshops, and in personal consultation on treatment units. With professional supervision, modular treatment is conducted by Specialists, Psychiatric Aides, and Charge Aides, job classifications paying $6765 to $10,127 a year. Patients spend six to eight hours a day attending classes conducted by unit staff who employ treatment modules or packages within a skill-building framework. The role of paraprofessionals in mental health is dealt with at greater length in Chapters 8, 9, and 10.

ROLE OF PROFESSIONALS

In settings like public mental institutions, which are staffed with three times as many paraprofessionals as professionals, where treatment staff to patient ratios are less than one-to-one (274 to 371 in the research and training facility here), and where physicians are sometimes not fluent in the English language, it is important to delineate clearly the roles of paraprofessionals and professionals. All treatment, research, and training that can be delegated is provided by paraprofessionals, since only they can provide enough direct service contact hours to deal with the large volume of patients on a regular basis. Professionals supervise the paraprofessionals; they limit their own direct personal treatment of patients to those areas which no other staff can perform, such as prescribing medications. Primarily, professionals direct, supervise, manage, and monitor all activities of paraprofessionals, consult with staff, develop new treatment, management, and assessment techniques, train students, develop training materials, and evaluate the effectiveness and efficiency of the program. This subject is dealt with at great length in Chapters 8 and 9.

CONCERNS OF PROFESSIONALS

Physicians, nurses and other professionals have expressed concern about training paraprofessionals to utilize behavior management and psychoeducational treatment techniques. They feel threatened that professionals will lose not only status, but also private patients to these MHWs. However, once nurses, physicians or other professionals themselves have attended the course that the paraprofessionals receive, and understand the principles and techniques used, their worries disappear. There is no way that a brief course will prepare a high school graduate to compete in private practice with a physician, nurse, or other professional. Nevertheless, the course does prepare the employee to teach a component of a module, and thus to extend the reach of the professional who is supervising the care of the patients. In fact, the system-wide association that accredits continuing education for nursing personnel has made the modular psychoeducational program described here their number one accredited course. Officers of District Branches and Members of the Assembly of the American Psychiatric Association have commended the modular approach and its developers to national authorities.

PSYCHOEDUCATION

Psychoeducational treatment combines psychological and educational methods to teach patients personal and social skills. It combines structured educational curricula with lesson plans, didactic teaching, and exercises to facilitate the application of knowledge about the skills to be learned; behavioral psychology and operant conditioning are employed to teach the skills.

Three features characterize the psychoeducational approach to therapy. (1) The therapist assumes the role of educator and trainer; he uses the treatment situation as an instructional setting to teach both the knowledge and the performance of the skills to be learned. (2) The patient assumes the role of a student who is an active participant in learning to enhance his skills; he may also assist others in the learning of new behaviors—he is not the passive recipient of a "cure," but is responsible for his own development. (3) In psychoeducation, lesson plans describe and delimit the content of each meeting at the onset of training, and each session has a planned agenda; this approach facilitates its use by therapists with a wide range of skills.[1]

Psychoeducational treatment is most effective when conducted in a classroom group, particularly if patients have varying degrees of dysfunction in the same behavioral skill areas. Each patient benefits from the information and instruction provided by the teacher-therapist. Patients may learn skills from fellow patients; they may aid each other in improving skills by providing information and feedback and by modeling appropriate personal and social behaviors.

Categories of Skill Enhancement Modules

Within each of the following broad categories, levels of skills can be differentiated. A few samples will clarify the types of skills which fall into each category.

Survival skills comprise behaviors essential to safety and life. The self-injurious behavior of an autistic child or the confused wandering of a disoriented elderly patient requires treatment at the level of survival skills.

Daily living skills include basic self-care activities, such as dressing, grooming, and eating. At a higher level, these self-help skills include doing laundry and handling finances.

Personal and social skills include the self-management of affective responses, coping and problem-solving skills, as well as interpersonal communication, assertion, cooperation, and proper social behavior.

Academic and vocational skills are achievement-oriented skills, such as those required for competence in school or on the job. These include effective study habits and classroom decorum, as well as securing and maintaining gainful employment.

Leisure skills involve the constructive and pleasurable use of leisure time. These skills are required by those patients who are social isolates and who involve themselves in potentially harmful situations and activities.

Cognitive skills are those dealing with forming or restructuring internal thought processes or belief systems. Depression training and anxiety management treat these processes.

Integrative skills deal with such areas as clarifying values, building self-esteem, setting goals, and measuring personal achievements. Many ungoverned adolescents and psychotic adults have never gained or have lost the ability to give their lives a sense of purpose and direction. These modules, which have recently been introduced, are planned to help them develop these abilities.

Different combinations of modules are required by patients of various ages, degree of chronicity, and severity of illness. Patients are grouped for psychoeducational treatment into three major program areas, those for the elderly aged 55 and over, the adults age 19–54, and children and adolescents age 18 and below. Programs for the elderly emphasize the development of leisure skills, since few if any of this population will be able to acquire gainful employment in a competitive job market. They will usually be receiving transfer payments and will be in contact with human service workers from state divisions of Aging Services when they leave the hospital.

Younger adults may enter the employment field and, thus, their programs usually involve Vocational Rehabilitation personnel and services. Children and adolescents are still dependent upon their parents and foster parents, who are therefore included in the treatment. Their treatment also involves the formal educational system and agencies like Social and Economic Services, which serve problem children and their families.

Family therapy is also available in the treatment of hospitalized adult patients. Family therapy is unusual in the care of schizophrenics. Mosher and Keith[7] found only three controlled studies of the effectiveness of family therapy with schizophrenics. Reporting on the needs of families of chronic mental patients, Hatfield[8] writes

. . . almost nowhere is the family identified as an important part of the treatment and rehabilitation team. This seems like a strange omission since many patients de-

Table 2-1

Skills taught in modular classes to patients of different ages and their families

Categories of skills	Components	Elderly	Young adults	Chronic adults	Adolescents	Children	Families
Survival skills	Medication training	X	X	X			X
	Personal information	X			X		
	Compliant behavior	X	X	X	X	X	X
Daily living skills	Personal hygiene/eating/toilet	X		X	X	X	X
	Home care	X	X	X	X	X	X
	Independent living	X	X	X	X		
Personal/social skills	Managing stress		X	X			
	Communicating	X	X	X	X	X	X
	Personal health	X	X	X	X		
	Problem solving	X	X	X	X		X
	Asserting	X	X	X	X		X
	Negotiating		X		X		X
	Relaxing	X	X				X
	Sex role		X		X		
	Peer support		X	X	X		X
	Leadership		X				
Academic/vocational skills		X	X	X	X	X	
Leisure skills		X	X	X	X	X	X
Self-integrative skills	Building self-esteem	X					
	Clarifying values		X		X		X
	Goal setting		X	X			
	Measuring personal achievement				X		
Cognitive skills	Managing anxiety and depression	X	X	X			X

pend heavily upon relatives. It has been estimated that as many as two-thirds of released patients return to their families . . . others found that the family was the primary resource for the patient.

Table 2-1 shows the categories of modules presently used with patients of various age groups and their families.

Assessment

Professionals have developed assessment batteries that include (1) standard psychosocial histories, (2) general measures of psychosocial functioning, (3) specific measurements of current functioning within each of the modular areas, and (4) instruments that measure the level of community or environmental support the patient receives. Staff who administer these instruments do not require a master's or doctoral degree in psychology. Like the teaching staff, they have been trained by professionals to administer, score, code, and fill in the assessment tests.

In addition to medical diagnosis and treatment, each patient receives an initial behavioral assessment upon admission and then periodic reassessments about every four weeks. Individual patients are assigned to classes according to measured deficiencies in their skills. During treatment, standardized assessments with psychosocial rating scales and proficiency gauges, and specific ones related to individual problems, tell how well the patient is progressing toward discharge. Final assessment precedes discharge. Follow-up instruments are also administered after discharge to measure patient progress upon return to the community.

All of the assessment instruments serve both clinical and program evaluation purposes. They provide feedback to the staff that helps to sustain a high level of effort and morale. Discharge is indicated when the patient has acquired sufficient skill to function efficiently with noninstitutional community sources of support. For example, a patient who has learned to handle finances, keep house, and prepare meals, among other activities, may be considered ready for independent living.

Not every patient may achieve the same level of skill, however. Assessments objectively reveal the degree to which each learns skills, information that is crucial to proper placement upon discharge. If a particular patient needs help in taking his medicine, for example, then a placement must be found that provides this service. Placement is built into the entire treatment program. From the initial assessments to the final interview, all training and assessment are placement oriented and placement relevant; and vice versa, all assessment measures are validated by their relationship to objective criteria such as their usefulness in predicting successful placements. Those instruments with low correlations are replaced.

Modular Psychoeducation in Treatment Programming

In many facilities a great number of patients may spend large blocks of unstructured time passively sitting in chairs lined up along the walls of the treatment unit or in front of the television set. Modular treatment and training can fill these large empty gaps in the patients' treatment programs. Adequate medical and nursing care that addresses patients' acute problems can be provided in a relatively few hours each day; the remainder of their waking time can be devoted to carefully planned psychoeducational programs that enhance their skills, improve their supports, and increase their ability to enjoy their leisure. Their psychoeducation may include selected TV viewing with follow-up discussion of current events, planned sitting in active conversational groups, and individualized use of free time that provides a well-earned rest. Every patient's treatment plan, derived from assessing individual problems, strengths, and skills deficits, should include systematic skill enhancement among its goals and objectives, and regular assessment to measure progress.

Bedell et al.[9] have developed a Problem Rating Scale (PRS) to assess a variety of personal and social phenomena rated as problems for psychiatric patients. Higher scores in the PRS denote greater pathology in 15 categories—the areas of alcohol/drug abuse, anxiety, confusion, depression, education, household management, interpersonal involvement, outside social involvement, personal adjustment, physical complaints, relation to children, self-definition, sexuality, suicide, and work.

Community Support Training

Modular programs of training also have been developed for persons in the community who provide environmental support to psychiatric patients. For example, the Gerontology Project staff provides training for Adult Services personnel, often delivered in classes utilizing training modules. Training of community service workers in various agencies is not only related to the care of specific patients, it is also part of the dissemination efforts in facilities that include training along with service and research in their mission. Written training packages for workers in mental health and other human services agencies are tried out and assessed locally. Those that prove successful are disseminated through workshops and consultations.

Individualized Behavioral Treatment

In addition to behavioral deficits that can be dealt with by modules, many patients have idiosyncratic problems. Extremely bizarre behaviors cannot be managed by modules and group treatment at present, but require individualized behavior management. Staff learn to use these techniques, as well as the modular skill-building methods, in a 30-hour in-service training course, which they take along with their medical and nursing training upon beginning employment. Parents and foster parents also receive similar training.[10,11] They learn to manage their children's problem behaviors in the home, to reinforce the gains their children make in the treatment program, and to maintain them when they leave the treatment facility. The content of these courses is outlined in Chapter 10.

The first step in therapeutic behavior management is an objective assessment of the patient's repertoire of behaviors. Some, of course, will be adequate. Behavior management focuses on behavioral extremes; it decreases inappropriate behaviors and/or increases weak or nonexistent adaptive skills. The second step is to identify and define the target behaviors that will become the objectives of the treatment plan. Precise definitions are very important, because all staff must be able to observe and record the same specific behaviors in order to measure the patient's progress. The patient also should be helped to understand why these target behaviors have been selected (e.g., "Your habit of spitting at others when you don't get your way is unacceptable and will not be rewarded; at the same time, you need to learn more effective ways of asserting yourself in dealing with people"). Here the modular program is especially helpful since patients can be assigned to classes, such as assertion training, where their assessments have shown they have defects and where the target behavior is defined in advance.

Before a treatment plan is implemented, however, staff gather baseline data by objectively observing and recording the occurrence of the target behaviors over a specified period of time. Exact accounting of frequency of extreme behaviors avoids misinterpretation of an isolated or rare behavior. Environmental antecedents of behavior may also be observed and often help in formulating the treatment plan. Baseline data are essential reference points for charting repeated observations during treatment to determine whether target behaviors are actually increasing or decreasing. Treatment plans that do not produce the desired behavioral objectives must be revised.

Repeated assessments during the course of treatment not only provide a record of an individual patient's progress, but also indicate that treatment may be ended when the behavioral objectives have been achieved. Collectively, these data make it possible to carry out evaluative research that demonstrates the overall effectiveness of various modules and programs. These records of treatments and results also meet the requirements for accountability and accreditation.

Disruptive behaviors are particularly troublesome to manage. A standard set of psychological techniques for reducing or eliminating violence and other unacceptable behaviors includes the following behavioral procedures.

Extinction of inappropriate behavior.   Extinction is effective with behaviors that are maintained by staff attention. Constant crying, whining, or engaging in bizarre verbal behaviors often respond to withdrawal of attention.

Response cost.   Examples include missing a ride to a party because of a delay in getting dressed, losing privileges for stealing, and losing tokens for abusive language when tokens are earned through using polite language.

Time-out.   The patient is removed from the classroom because of disruptive behavior. In exclusion time-out the patient sits alone for three to five minutes where the class cannot be seen.

Contingent observation.   The patient is removed from an activity but required to observe the appropriate behavior of others in the class. The patient rejoins the activity after a specified period of observation, having promised to behave appropriately. (Contingent observation is essentially exclusion time-out plus the educational component of observation.)

Differential reinforcement of other behavior.   This procedure is useful for decreasing self-injurious behavior, since appropriate behaviors are strengthened concurrently. Differential reinforcement is used in token economies where patients receive tokens for engaging in appropriate behavior (being on time or practicing a skill) and are fined for inappropriate behavior.

Overcorrection.   These procedures require patients to rectify the effects of their destructive behavior. In household orderliness training the patient learns the proper care of property; he not only corrects the damage (e.g., repositions an overturned chair), but also straightens the remaining objects in the class.

Required relaxation (quiet training).   Quiet training generally consists of going to bed immediately and lying down for a specified period of time following an object-throwing, screaming episode, or some other disruptive behavior.

COMBINING DIFFERENT THERAPIES IN THE TREATMENT PROCESS

Program planning recognizes the changing needs of patients as they progress in the treatment process. In the first, acute phase, Period A in Figure 2-1, treatment for patients who are overtly psychotic and may be exhibiting behavioral excesses emphasizes (1) medical and (2) behavioral

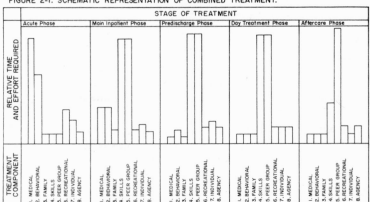

Fig. 2-1.   Schematic representation of combined treatment. This figure illustrates the relative importance of different components in various periods of the treatment process. Patients may not participate in every phase shown; in particular, they may never enter day treatment. However, this schema serves to illustrate the generalized program of treatment received by most patients.

components. Well-planned scheduling of daily activities (see Table 14-1.), which addresses patients' individual requirements as well as their stage in therapy, helps keep disruptive behavior to a minimum, and reduces the need for such behavioral methods as time out from positive reinforcement and seclusion. When required, however, these procedures are made part of the individual's treatment plan. Medical examination and treatment, initially stressing the use of major psychotropics, and behavioral management techniques, especially differential reinforcement of other competing behaviors and staff-managed token economies, help bring aggression, physical violence, and psychotic behavior under control. Medications are generally needed more frequently with adults, and behavioral procedures with children. These procedures prepare the patients for the main inpatient phase—Period B.

Period B concentrates on (4) modular skill building and self-help and (5) peer management and support. Family Therapy (3) continues; it is most important with children, especially younger ones where parent training may be a major component of the overall treatment plan, both during the hospital stay and in maintaining the child's behavioral gains after discharge (see Chapter 13). Psychotherapeutic games (see Chapter 7) are often used with other didactic and practice sessions for teaching skills.

In the predischarge and day treatment phases of treatment, Periods C and D, patients become increasingly responsible for their own and other patients' treatment. Self-medication with reduced doses of psychotropics and peer management responsibilities move to the fore. Throughout all periods, patients engage in (6) recreational and other activities. Early in treatment, patients who are operating at low functional levels engage primarily in recreations where few demands are made on their performance. As they reach higher levels of functioning, they move up to psychoeducational skill-building programs, which take over some of the time for recreation. Patients now begin to participate in leisure skills training, where they perform actively as students in classes.

Throughout the entire treatment program (7) individual counseling continues. Patients of average or better intelligence, whose self-confidence has grown sufficiently as a result of their increased skills, improved performance, and growing peer and other supports, and who can handle insights, may receive dynamic therapy. But all patients, regardless of degree of impairment in skills and intelligence, learn basic communication, tactful self-assertion, and problem-solving skills; they are taught to apply these in coping with their own personal day-to-day problems.

After discharge, in Period E, sessions of counseling and psychotherapy decrease from daily to weekly or less in the community; however, the natural and peer support groups take up the slack by providing counseling and goal-directed services to expatients, as described in the next chapter. Now, productive behavior has replaced disruptive; newly learned skills are maintained by the individual patients themselves, by the peer group, the family, and by (8) community groups, including employers, teachers, and foster home, boarding home, and congregate living facility managers—all of whom have been consulting with the research and training center staff throughout the treatment process. Many have received special training in behavioral and modular psychoeducational methods in workshops and personal consultations.

Involving Community Agencies and Personnel

In the acute phase of treatment, Period A, research and training facility staff confer with community personnel largely to gather information regarding patients that contributes to planning individual treatments. Community therapists, mental health centers, and others exchange knowledge about patients' social, military, legal, vocational, financial, and educational histories.

Social agency staff are taught to participate actively with treatment staff in the main therapeutic phase, Period B. They collaborate in providing educational and vocational training and activities, legal and financial aid, and other services like aid for dependent children.

This collaboration continues in Periods C and D as the patients get ready for discharge and for reentering community life. Residential treatment staff, primarily paraprofessionals, arrange with community personnel for housing, financing, and medical, dental, and continuing psychiatric care; for recreation, religious services, and for the patients to join community groups like Parents Without Partners and Alcoholics Anonymous.

After discharge, in Period E, research and training center staff collaborate with community groups in providing peer support and assessment and evaluation; they continue to serve as trainers and consultants, both in the center and in home and site visits, to schools, employers, and sheltered workshops; to foster homes, boarding homes, congregate living facilities, and foster parents; and to Community Mental Health Centers (CMHCs) and individual therapists to the fullest extent possible considering the time and resources available.

Research and training center staff and patients actively developed these integrated programs, initially with resistence from some administrative supervisors, who instructed them to focus on inpatient treatment services and to leave community programs to other agencies in the fragmented nonsystem. Staff successes in developing a patient peer group community network (see Chapter 3), in disseminating the programs, in obtaining grants for community programs, in evaluating and demonstrating the effectiveness of the treatments, as well as in benefiting the patients themselves, have gradually gained community recognition and support for integrating services rather than leaving them fragmented.

MODULAR TRAINING AND INDIVIDUAL TREATMENT: A MATRIX ORGANIZATION

Skill-enhancing modular training occurs within an overall treatment environment. To be effective, modular training must be conducted as a component of a total patient care program. All elements are mutually complementary, one reinforcing the other. For example, if a patient is receiving Personal Hygiene Training in Activities of Daily Living-I (ADL I), his daily ward routine must be modified so that he can practice bathing or shaving independently. Likewise, changes in medication can cause changes in behavior or in cognitive functioning that bear directly on performance in modular training. A patient's attendance in a training group is partly based, therefore, on his current medical treatment plan, and coordinated according to his total condition. Similarly, mandatory attendance in modular training groups may interfere with his medical treatment goals. In short, modular training must be an integral part of a total treatment program, and not operate independently from the rest of his treatment.

A good way to integrate modular training into the total treatment program is for both to be under common managerial and supervisory responsibility. For example, the Project Coordinator must have as much responsibility for modular training as for seeing that patients consult their physician for medications. All staff who provide direct care or who affect treatment plans must be as invested in modular training as they are in other components of patient care. Two major day-to-day methods integrate this operation: (1) The treatment team meets regularly to review the patient's total condition, including his progress in modular training. (2) Each member of the treatment staff, regardless of organization function or status, accepts modular responsibilities as trainer, observer, assessor, or coordinator (see Figs. 9-2 and 9-3).

Each staff person, therefore, has two role assignments, one as a member of the treatment team with a functional classification (i.e., head nurse, psychiatric aide, physician, licensed practical nurse (LPN), psychologist, and another in the modular training organization (module program supervisor, module coordinator, trainer, observer, or assessor). The duties of the latter three roles are obvious: conducts training, observes and records patient behavior, and conducts the periodic assessments. The former two roles involve the following activities.

Module Program Supervisor (Training Program Coordinator)

PROGRAM DETERMINATION

1. Decides which modules will be taught.
2. Plans when and where modules will be taught.
3. Knows what materials will be used.
4. Determines what assessments will be made.

PROGRAM STAFFING

1. Selects module coordinators.
2. Assigns trainers/observers/assessors (coordinates with ward supervisors).
3. Determines what training is required and who will provide it (cooperates with staff development and ward supervisor).
4. Resolves scheduling conflicts and provides for adequate vacation, shift, holiday coverage.
5. Monitors staff performance and provides feedback.

PROGRAM ADMINISTRATION

1. Determines what assessment and sessional data are required.
2. Decides who will record them; how and when they will be entered in client chart.
3. Determines which clients will attend what module.
4. Decides what procedures will be used to assess client "graduation."
5. Integrates module training with discharge/placement planning.

PROGRAM TREATMENT INTEGRATION

1. Attends treatment team meetings and reports on patient module performance.
2. Reviews individual patient performance in modules with each module coordinator.
3. Makes recommendations for patients to enter, graduate, or drop modules.

Modular Coordinator

MODULE DOCUMENTATION

1. Fully documents module objective, patient behavior goals, training methods and techniques, facility and materials requirements, sessional and periodic measurements and assessments, patient admission and graduation criteria, and record keeping and administrative procedures.
2. Assures that patient modular performance is properly recorded and entered in chart.
3. Maintains record of patients who have taken module and their performance.

MODULE STAFF

1. Trains trainers, observers, and assessors.
2. Assures each training session is properly staffed.
3. Monitors staff performance, observers, and assessors as required.

MODULE ADMINISTRATION

1. Maintains module and staff assignment schedules.
2. Maintains client training schedules.
3. Recommends admission, graduation, or termination of client's participation in the module.
4. Reports on client's performance as requested and participates in treatment and placement planning.

The above statements of duties, tasks, and responsibilities are general guides. They are not all inclusive, and are modified and supplemented to meet individual differences in programs, facilities, personnel, and patients served.

Assignments are made on the basis of individual competencies, personal preferences, and emotional investment in some particular type of skill training. A clinical psychologist, for example, may be the assessor for a cognitive behavior module because of research interest in this difficult measurement area. In this role the psychologist may report to an LPN who is the coordinator for Self-Esteem Training because the latter has received special training or has acquired experience in leading such groups. In short, module assignments cut across organizational and professional roles, and distinctions concentrate on specific tasks and provide an integrating mechanism that is patient-treatment oriented. Most staff fill some module training role. This use of matrix organization provides for an efficient utilization of staff.

Changing Modules

When assessment and evaluation show that a specific module is ineffective, it can be removed from the program without interrupting the flow of patient care. The whole treatment program does not need to come to a halt in order for a more promising module to replace an older, less useful one. The modular treatment approach, therefore, lends itself to continued upgrading as improvements in modules increase the effectiveness and quality of the components.

EVALUATION

These treatment programs, since they primarily are using paraprofessionals, are not costly to implement. Patients who have been trained to take care of themselves, furthermore, are cheaper to support after they return to the community than when they were residing in the state hospitals. After training in personal information and restoration of their self-esteem, plus training in leisure skills, communication, self-assertion, problem-solving, and other areas, they lead happy and interesting lives in their new homes in the community.

Effectiveness

The modular treatment program was compared by use of a quasi-experimental design to a traditional therapeutic program at a state hospital. In 1976, 129 elderly patients were selected from among those hospitalized at Hospital A. Seventy volunteered for transfer for modular treatment; 59 voluntarily remained at Hospital A. Demographic and diagnostic data indicated that the two groups were fairly well matched. Both groups of patients had previously resided at Hospital A an average of two years. Data comparing outcomes of treatment at the two facilities are shown in Tables 2-2 and 2-3.

Those who entered modular care fared better than those who did not. After a shorter average period of treatment (17.2 versus 21.7 weeks), a significantly larger percentage of the modular treatment group were discharged than those who remained in traditional care (74 percent versus 53 percent). A major difference between the two treatment outcomes was that six times

Table 2-2
Effectiveness of modular treatment with gerontology patients

	Modular treatment	Traditional treatment
Number of patients	70	59
Effectiveness		
Mean length of stay before discharge (weeks)	17.2	21.7
Discharged from hospital (percentage)	74	53
Rehospitalization rates (percentage)	4	29

as large a percentage of the modular program's discharged patients (30 percent versus 5 percent of those in traditional treatment), moved into local boarding or foster homes. Twenty-three percent of those who underwent modular treatment were discharged to independent living; only seven percent of those under traditional treatment were able to live independently. Finally, eight months on the average after discharge, only four percent of the patients who received modular care needed reinstitutionalization, less than one-seventh of the 29 percent who required readmission after discharge from the group that chose to remain in traditional state hospital care. None of the elderly patients treated successfully by the modular approach were sent to live in nursing homes.

A year after discharge, 77.4 percent of elderly chronically ill mental patients were still responding well to modular treatment. They were remaining in noninstitutional community settings. In contrast, only 23.9 percent of those treated by traditional methods were not back in an institution after one year.[12]

Individual follow-up psychosocial assessments of patients after discharge, and interviews with significant persons in their homes, point to the continued effectiveness of the modular treatment program. The assessments

Table 2-3
Discharge destination of gerontology patients by type of treatment

	Modular treatment (percentage)	Traditional treatment (percentage)
Destination		
Independent living	23	7
Boarding or foster homes	30	5
Not discharged from hospital	26	47
Living with family	17	34
Other	4	7
Total	100	100

Note: Fewer patients who volunteered for modular treatment had families.

show that the majority of elderly patients are not merely derelicts, clustered in slum neighborhoods, but are living in locations throughout the community where they participate in a variety of social activities. At discharge, staff set therapeutic goals for the patients to achieve in the subsequent three-month period. The evaluations show that the patients have done well at attaining thes goals.

Neither the comparison study nor the post discharge follow-up data can pinpoint modular training as the unique variable that produced the remarkable and significant results. Ongoing research is seeking greater precision in isolating and identifying the relationships more fully. What can be stated is that a program that utilized modular training as the predominant treatment modality was more effective than traditional state hospital treatment; it reduced recidivism significantly and helped former patients who had spent nearly two years of their lives in a state hospital to adjust well to normal community living. Some other variables that may account for these results include the milieu of this program, unknown patient selection criteria, or higher levels of staff motivation and treatment effort.

EVALUATION OF SKILLS BUILDING WITH ADULT
PATIENTS

Results from evaluative studies point to the effectiveness of modular skill building in enhancing the living and coping skills of adult mental patients. A series of studies by Bedell, Archer, Marlowe, and associates[9,13-15] evaluated the overall effectiveness of the modules on personality characteristics of adult patients. Patients were tested at admission and again at discharge with the Rotter Internal External Locus of Control (I-E) Scale[16] and the Spielberger, Gorsuch, and Lushene State-Trait Anxiety Inventory (STAI) Trait Anxiety Scale.[17] In contrast to admission I-E mean scores of 9.71, the patient's discharge I-E mean score of 8.10 was significantly more internal ($p < .01$). This indicates that after completing a six week treatment program patients expected to exercise significantly more personal control over important reinforcers in their lives than they did at admission.[13] Trait anxiety (A-Trait) was also significantly reduced as a result of six weeks of treatment from an admission A-Trait mean level of 50.71 to a discharge mean of 46.69 ($p < .01$).

In later investigations, the effectiveness of two specific modules (problem solving and depression management) were examined. Bedell et al.[9] compared the pre- and post-test performance of patients receiving a six-week problem-solving module in terms of a knowledge inventory of problem-solving skills and performance ratings in a simulated problem-solving situation. A control group, matched on pretest scores, was also included in data analyses. Results showed that experimental problem-solving patients improved significantly more than controls on both knowledge ($p < .05$) and behavioral performance ($p < .01$) measures.

Vagg et al.[14] examined the effectiveness of the depression management module using multiple depression measures that included both behavioral ratings and standardized self-report assessments. As in the problem-solving study, pre- and post-test depression scores were compared both for subjects receiving six weeks of cognitively oriented depression management training and for control subjects receiving the standard treatment modules with the exclusion of the depression module. Results demonstrated significant reductions in the experimental depression module group. The improvement showed a consistent pattern across depression measures and was significantly greater than improvement in the control group patients. Additional evaluations suggest that patients significantly strengthen their communication skills, learn relaxation skills, and acquire more accurate sexual knowledge as a function of modular treatment.

COST EFFECTIVENESS

The program for young adults is a five weekday, four weeknight regimen in which patients leave the research and training center each weekend and return to their community residences. The data reported above were collected after the sixth treatment week, after 30 days and 24 nights of residential psychoeducational treatment. This project is conducted by a typical state hospital unit staff of 23 personnel—1 psychiatrist, 6 nurses, 2 social workers, 1 secretary, and 13 paraprofessionals—and their salaries totaled $243,000 per annum in 1978–1979. Up to 32 patients were treated on this unit at a time. In 1978–1979 the team treated 178 patients for up to nine weeks of residential care (45 days, 36 nights) at an average treatment team personnel cost of $1806 per patient. This amounts to $35.57 a day for treatment-team costs per patient completing the program. Adding expense costs, the figure amounts to approximately $45 a day. Compare this cost with those reported in 1979 for other public psychiatric institutions: state hospitals ($60.00 a day),[18] municipal hospitals ($100 a day),[19] community mental health centers ($255 a day).[18]

Measurable, significant, and meaningful improvements occurred with psychiatric patients within six weeks (30 days and 24 nights of residential care). This fact is important to health authorities, since insurance carriers now offer up to 30 days and nights of residential care.

PREDICTION OF SUCCESSFUL
DEINSTITUTIONALIZATION

Of special importance will be the relationships found, if any, between scores on assessment measures administered prior to or early in treatment and subsequent criteria—outcomes of treatment, successes and failures, as well as dropouts. With major deinstitutionalization efforts throughout the nation, it will be useful to know whether the patients who do not benefit from these treatment methods and who require rehospitalization can be identified early.

Limitations

PATIENT SELECTION

All patients in these treatment programs are volunteers for research. Adults sign informed consent forms for human experimentation, as do parents of minors and guardians of legal incompetents. Results with all patients, experimentals, and controls must be interpreted with the reservation in mind that they include findings from self-selected samples. Because of construction features and the location of the treatment buildings, bedridden patients cannot be accepted for treatment, nor those who are dangerous to themselves or others, or unable to save themselves in case of a fire or other life-threatening emergency. Nevertheless, the patients treated include the vast majority of chronically ill, low income, mental patients requiring help in the state hospital system in the catchment area served.

EDUCATION OF STAFF

These modular training and research programs are being developed in a treatment facility located on a university campus. This location affects the treatment programs. Although the level of education and experience required for employment and the salaries received by the staff are modest, college students and graduates actively compete for low-level staff positions. The true test of the effectiveness of these programs will come when results of psychoeducational efforts at rural state hospitals and elsewhere are analyzed. Programs are being implemented in these settings, data are being collected, and the results and findings will be reported. Each of the state hospitals now has a community college human service program conducted on its grounds. State hospital staff are receiving training in the psychoeducational modular approach that utilizes components of the modular training series. The modular program for gerontology patients has been transferred in full to state hospitals and early results have been promising (see Chapter 10).

PATIENT DROPOUTS

Two patients were recently talking about insanity. They were overheard by a staff member as one spoke to the other. "I've made up my mind," he stated. "I've decided to stay insane for the rest of my life. At least I can handle that."

Psychoeducational learning requires effort by patients; many chose not to make the effort. Patients drop out of psychoeducational programs just as they do out of formal schooling in high school and college. Thirty-one percent of young adults, for example, dropped out of treatment; so did 21 percent of the elderly patients transferred from the state hospital. Furthermore, others refused the offer to participate in the program. Several state hospital patients did not hesitate to state their reasons: They had no wish to leave the shelter of the asylum. They preferred to follow their favorite soap operas on television each day.

Greenblatt[20] points out that, in addition to protecting patients' rights, it is time to consider their responsibilities. In his opinion, patients should be responsible for (1) learning the rules and regulations of the institution in which they reside, (2) cooperating in treatment, (3) refraining from destructive and violent behavior, (4) joining in patient councils and patient government in order to improve the therapeutic program, (5) learning the skills of successful living in ward society and in the world outside, (6) mastering a useful occupation and making progress toward becoming self-supporting, and (7) learning to identify early signs of recurring illness. These are some of the components of the modular skills training programs.

DISCUSSION

A modular method of treating psychiatric patients in classes designed and supervised by professionals utilizes individualized assessment and treatment programs, skill-building modules, and paraprofessionals as teachers. It appears to offer an effective, inexpensive technology for augmenting psychiatric treatment. Initial findings indicate that psychoeducational treatment assists in deinstitutionalizing elderly patients and maintaining them successfully in meaningful community lives or activities. Later chapters will show how modular treatment diverts elderly patients from hospitalization, provides a means of treating seriously disturbed autistic and other chronically ill children and adolescents, and prepares chronically ill adult mental patients to return from the mental hospital and remain in the community.

Modular psychiatric skills-building treatment, along with the supports-building techniques discussed in the next chapter, prepares many poorly communicative chronic patients, whom psychotherapists often find unappealing and difficult to treat, to become more amenable to dynamic individual and group approaches. After learning techniques for improving their communication, for solving problems, for asserting, and for keeping their symptoms under control with the help of behavioral and self-medication training, after beginning to set personal goals and to strive for them with the help of their community network of peers, and for developing the necessary vocational and educational abilities, many become promising candidates for outpatient dynamic psychotherapy. With the help of individual or group psychotherapy in the private psychotherapist's office or the community mental health center, they can custom-tailor the knowledge and skill they gained in modular classes to fit their own individual circumstances.

The programs described, when presented in a modular fashion in a series of workshops, have attracted the interest of mental health and other human service personnel, who gather from all over the area periodically to attend training sessions. Returning to their own facilities, they select modular components of each program for use in their own community settings.

Dissemination

PSYCHOEDUCATIONAL TRAINING OF MENTAL
HEALTH AND OTHER HUMAN SERVICE WORKERS

Many previous reports have described the difficulties encountered in establishing behavioral programs in mental hospitals, public schools, and correctional institutions. They often work well with limited subject groups, utilizing unique facilities and employing individually trained staff, but their value may be challenged if they are suited only for special laboratory-type settings. Yet, if a program of treatment is to be effective in a system for deinstitutionalizing patients or diverting them at young ages from institutional care, it must be disseminated widely and must receive acceptance from those in the institutions and facilities who would use it.

A stumbling block to implementation is that behavioral therapies require nurses, activities therapists, and psychiatric aides to practice an art that they are ill trained to perform. They have not learned in their previous schooling to conceptualize a mental health problem as a deficit in skills that can be treated by training and education (skills building). Thus, they are not prepared to make sophisticated judgments such as (1) how can you operationalize the behavioral skill to be taught? (2) what is the proper contingency to be introduced? (3) who will evoke the contingency and how often? (4) how do you elicit the desired behavior? (5) how do you shape the behavior? (6) when is a prompt necessary? and (7) when does a behavior represent an approximation and therefore warrant reinforcement? Subsequent chapters show how personnel acquire this preparation and training.

REFERENCES

1. Bedell JR, Weathers LR: A psycho-educational model for skill training: therapist-facilitated and game-facilitated applications, in Upper D, Ross SM (Eds): Behavioral Group Therapy, 1979: An Annual Review. Champaign, Ill., Research Press, 1979, pp 201–235
2. Bates HD: Proposal for a gerontological assessment treatment and training project at the Florida Mental Health Institute. Tampa, Fla., 1975
3. Bates HD (Ed): Gerontology Project Staff Training Manual and Workbook. Tampa, Fla., Florida Mental Health Institute, 1975
4. Gordon R, Patterson R, Bates H, et al: Modular treatment and training. Career Education for Mental Health Workers Project: Monograph Series No. 2, Report No. 2. Tampa, Fla.,

Human Resources Institute, College of Social and Behavioral Sciences, University of South Florida, April 1979

5. Slater AL, Gordon KK, Gordon RE: Role and task differences of mental health workers. Career Education for Mental Health Workers: Occasional Paper Series, Report No. 1. Tampa, Fla., University of South Florida, 1978

6. Slater AL, Gordon K, Redcay S (Eds): Human Service Instructional Series, Career Education for Mental Health Workers Project, Human Resources Institute. Module No. 1: Human Relation Skills; Module No. 2: Interviewing and Influencing Skills; Module No. 3: Psychosocial Assessment; Module No. 4: Techniques of Intervention; Module No. 5: Integrative Seminar in Human Service; Module No. 6: Health Assessment. Tampa, Fla., University of South Florida, 1978

7. Mosher LR, Keith SJ: Research on the psychosocial treatment of schizophrenia: A summary report. Am J Psychiatry 136:623, 1979

8. Hatfield AB: The family as partner in the treatment of mental illness. Hosp Community Psychiatry 30:327, 1979

9. Bedell JR, Archer RP, Marlowe HA: A description and evaluation of a problem solving skills training program, in Upper D, Ross SM (Eds): Annual Review of Behavior Group Therapy, Vol. 2. Champaign, Ill., Research Press, 1979

10. Patteron R, Jackson G: Behavior Management with the Elderly, Gerontology Program. Tampa, Fla., Florida Mental Health Institute, 1979

11. Boyd A: Behavior Management Training Manual, Child Adolescent Program. Tampa, Fla., Florida Mental Health Institute, 1979

12. Patterson RL, Jackson GM: Behavior modification with the elderly, in Hersen M, et al (Ed): Progress in Behavior Modification, Vol. 7. New York, Academic Press, 1980

13. Archer RP, Bedell JR, Amuso K: Interrelationships and changes in locus of control and trait anxiety among residential psychiatric inpatients. Tampa, Fla., Florida Mental Health Institute (Unpublished manuscript)

14. Vagg P, Archer RP, Bedell JR, et al: A comparison of cognitive and behavioral treatments of depression. Tampa, Fla., Florida Mental Health Institute (Unpublished manuscript)

15. Archer RP, Bedell JR, Amuso KF: Personality, demographic and intellectual variables related to discharge readiness. J Psychol 104:67–74, 1980

16. Rotter JB: Generalized expectancies for internal versus external control of reinforcement. Psychol Monogr 80, 1966

17. Spielberger CD, Gorsuch RL, Lushene RE: STAI Manual for the State-Trait Anxiety Inventory. Palo Alto, Calif., Consulting Psychologists Press, 1979

18. Glickman MD: The continuing demedicalization of psychiatry. Psychiatric Opinion 16:15–21, 1979

19. Koz G: Catch 22: The psychiatrist in the state hospital. Psychiatic Annals, 9:47–54, 1979

20. Greenblatt M: A page from a psychiatrist's journal. Psychiatric Opinion, 15:2, 1978

3
Reducing Rehospitalization of Mental Patients by Peer Management and Support

This chapter describes programs for reducing rehospitalization of former state mental institution patients and for improving the quality of their lives in the community. It focuses principally upon peer management and support systems developed for treating patients both while they are in the hospital and after discharge. Evaluations of these treatment methods have shown them to be effective in reducing rehospitalization; perhaps they might be incorporated into deinstitutionalization efforts nationwide. Such a peer management and support approach assumes that it is therapeutic for patients to have responsibilities and for them to help each other to the fullest possible extent. Patients do not develop the feelings of helplessness and inadequacy that they do when they must depend on staff alone for treatment and emotional support. A variety of peer-support and peer-management techniques are integral components of treatment plans, including residential, day-treatment, and long-term community programs. Each program is structured in such a way that patients are encouraged to assume responsible roles and staff are prevented from behaving in a "debilitatingly helpful" manner.

We appreciate the statistical assistance provided by Dr. Albert Rust. Portions of this chapter appeared originally in Gordon R, Edmunson E, Bedell J, et al: Utilizing peer management and support to reduce rehospitalization of mental patients. J Florida Med Assoc 66:927–933, 1979, and are reprinted with permission.

DEVELOPING SUPPORT SYSTEMS

Although the average person has a large circle of family, friends, school-mates, and coworkers, most hospitalized mental patients' support systems may be limited to immediate family members. Sometimes, especially after the patient has been repeatedly hospitalized, a family may offer no support at all. Loss of support and assistance from family and friends contributes to the development of emotional disorder; its restoration plays a significant part both in patients' regaining emotional serenity and, in controlled experiments, in the prevention of emotional distress.[1]

Although the normal community resident maintains a fairly even relationship with people in his support network, giving assistance as well as receiving it, the relationships of mental patients are often less reciprocal. The patient receives support from others, but seldom is able to return it. Pattison[2] has shown that normal people have an average social network of approximately 25 people, neurotics can rely upon 10–18 people, but psychotics usually have only 4–5 people in their support systems.

Tolsdorf[3] compared the social networks and coping processes of recently hospitalized psychiatric patients and recently hospitalized medical patients with no psychiatric problems ("normals"). In contrast to the normals, the psychiatric patients' network had fewer intimate relationships, made up of proportionally fewer members who were outside of the family, and were more often controlled and dominated by their network members. Given these network characteristics, it was not surprising to find that the psychiatric patients were reluctant to draw on their network for support. By contrast, the normal medical patients had positive feelings for their network and sought out the support and help of others when needed. Tolsdorf found that when the normal group experienced stress they first relied on their own strengths to cope; if these were not sufficient, they turned to their support system. In all cases this strategy kept the stress situation manageable. Tolsdorf's study shows that people without an adequate network of people to whom they may turn are at much greater risk than people with a solid support system.

> . . . the psychiatric subjects experienced some significant life stress with which they attempted to cope by using their own defenses. When this strategy failed, they chose not to mobilize their networks, relying instead on their own resources, which had already been shown to be inadequate. This resulted in more failure, higher anxiety, a drop in performance and self-esteem followed eventually by a psychotic episode (p. 415).[3]

Previous research with maternity groups led us to expect that peer support might reduce chronic mental patients' need for rehospitalization. In a series of investigations that compared treatment methods, we found that when women who had sought psychiatric help for emotional disorders associated with childbearing received instruction in building supports along with their other treatment, they responded more quickly and required only out patient treatment. The mean number of treatment sessions for 24 women with postpartum mental disturbances who received only dynamic therapy was 45; for 36 patients who additionally received social psychotherapy, the mean number of sessions was six. Of the 24 women who received only dynamic therapy, 43 percent required mental hospitalization; of the 36 women who were shown how to obtain supports and to increase their coping skills, zero required hospitalization.[4]

In a comparison group of women who also required psychiatric help, but apart from the childbearing period, 13 percent of 60 of these women who received only dynamic psychotherapy required hospitalization, as compared to 14 percent of 51 who also received social psychotherapy, including instruction in building social supports.[4] Women whose problems were related to pregnancy had a readily available natural support group—other women with young babies and female relatives and friends who were experienced with young children. Women whose emotional distress arose apart from pregnancy had a great variety of social problems; no single organization existed in the 1950s from which they could obtain all the kinds of supports required. The women's movement of the 1960s and 1970s now provides many needed services to women.[5,6]

The relationship of instruction to the prevention of perinatal distress and mental illness was investigated. We examined steps that expectant and new mothers took to cope with bringing a new child into their lives. Classroom instructions were developed from systematic comparisons of the lives of women who were hospitalized for mental illness related to pregnancy and childbearing, normal perinatal women, and women who were treated as outpatients in psychiatric practice. The changes the instructed women made, which significantly discriminated between women who had no postpartum emotional problems and those who suffered emotional distress and illness, were related to increasing their supports. The instructions provided in information about the benefits of five types of supports—emotional, recreational, informational, instrumental, and services. Seventy percent of women in the instructed classes increased their numbers of friends among their peers (other women with young children), as compared to 46 percent of matched, uninstructed controls (p < .01) and 14 percent of those who suffered emotional disturbance (p < .001). Instructed women also obtained significantly more help and support after the baby's birth from their female relatives and from their husbands. These changes resulted in significantly better emotional response following delivery (p < .02 in both cases).[7,8]

Follow-up studies four to six years after these same women had given birth to their babies revealed that the gains made by the instructed women were retained: They still were better adjusted emotionally than the matched controls. They had gone ahead to give birth to significantly more children, and had encountered fewer serious marital, health, and sex problems in their subsequent lives.[8]

These findings were widely disseminated to obstetrical practitioners (in scientific meetings, the state medical journal, and the obstetrical literature) and to women (in national magazines and a best-selling book).[9-12] Preventive instructions based on these studies, which emphasized the importance of support for new mothers from peers, husband, and family, became part of the program of the International Childbirth Education Association and other women's organizations.[11]

A striking decrease in numbers of patients with emotional disorders related to childbearing occurred in the state (New Jersey) where the research was conducted and most widely disseminated (from six percent of psychiatric outpatients in the 1950s to less than one percent in the 1960s). Although the overall homicide rate remained stable in the state, there was a remarkable decline in infanticide, which paralleled the decrease in maternity mental disorders. From a mean rate of 4.9 in the 1951–1959 period, it plummeted to 1.6 per 100,000 in 1960.[13]

These findings about the benefits of peer support and training for coping with the role of new motherhood were encouraging. They suggested that a similar systematic approach to training chronic mental patients in peer support might provide long-term benefits in improving the quality of their lives and in reducing their need for further hospitalization. When we were provided the opportunity to develop innovative and inexpensive treatment and management programs for a state's mental health system in the present setting, we drew upon this successful experience in the use of peer support in treatment and prevention of postpartum emotional disorder to investigate whether programs of peer management and support might provide a major contribution in the treatment of the chronically ill mental patient both in residential and in community follow-up care.

Most mental hospitals refer discharged patients back to their private psychiatrists or to community mental health centers (CMHCs). This approach has been only partially successful. Traditionally the mental health service delivery system has focused on shoring up a patient's internal resources (i.e., improving skills, promoting insight, psychotropic medications). Because of the demonstrated importance of support systems, several peer managed programs have been developed that, in addition to developing a patient's internal resources, also increase his external resources through the formation of a viable support system.

Professionals cannot begin to supply the psychosocial support that patients need. Supplementing the patient's limited support system of family and old friends with a new support network of fellow patients, teaching CHMC or hospital staff to provide modular training, and training patients and staff in peer management and support, offer promise for maintaining the chronic mental patient in the community.

PEER MANAGEMENT FOR CHRONICALLY DISABLED PATIENTS

To teach former hospital patients to provide peer management and support for each other in the community, they were first given training in their residential treatment. Initially, the peer management approach developed by Fairweather[14] was replicated. During their residential stay, patients progressed through a four-level system in which each succeeding level required a higher level of function. Since this program will be described more fully in Chapter 14, a lengthy description will not be included here. Briefly, each patient on the treatment unit was assigned to a small peer group. Each group met daily, without staff members present, to discuss the previous day's activities and the progress of individual patients. At these meetings the group provided feedback to members and helped individuals with problem solving and life planning; it also provided incentives for positive behavior change. Staff members served as role models, facilitators, and as feedback "instruments" to help the group focus on maladaptive behaviors. The group made recommendations to the staff regarding money and passes for members who showed satisfactory participation in the program. In making recommendations, members considered the current step-level of each patient and his/her rate of progress.

Effectivenes of Peer Management

One hundred and eleven patients were divided into two groups crossmatched on the basis of age, sex, and diagnostic category (psychotic or nonpsychotic) The peer management experimental group (n = 63) participated in the peer support program; the other, the controls (n = 48), in a program of traditional psychiatric rehabilitative therapy. Eighteen months after discharge, 35 percent of the experimental group were rehospitalized, as compared to 53 percent of the control group.[15] The rehospitalization rate of the control group is compatible with the average rehospitalization rate in the nation. Recidivism rates of 50–55 percent eighteen months after discharge are the rule and may be considered "base-rate data."[16] Furthermore, the mean number of days of rehospitalization for patients in the experimental group was 53.28; for the traditional therapy group it was 121.27, more than twice as large.

Findings from this first study encouraged further applications of peer management and social support approaches. A token economy program was developed and used with residential patients to ready them for a community support program for discharged patients.

PEER MANAGEMENT IN A TOKEN ECONOMY PROGRAM (TEP)

A peer-managed Token Economy Program (TEP) for motivating patients' performance, decreasing their behavioral abnormalities, and for training them in group management and support provides the final phase of treatment received by a group of residential psychiatric patients before they are discharged to the community. These patients are adults age 18–45 who are treated in an intensive nine-week (five days per week) skills and supports training residential program. Sixty-six percent of the patients had been diagnosed as psychotic, 15 percent with character disorders, and 19 percent with neurotic disorders. None were included who had received a primary diagnosis of mental retardation, organic brain syndrome, or substance addiction. The peer-managed TEP is a modification of the Fairweather small group. It provides more structure, so that operation of the program is not dependent on the talent of any one patient. Also, it incorporates more clearly defined treatment goals, uses behavioral methods, and is designed as a program to provide transition to community living once community discharge becomes feasible for the patients.

The TEP provides patients with a structure within which they practice being responsible and independent and learn behaviors needed for community living. In a sheltered setting where they can make mistakes without catastrophic repercussions, patients rely on their own resources to learn new skills, solve problems, manage difficulties, and prepare for life in the community.

The TEP is organized like a business corporation in which patients' management responsibilities, earnings, and spending are clearly defined, and each patient takes charge of a specific area of the TEP's operation. Patients are elected by their peers to be Director and Assistant Director of the TEP. These individuals are responsible for conducting all daily meetings and for facilitating the smooth operation of the token economy. Another patient, the Director of Target Behaviors, reviews and summarizes each patient's performance of individually targeted behaviors, and the Director of Groups evaluates patients' attendance and participation in therapy groups. Each of the 10 to 12 patients involved in treatment during the last three weeks of the program is given a clear and defined role in the management of the token economy. Every job in the organization is important, and every patient is held responsible for proper conduct of the job. The importance of patients' being given leadership responsibilities and managerial duties, and receiving recognition for achievement for their performance of these functions, is borne out by experimental evidence that will be reported in Chapter 14.

In daily formal meetings, patients resolve their own problems, assign tasks, give each other feedback and reinforcement on performance, and plan group activities. The role of the staff is to give written feedback to the group on individual performance of assigned tasks. Staff do not solve patients' problems nor in any way provide traditional counseling. Tokens may be spent individually or for group activities.

A community store on the treatment unit sells toilet articles, food, books, clothing, etc., in exchange for tokens. Entertainment, outings, and other social events are also available.

Patients may earn tokens for performance in any of three areas: (1) for participating in modular psychoeducational classes such as communications, problem solving, assertion, and others listed in Table 2-1; (2) for performing therapeutic tasks that are addressed to each patient's specific personal problems or problem behaviors ("initiate a two-minute conversation" or "make three positive statements about yourself"); and (3) for completing tasks that aid the transition to community life ("find the city bus route from your home to the nearest Community Mental Health Center" or "organize and participate in a car wash").

Results with TEP

Bedell and Archer[17] compared the effects of three different methods of reinforcement on patient performance in the peer-managed TEP. In the "peer reinforcement" condition, information on their performance was reviewed by the peer group at their daily meeting, and token points were assigned to each patient according to the group's evaluation of this feedback. In the "staff reinforcement" condition, written reports on each patient's performance were reviewed by the Staff Coordinator, who assigned token points to each patient on the basis of actual performance, but without any input from the patients present at the daily meeting. In the "noncontingent reinforcement" control condition, the written feedback was distributed to patients at the meeting, but was not discussed nor considered when tokens were awarded; instead, each patient received a fixed and identical number of points each day, regardless of performance.

Both the peer-reinforced and the staff-reinforced groups performed significantly better than the noncontingent-reinforced control group in terms of their attendance in treatment groups. These results clearly indicate that contingent token reinforcement was an important factor in determining patient performance, but that this reinforcement may be provided by either peers or professional staff with equal effect.

Bedell and Archer[18] measured patients' performance on the Problem

Rating Scale and the Discharge Readiness Inventory,[19] which were first administered before they entered the TEP and again three weeks later upon completing the program. Results of the analysis indicated that patients were rated by staff as having significantly less severe psychosocial problems on the Problem Rating Scale after completing the TEP than before entering the program ($p < .001$), significantly greater Community Adjustment Potential on the Discharge Readiness Inventory after completing the peer management program than before entry ($p < .05$), and greater psychosocial adequacy after completing the program than before entry ($p < .05$). It is important to note that these improvements in adjustment occurred after the relatively brief span of three weeks of treatment. Thus, this peer management and support TEP model significantly affected patient performance and adjustment ratings over a relatively short period of treatment and resulted in significant benefits.

Clinical observations of the program also point to its effectiveness. The patients were active and goal-oriented. Their efforts were clinically relevant to them and were individualized to meet their needs. Patients helped each other to complete tasks and to attend therapy groups, and generally provided support for each other. Rarely were TEP patients uninvolved or simply unoccupied on the residential unit. In the "noncontingent reinforcement" control group, on the other hand, lethargic, "institutional" behavior was frequently observed.

The cost-efficiency of the peer-managed TEP is apparent. Only one staff member, working in conjunction with 12 patients, supplied nearly all of the professional support necessary to operate a broad-based program on a 24-hour-a-day residential treatment unit. A limited amount of clinical support was required from the professional staff of a contemporary staff-managed unit. This support, however, was easily assumed and did not require that additional staff be hired to supply these services to the peer-managed TEP.

The TEP is an approximation of community living; it requires more active coping and community skill than traditional residential treatment, but it is not as difficult as actual independent community life. TEP is used as a transitional peer mangement and support treatment program to facilitate patient movement from institutional living into a community support program—the Community Network Development (CND).

PEER SUPPORT FOR COMMUNITY RESIDENTS: COMMUNITY NETWORK DEVELOPMENT (CND) PROJECT

CND seeks to increase the amount of peer support available to patient members by arranging a variety of programs and activities where members can meet, socialize, and work together in a positively reinforcing atmosphere.

Because emphasis is on peer support rather than on professional support, CND employs members of the network as activities organizers and managers. CND staff begin preparing patients for the transition from residential treatment to community life during the last weeks of their residential treatment. Staff train patients in pre-employment skills, peer counseling, group leadership, and community living skills, as well as review patient plans regarding housing, employment, finances, and medical follow-up.

Pre-employment Skills Training

Patients learn how and where to look for a job; how to express themselves well nonverbally in an interview; how to dress appropriately for the interview; how to make an employer aware of their assets; and how to deal with such sensitive questions as, "Have you ever been hospitalized?" or "Have you ever been arrested?"

Peer Counseling Training

Patients learn to counsel each other. They learn to listen, give, and receive feedback, and to use positive reinforcement. CND staff observe patients as they are being trained and learn which patients are most effective as peer counselors.

Group Leadership Skills Training

Patients learn group work and leardership, skills that increase their ability to interact effectively with people on the job, in their families, and among their friends. Training includes didactic lessons on leadership, discussions of experiences group members have had in which they made use of leadership qualities, and videotaped role plays of leadership situations. Each group member plans an agenda for a meeting, defines the role that other members will represent, presents the agenda to the group, and finally runs a meeting.

Community Living Skills Training

Because patients often lack the basic living skills necessary to manage their lives effectively, CND has developed a series of programmed instruction modules designed to teach these new skills. When people join CND, they receive copies of these modules with their orientation manuals. The modules cover how to find a place to live, how to obtain assistance from agencies, how to manage money, how to develop leisure skills, and how to ride a bus. Each booklet is designed so that it can be used by CND members to obtain general information or as a resource when a specific need arises.

Selection of Community Area Managers
(CAMs) and a Network Director

Patients apply to become a CAM or Network Director, and staff make selections from applicants on the basis of personal qualities (overall emotional adjustment and motivation) and practical matters (possession of a current driver's license, a car, and a telephone). The CAMs and Director receive special training as managers and, after discharge from the residential unit, are hired at the minimum wage for 20–30 hours of work per week. The Network Director coordinates the activities of three or four community area groups, each managed by a CAM. The CAMs and Network Director receive Peer Counseling manuals. These describe 10 of the most common problems that patients may encounter in the community: problems dealing with (1) employment, (2) housing, (3) financial assistance, (4) noninvolvement in the group, (5) suicidal tendencies, (6) training and education, (7) transportation, (8) recreation, (9) patient crisis and instability, and (10) health. The manual details step-by-step solutions to each problem and provides a Referral Resource File with addresses and telephone numbers of local helping agencies.

CND Program

The CAMs' work with members is supervised regularly by a CND staff member, who also provides clinical back-up should the CAMs encounter problems beyond their skill level.

The CAMs organize and lead weekly Area Meetings of between 20 and 50 members. They provide peer counseling and referral information when needed, and facilitate goal-planning sessions with group members. They meet with a staff member weekly to report on activities, problems, and accomplishments, and to receive training, consultation, and supervision. They attend monthly Network Meetings in which CND staff and patients participate. They organize business or fund-raising activities, call or visit group members each week, assist group members in times of crisis, and generate a positive attitude among group members.

Area Group Meeting

Meetings always include an activity such as enjoying a picnic, playing a game, eating lunch together, going shopping together, etc. A member who has no transportation is picked up by another CND member and taken to the meeting and activity. Members are encouraged to contact each other socially between meetings to reinforce their social skills and to aid group cohesion.

CND members from the entire Network gather once a month at a meeting that is primarily social in nature. The Network Meeting keeps members from different areas in contact, maintaining a sizeable support system for the patients.

Fund-raising events earn money that is used to sponsor recreational activities. Trips to amusement parks, for example, are paid from monies generated by the fund-raising projects, which include car washes, a catering service for conferences, bake sales, garage sales, and other events.

Many members now call each other just to talk and get together because they enjoy each other's company. They befriend each other when problems arise and help each other solve them. Through the informal network of friendships that CND helps to create, patients have provided temporary housing to fellow peers when difficulties arise in their home situation. They have helped each other get jobs, and have loaned each other money. They encourage each other to take their medications and keep their mental health center appointments; members with cars drive those without transportation to obtain these services.

EFFECTIVENESS OF THE COMMUNITY NETWORK DEVELOPMENT (CND) PROGRAM

Eighty former residential patients were contacted at an average of 10 months after discharge from residential care. Although patients with prior hospitalizations of both long and short duration are admitted into the CND program, only patients with less than four months in-patient hospital experience prior to their present admission were included in the experiment described here. While in residence, all 80 patients had received intensive psychoeducational treatment that included modular life-skills training and peer-managed TEP training. During the last two of their nine weeks of residence, however, the patients had been randomly divided into two groups. Patients in the control group were referred only to traditional aftercare services (i.e. their private therapist or a local community mental health center). Patients in the experimental group (CND) were also referred to the CND program and became part of the peer support network.

Ten months after discharge, one-half as many patients in the CND group required rehospitalization as compared with the control group (17.5% vs. 35%). Even if rehospitalized, the CND patients, on the average, required less than one-third as many days of rehospitalization (7.0 vs. 24.6). A significantly greater percentage of CND members (52.5% vs. 26%) were able to function without any mental health system contact. Finally, as compared with the control group, the CND members required far fewer total hours of outpatient psychiatric care (201 vs. 1158).[20]

DISCUSSION

Peer management and support, as part of a system of care that includes modular life-skills training and training in self-medication, has taught many of the least self-sufficient segment of the population—previously institutionalized mental patients—to be more independent and to take more responsibility in caring for themselves and each other. Furthermore, it is less expensive than professional management. When used solely in a residential setting, peer management reduced recidivism among patients after their discharge. When combined with a token economy, peer management was as effective as staff management in effecting improvement in patients' behavior, but was less costly since it required fewer staff. Peer support in a community aftercare setting cut the costs of days of rehospitalization by two-thirds, and the costs of hours of outpatient contact by nearly five-sixths.

REFERENCES

1. Gordon RE: Prevention of Postpartum Emotional Difficulties. Ann Arbor, Mich., University Microfilms, 1961
2. Pattison, EM: Clinical social system interventions. Psychiatry Digest 38:25–33, 1977
3. Tolsdorf C: Social networks, support, and coping. Fam Proc 15:407–417, 1976
4. Gordon RE, Gordon KK: Prediction and treatment of emotional disorders of pregnancy. Am J Obstet Gynecol 77:1074–1133, 1959
5. Gordon RE, Gordon KK, Gunther M: The Split Level Trap. New York, Bernard Geis Associates, 1961 (New York, Dell, 1962, 1964; Good Housekeeping, December 1960)
6. Friedan B: The Feminine Mystique. New York, Norton, 1963
7. Gordon RE, Gordon KK: Social factors in the prevention of postpartum emotional problems. Obstet Gynecol 15:443–448, 1960
8. Gordon RE, Kapostins EE, Gordon KK: Factors in postpartum emotional adjustment. Obstet Gynecol 25:156–166, 1965
9. Gordon RE, Gordon KK: Some social psychiatric aspects of pregnancy and childbearing. J Med Soc NJ 54:569–572, 1957
10. Gordon RE, Gordon KK, Gunther M: The Split Level Trap, in Brazzell C (Ed): Teaching Materials Currently Used in Mental Health Work Training Programs. Atlanta, Ga., Southern Regional Education Board, 1974, p 39
11. Haire D, Haire J: Implementing Family-Centered Maternity Care with a Central Nursery. Hillside, N.J., International Childbirth Education Association, 1968, pp II–15, 16, IV–13
12. Boston Women's Health Book Collective: Our Bodies, Ourselves: A Book by and for Women. New York, Simon and Schuster, 1973, pp 306–308
13. Gordon RE, Gordon KK: The psychiatric problems of the 1960s. Int J Soc Psychiatry 10:223–231, 1964
14. Fairweather GW (Ed): Social psychology in treating mental illness. New York, John Wiley & Sons, 1964
15. Stone A, Donoghue B, Rust A, et al: Peer management inpatient treatment of chronic psychiatric patients: A controlled study with follow up. Presented at Southeastern Psychological Assn, New Orleans, 1979

16. Anthony WA, Buell GJ, Sherratt S, et al: Efficacy of psychiatric rehabilitation. Psychol Bull 78:447–456, 1972
17. Bedell JR, Archer RP: Peer Managed Token Economies: Evaluation and Description. Tampa, Fla., Florida Mental Health Institute, 1979
18. Bedell JR, Archer RP, Marlowe HA: A description and evaluation of a problem-solving skills training program, in Upper D, Ross SM (Eds): Annual Review of Behavior Group Therapy, vol. 2. Washington, D.C., Research Press (in press)
19. Hogarty GE, Ulrich R: The discharge readiness inventory. Arch Gen Psychiatry 26:419–426, 1972
20. Edmunson E, Bedell J, Archer R, et al: The community network development project: Skill building and peer support, in Slotnick RS, Jeger A (Eds): Community Mental Health: A Behavioral-Ecological Perspective. New York, Plenum Press (in press)

Morton Cohen, Jeffrey R. Bedell
Lawrence R. Weathers, Susan Fertig
Julia Adams, Richard E. Gordon
Katherine Gordon

4
Training Patients in Self-Medication

In 1975, a typical patient left a public mental hospital with prescriptions for a half dozen different psychotropic medications and no clear understanding of why they were needed, what was their effect, nor how to take them. Frequently, the total cost of medications was eight to ten times greater than it needed to be. Sometimes the drugs may have been incompatible with each other. The confused and poorly motivated patient may have discontinued taking medications altogether and, as a result, ended up being rehospitalized. A treatment system for remedying these problems will be presented in the following sections. It includes the unit dose procedure, periodic review of medications, the single daily dose regimen, polypharmacy reduction, decreased use of concentrates, and patient self-medication training.[1]

UNIT DOSE PROCEDURE

Traditionally, ward nurses dispense medications to hospital patients from bulk quantities kept at the nursing station or from specific supplies for individual patients. Under unit dose, all medications for the day for every patient are prepared in the pharmacy in individually labeled packets. These are sent to each floor in special carts that contain drawers labeled with each patient's name and room number.

Portions of this chapter appeared originally in Cohen M, Gordon R, Adams J, et al: Single bedtime dose self-medication system (Hosp Community Psychiatry 30:30–33, 1979), and are reprinted with permission.

Evaluation of unit dose has demonstrated that it is markedly superior to the traditional method. The unit dose procedure accounts for every dose of medication, minimizing the possibility of diversion or pilferage. It eliminates the necessity of disposing of partially used medications that are left over when a patient's treatment is changed or discontinued, and cuts drug costs. The possibility of error in type of medication administered, dosage, or time of administration is reduced. Nurses save time that can be used to perform other duties. The Joint Commission on Accreditation of Hospitals and the Federal Drug Enforcement Administration recommend this drug distribution concept. The Hartford Insurance Company offers reduced malpractice insurance rates to hospitals operating on unit dose because of the reduction in medication error.

PERIODIC REVIEW OF MEDICATIONS

Upon admission each patient continues to receive his current medication for 24 hours. The clinical pharmacist conducts a medication interview with each new patient to discuss all medications he received in the past year. After the admission physical is completed, the physician and pharmacist meet and review the patient's past utilization of drugs and possible allergies, as well as interactions, side effects, and other information about medicating the patient.

After the physician has selected a drug regimen, orders are sent to the pharmacy where the patient's drug profile and laboratory findings are monitored for drug incompatibilities. Throughout the patient's treatment, the team of physicians, nurses, project directors, and clinical consultant pharmacists conduct weekly medication reviews on every patient, a practice which not only protects the patient but also results in further financial economies. Benefits arise from the effort of the treatment team in these discussions to reduce to a minimum the number of different psychotropic medications the patient takes. They attempt to place patients on single bedtime medications and to eliminate polypharmacy and the use of concentrates. Finally, staff strive to persuade patients to cooperate in taking oral medications rather than to require injections.

SINGLE DAILY DOSE REGIMEN

With many drugs that are effective in the body for short periods of time, it has been common practice to divide a specific amount of drug into equal doses and to administer it three to six times daily. Certain psychotropic drugs (the antipsychotics and antidepressants), however, accumulate in body tissue and retain their effectiveness for relatively long periods of time. These characteristics render them useful in a single daily dose given at bedtime. No significant therapeutic effects favor multiple dosages of these medications. There are, however, many advantages for the patient to a single bedtime dose. The drowsiness and sedation that accompany the single large dose are beneficial for sleep. Undesirable side effects such as orthostatic hypotension, dry mouth, and visual blurring are reduced, as these effects peak in approximately four hours while the patient is sleeping. Because of their long-lasting properties, the drugs may be discontinued for short periods of time, so that on weekend passes the patient can discontinue the drug entirely and resume taking it upon returning to the hospital. The single bedtime dose means fewer tablets taken less frequently, resulting in a reduced feeling of drug dependency. Fewer and milder side effects occur, and the patient needs fewer other drugs, such as sedatives and anti-Parkinsonism preparations. Patients obtaining only a bedtime medication receive fewer reminders that they are sick than those whose regimen requires three to five daily timeouts for medications. During the day, furthermore, when most psychosocial treatment takes place, the patient feels the benefit of increased physical and mental efficiency.

The nursing and medical staff also benefit from the single daily dose regimen, since the time spent in administering drugs is reduced. On a 32-bed psychiatric unit the savings in nursing time alone is approximately 550 hours annually, time that can be spent effectively in other therapeutic activities. There is less need to pay attention to relieving distressing side effects of medications and better control over the dosage time when the drugs are dispensed only once daily.

Finally, financial savings are substantial with the single daily dose regimen. A single large dose is considerably less expensive than multiple small doses. For example, Mellaril (thioridazine), 50mg. q.i.d. costs the hospital 28 cents a day. The same amount administered in one 200mg dose costs 12 cents daily, a savings of 57 percent.

POLYPHARMACY REDUCTION

Polypharmacy is the prescribing of two or more drugs from the same class of therapeutics. There is no conclusive evidence that combinations of psychotropic drugs are more effective than carefully selected single drugs, but there are a number of disadvantages to the use of such combinations. The greater the number of different medications a patient receives, the greater is the likelihood that he will suffer an adverse drug reaction due to interaction effects and toxicity of various drug mixtures. In the event of toxicity or an adverse reaction, it may be difficult to determine which of the patient's many medications to adjust or eliminate. The chance of error in medication is increased with polypharmacy and is compounded when patients are discharged

Table 4-1
Examples of polypharmacy reduction

Admission regimen	Discharge Regimen
Patient A	
Presamine 100 mg bid (imipramine) Stelazine 2 mg tid (trifluoperazine) Thorazine 50 mg am (chlorpromazine) Thorazine 100 mg hs (chlorpromazine) Valium 5 mg hs (diazepam) Cogentin 2 mg qd (benztropin) Benadryl 50 mg tid (diphenhydramin) Cost $1.84	Stelazine 5 mg tid (trifluoperazine) Tofranil 50 mg hs (imipramine) Cost $0.27
Patient B	
Haldol 10 mg qid (haloperidol) Thorazine 200 mg qid (chlorpromazine) Artane 5 mg qid (trihexyphenidyl) Thorazine concentrate 150 mg qid (chlopromazine) Valium 5 mg im prn (2qd) (diazepam) Valium 5 mg qid (diazepam) Presamine 250 mg hs (imipramine) Cost $2.66	Thorazine 300 mg tid (chlorpromazine) Cost $0.35

from the hospital and have to assume responsibility for taking their own medications. Polypharmacy is also responsible for unnecessary expense, since many small doses of a number of drugs generally cost far more than an equivalent single dose of one drug.

Examples of typical medication profiles of patients admitted in 1975 dramatize the simplification and savings (1975 costs) that result from the elimination of polypharmacy (Table 4-1).

Incoming patients taking a combination of psychotropic drugs, such as those shown in Table 4-1, are placed on a single drug after observation for 24 hours on their intake regimen. Their response is monitored while the drug is titrated to its proper dosage level. Only after a period of careful observation and adjustment is a drug ruled out if it is not effective, or if undesirable side effects are noted. Then a different drug is prescribed. These patients were admitted in 1975. If they were admitted today, after experience for over four years with the success of the single bedtime dose, they probably would have been discharged on this regimen. If so, the costs for Patient A would be reduced further to 20 cents per day.

DECREASED USE OF CONCENTRATES

Concentrates (medications in liquid form) are more costly to prepare and distribute than the same drug in pill or capsule form. Haldol (haloperidol) concentrate 5 mg, for example, costs the state 35 cents for a unit dose; the 5 mg tablet costs only 13 cents. The comparative cost of Mellaril (thioridazine) 200 mg are 25 cents and 12 cents, and of Thorazine (chlorpromazine) 200 mg are 19 cents and 5.5 cents. Despite the cost, physicians must prescribe concentrates to patients who "cheek" medications (pretend to take a pill and later spit it out). Other patients receive concentrates because, for physical or psychological reasons, they are unable to swallow pills. Patients, once started on concentrates, often continue to take them long after the need has passed, resulting in unnecessarily high drug costs. At the weekly medication reviews, the staff continuously reassess patients' progress to determine if concentrates are still needed. Whenever possible they convert the patient's medication to pill or capsule form.

COST EFFICIENCY

The unit dose procedure and single bedtime dose regimen contribute to increased efficiency and reduced medication costs in the management of psychiatric patients. The cost reduction achieved is impressive. In 1975, the first 64 patients, age 18–54, who transferred out of other mental hospitals into the research and training facility when its first adult program opened, were on drug regimens that cost an average of $2.11 per day. The use of unit dose and beginning reduction of polypharmacy immediately cut these patients' medication costs within a few days to 90 cents per patient per day. Weekly medication reviews have resulted in a continued decrease in polypharmacy and the use of concentrates, and an increased reliance on single bedtime dose medications. By August 1977, the average daily drug cost per patient was reduced to 30 cents. These figures provide a daily savings in costs of approximately $1.80. Extrapolating to the more than 3000 patients between the ages of 18 and 55 currently residing in the state's mental hospitals, potential savings could amount to more than $1,800,000 per year. (Children and older patients were excluded from these calculations since they were not part of the patient sample on which this analysis is based.)

Safety and efficiency in the use of pharmaceuticals is increased, expenses are reduced, and nursing time is released for behavioral training or training patients in self-medication and other skills.

SELF-MEDICATION TRAINING

When patients leave a state hospital with instructions to take a large number of different medications, many fail to do so properly, or cease to take their medications altogether. They soon need to return to the hospital.

Discontinuation of medication is a major cause of recidivism among schizophrenics, and nearly 50 percent of patients admitted to public mental hospitals each year are recidivists. Furthermore, illness and even death can befall persons who combine psychotropic medications with other substances, such as alcohol. Simply telling a departing patient to take medications as prescribed and to avoid combining them with certain other drugs often is ineffective. To gain genuine understanding so that they become responsible self-medicators, patients need training and practice in the use of drugs.

Self-Medication Training is facilitated by the single bedtime dose regimen. Patients who are taking only one or two tablets or capsules at bedtime are much easier to train in self-medication than those receiving five or six different medications in 15 to 20 pills at varying intervals throughout the whole day. Once patients have been stabilized on a single bedtime medication, they are ready to begin learning how to manage their own medications independently, in preparation for leaving the hospital.

In the first component of self-medication training patients spend two hours a week in a psychoeducational "drug group." In these sessions they receive information about drugs in general and about the specific medications they are taking. They play educational games developed by staff, "Name That Pill" and "Meds Bingo." These help capture patients' interest and motivate their learning about medications. At the end of this first medication training period, patients learn to identify their medication by name; describe the medication's therapeutic effects, side effects, and interaction effects with other drugs; list precautions to be taken in the use of their medication; and name the dosage and frequency of their medication. During the initial learning phase, patients continue to receive their drugs from the nursing station in the single daily dose manner, except that the nurse, in addition to supplying the medication, also identifies it and provides the patients with information about it. This effort augments the learning taking place in the drug group.

The next stage of self-medication training requires the patients to assume more responsibility for correct self-administration of their medications. They are required to appear at the nursing station at the proper time, to select the appropriate medication from a tray, and to give the nurse complete information about it.

Patients in their final training period are given full responsibility for their medication, which they keep in a locked drawer in their room. At the proper time they take their drugs to the nursing station, swallow them in the presence of the nurse, and tell her about what they are taking. On weekends they independently take their medication at home rather than go drug free. When they return, their supply is counted to check whether the correct number of drugs has been consumed. The self-medication behavior developed through this graduated practice prepares the patients for the unsupervised situation they experience upon being discharged to the community.

Self-medication training results in more responsible drug use and decreased hospital recidivism due to inability to continue the prescribed medical regimen independently. Since each patient-day of care cost over $30 (in 1975–1976), reduced recidivism through responsible patient self-medication potentially saves more than $10,000 per year in state hospital costs alone for every recidivist who remains in the community; savings are greater today with the added costs of inflation.

IMPLEMENTING SELF-MEDICATION TRAINING

In many settings, such as public mental and retardation facilities, pharmacists and physicians may hesitate to encourage self-medication by patients. Many are not educated in behavioral approaches, and have not observed the advantages that counterbalance the risks. On the other hand, professional staff who have received psychosocial and behavioral training may readily recognize the benefits of single bedtime dose medications in reducing the likelihood of adverse drug interactions or of drowsiness that interferes with patients' learning new skills. They appreciate the merits of this medication system for training patients to manage their own medications and the potential for reducing recidivism. Psychologically trained nurses recognize the need to prepare patients gradually for discharge by giving them medications to take home on weekend passes and, in the later states of their residential treatment, letting patients keep medications in their own possession on the unit for supervised self-administration. Thus, these nurses may serve as links, "bridge persons," between physicians, pharmacists, and other nurses, on the one hand, who are worried about the medico-legal implications of leaving medications with patients on the treatment units, and psychoeducators, on the other hand, who want to teach the patients to take responsibility for managing their own drugs. In staff conferences and weekly medication reviews, it is often the specially trained nurse who is best qualified to suggest which patients are ready for self-administration of medications. As was previously noted, the single-daily dose regimen frees up nursing time that can then be used for behavioral and other skills training of patients, including in self-medication.

Nurses who are educated to provide this training in addition to their regular nursing duties find themselves performing two different kinds of jobs, and working for two different bosses, a situation that will be discussed more fully in Chapter 9. When a person is working in two jobs and for two chains of command, problems are resolved when bridge persons are placed in the role of project coordinator, as in Figures 9-2 and 9-3. Nurses are often given this job after they have received training in psychobehavioral techniques.

No nursing positions are usually available in the table of organization to which the nurse can be promoted after she improves her psychoeducational skills. But she can often qualify now for a better-paying nonnursing position such as that of a social service worker. In this new position a conflict may arise as to her legal right to perform nursing duties on the unit. Under the Pharmacy Act she is not recognized as a licensed nurse, since she is neither in a supervisory nor a charge nurse position. Thus she cannot obtain medications from the pharmacy.

This problem has been resolved in cooperation with the Florida State Board of Nursing: The nurse must primarily practice within the state job classification in which she was hired and perform the duties of a social service worker as spelled out in her job description; in this role she reports up the psychoeducational chain of command. In addition she can perform limited duties of a licensed nurse when she is not occupied with her social service duties; here she is supervised by the nursing and health services administrative hierarchy. Although filling a social service position, she remains a nurse and has a right to utilize her nursing expertise in consultations and in teaching with nurses, to discuss psychotropic medications and other medical issues with the psychiatrist, and to provide direct nursing care to patients in an emergency in the absence of other nursing personnel. Furthermore, she can teach nursing students, who often are encouraged by their faculty to do internships under her supervision in order to broaden their understanding of biomedical, psychoeducational, consultative, and administrative nursing responsibilities. Under matrix management, many nursing staff members perform more than one job; most are eager to add nursing and psychoeducational training, consultation, and assessment to their nursing treatment duties.

SUMMARY

This chapter describes a medication system for patients with major psychiatric disorders. It utilizes the unit dose procedure during the first part of residential treatment. Regular medication reviews by physicians, nurses, behavior therapists, and clinical pharmacists reduce polypharmacy and lead to the single daily dose regimen. They curtail the use of liquid concentrates and parenteral drugs. Once patients have been stabilized on a single bedtime oral medication regimen, they are trained to manage their own medications independently in preparation for discharge from the hospital. The treatment system is effective and has produced savings of up to 90 percent in medication costs. It has won the support of staff and cooperation of patients, and is gaining acceptance statewide in mental health and retardation facilities.

In our experience nurses who have received special training in psychoeducational treatment techniques can serve as bridge persons between psychoeducators and pharmacists and physicians.

The treatment system shapes independent self-medication behavior in those patients about to re-enter the community, and may lead to reduced recidivism. This system is not limited to treatment of psychiatric patients in state hospitals. Private patients, those in community mental health centers, and others can benefit from the approaches described. This smoothly functioning system, developed at the research and training center, serves as a model for other facilities throughout the mental health system. In particular, it helps chronic recidivists who have previously assumed that they must go back to the hospital to get over a new acute phase of their mental illness; they learn that they merely need to get the dosages of their psychotropic medications readjusted.

REFERENCES

1. DiMascio A, Goldberg HL: Emotional Disorders: An Outline to Diagnosis and Pharmacological Treatment. Oradell, N.J., Medical Economics Co., 1977

Richard E. Gordon, Carolyn J. Hursch
Philip W. Drash, Joseph W. Evans
Katherine K. Gordon

5

Measuring Progress in Psychiatric Treatments and Programs with Proficiency Gauges and Psychosocial Rating Scales

Psychiatric treatment has recently been criticized on several grounds. As noted by Bassuk and Gersen,[1] most of the therapeutic methods used are not well defined; there is only a small body of data on the efficacy of particular techniques; and there are no guidelines for establishing comprehensive systems for the delivery of mental health care to disadvantaged people who may require interventions not practiced by many psychiatrists. According to Braceland,[2] psychiatric practice is being threatened by these failings. He quotes members of Congress who have asked psychiatry's leaders: "Is there any way of assessing what kind of treatment Mr. X needs? Can you tell us if it does any good? When does anybody finish treatment? You psychiatrists have trained indigenous workers; you told us last decade that they are doing well. Aren't they doing well now?"

The Harvard Case Report[3] makes a similar set of comments about program evaluation in the human service agency:

There is no baseline data for comparing program quality. . . . There are no annual evaluations of program areas with fundamental measures of program performance . . . . There are no surveys of client satisfaction with program services (p. 9).

The research and training facility's therapeutic approach provides data-based treatment procedures for psychiatric patients, and supplies answers to some of these questions and criticisms. A comprehensive program that combines medical-psychiatric treatment with psychoeducational modular skills building and behavior management is effective in treating disadvantaged, chronically ill mental patients of all ages.

PSYCHOEDUCATIONAL ASSESSMENT

The modular approach provides a treatment technique in which patients' abilities and supports are assessed at regular intervals. Assignment of patients to specific classes is based on pretests. Levels of impairment are readily tested before, during, and after treatment; so are numbers and quality of personal and environmental supports.

Objective assessments of patient performance provide valid and reliable measures of progress in treatment. Previously standardized psychosocial rating scales and staff-developed proficiency gauges administered by paraprofessionals measure group and individual progress in treatment. Patient performance is plotted in treatment records on graphs similar to those used for depicting chemical and psysiological variables such as body temperature, blood pressure, blood sugar, etc. These graphs can be interpreted easily by clinical treatment personnel, and patient improvement can be determined at

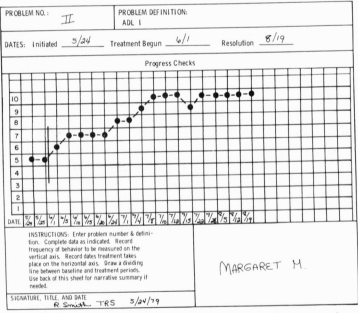

Fig. 5-1. Proficiency Gauge for ADL-1: A graph for presenting progress in activities of daily living in the elderly, and instructions for assessing proficiency.

Table 5-1

Scoresheet for ADL-1, and instructions for scoring a patient's performance.

Instructions for rating:

Observe the client performing the following skills. Place the number corresponding to the client's present level of function in the blank preceding each skill. Women start with one point.

1. Performs skill independently and correctly.
0. Does not perform skill independently or correctly. Indicate N/A if the item is not applicable.

i. Oral hygiene
    _____cleans teeth and dentures daily
ii. Bathing
    _____operates bathroom equipment
    _____bathes regularly (partially or fully)
    _____cleans and groom hair
    _____shaves neat (men only)
iii. Nail care
    _____grooms fingernails neatly
    _____grooms toenails neatly
iv. Personal eating habits
    _____eats with proper care
    _____follows basic table manners

a glance. Finally, aggregate scores from patient and family assessments provide data for overall program evaluation.

Proficiency Gauges

Proficiency gauges are assessment instruments with graduated scales that measure the quantity of the person's knowledge or skill in a specific area of behavior according to a standardized system. They demonstrate competency achieved as a result of psychoeducation; when administered over time they monitor the progress the patient makes in treatment or training. Pooled scores can be used to evaluate a program of treatment. Each module's specific proficiency gauge is included as part of its manual (see Appendix). Assessment scores are plotted on graphs that are included in the patient's treatment record. Figure 5-1 presents a graph of an elderly patient's progress in Activities of Daily Living training. It shows the standardized scale used to gauge her skill and progress. Table 5-1 provides the scale items developed by Harrell, et al.[4] for testing the patient, and the instructions to the staff member performing the measurement. Note that the patient reached an optimum level of performance on the skills measured, indicating that this training could be ended. When patients' curves flatten out at a point below the optimum, and do not improve with further training, this too indicates that treatment of this specific skill can end.

Standardized Psychosocial Behavior Rating Scales

Rating scales that have been validated previously and utilized extensively elsewhere are used both to measure treatment outcomes and to quantify overall patient and program progress. Some of the scales used with adult and elderly patients are described below.

The Nurses Observation Scale for Inpatient Evaluation (NOSIE-30) measures behavioral change.[5,6] It contains six subscales. *Social Competence* contains items, such as "Shaves himself, Makes his own bed, Knows where he is," that measure orientation and performance of daily living tasks. *Social Interest* measures sociability ("Talks about happenings on the ward, Stays by himself"). *Personal Neatness* includes "Keeps his clothes neat, Is messy in his eating habits." *Irritability* is indicated by items such as "Is impatient. Shouts and yells." *Manifest Psychosis* includes psychotic symptoms ("Giggles or smiles to himself without apparent reason. Assumes strange expressions, pos-

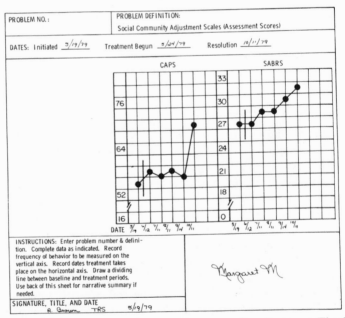

Fig. 5-2.   Graphic presentation of progress in community adjustment. The CAP and SABRS scales are standard psychosocial rating instruments.[8,9]

tures, or movement. Hears things that are not there"). *Retardation* means slowing of movment and not mental or intellectual retardation (sample items include "Sleeps, unless directed into activity" and "Is slow moving or sluggish").

The *Community Adjustment Potential Scale (CAP)*[6] and the *Social Adjustment Behavior Rating Scale (SABRS)* [7] measure, respectively, discharge readiness and level of social adjustment. The CAP tests judgment and ability to communicate, which increase the patient's interpersonal skills outside the hospital. The SABRS includes items such as "Does not usually respond when people talk to him"; "knows the names of a few other people"; and "talks easily with the ward attendants."

These three rating scales provide the kind of information that treatment personnel need for making important administrative and clinical decisions. They answer questions like: "What is the patient's overall social adjustment? Is he ready for discharge? Can he move to a higher treatment level?"

Figure 5-2 shows the progress made by an elderly patient, whose case history will be described in Chapter 15, on the CAP and SABRS behavior rating scales.

Functional Behavior Checklist for Measuring Children's Performance

Since 1976 Hung and his associates[8] have been developing a Functional Behavior Checklist for measuring the performance of preschool, autistic, and developmentally disabled children in 22 areas of functional skill. The instrument is not standardized, but it can be used to evaluate a child's progress over time and to compare the performance of matched groups of children receiving different types of treatment. The checklist has been shown to be 80 percent reliable.

COMMENT ON STANDARDIZED PSYCHOSOCIAL
RATING SCALES, TARGET BEHAVIORS, AND
PROFICIENCY GAUGES

Patterson and his associates[9] point out that standardized psychosocial rating scales suffer from being imprecise with respect to individual target behaviors, and from requiring extensive periods of observation. Therefore, they are used in the assessment programs to measure overall treatment and program progress at relatively long intervals, such as at the beginning of treatment, at the end of each month, and at discharge.

In behavior modification, target behaviors are used in formulating individual treatment plans and monitoring individual progress. There are problems here too, however. Individualized measures are costly and time-consuming to develop, and their validity is not usually tested. Their development requires a relatively high level of staff expertise and, once defined, individual target behaviors are useful only with the person for whom they were developed. They may require extended periods of observation and, since they are individualized, it is difficult to combine them for the purpose of program evaluation.[9]

Proficiency gauges, which assess functional deficiencies of the mentally ill and progress in developing proficiencies, overcome many of these obstacles. They point at specific target behaviors. Staff with little academic training can use them, and they take only a half hour or less to administer. Their use is not limited to a single or a few individuals, and scores on many patients can be aggregated for program evaluation. Test-retest reliability, interrater reliability, and convergent and discriminant validity are satisfactory.[9]

Assessing Supports

Edmunson, Weinberg, and their associations[10-12] are evaluating the usefulness of a process for measuring networks and patients' success in improving their supports during psychoeducational treatment. Before treatment begins, they assess patients' networks in the following manner: The patients name their fiancé (or fiancée) or special, intimate friend or spouse, if any. Next they add all persons, both family and friends, who live in their household. Then they list the names of anyone else upon whom they can rely to look after their home when they leave town. The names are included of everyone to whom they talk and those who talk to them about work problems. The patients continue by adding the names of persons with whom they have dined, visited, or engaged in other social activities, and those with whom they have gotten together to share hobbies and spare time activities within the past three months. The names are included of those to whom they turn or who turn to them (excluding mental health professionals) with a personal problem, a worry, or when another person's opinion or judgment is valued for making an important decision. The list continues with the names of persons from whom they could borrow a large sum of money, if necessary. Finally, the patients add any other names of persons whom they consider important in their lives.

After weeding out imaginary, symbolic, unrealistic names (chronically ill mental patients sometimes include the names of Billy Graham, Jimmy Carter, Jesus Christ, etc., in their lists), the researchers determine the density of the network (the number of persons who know each other; the amount of reciprocity, how much give and take there is between the patient and each relative or friend; the number of stress-producing persons; the sex of each member; and the relative importance of each person).

Research has shown that progress in support building is related to increase in network size: a good network should contain at least 20–30 members to provide adequate support;[13] increases in non-kin members: a majority of members should not be the patients' kin;[14] moderation in density: psychot-

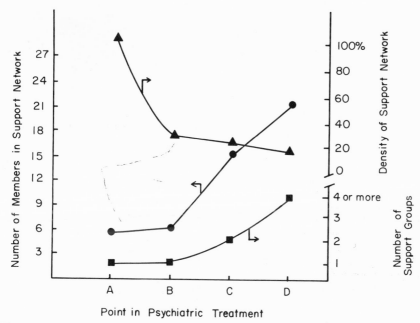

Point in Psychiatric Treatment

Fig. 5-3.   Graphs showing increasing success of a patient, Suella P., in building supports during treatment. Density is determined by counting the numbers of members
who know each other and dividing this number by the number of possible combinations. The latter is calculated from the formula $C = N (N-1)/2$, where C is the number of combinations possible and N the number of members in the network.

ics' networks are usually dense and constricting (probably about one-half of
the members should know each other); decreases in troublesome members;
increases in reciprocal relationships: patients who receive support but do not
reciprocate gradually lose their friends;[11] increases in numbers of groups of
members;[15] decreases in dependence upon key linking persons whose loss
from the network would isolate groups from each other; increases in both
close and distant relationships; increases in availability of members both geographically and emotionally; increases in amount of support between members; and increases in the patients' accepting leadership and helping roles in
the network: Edmunson and her co-workers[12] have found that patients' self-
esteem is bolstered and their need for rehospitalization is reduced when they
hold leadership responsibilities in the CND, as long as they can rely upon
professional and paraprofessional backup support when needed. Many of
these features of patients' support networks may be plotted on graphs. These
graphs showing patients' progress in treatment can be made part of the clinical record. An example made from Suella P's record is shown in Figure 5-
3, and discussed in the next chapter.

Table 5-2
Severity Scale: Level of educational restriction required by child/adolescent patients

Least restrictive setting	Level I	Regular school (private or public)
	Level II	Regular school plus supportive services (periodic visits to school counselor)
	Level III	Regular school plus residential treatment facility (group home, family teaching home, foster home, etc.)
	Level IV	Full-time special school and/or supportive services, living in the home
	Level V	Full-time residential setting for emotional handicap and attending regular school (with or without supportive services)
	Level VI	Intermittent school suspensions and living at home
Most restrictive setting	Level VII	Intermittent school suspensions and residential treatment facility
	Level VIII	Continuous school suspensions (home bound)
	Level IX	Intermittent hospitalization for emotional disturbance and living home (regular or special school)
	Level X	Continuous residential treatment setting and school on site
	Level XI	Continuous residential treatment setting and incapable of attending school

(Level of restriction — arranged from Least restrictive setting to Most restrictive setting)

Measuring Behavioral Excesses

Standardized scales to assess behavioral excesses are difficult to develop. For example, the control of head banging, destructive violence, hyperactivity, running away from home, etc., are major problems with child and adolescent mental patients. Drash and Hung are attempting to develop standardized severity scales to assess progress in bringing these abnormal behaviors under control.[15] These measure how the patient's behavior affects his adjustment to the environment. For example, they are developing a scale for measuring severity of emotional handicap as it affects educational placement setting. Table 5-2 presents the scale in its present form. When combined with other objective measures of adjustment in the home and community, this type of instrument provides a potentially useful, quantitative indicant of a child or adolescent patient's pretreatment condition and subsequent outcome with therapy.

Paraprofessional staff on the treatment units have no difficulty in learning to administer proficiency gauges. As part of their initial training on beginning service, they are taught the procedures, just as they are taught to administer a thermometer to measure a patient's temperature. They learn to record findings and to plot data on the progress graph in the patient's clinical chart.

The overall system for assessing patients' behavioral progress and for evaluating modules and programs will be described in the following section.

THEORETICAL FRAMEWORK

The theoretical basis underlying the entire assessment approach rests on a model proposed by Brunswik in 1956,[16] later fitted with a method for statistical analysis by Hursch, Hammond, and Hursch,[17] and since then applied to a wide variety of situations. This model relies upon the specific, observed behaviors from which predictions of future behavior are made. Whether or not these predictions are right, and to what extent they are inaccurate, can be determined by the actual outcome at some later time.

Patients in a mental hospital engage in behaviors (predictors) that are observed by the mental health professional and paraprofessional staff attending them. At some point, these clinical staff personnel are required to make a decision (prediction) regarding the patients' ability to conduct themselves appropriately in the outside world, i.e., to either discharge them or continue to treat them. If the patients are released from hospital care, their conduct outside the hospital over a period of time (the criterion) either confirms or denies that the prediction was correct.

Because the measures of mental health have traditionally been loosely specified, predictions of normalcy (as evidenced by discharge from the hospital) are only haphazardly based upon observations of the patients' behavior in the hospital. Since these observations are usually informal and unspecified, it is impossible to determine which behavioral cues were incorrectly interpreted (weighted); in fact, it is often impossible to find out what cues even entered into the judgment. In most cases, behavior outside the hospital is not followed, so that unless the former patient is returned to the hospital, there is no way of knowing whether or not the prediction was correct, i.e., whether or not the decision to release the patient at a given time was appropriate.

Brunswik's "lens" model, on the other hand, requires that (1) the cues that serve as predictors must be specified, (2) judgment is made of degree of success based upon the specified predictors, and (3) a follow-up is conducted after the patient leaves the hospital so that the judgment may be evaluated in terms of the outcome. It also allows for an analysis of the judgment process, and of the validity of the predictors being used so that useless behavioral cues may gradually be eliminated from consideration, in favor of cues with higher predictive value.

The structure and use of the model are as follows: The physical model is a lens that is convex on both sides. Enclosed within this lens are the specific, observed behavioral cues that are exhibited by the patient. They are depicted as enclosed within the lens because these pieces of behavior are all that the clinician has by which to make a decision. The patient's "overall social adjustment," his "readiness to move to a higher treatment level," and his "readiness for discharge" are all concepts abstracted from a composite of observed behavioral cues; but it is these distal concepts upon which mental health personnel are required to render a judgment.

The cues, which in the present context are test results on proficiency gauges and psychosocial rating scales, transmit certain meanings to the treatment staff, and thereby become predictors. From them staff form a concept such as "the patient's ability to live outside of the hospital setting." If the clinical staff gives the patient a high enough rating on this concept (the distal variable), then the patient is released and takes up life in the community.

Six months later, for example, the patient is again tested on a set of behavioral indices, which together make up the concept "ability to live in the outside world." This is the concept that the clinical staff was attempting to predict six months earlier; but, at this point, the fact is established, and we can determine by the test results to what degree the patient is exhibiting such an ability. This, then, is the true value of the "distal variable," and by comparing it with the clinical prediction, we can ascertain how accurate that prediction was. A simple correlation of the prediction with the patient's degree of success in living in the community will show the extent of accuracy. Further analysis of the relationship between the original predictors and the prediction itself will show what caused the prediction to be inaccurate. Thus, the lens model for this situation looks like the illustration shown in Figure 5-4.

It can be seen that the "rays" emanating from the left side of the lens converge at a focal point that is the clinical staff's summation of the patient's condition. This is expressed as a prediction of the patient's degree of success in living outside the hospital setting. On the right side of the lens, the corresponding rays converge on the distal variable itself, which is the fact, six months later, of whether or not, and to what degree, the patient actually could succeed in carrying on his life outside the hospital. Thus, if the clinical staff correctly interpret the predictor variables (and if the latter actually do bear a relationship to the distal variable), the prediction will be the same as the distal variable, i.e., correct.

What if the prediction is not correct? This is where the statistical analysis of Hursch et al.[17] becomes important. The above is a multivariate situation, where the predictor variables may be entered into a multiple regression equation, with the distal variable serving as the criterion. This can be done

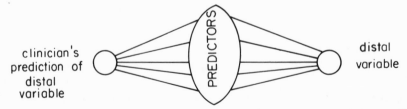

Fig. 5-4. Brunswig lens model used in clinical prediction of treatment outcome. The predictors are test results during hospital stay, and the distal variable is a test result 6 months after release, which indicates the patient's ability to live in the community.

on either side of the lens so that the predictors and the clinical staff's estimate of the distal variable can form one regression equation. The same predictors and actual value of the distal variable can then be used to form a second regression equation. When this is done, the weightings given each predictor variable by the clinical staff may be compared with the correct weightings in the regression equation by use of the true distal variable. If the treatment staff's overall estimate of the distal variable is not correct, then this will be reflected by an incorrect weighting of one or more of the predictor variables. When treatment staff receive feedback on these incorrect weightings, they can gradually be trained to weight them correctly, and thus to make more accurate assessments, i.e., predictions.

Since the above analysis may imply only strictly linear relationships between predictors and the criterion, Hursch et al.[17] added a further refinement designed to pick up the nonlinearity that may occur within the system. For a complete explanation of this refinement, the reader should refer to their original publication; their statistical model is shown in Figure 5-5.

By patterning its work after a model of this type, the research and training facility bases patient assessments on the results of objective tests rather than upon loosely specified opinions of progress. However beneficial a treatment may appear to be while the patient is in the hospital, its merit can only be determined by careful follow-up and retesting after the patient has returned to community life.

The weightings on the predictor variables are particularly important in light of the fact that psychological tests all have less than perfect validity, i.e., may have only a partial relationship to the skill or ability they purport to measure. Also, clinicians tend to base their assessments on the results of a "favorite" test, often without regard to the low predictive value of that test.

With the lens model, the value of each test result in predicting the criterion can be derived from the multiple regression equation. Thus, if a test has only very low validity in the hospital situation, the clinical staff can be shown this, and can be advised to give very little weight to the results of such a test. Also, because the model also derives the intercorrelations between tests (or, if only one test is used between the items on a test), if two tests are highly intercorrelated they are testing the same thing, and one of them may be discarded, thus saving the time necessary to administer and score such a test. Perhaps comprehensive tests like the NOSIE-30, which are time-consuming to administer, will be replaced by briefer proficiency gauges that measure only each patient's specific strengths and weaknesses.

The model also shows staff where there are gaps in their test batteries; when the individual and multiple correlations are low they must find or develop better test instruments. In summary, the use of this model and its statistical applications, allows for considerably deeper analysis of the results of treatment than has heretofore been possible. It also has broad implications for the training of treatment staffs.

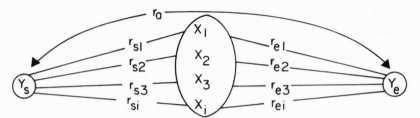

Fig. 5-5.   Statistical model developed by Hursch, Hammond, and Hursch[17] as applied to clinical treatment settings.

Y_s = the clinician's prediction of the distal variable
Y_e = the actual value of the distal variable
r_a = correlation of clinician's prediction with actual fact (accuracy)
X_1, X_2, X_3, X_i = the predictors, i.e., in-hospital test scores
$r_{s1}, r_{s2}, r_{s3}, r_{si}$ = correlations of individual predictors with the clinician's prediction of the distal variable
$r_{e1}, r_{e2}, r_{e3}, r_{ei}$ = correlations of individual predictors with actual distal variable

Then: if we assume that Y_e, Y_s, $X_1 \ldots X_n$ are standardized random variables (i.e. their mean is zero and their variance is 1), and that

$$\text{Correlation } (Y_e, X_i) = r_{ei}$$
$$\text{Correlation } (Y_s, X_i) = r_{si}$$

Let R_e be the multiple correlation of Y_e and $(X_1, \ldots X_n)$ on the distal variable side,
Let R_s be the multiple correlation of Y_s and $(X_1, \ldots X_n)$ on the clinician's prediction side.
Under these assumptions

$$Y_e = (B_{e,1}X_1 + \ldots + B_{e,n}X_n) + Z_e$$
$$Y_x = (B_{s,1}X_1 + \ldots + B_{s,n}X_n) + Z_s$$

where the quantities in parentheses represent the regressions, and Z_e and Z_s are the residual that are uncorrelated with any of the regression variables $(X_1, \ldots X_n)$

PSYCHOSOCIAL DATA COLLECTION

A standard procedure for the routine collection of data by staff of the research and training center's Gerontology Program was developed by Penner[18] with support from Title XX training funds. These data are systematically collected from the time the patient enters treatment until one year after discharge and are used to establish norms on demographic characteristics, social skills, and level of psychosocial functioning of patients; to track an individual patient's progress throughout treatment and his status after discharge; and to evaluate the effectiveness both of individual modules and of the entire project. These assessments provide data for planning patient treatments, making discharge and placement decisions, and evaluating post discharge status; they also provide a record for evaluating projects, modules, treatments, and changes as a function of time.

Data collection is individualized, as it would be in a typical clinical treatment setting. Periodic assessments are conducted on each treatment unit by paraprofessionals. These measures accurately reflect the length of a patient's stay in the program, the progress of the patient in the program, and the individualized treatment plan for the patient. Data collected from different patients are combined and statistically reduced for the purpose of evaluating individual modules and the overall program.[18]

Pattern of Psychosocial Data Collection During Treatment

Patients are assessed during the first full week in treatment and at the end of each three weeks of treatment. When the patient is ready for discharge, a final assessment is conducted. At the time of intake, all patients receive assessments by means of a standard set of proficiency gauges and psychosocial measures that are specific to their age group and treatment project.

Data are collected on all patients as they progress through treatment. A patient's participation in a module is not terminated until his proficiency has been measured. When this assessment indicates that patient has reached the criterion (or criteria) for graduation, she/he stops attending the module, and this assessment becomes the final progress assessment. Treatment continues during the week of a progress assessment. During an assessment week, patients are rated on the CAP, NOSIE-30, and SABRS, and all modules in which they are currently enrolled. Discharge assessments take place within a week to ten days before the patient leaves treatment.

Follow-up

Follow-up information is collected on patients after they have left the treatment phase of the program. The goals of follow-up are to monitor the pychosocial status of the patients after they leave the program, and to provide the data base for the evaluation of the long-term effects of the program.

Patients are interviewed one, three, six, and twelve months after they leave the program. In the face-to-face interview, the patient's status is once again assessed with both proficiency gauges and global psychosocial scales, and the patient's satisfaction with treatment is measured.[18]

A relative or friend of the patient is also interviewed with the patient's permission on an informed consent form. This person also signs an informed consent form, and then fills out a modified NOSIE-30, which describes how the patient appears to him/her at the time of the follow-up assessment.

Out-of-area patients are contacted by telephone for each of the four follow-up sessions, and an abridged social history obtained.[18]

Reporting

Data are collected for regular periodic reports (monthly, quarterly, and annually), as well as for program evaluation. Projects that relied solely on the computer for storing and generating these reports were less reliable in the research and training center's early years of existence than were those where data were compiled by hand and reported by designated individuals.

DEVELOPING PROFICIENCY GAUGES

A standardized interaction procedure utilized by the Child and Adolescent Program trains children in three skills: greeting a guest, answering the telephone, and behaving appropriately when a guest departs.[19] This type of training begins immediately when the child enters treatment. The sessions include baseline observation, instruction with cards, and teaching interaction. Repeated assessments measure progress.

Baseline Condition

During this initial assessment, the children are asked to engage in each of the three behaviors. They respond to instructions: "Please answer the door." "Please answer the telephone." "Please help our guest leave now." Examples of baseline results appear in Figure 5-6. The data show that the child lacked some components of the three target skills upon entering the program. The standard pretreatment assessment is performed by counting the numbers of the component parts of each skill that the child performs correctly (see Table 5-3).

Psychoeducational Training

The children next are given cards containing the written instructions shown in Table 5-3. These are the components of the skills that they will learn and on which their performance will be assessed. The manner in which these skills are to be carried out is explained. The children read the instructions and ask questions until they understand them. They keep the instruction cards and refer to them when necessary.

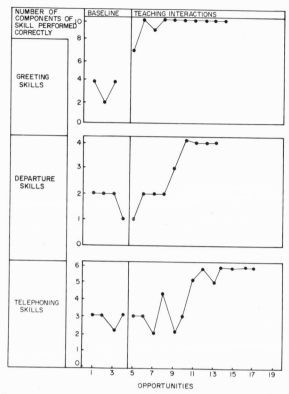

Fig. 5-6.   Graphs displaying a child's progress in developing several psychosocial skills.

The children then receive structured training in the appropriate use of the components of the three social skills. This procedure follows the teaching interaction sequence described by Maloney et al.,[20] and basically employs four elements—instruction, modeling, rehearsal, and reinforcement. Each child is taught to a 100 percent criterion in one initial training session. Repeated training occurs when the child fails to maintain a perfect pattern of responses over time. Figure 5-6 shows a typical 10-year-old patient's progress in treatment as measured by a proficiency gauge that the children's program is developing.

Complexity of Proficiency Gauges

Initial success has been achieved in developing preficiency gauges for simple skills like communicating, or learning personal information or skills of daily living. In time, we expect to develop valid and reliable measures for

Table 5-3
Written instruction card

Greeting Skills
 1. Say "Hi" or "Hello."
 2. Introduce yourself ("How do you do," and/or "I'm James").
 3. Look the person in the eye.
 4. Talk loud enough for the person to hear you.
 5. Smile.
 6. Put your hand out and shake the person's hand.
 7. Invite the guest into the house.
 8. Offer a seat.
 9. Offer something to eat and/or drink.
10. Offer help in finding a person or materials.

Departure Skills
 1. Say you are glad to have met the guest or to have seen her/him again.
 2. Walk guest to the door and shake hands if possible.
 3. Invite the guest to come back again.
 4. Say "Goodbye."

Telephone Skills
 1. Say "Hello."
 2. Identify the residence and yourself ("Children's Cottage, James speaking").
 3. Find the person the caller wants to speak to,
                    -or-
    Take a message if necessary.
 4. Thank the caller for calling.
 5. Say "Goodbye."
 6. Hang up the receiver gently, without a "clang" noise.

These 20 steps include all the component parts of three psychosocial skills taught children. Scores are obtained by counting the number of steps the child performs correctly for each skill. These assessments gauge the extent of the child's proficiency in the skill.

more complex skills like problem-solving or integrating several skills. Bedell and Archer are beginning to achieve some success in this effort (see Chapter 14).

RELIABILITY AND VALIDITY OF PROFICIENCY GAUGES

Patterson et al.[9] have reported on reliability and validity of proficiency gauges developed by the research and training center's Gerontology Program. They describe an investigation of three instruments that measure Intellectual Competence, Conversational Skills, and Personal Hygiene Skills.

Intellectual Competence is measured on a list of ten items of personal information that tell a client's orientation for time, place, and person. It includes items such as: "What is your name?" "Who is your doctor?" "What month is it?" "What is the name of this place?"

Conversational Skills are measured by observing patients in a social setting for 30 seconds. Five observations are made per patient, and a record kept of whether the patient is speaking to someone.

Personal Hygiene Skills are gauged by ten activities of daily living. Self-report and observational data are recorded on mouth care, cleanliness, and eating behavior. For example, patients are asked when they last brushed their teeth or cleaned their dentures. The assessor then inspects the patient to check whether these behaviors have been carried out. These assessments require about ten to fifteen minutes per patient.

Measurements on proficiency gauges developed by the gerontology staff were correlated with scores on three comparable subscales of the NOSIE-30 (Social Competence, which measures intellectual competence; Social Interest, which measures conversational skills; and Neatness, which assesses personal hygiene). Inter-rater reliabilities for personal hygiene, intellectual competence, and conversation (as measured by the method of exact agreement) were 93 percent, 100 percent, and 89 percent, respectively, as reported by Patterson et al.[9] Five of the six test-retest reliability correlations were in excess of 0.60, and one was 0.53. Convergent validity was determined by correlating proficiency gauge measures with their NOSIE-30 counterparts. These ranged from 0.43 to 0.57 (p < .01 for all three correlations).[9]

The data show that stability, reliability, and both concurrent and face validity are high for the standardized global psychosocial assessment scales.

Proficiency Gauges Developed Elsewhere

Connor and Gordon[21] have developed a behavioral instrument for gauging proficiency in assertion. This Psychiatric Assertion Test (PAT), which paraprofessionals can administer, contains 20 items consisting of scene descriptions and cue lines to which patients respond. The inter-rater reliability of the PAT is 0.97.

Proficiency gauges that measure assertion, activities of daily living, communication, problem solving, and other psychosocial skills will, we believe, shortly become major clinical measures of progress in psychiatric treatment. A number of these instruments that currently are available are described in the Handbook of Behavioral Assessment.[22]

DISCUSSION

Many psychiatrists have criticized efforts to objectify quality of psychiatric care, which they consider premature. They assert that they are being forced to treat charts and not patients, and that too much time is now being spent on some charting requirements. Certainly, the procedures described here are not overly burdensome once paraprofessional staff have learned to perform them and clinicians to interpret them. The benefits to the clinician as well as to the program evaluator are obvious: the patient's graphs in his clinical chart clearly show the progress made and how much further the patient must go to achieve the targeted goal.

An obstacle to the continued development and use of the procedures described, however, is the limited training in quantitative methods, assessment, and evaluation that most mental health and human service personnel receive. This gap in their education can be filled, and Chapter 10 shows how it is being done.

SUMMARY AND CONCLUSIONS

The findings of the present chapter suggest tentative answers to the kinds of questions posed in the introductory paragraphs of this chapter.

Who can be covered by mental health insurance? Programs using modular skill training and individualized behavior management to augment medical treatment benefit most chronically ill and other mental patients of all ages. The programs also divert persons who are at high risk for chronic mental illness from hospitalization. Poverty and other disadvantages need not limit the effectiveness of the combined treatment approach.

What kind of treatment does a given patient need? Impairments and behavioral excesses are tested on admission, along with other medical and psychiatric examinations; treatment is determined and prescribed in advance.

Can progress be determined? Progress in skill-building is assessed by paraprofessionals on objective tests at every stage of treatment, and plotted graphically in the patient's record. Standardized tests gauge improvements in both global performance and proficiency in specific skills. Both program and individual progress can be assessed.

When does treatment end? Clearly stated objective end points for treatment are stated in advance, and progress toward them is measured regularly on standardized scales. Program evaluations show that, although patients continue to progress with psychoeducational treatment, the greatest benefit takes place for most elderly persons in the first four weeks of residential care, a period of treatment covered by many insurance policies.

Who does treatment? Psychiatrists, general physicians, and other professionals provide medical care and individualized behavioral treatments that require graduate training. Paraprofessionals supervised by professionals provide the bulk of routine, standardized modular treatment in psychoeducational classes.

What is the role of indigenous workers? State hospital and other indigenous mental health workers, who speak the same language as the patients, as well as the patients themselves, provide most of these innovative treatments and assessments. Professionals provide them with training, supervision, direction, consultation, and back-up support, as needed. Since the mental health workers teach the patients in addition to performing their other regular ward duties, additional expenses are minimal. By learning to administer proficiency gauges and standardized psychosocial assessment scales, indigenous workers measure the progress patients make in treatment and help document the effectiveness of psychiatric treatment.

REFERENCES

1. Bassuk EL, Gerson S: Deinstitutionalization and mental health services. Sci Am 238:46–53, 1978
2. Braceland FJ: Dear doctor: It's later than you think! Psychiatric Ann 9:8, 1979
3. Whitman D: Reorganization of Florida's human services agency. Kennedy School of Government Case Program, C95-80-040. Cambridge, Mass., Harvard University, 1980
4. Harrell T, Smith G, Piroch J, et al: Activities of Daily Living, Level 1. Gerontology Program. Tampa, Fla., Florida Mental Health Institute, 1979
5. Honigfeld G, Gillis RD, Klett CJ: NOSIE-30, A treatment sensitive ward behavior scale. Psychol Rep 19:180–182, 1966
6. Hogarty GE, Ulrich R: The discharge readiness inventory. Arch Gen Psychiatry 26: 419–426, 1972
7. Aumack L: Social adjustment behavior rating scale. J Clin Psychol 13:436–441, 1962
8. Hung D: The Functional Behavior Checklist. Tampa, Fla., Florida Mental Health Institute, 1979
9. Patterson RL, Penner L, Eberly D, et al: Behavioral assessments of intellectual competence, conversation skills, and personal hygiene skills of elderly persons. Poster session presented at 2nd Annual NOVA University Conference on Aging. January, 1980
10. Edmunson E, Kinder C, Marlowe A (Eds): Peer Support Systems: Concepts, Prototypes, and Developmental Techniques. Tampa, Fla., Florida Mental Health Institute, 1979
11. Edmunson E, Weinberg R, Phillips C, et al: Social networks and support systems of mental health clients and staff. Paper present at the Annual Convention of the Southeastern Psychological Association, Ft. Lauderdale, Fla. 1980
12. Gordon RE, Edmunson E, Wolfe A, et al: Course #60: The use of networks and social support in therapy. 133rd Annual Meeting, Am. Psychiatr Assoc, San Francisco, Calif., May 1980
13. Pattison EM, Llamas R, Hurd G: Social network mediation of anxiety. Psychiatric Ann: 56–67, 1979
14. Pattison EM: Clinical applications of social network concepts to mental health. Paper presented at the Fourth Annual Colloquium on Social Networks, Manoa, Hawaii, December, 1977
15. Drash P: Personal communication, April 11, 1980
16. Brunswik, E: Perception and the Representation Design of Psychological Experiments, Berkeley, University of California Press, 1956
17. Hursch, CJ, Hammond, KR, Hursch JL: Some methodological considerations in multiple-cue probability studies. Psychol Rev: 71:42–60, 1964

18. Penner L: The data collection system. FMHI evaluation procedure manual. Unpublished manuscript. Tampa, Fla., Florida Mental Health Institute, February 9, 1979

19. Ford D, Evans JH, Devorbian L: Teaching interaction procedures: Effects upon the learning of social skills by an emotionally disturbed child. (submitted for publication)

20. Maloney DM, Phillips EL, Fixsen DL, et al: Training techniques for staff in group homes for juvenile offenders: An analysis. Criminal Justice Behav 2:195–216, 1975

21. Conner WH, Gordon PM: Psychiatric assertion test: Behavioral and psychiatric considerations. Presented at the meeting of the Midwestern Psychological Assoc., Chicago, May, 1978

22. Ciminero AR, Calhoun KS, Adams HE: Handbook of Behavioral Assessment. New York, Wiley-Interscience, 1977

6
Filling the Gaps in the Treatment of the Individual Patient

At this juncture we have enough general information about the new treatment programs to see how they apply in the case introduced in the first chapter, of Suella P., the chronically ill 25-year-old separated mother of a small daughter, who had been admitted to public mental hospitals on four separate occasions over the past seven years of her life. This chapter will discuss in broad outline her program of treatment from the perspective of four different conceptual models—the medical pharmacological, the behavioral skill enhancing, the psychosocial supports building, and the psychodynamic insight giving. This presentation will show how these four treatment approaches are combined into integrated treatment plans where the patient gains personal control of her life, her emotions, and her thoughts, and also receives both continuous support from friends and backup assistance from professionals.

Before considering Suella's treatment, let us consider what the Harvard Case Report[1] says about the services patients are receiving. (Descriptions of a mental hospital and other institutions and the treatment in them will appear later in the chapter on matrix management.)

The director of a mental health clinic states, "the system is arranged in such a way that there are too many bosses to get things done . . ." (p. 35). An attorney who is head of a legal services unit that deals with health and welfare problems in the public sector explains, "Clients are still getting the runaround because the staff is not adequately trained about what is available. . . . We had a situation, for example, with a woman who was an AFDC recipient with a clear mental problem; she was an episodic schizophrenic. I saw her record, it must have been a foot thick. This woman started yelling at her worker—not being physically violent—and the worker just terminated her case and threw her out of her office. I sat down to talk with this worker. I said,

'Didn't you realize this woman had problems?' 'No.' 'Did you ever think of getting her to a psychiatrist ...?' 'No.' ... That type of thing is not infrequent in my experience" (p. 35–36). "... A clear majority of the [veteran social] workers interviewed felt that reorganization was detracting from the quality of service delivery ..." (p. 37). However, although legislators were (and are) strong supporters of reorganization, they and outside experts compiled evidence that "... complaints about service ... had origins in problems which predated reorganization, but the continuance of these problems into the post-reorganization period lent some credence to claims that reorganization had not touched ... fundamental problems" (p. 11).

Now look at Suella's case, and see what kinds of services she needed and what the programs described in the early chapters of this book had to offer her and the many patients like her. We consider her treatment first from the perspective of the biomedical model.

BIOMEDICAL MODEL

Suella's disorder is a functional psychosis that responds to antipsychotic medications. She needed to understand her medications better and to know how, why, and when to take them. A cooperative patient, she easily learned all that was necessary for successful self-medication.

Suella responded well to single bedtime doses of major tranquilizers. These helped her sleep well, and thus controlled some of her most troublesome symptoms: her tendency to dwell on problems at nighttime, to lose sleep, and to begin to hallucinate. With tranquilizers to help her sleep and to calm her nerves, and training in problem-solving in the daytime to help her plan and cope with her difficulties, she immediately began to improve. Her more flagrant psychotic symptoms—her auditory hallucinations and her withdrawal—abated.

It is possible that a good medical regimen might have aborted several of Suella's acute psychotic episodes that resulted in her requiring hospitalization. In any event, medications brought her back in touch with reality. She could then cooperate in her psychological treatments.

BEHAVIORAL MODEL

Let us look now at her case from the behavioral skill-building conceptual model for evaluating patients and planning their treatment.

(1) Suella's disordered behavior and thinking are precipitated by antecedent biological and cultural events: her loss or threatened loss of emotional relationships with both her husband and her child, her becoming a mother—a new role for which she was unequipped by background experience and for which no one provided her with present-day training. (2) Her waitress jobs

provided her with social contacts that counteracted the isolation and rejection, as well as self-doubt she felt as a farm housewife. (3) Suella's deficits in skills—in communication, assertion, problem-solving, relaxation, and the use of leisure—impaired her ability to cope with her problems. (4) Her brother-in-law's sexual harassment stirred feelings of anxiety and guilt over her premarital affairs.

(5) Suella's willingness to work hard, her perseverance both in the home and on the job were valuable personal assets that would be useful to her rehabilitation. Even though her relatives had not provided her with a sense of security, they had taught her persistence at work and had inured her to hardship, skills that many patients have not acquired before they enter therapy. In these respects she was better off than most chronic mental patients. She continued to seek treatment at the clinic despite being confused, and at least got to talk to staff and patients. Her persistence at work helped keep a roof over her head in her aunts' and uncles' homes as a child and, later, provided her with financial security and a measure of social acceptance from the people she met at work. This perseverance and reliability can be generalized to her learning in modular classes and gaining respect from fellow patients.

Suella participated actively in her residential classes of skill-building treatment, and learned techniques for communicating better, asserting herself effectively, and solving problems. She also learned how to counsel other patients and friends, how to provide leadership, and how to use her leisure and to relax. Sexuality training also helped her to reassess her own values and to reduce her feelings of guilt over her conduct prior to meeting Tom. The purpose of this training was similar to what the therapist in her clinic group was trying to achieve; but the careful design of the sexuality classes, and their systematic and structured approach to the subject matter, did not embarrass and confuse her. Instead, it gradually helped to reduce and extinguish her anxiety and guilt over events in her past. [2]

(6) Suella's inconsistent and often conflicting psychiatric treatment, with her repeated hospitalizations, were damaging her life: they contributed to the break up of her marriage and were leading to her losing her child. They were destroying her self-confidence, adding to her fears, and making her rehabilitation increasingly difficult as she lost trust in her therapists. The hospital staff knew that patients like Suella who had been hospitalized many times were hard to place in the community, especially if they were separated or divorced, and had no families to support them; they were quite satisfied with Suella's living with Marsha as the best plan available. The clinic personnel, on the other hand, dealt with patients who were less severely impaired. They were threatened by Suella's behavior when she was psychotic and were truly concerned that she might harm her child.[3] There is a slight risk that a patient like Suella would be a danger to others, possibly as part of a sequence of be-

havior where she was harming herself, since she tended to be self-destructive when mentally disturbed. It is conceivable that Suella might have taken Mary Ellen with her to be purified in the bay waters. But Suella was not likely to harm someone she loved when she was happy, as she had been with Marsha and her child. Suella became psychotic and potentially dangerous to herself and others when she was losing loved ones; the clinic's action in stirring up proceedings to take Mary Ellen away from her was just such a situation.

(7) Assertion training taught her to ask that people consider what she wanted, including, of course, to keep her daughter.

As Suella learned to speak up in communications classes, she began to explain her feelings about her daughter and Marsha, her job and her marriage, and her worries that the psychiatric treatment she was receiving was making her worse. Her classes in solving problem showed her the techniques for resolving conflicts, and provided her with practise in tackling some of her own problems. Training in relaxation, in combination with psychotropic medications, helped her gain refreshing sleep.

(8) Anxiety and depression training taught Suella how to shunt away her negative thinking and resulting bad feelings about herself.[2]

Comparison of Conventional Dynamic Group Psychotherapy and Modular Psychoeducational Treatment

Group psychotherapy is relatively unstructured, and generally chooses its own directions. The group does not focus upon achieving specific operationally defined behavioral goals. The underlying principles of the group process are that freedom of expression promotes group feedback. Participants learn about relationships with other persons from discussion with each other and the group's leader, and develop new ways of interacting and coping with personal problems. This process is limited in general by the knowledge and skills of the patient participants and the group leader. The topics may or may not be relevant on any given day to an individual patient's needs.

The modular psychoeducational approach is based on empirical data resulting from the scientific study of behavior. This approach concentrates on behaviors the patient is using to adapt to the environment rather than on exploring underlying causes. Specific target behaviors for each individual are established by assessment and, along with the treatment methods to be employed, are operationally defined. The effectiveness of modular therapy is assessed scientifically, monitored repeatedly, and empirically determined.

In group psychotherapy, patients freely discuss historical information about their lives or whatever problems interest them at the moment. A more verbal, more aggressive patient may preempt a comparatively large part of the therapy session despite efforts of the leader to be fair to all the members. Discussion is directly related to specific problems that patients in the group are facing at the moment.

Psychoeducation covers a specific content in a preplanned curriculum with a schedule of subjects. Psychoeducation is less time-consuming, more efficient, but narrower in scope. It takes up problems sytematically, one-by-one, pointing out techniques for solving them or managing them, and training patients how to cope with them in an orderly manner, utilizing both cognitive and expressive, role-play components.

In traditional psychotherapy, patients generally work out their own solutions, although therapists will point the way, instruct patients, or lead them to a solution, but not in any systematic manner.

Psychoeducational modules are developed in a structured fashion that allows for continuous evaluation of their effectiveness as measured by patient progress. Improvements are made in each module as new data emerge from psychological and educational researches.

Traditional psychotherapy is unsystematic in comparison to psychoeducation. In the former, important problem areas may be dealt with randomly or not at all. Because of dynamic therapy's orientation to acute or crisis situations or topics that interest patients at the moment, important difficulties may never come up for discussion, and may be completely ignored. Certain human needs (e.g., political and spiritual) are not yet included in the psychoeducational program, however. These must be addressed in traditional psychotherapeutic sessions. Psychoeducation assesses every patients' strengths and weaknesses and systematically corrects measured handicaps in the area where staff have developed treatment modules.

Traditional dynamic psychotherapy depends very heavily upon the experience, maturity, and theoretical interest of the therapist. Clinicians vary in their skills in problem solving, for example, and thus therapy is inconsistent from therapist to therapist.

The psychoeducational approach provides a highly consistent, predetermined, standard therapy in each module regardless of who is leading the class. Novice paraprofessionals provide much the same treatment as seasoned professionals.

A large number of patients can be treated with the psychoeducational approach in a shorter period of time than with the traditional approach. In the former, as many as 32 patients have been treated in a modular psychoeducational gaming session. The maximum size for a therapeutic group in dynamic treatment is one-half as large or less, about 8–16 patients.

Low income chronic schizophrenics, who make up the majority of patients treated in public institutions, are poor candidates for dynamic therapy as a rule. They communicate poorly and soon exhaust most dynamic therapists because of their apathy, or the poor quality of their responding. Psychoeducational treatment reaches these patients effectively.

Traditional psychotherapy relies entirely upon verbal interaction; patients and therapists only talk about situations and behaviors; patients do not practice real behaviors in the treatment session and receive systematic reinforcement for learning. (Sometimes therapists will provide this training; when they do, they are utilizing behavioral techniques. This is fine, and should be encouraged, but it is not dynamic therapy.)

Psychoeducation uses modeling, shaping, role-play, practice, rehearsal, and other learning principles to change behavior.

Dynamic psychotherapy is often a long-term process in which patients may discuss an issue for months without resolving the problem.

Psychoeducational treatment can be a time-limited procedure. Patients can learn a specific skill in a matter of hours, days, or weeks; they can complete a full program of treatment with measurable results in a nine-week period.

Although dynamic psychotherapy requires highly skilled professional training and fairly intelligent, verbal, less impaired patients, it is more finely attuned to the specific needs of the individual patient. The patient who already is competent in communication, or is obtaining training in this and other skills, may benefit from dynamic, insight-giving therapy. A later section of this chapter will show how combinations of psychoeducational and dynamic therapy, along with medication and peer support, provided Suella with a most effective treatment regimen.

We return now to Suella's case history to see what peer management and support, and the psychosocial approach to treatment had to offer her. It is useful to remember the data from the authors' studies with women who developed mental disorders related to childbearing. Fully 43 percent had required hospitalization when provided only with psychodynamically oriented psychotherapy. Once supports and skills building were added to dynamic psychotherapy, none of the patients required hospitalization. When they could join new mothers' groups, get help from their female relatives and their husbands, in addition to receiving insight and psychotropic medications, they rapidly recovered. They needed an average of only six psychiatric out-patient sessions. Suella's case, however, is more complicated than most postpartum emotional breakdowns. She had suffered a number of psychotic episodes at other periods prior to and following maternity. Nevertheless, what can psychosocial therapy do for her, when added to her behavioral and medical treatment?

PSYCHOSOCIAL MODEL

(1) Suella's problems result from a series of stressful life events. She was sensitized in early childhood by her mother's desertion, and later by her lack of a stable home. She was pressurized by the lack of social supports and the brainwashing she received from her brother-in-law, Erwin. Her acute psychotic episodes were precipitated by the loss or threatened loss of persons in her support group.[4,5] (2) She had few natural social supports—no close family and only one friend, who also was a mental patient—to assist her, particularly in her new role as a mother. (3) Her professional supports were inconsistent and conflicting.

Little can be done at this late date to relieve Suella's early life stress—her sensitizers; but a great deal can be changed for the better in her present situation: both her pressurizers and her precipitators can be reduced.[4,6] The token economy program and community network development discharge preparation provided her with peer support, counseling, leadership, and community living skills, and showed her how to reinforce others in working towards individual and group goals and target behaviors.

Suella also needed professional support. Early in her residential stay, Suella learned from her problem-solving peer group that legal aid was available at no cost to persons in her position and that, if she wished, they would help her to obtain the services of a lawyer.

Suella at first was reluctant to speak to an attorney because she did not believe that anything could be done to help her keep Mary Ellen. Besides, she was afraid to visit the law offices. When told that she had every reason and every right to find out what could be done to keep her child, and that a fellow patient who had already made use of their services would accompany her to the lawyers' offices as often as needed, and would model law client behavior for her, Suella agreed to give the law a try.

The attorneys were interested in Suella's problem. After her initial visit they invited her to return for two more conferences. Both times she returned alone. Once they confirmed with the research and training center staff that Suella would be discharged soon, that she had a home, a job, and someone to help with Mary Ellen, they told her that she had an excellent case. The lawyers felt confident that they could prevent her losing custody of her daughter, since there was no indication that Suella was not doing a good job as a mother. When the opposing attorneys realized that Suella was going to fight to keep Mary Ellen, and that the research and training center's experts were ready to testify that she was capable of managing her child, they dropped the case. Suella had received competent professional support from attorneys; she obtained it not by the intervention of staff but by her own and her peers' efforts. This last fact is crucial to her treatment: it enhances self-help and peer support.

After discharge from residential treatment, Suella became one of the most active members of the CND, which also welcomed Marsha into its membership.

Because she had a telephone, a VW "bug," and a valid driver's license, she held an essential, responsible, and respected position in CND—she chauffeured four members from her area to the weekly meetings. A hard worker and a good cook, Suella was a key member of the food service brigade. She earned words of praise and appreciation from the other CND members for her cooking and driving abilities.

One of Suella's CND friends invited her and Marsha to attend a local church that also had a Sunday kindergarten for Mary Ellen. Here the little family made a new circle of friends, and Suella began to fulfill a lifelong need for a religion to give order and meaning to her life; this need had expressed itself symbolically during her psychotic episodes. Although Suella's religious training was minimal, she volunteered to help with the kindergarten. There she began her own religious education by reading Bible stories to the children. She met other parents in church and Sunday school, and exchanged child-rearing experiences and ideas with them. Few of these people, if any, had been hospitalized for severe emotional stress. Suella behaved no differently than any of them. She conversed freely, utilizing her developing communication skills, and made cakes and pies that everyone enjoyed at church socials. She was treated as a normal member of the group, no different than anyone else. Gradually her fears of being a permanent mental patient extinguished as she associated with normal people and saw she was really not very different from them.

It is possible that, if Suella had joined an expectant mothers' support group prior to her daughter's birth, she might not have become psychotic in the postpartum period. Such organizations have proliferated following our research reports of the 1950s and early 1960s. They serve a variety of purposes, but all provide one major function: mutual support at a critical period of life change. An expectant parents' and/or new mothers' group might have provided Suella with the companionship she craved, the baby-care formation she sought, and the practical assistance she occasionally needed that together might have prevented her developing a postpartum disorder. For in fact, like spraying oil on mosquito breeding swamps prevents malaria, mutual support groups prevent emotional breakdown.

PSYCHODYNAMIC MODEL

Now we will consider the psychodynamic perspective in Suella's case, to see how this model relates to her treatment as well as to the other three models in her combined program of care.

(1) Suella' giving birth to a female child was a precipitating event that reactivated unresolved conflict with her own mother. (2) Her problem also represents in part a manifestation of unresolved grief over repeated rejections, losses, or threatened losses of loved ones. (3) Her illnesses often arose during

developmental crises when she entered new phases of her life cycle—marriage, divorce, motherhood, separation—for which her past had not prepared her adequately.

Once medications had calmed her down so she could begin to think more clearly, once she had developed better communicating, asserting, and problem-solving skills, and a broader perspective on her sexuality, once she had joined support groups of friends upon whom she could rely for fun and aid—both fellow patients with similar mental problems and fellow single parents with similar problems with children—and once she could use her rational powers to prevent herself from sinking into an emotional morass of isolation, confusion, and guilt, Suella began to discuss her personal conflicts with her primary paraprofessional counselor, with her patient peer group, and with professionals and fellow patients in group therapy. Now, with the emotional serenity to look at herself and her life in perspective, and with the cognitive and psychosocial tools—the conceptual ideas and the communication skills—to understand and to express feelings, she could begin to benefit from dynamic psychotherapy. Like many chronically ill mental patients who have learned to communicate better, to assert themselves more skillfully, and to solve problems in a systematic fashion as a result of modular skill building, and who have begun to gain social support and enjoyment of their leisure by joining CND groups, Suella became a good candidate for dynamic psychotherapy.

While still in the hospital she received both individual and group therapy. After leaving residential care, she continued to utilize the CND's goal planning sessions to help her find answers to many of her problems. After she went back to work and was receiving a regular income, she obtained bimonthly services from an experienced private psychotherapist who helped her polish her skills and customize what she had learned in her psychoeducational classes. The therapist coached her personally in adapting her new general knowledge increasingly effectively to use in her own specific circumstances. Dynamic insights were combined in her case as in others with the proper use of psychotropic medications, and with behavior management, psychoeducation, and sociocultural support in a number of ways. Some of these are the following:

1. *By describing each problem and clarifying its dynamic relationship to events in her past life and present experience, Suella saw how her problems were associated with her loss of human relationships. She saw, for example, how her feeling abandoned led to her periodic mental breakdowns. This insight by itself does not relieve the problem but it helps to motivate her skill and support-building effort. She realized how her overcompliance, childlike obedience, and unassertiveness resulted in people's exploiting her; how her poor relationship with her father and her father-surrogates provided her with an inadequate background for selecting suitable husbands. Her need for affection made her vulnerable to any male who told her he loved her. She could not discriminate well between reliable men and unsuitable*

ones, and suffered from this deficiency. Insight into her own problems helped her recognize these gaps in her personal skills. Her psychoeducational courses not only helped her to improve her abilities in these areas where insights showed her how her handicap hurt her, they also showed her how to compare people in their assertiveness, their industriousness, reliability, and perseverance, and thus helped improve her ability to select friends. As she developed loyal friends in the CND and elsewhere, she felt less desperate and vulnerable in her quest for a permanent mate.

2. *Suella gained insight into how her lack of self-confidence and low self-esteem made her easily confused by the mixed messages she had received in the clinic psychotherapy group. By reassessing her own abilities and systematically improving them in class, she developed confidence in her own capabilities. She learned that by improving her personal skills and resources step-by-step she could improve her realistic position in life. With assistance and reinforcement from her support groups, she increasingly realized that she could gain power over her personal environment and destiny and control over her own life. As a result, her self-esteem soared.*

This success of combined insight and skill/support building therapy with severely disturbed patients stems from the fact that the treatments are complementary. Chronically ill mental patients usually suffer many gaps in their skills and their support; further, they have failed in so many of their efforts, that they have lost motivation to keep trying. Insight supplies understanding and helps restore motivation; skill training and supports provide the tools for them to correct their deficits, and the rewards to reinforce their efforts. Insight therapy alone, without filling the gaps in skills and supports to correct deficits and to maintain improvements, has not generally helped chronically ill mental patients. They have few skills lying nascent in their behavioral repertoires just awaiting removal of emotional blocks. Insight alone just makes many of these patients realize their incompetencies; for this reason, it can do them more harm than good. When skills training and support networks are available, however, insight can spur effort to utilize these resources fully.

3. *Insight helped Suella to discriminate between painful past experiences, such as her problems with her brother-in-law, that are no longer any danger to her in the present, and painful memories and thoughts about them. The memories are separated from the pain by repetition and discussion, and the pain extinguished in time.*

4. *Suella benefited by remembering how impressed she had been as a child by observing total immersion in baptismal ceremonies she attended. She began to understand why she felt so impelled to immerse herself when she felt under stress. Her thoughts were also related to feeling dirty sexually, feelings that began when she was a child, and that had been confused in her mind with wanting companionship and friendship, as well as permanent, dependable loved ones. The course in sex attitudes relieved her great-*

ly as she remembered and discussed these personal experiences and feelings.

5. *Suella also learned how her behavior affected others. Both her fellow patients in her group and her therapists let her know that her passivity and unsmiling countenance were handicaps. Role play and behavioral rehearsal helped her correct these defects.*

6. *Suella had been confused by the conflicting advice she received in her previous therapy. As a rule, experienced therapists do not give advice. Instead, they provide information, insight, and training. Patients are provided with various options and an estimation of the probability of success of whichever course they choose. In problem-solving training, for example, they are helped to generate a large number of alternative solutions to a problem. Then they are shown how to evaluate the alternatives. Finally, they choose the solution that, in their own estimation, best fits their personal circumstances. Much of Suella's problem with others—Tom, his family, her fellow patients, and her therapists—was in feeling that she must follow their advice and permit them to control her. Instead, she learned to welcome their ideas and suggestions, to weigh the pros and cons, and to select the alternative that in her own judgment suited her situation best. Thus she gained personal control over her own life.*

7. *Dynamic psychotherapy gave Suella insight into many problems with her marriage to Tom. She realized that Tom was as weak and passive as she. Part of their trouble stemmed from his letting his mother and older brother dominate him. Ultimately, he allowed them to break up the marriage rather than work with her in family therapy to fill the gaps in both his and her skills, in their mutual marital supports, and in their network of friends in the community.*

Diagramming Supports

Suella's success in building supports can be shown by the graphs presented in Figure 5-3 and the diagrams of Figure 6-1. Example 6-1a and point A in Figure 5-3 measure her network at the time she gave birth to Mary Ellen. She had lost her few friends at work and was totally dependent through Tom upon his family whose attitude toward her was destructive. Since everyone knew everyone else, the density was 100 percent.

Figure 6-1b and point B in Figure 5-3 illustrate her network at the time of her last hospital admission after being rescued from the bay. Her supports consisted of her immediate personal circle of Marsha and Mary Ellen plus a small group consisting of three waitresses and her boss at work; she obtained material support from the latter—an income—and also gained freedom from loneliness and boredom. She offered little else besides her performance at work to these people.

In the diagram in Figure 6-1c and at point C in Figure 5-3, Suella had

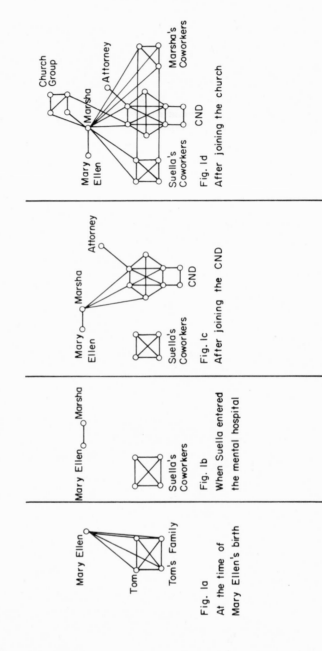

Fig. 6-1. Diagrams of Suella P.'s support networks as she progressed in treatment.

104

begun to make progress in building supports by joining the CND; in it her role was reciprocal, since she held several responsibilities. She had eight CND friends with whom she felt especially close. Her network now consisted of 15 persons and two groups (her work group and her CND group), and also a very important additional person—her attorney, who was helping her get rid of a major stress in her life.

When Suella's individual therapist saw Figures 6-1b and c and asked her why she had not introduced Marsha to her fellow waitresses at work, Suella replied that Marsha's and her schedules and need to look after Mary Ellen prevented both of them from visiting the other's place of work. The therapist asked why Marsha and she did not invite some of the other waitresses and secretaries from Marsha's office to their home, or to go on picnics or other outings together on days off. Suella replied that the thought had never occurred to her. Before joining CND, neither she nor Marsha had ever tried to make friends with other women besides each other. Neither of their families had allowed them to bring girlfriends home when they were younger, and they had never learned to make friends with groups of women later in their lives; their only friends were boyfriends. As her leisure time skills and her confidence in them mounted as a result of her participation in psychoeducational classes and the CND, and she became aware of the deficiencies in both their support systems, Suella plugged this major gap in her and Marsha's lives. By linking their two co-worker groups, Marsha and Suella increased the numbers of persons both could call upon in case of crisis. Suella's support system, shown at point D in Figure 5-3 and in Figure 6-1d, includes this change as well as adds her new church circle.

Note that Suella can now turn to over 20 persons for a variety of emotional, material, leisure-time, and other supports. However, there are still minor defects in her network which she can repair in time: Her network is not sufficiently dense; few members of her different support groups know each other. Further, the network is highly dependent upon Marsha. Suella would do well to join up some friends from her church and co-worker circles.

TREATMENT PLANNING

We have used Suella's case to illustrate how a variety of approaches and therapeutic models are combined in the care of the chronically ill mental patient. We now examine her situation from the perspective of the staff who were treating her, and describe the treatment plans they developed for the several periods in her treatment process. Her treatment plans illustrate how the combined program fills the gaps in the hospital and community care of adult, elderly, child, and adolescent patients. The diagram shown in Figure 2-1 helps in planning for each phase of patient care.

Acute Phase

Initially Suella was withdrawn, delusional, hallucinating, and likely to harm herself. The initial goals of her treatment plan were to help her sleep, to restore her sanity, and to guard against her harming herself in her psychotic state. After completing her physical assessment, her physician ordered her tranquilizers with heavy bedtime doses, and placed her on suicidal precautions that included one-to-one observation by the mental health worker who would become her primary therapist. The second day of her hospital stay, once she had had a full night's sleep, she was started by her treatment team in a full program of recreational and other activities (See Table 14-1). *Her medications and this highly structured schedule of activities, which included companionship and reassurance by her primary therapist, rapidly helped to calm her and to reduce the extremes of her psychotic behavior and thinking. She appeared more relaxed and less frantic.*

None of Suella's legal family were interested in her, so a social service worker was assigned to interview Marsha to obtain Suella's immediate past history. The worker also obtained further information from the CMHC where Suella had previously been treated. Marsha and the worker arranged for Mary Ellen to attend a nursery while Marsha was at work each day. The worker also reassured Marsha that she would look into holding off the legal processes regarding the child's custody. Within less than a week Suella was rational and no longer suicidal. She was ready to begin Phase B of her treatment plan.

Main Inpatient Phase of Treatment

Suella's assessments included measurements on proficiency gauges and standardized psychosocial rating scales, in addition to physical and other psychiatric evaluations. Once these were collected in her record, her treatment team began to develop a new plan for Suella. Treatment goals were written that were observable, measurable, and time referenced. Responsibility for each intervention and procedure was assigned to the most appropriately trained member of the multidisciplinary team, with her primary therapist coordinating these efforts. Suella's treatment plan gave first priority to her deficits in communication, assertion, and relaxation skills. Later she had training in peer management and support, problem solving, and anxiety and depression management. Her skills building continued with training for the use of leisure time and sexuality training. Because of Suella's many strengths—her perseverence, reliability, willingness to work hard, and inurement—she was assigned for special leadership training. As soon as she learned to speak up, she began to prompt and reinforce other patients' behavior in the token economy program.

Meanwhile, Suella continued to work with her primary therapist in applying what she was learning in class to solving her individual problems. Since she was no longer suicidal, her physician took her off precautions, and her treat-

ment team added weekend home visits to her plan. This included "family" therapy with Marsha, who met with Suella and the social service worker late each Friday afternoon when she came to take Suella home. They went over what Suella had learned during the week, and discussed what she was expected to practice at home. When Marsha brought her back to the facility at the end of the weekend, they reported to the social service worker on what Suella had accomplished.

During this period, Suella's more experienced patient peers also became involved in her treatment. In particular, they encouraged and assisted her preparing for her first visits to the attorney who helped her resolve her legal problem regarding Mary Ellen's custody. Having completed medication training, having slept well for weeks, and having been relieved of her anxiety and confusion, Suella was ready for the physician to decrease her medications to a single bedtime dose. After six weeks of treatment, which included only 30 days of inpatient hospital care, Suella could enter Phase C, the Predischarge Phase of her treatment.

Predischarge Phase

Suella's treatment plan now called for her to assume an active part not only in her own care but in that of other patients. She became a member leader in the CND, and an officer in the peer managed Token Economy Program (TEP). Both in goal planning in the CND and in individual sessions with her primary therapist she gained increasing insights into her problems, including her need to join her friends at work with Marsha's support group. (See Figure 6-1d.) She now began to plan with Marsha and her employer to go home and back to work. With the attorney's help, she resolved her legal problems. The progress she had made enabled Suella to skip Day Treatment, return to work, and enter the Follow-up Phase of treatment.

Aftercare Phase

Suella's discharge plan called for her to continue as a leader in her area CND, with which she had already become involved while still an inpatient. She continued to improve her support group by joining a church. This move also filled her need for religion in her life, which she came to understand as a result of the dynamic therapy that she was now obtaining from a private psychotherapist.

COMMENT

Does Suella really need dynamic therapy? Can she not learn everything from her peers and her classes? How long should Suella continue to obtain individual psychotherapy? How long should she receive medications? When can she leave the CND? Complete answers are not yet available to these questions, but they will be eventually, since the subjects are being investigated. The matter of patients remaining in the CND will be discussed in Chapter 14, but some experience with continued psychotherapy can be related here. We conducted an experiment[7] with 106 former mental patients all of whom had successfully completed a program of outpatient treatment. Approximately half the patients, the controls, were told to return for more treatment only if they needed further help. The other half, the experimentals, were invited to participate in regular prescheduled professional psychotherapeutic consultations, even though they were having no difficulties. They came for conferences with the doctor every three to six months. The experimental group of patients welcomed the opportunity to review their lives periodically—their problems, plans, crises, and goals; evaluations showed that they benefited significantly from it. Objective indicators in their lives—significantly improved incomes, marriages, and educations, as well as decreased legal entanglements—pointed to the progress they made in comparison to the control groups who were not given the option to preschedule regular professional appointments (p < .001). In the long run, those patients in the control group who subsequently required follow-up psychiatric treatment needed many more sessions than did those experimentals who saw the psychiatrist two to four times each year. Putting aside the pain and suffering, the treatment costs alone to the controls were far greater than those of the experimentals.

This study concluded that perhaps mental patients are like diabetics, hypertensives, and others with psychosomatic physical disorders for whom periodic reassessments serve to control their diseases and reduce serious complications. Like yearly consultations with their accountant and their attorney help many prudent people to keep out of financial, tax, and legal difficulties, periodic consultations with their psychotherapist help foresighted patients to avoid overwhelming stress and to enrich their lives.

REFERENCES

1. Whitman D: Reorganization of Florida's human services agency. Kennedy School of Government Case Program, C95-80-040, Cambridge, Mass., Harvard University, 1980
2. Gordon RE, Gordon KK, Gunther M: The Split-Level Trap. New York, B. Geis, 1961
3. Gordon RE: The psychiatric emergency: Good intentions vs. good sense. Consultant 1:34–38, 1962
4. Gordon RE, Singer M, Gordon KK: Social psychological stress. Arch Gen Psychiatry 4:459, 1961
5. Holmes TH, Rahe RH: The social readjustment rating scale. J Psychosom Res 11:213–218, 1967
6. Gordon RE: Sociodynamics and psychothapy. AMA Arch Neurol Psychiatry 81:486–503, 1959
7. Gordon RE: Is short-term psychotherapy enough? J Med Soc NJ 63:41–44, 1966

Lawrence Weathers, Jeffrey R. Bedell
Herbert Marlowe, Richard E. Gordon
Julia Adams, Valerie Reed
Jo Palmer, Katherine K. Gordon

7

Using Psychotherapeutic Games to Train Patients' Skills

"Tell the group what you would change about yourself if you could change one thing." This request for self-disclosure is one of many a psychiatric patient might select when drawing a card in "Talk One," a psychotherapeutic game employed on a residential treatment unit at a mental hospital in Florida.

Gaming has a long history dating back to the Prussion war games, which were analogous to chess. Contemporary adaptations of games have been applied in educational and business settings as tools for teaching and assessment.[1,2] Because games can provide a simulated life experience, they offer an innovative approach to skills training in psychotherapy.[3] Gaming also provides a useful research environment, because the structure of the game controls what takes place in the therapeutic situation, thus the extent to which the game reflects the real world can be manipulated.[4] We are all familiar with the function that educational games have in the development of the healthy individual. An educational game is one that is simultaneously playful, joyful, and instructional. In short, participants have fun and learn at the same time. Children's group games build upon this foundation by encouraging the development of more complex interpersonal skills. Adult games provide the opportunity for individuals to both practice and enjoy social skills. Therapeutic board games serve the same general function as conventional educational

Portions of this chapter appeared originally in Weathers L, Bedell J, Marlowe H, et al: Psychotherapeutic games (J Florida Med Assoc 65:891–896, 1978), and are reprinted with permission.

games but are especially designed to build or rebuild the inadequate social skills of mentally ill patients. Presently, therapeutic board games are a prominent part of the comprehensive treatment programs that have been developed for adolescent and young adult patients at the center. The major objective of these games is to teach skills that have often been assessed as deficient in these populations. Specifically, a gaming format is used to deliver training in communication, assertion, problem-solving, sexuality, self-medication, leisure time utilization, and family life. Not only are therapeutic board games less threatening than traditional modes of intervention, they have also been demonstrated to be significantly cost effective. In treatment, games are applicable in a wide variety of settings, designed to encourage psychological growth and the development of a variety of skills, cost efficient because as many as 32 patient at a time are engaged in treatment by a single mental health worker with one or two years of college education, "fun" because they provide a relaxed and highly motivating environment for the acquisition of skills, quantifiable because in each game participants' scores provide a convenient measure of patient progress over a series of group sessions, and self-motivating because players help themselves and other participants. The last point should be emphasized because the structure of the game discourages patients' dependence upon staff, a problem that often develops in residential treatment.

FORMAT OF GAMES

The treatment model used with the therapeutic games combines lectures and practice. A typical three-hour gaming session explains the games objectives, reviews the skills involved, plays the game, and discusses the experience. The games themselves share a variety of common elements. Even though they differ in specific objectives and in content, there are several standard features. The four basic components are scorekeeping devices such as points or a marker to move around a playing board; a process of assigning tasks to participants such as drawing cards, playing roles, or following rules; a peer grading procedure to score each patient's response; and stimulus items that elicit practice.

Patient Participation

Players participate according to the rules of the game and, in addition, assume roles such as game manager, banker, vote caller, and vote recorder. After the operation and rationale of the game have been explained by a staff member, players are responsible for organizing and managing the group experience.

This peer management model is an integral part of several treatment programs. The model assumes that it is therapeutic for patients to have responsibilities and for them to help each other to the fullest possible extent in the treatment program. When patients must depend on staff, their feelings of helplessness and inadequacy are reinforced. This model helps avoid that problem. The games' structure, concreteness, and simplicity enable patients to interact therapeutically with each other. The content and process are designed so that a patient's self-esteem is enhanced rather than diminished. Furthermore, peer pressure ensures active participation of everyone, both in taking turns in playing and in grading other players' responses. A patient whose attention is distracted by hallucinations, for example, receives continued reminders from other patients to participate. "Come on, George, pay attention. It's your turn!" "Wake up, Phyllis. Grade George's answer!"

Staff Participation

Staff participation in gaming therapy is minimal and requires little sophisticated training. As part of their in-service training, the staff members are instructed in the operation and rationale for each game. They provide didactic instruction to patients regarding the skill being taught in each game session and explain rules for conducting each therapy game to patients. The staff members usually observe while patients operate the game according to rules. The patients instruct and provide feedback to each other in accordance with the clear guidelines outlined by staff and provided in written form with the game. Occasionally, staff serve as referees helping interpret rules while the game is in progress, resolving disagreements between player regarding matters like accuracy of a vote, and explaining the meaning of a stimulus item or other procedure in the game. Experience indicates that patients require little help when operating the games. On occasion, when staff members are delayed in attending a session, the patients proceed to set up the games and commence play quite effectively without them.

Figure 7-1 shows that the procedures for "selecting behavior from hierarchy," "modeling behavior," and "assembling skills" proceed in an identical manner for both leader-led treatment and gaming. Critical elements in skills enhancement based on experimental learning research, such as prompting, rehearsing, shaping, and providing feedback for differential reenforcement, are built into the structure and content of the game; they require no participation of the group leader. Minimally trained therapists can perform as well as experienced professionals, since they are called on to do little more than set up, explain, and proctor the game. In many treatment settings, such as when language may introduce a barrier between foreign born therapists and state hospital patients, gameplaying may increase the quality of psychotherapy available to patients. It certainly increases cost-effectiveness and consistency in the treatment process. The high level of structure and independent oper-

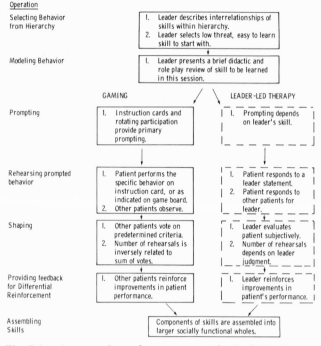

Fig. 7-1.   A comparison of contemporary leader-led and game procedures for skill enhancements.

ation of the game does not accommodate therapist modification to suit individual client needs; however, if highly skilled therapists are available to make sophisticated clinical discriminations, individual sessions may be conducted to supplement the gaming sessions.

In order to maintain a high level of interest, to present a continuing challenge, and also to build skills in a stepwise fashion, some games are arranged in series, with beginning games teaching basic skills and later games demanding more sophisticated interpretations and interactions. The communications game series will serve to illustrate the game therapy model.

COMMUNICATION GAMES

Eight board games of increasing difficulty facilitate learning of three basic communication skills. These are self-disclosure, listening, and feedback.[5,6] Each of these skills is fundamental to effective interpersonal relationships. Didactic lectures teach patients these concepts, alert them to "road blocks" that prevent effective communication, and explain nonverbal communication through the use of body language.

Self-Disclosure Games

The first skill introduced is self-disclosure, a means of communicating to others one's thoughts or beliefs. Two games, "Who I Am" and "Talk One," get players to talk about themselves by using "I" messages (speaking in the first person as opposed to making global statements). The first, "Who I Am," increases awareness of interests and associated feelings. The materials consist of one "Who I Am" board for each group of four players, a set of "Who I Am" cards, $1000 in play money, and four sets of vote cards. The player selected as Game Manager sets up the game and reads a statement to the group that each card contains a word that is associated with people and that has impact on their lives. The cards contain words such as "garden," "sister," "religion." The circular board is divided into three color coded segments, each relevant to the player's feelings about the card—"bad," "neutral," and "good." Each segment cuts through three concentric circles labeled "very little," "some," and "very much," which apply to the importance of the word to the player. The first round starts when the shortest player (or youngest, or oldest) draws a card from the deck, looks at the word, rates its importance, and identifies the appropriate color coded section of the circle— "very little" as an example. Next the player decides what his/her feelings are about the word—"neutral" for instance—and places the card on the appropriate section of the board. Finally, the player explains to the group why it was placed there and how he/she feels about its being on that particular spot. The Vote Caller then calls for a vote card ("0" = poor response, "1" = acceptable response, "2" = excellent response) and places it face down in front of him. When all decisions are made, the cards are turned over.

Votes are cast according to a clearly defined outline for rating self-disclosure. The most complete response includes the following components: (1) acceptance of ownership of the statement by using "I"; (2) behavioral specificity, defining clearly what specific people and situational factors are important, rather than making vague or global remarks; (3) inclusion of how the speaker feels, what affect (happy, sad, angry, content) is associated with the area in question; (4) clarity as to the speaker's wish or desire regarding the future of the person, experience, or activity introduced by the word. Would the speaker like to continue unchanged? Would he/she like things to be modified somewhat?

The Vote Recorder sums and records the votes, and the player receives from the Banker a payment in play money equal to the total votes received. The round continues with the player to the starter's right relocating the same card to reflect his own interest and feelings. This continues until all four players have responded to the card. A new card is then drawn and a new round begins. The game ends when the allotted time period is up, and the player with the most play money wins.

Experience has shown that the games are so effective in maintaining patients' interest that they often want to continue playing after the allotted three-hour time period has expired. This is especially true at state hospitals where patients frequently request an opportunity to play the games. For many patients the game setting represents the first time in their life that they have held a position entailing responsibility, where they sense they are doing something important. Their self-sufficiency is enhanced as they give and receive feedback; they develop feelings of mastery from learning to do something well and having their accomplishment confirmed.

All the communications games are structured so that the patients begin with relatively low level challenges and progress to situations requiring greater risk-taking or more complex skills. For example in "Talk One," at the least difficult level, the patient may be asked to tell the group about his/her favorite time of day, or how he/ feels about sports. At the middle level, he/she may draw a card requiring that he/she describe the unhappiest moment in his/her life, or the hardest thing he/she ever had to do. At the most difficult level, self-disclosure is pushed to the limit with cards that ask the patient to tell the group about what he/she is most ashamed about in his/her sexual adequacy (see Table 7-1).

Listening Skills Games

The Listening Skills games follow a similar pattern. In "Listening One" and "Listening Two" the focus is on the basic communication skills of paraphrasing, asking open questions, and reflecting feelings. Paraphrasing is repeating what another patient says using different words. An open question is one that helps the patient explore his own interests and feelings more fully, rather than forcing a "yes" or "no" response, or any certain answer. Reflecting feelings involves a patient expressing understanding of how another patient feels about what he/she is saying.

The game is initiated when one player draws a "statement" card that instructs the patient to roleplay a simple situation. The situation may be relatively innocuous such as, "I can't believe this Florida weather," a serious concern as, "I often worry about what will happen when I die," or an aggressive comment like, "In your ear, wise guy." A second player, selected by a roll of dice, draws an "instruction" card, which tells him to paraphrase the statement, ask an open question, or reflect the feeling. The other players vote on the adequacy of the response, and points are awarded accordingly. Here again, specific outlines for evaluating the patient's response are provided to guide the voting.

Table 7-1

Examples of stimulus cards in the psychotherapeutic game—"Talk One." The cards are presented with the least difficult challenges first, and the most difficult last.

YELLOW (Least difficult level)
1. Tell the group about your hobbies.
2. Describe how you feel about your height.
3. Describe how you feel about your hair.
4. Tell what your favorite time of day is (morning, afternoon, evening, night).
5. Tell the group about your personal religious views.

GREEN (Intermediate level)
1. Describe how you felt about your father as a child.
2. Describe one of your most embarrassing experiences as a child.
3. Tell the group what is missing most in your life now.
4. Tell the group about the description of a person with whom you have been or are in love.

RED (Most difficult level)
1. Tell the group about what you regard as the mistakes and failures your parents made in raising you.
2. Tell the group about characteristics of yourself that give you cause for pride and satisfaction.
3. Tell what you would change about yourself if you could change one thing.
4. Describe your feelings when you found out you would be coming to this treatment facility.

Feedback Games

Feedback is a special form of self-disclosure in which one patient reveals his reaction to another patient's behavior.[7] "Feedback One" and "Feedback Two" provide players with the opportunity to practice telling other players how they perceive them and how they interpret and experience their behavior.

Players draw cards that instruct them to provide feedback to another player. For example, instructions may be, "Tell the other person how you see him/her deal with embarrassment," or "Tell the other person what he/she does that you like best." A few cards instruct the player to make self-disclosure statements such as, "Tell the person on your right how you feel in giving him/her feedback." As in all the games, player votes determine the points scored.

In "Talk Two" all the major communications skills are practiced. One player self-discloses, his "partner" listens, and the remaining players give feedback, which determines the player's score and the movement of his marker on the game board. "Communications One" provides another synthesis, requiring players to practice feedback, I-messages, and active listening. By the end of a nine week program, patients have experienced intensive training in self-disclosure, active listening, and feedback skills, which helps them break through the communication barriers that have contributed to their psychiatric disability.

PROBLEM-SOLVING GAMES

Problem-solving is another skills training area where gaming therapy is being experimentally applied. In a short-term (9 weeks) program, problem-solving skills are taught simultaneously with communication skills. When longer periods of hospitalization with less intact patients are involved, communication skills might be taught first, as they are more basic and are required for effective problem-solving.[8]

The problem-solving sequence consists of six games that take patients through four aspects of problem-solving: Problem recognition, problem definition, alternatives generation, and decision. The problem recognition process teaches patients to acknowledge problems, accept responsibility for them, and establish priorities for dealing with them. In problem definition the patient learns to break down a problem into its component parts and to establish a goal-oriented approach to finding a solution. The objective of the alternatives generation process is to teach six different methods of developing possible solutions to problems: brainstorming,[9,10] producing an idea checklist, minimizing hindering factors or maximizing helping factors, changing frame of reference,[11] solving analogous problems, and problem diagraming.[12,1] Finally, in the decision process, alternative solutions are evaluated and the best one chosen.

In the problem-solving series a subjective component is being developed in which patient players learn to recognize and work through their personal real-life problems while playing the games. Four games and three simulation exercises are being developed along with supportive didactic materials. A "Problem Journal" is used so that the player's own problems can be carried through all four stages of problem solving. This format contrasts somewhat with that of communication games that focus mainly on a process-oriented approach. It also differs in that the problem-solving sequence uses a balanced program of simulations and games, rather than only the structured games format described in communications training. The advantage in including role-playing is that it more closely represents a real-life setting, with the patients acting out the problem's solution in addition to solving it cognitively. Role play simulations are used in several other skills training groups, including assertiveness training, nonverbal expression training, sex role education, as well as in traditional communication training.

ASSERTION SKILLS GAMES

Assertion skills are taught in a 23-session program that incorporates lectures, group discussion, videotape vignettes and responses, and role-playing. Six games are used to augment this training. They help patients learn to differentiate between passive assertive, and aggressive behaviors.[14] In assertion games, patients practice and experience making responses in these three styles.

Assertion II, for example, gives players a variety of role-play situations in which they are instructed to respond passively, aggressively, or assertively. Examples of some of the instructions are the following: (1) You are offered a good job in another state, but your spouse doesn't want to move; (2) After paying the TV repair bill, you find that the set now has the same problem as before, so you telephone the repairman; (3) You just got your friend's car in an accident, which was your fault, and now he/she is asking entirely too much in terms of compensation; (4) Your sibling has been watching TV all morning and now you want to watch a different show; and (5) Your boss is trying to get you to work late, and you've made plans for the evening. (See Table 7-2.)

A Game for Teaching Assertiveness to Adolescent Patients

Adolescents traditionally have difficulty in asserting themselves appropriately with parents, peers, siblings, teachers, and others in authority. Teenage patients in particular frequently use passive or aggressive modes of responding. Training in assertion helps modify their more negative behaviors. A game provides an appealing approach for teaching adolescents to distinguish and identify the three modes of behavior—assertion, aggression, and passivity. Since the situations that adolescents find most threatening differ considerably from those which confront adults, the game incorporates problems based on observations and reports of teachers, and on accounts gathered from the student-patients themselves.[15] A surprise element is also provided in which the adolescent patients can respond to a positive situation. Here are typical examples of instructions contained on the cards: (1) Ask someone for a date; (2) Tell your teacher you forgot your homework; (3) Tell the cop why you don't have your driver's license; (4) Ask your parents for a raise in your allowance; and (5) Tell a friend that you believe he has cheated you.

Surprise cards include the following: (1) Tell the person on your right one thing you like about him; (2) Tell the teacher what you really think about this game.

Table 7-2
Examples of stimulus cards from the game—"Assertion II."

The player opposite you is attacking you for just colliding with his/her car.

The player on your right is insulting your appearance.

You want very much to ask a player of the opposite sex to go out to dinner with you, but s/he isn't eager to accept.

The group is arguing excessively over which client is the least disturbed, and you'd like them to can it.

Your boss (player on left) has decided not to give you the raise you asked for.

The player opposite you has just told a very funny joke. Respond.

Your six-year-old child (player on your left) is annoying you and your guests.

You'd like to persuade the player on your left to help you push your stalled car off the road.

Your neighbor (player on right) is asking you for a loan of $100.

The player on your left is asking for some of your Coke, which you really want to finish yourself.

The player on your right is arguing against abortion, and you'd like to express your views, which are quite different.

The furious policeman opposite you is needlessly lecturing you how much trouble "all you young hippie-freaks" cause at these rock concerts.

The player opposite you is making gross noises.

The player on your right is chattering endlessly, and you wish it would stop.

The player opposite you is saying what a creep the Boss is and you feel differently.

You really like the new outfit worn by the player on your right, who now asks for your opinion.

Your roommate (on left) is listening to a rock show and you're trying to get some sleep.

Defining Assertion

A great deal of controversy swirls around the meaning of assertion, aggression, and passivity. We use these terms in the manner shown in Table 7-3, developed by Alberti,[16] where nonassertion means the same as passive behavior. In our previous writings,[17] we generally spoke of "tactful" self-assertion and "pushy" aggression. We believe these concepts, which consider the context, style, and consequences of the assertion, are less confusing. Table

7-4 presents definitions by Cameron et al.[18] They help clarify the meaning of assertive behaviors.

SELF-MEDICATION GAMES

Staff continue to find new uses for game therapy. "Meds Bingo" teaches drug classification, therapeutic effects, side effects, drug interactions, and precautions. In "Name that Pill" patients learn visual identification of different medications, and practice reciting the information they learned in "Meds Bingo." By the time they have finished with their self-medication training program, they have become informed and responsible self-medicators, prepared for unsupervised situations they will experience upon discharge. The importance of this training is obvious when one considers that a major cause of recidivism among chronic schizophrenics is discontinuation of the medication regimen.

The gaming model is being applied to other skills training programs such as the use of leisure time, heterosexual relationships, and family living. The gaming sequence and content are flexible and can be modified to suit the specific needs of a particular program. For example, the package can be expanded to include more elaborate simulations to provide a greater variety of experiences to participants. To add incentive, a token economy system can be tied into the game format by converting the play money won in the games into tokens that may be exchanged for toilet articles, food, and social events of interest to the patients.

DISCUSSION

Adaptability To Other Treatment Facilities

Most of the games now in use can be adapted to accommodate the needs of other treatment facilities. For example, the content of the communication series can be focused around the needs of geriatric patients, adolescents, detained criminals, and deinstitutionalized patients living in the community.

A number of treatment facilities have already begun using games in their programs both alone and with other skill-building procedures. Gaming's effect has sometimes been dramatic. Part of the communication games series was introduced to a group of chronic mentally ill offenders hospitalized in most part for at least two years in a state hospital forensic unit. Previously, a psychotherapy group had been running for two years with minimal interaction among or benefit to patients. Upon beginning to play therapeutic games, the patients began communicating actively, talking about themselves

Table 7-3
A model developed by Alaberti for differentiating assertive behavior[16]

"The Crib": A model for differentiating assertive behavior
Your actions may be labeled as . . .

	Non assertive	Assertive	Aggressive
WHEN THE SOCIETY OR CULTURE OR CONTEXT CALLS FOR . . .	Strength; "Cool;" Ambition; "Macho;" Drive; Self-Serving; Hardness; Toughness; Lack of regard for others.	Honesty; Forthrightness; Firmness; Courage; Directness; Caring; Respect for others; Equality in relationships.	Self-denial; Sacrifice; Quiet; Softness; Submission to others; "Not making waves;" "Staying in your place."
WHEN YOU FEEL THIS INTERNAL RESPONSE . . .	Emotional pain; failure to gain your goals; loneliness; Physical ailments (headaches, etc.); Low self-confidence; Low self-respect.	Good feeling; Accomplishment of your goals; Closeness (in long run—sometimes distance at first); Confidence; Self-respect; Affection; "I did all I could."	Guilt; Loneliness; Accomplishment of your goals; Distance from others; Power; Confidence; Low self-respect.
AND THE RESPONSE OF OTHERS IS . . .	Scorn; Derision; Lack of respect; Pity; "Winning;" Ignoring you; "Turning off."	Good feeling; Friendliness; Affection; Cooperation; Respect; Closeness; Openness. Or sometimes: Fear; Withdrawal Or sometimes: Anger; Dislike	Fear; Withdrawal; Submission; Avoidance OR Anger; Disrespect; Dislike; Hostility OR Firmness; Assertion; Resistance.
WHEN YOUR INTENT IS PRIMARILY TO . . .	Deny yourself; Avoid risks; Stay out of trouble; Put yourself down; Avoid hurting others; Avoid hurting yourself; Be liked; Hide your anger.	Express yourself; Reach out; Gain your goals; Show respect for others; Be honest and direct; Stand up for your rights; Express friendship or affection; Show your anger.	Express yourself; Dominate; "Set others straight;" Win; Do it your way; Gain your goals; Disregard others.

120

AND OTHERS INTERPRET THAT . . .	You are afraid you are a pushover; You don't believe in your ideas; You don't know what you're talking about.	You are confident; You are friendly; You are honest; You know your feelings; You respect yourself and others; You care.	You want to hurt others; You are thoughtless and rude; You are mean; You have no feelings; You are pompous.
WHEN YOU BEHAVE WITH . . .	Downcast eyes; Soft voice; Hesitation; Helpless gestures; Denying importance of the situation; Slumped posture; Words like "anything you want is okay with me," OR avoiding the situation altogether.	Direct eye contact; conversational voice level; Fluent speech; Firm gestures; Erect posture; "I" messages; Honesty; Positive statements; Direct response to the situation.	Glaring; Loud voice; Fluent/fast speech: Confrontation; Threatening gestures; Intimidating posture; Dishonesty; Impersonal messages.
AND OTHERS BEHAVE BY . . .	No eye contact; Not listening; Being pushy; Making unreasonable requests; Taking advantage of you; Disagreeing; Denying your requests; Head shaking; Manipulation.	Making eye contact; Interested conversation; Open posture & gestures; Listening; Forthright comments; Agreeing or disagreeing. OR SOMETIMES: giving in; OR SOMETIMES: aggression.	Backing away: Hesitating; Agreeing; Closed posture; Accepting; Giving in; Looking away or down; Head nodding OR counter aggression; glaring; hostile remarks; loud voice; threats; violence OR direct eye contact; firm posture and gestures; forthright comments.

From Alberti RE: Assertive behavior training: Definitions, overview, contributions, in Alberti RE (Ed): Assertiveness: Innovations, Applications, Issues. Copyright © 1977, Impact Publishers, Inc., San Luis Obispo, California. Reprinted by permission of the publisher.

Table 7-4
Definitions of passive, aggressive, and assertive behavior[18]

The following definitions imply clear-cut behavioral delineations. In practice, these behaviors can best be understood on a continuum with completely passive behavior on one end, completely aggressive behavior on the other, and assertive behavior in the middle. Occasionally, the lines are blurred. Assertion Training helps patients to develop awareness of assertive behavior, to distinguish between methods of assertion, to develop skill in assertion, and to choose behaviors that are appropriate to situations.

Passive Behavior: Not getting one's needs met, or getting them met indirectly through manipulation.

When a person acts in a passive manner, that person ignores or simply fails to express his rights, needs, or desires. The consequence is the abdication of his rights. However, passive individuals sometimes get their needs met through manipulation. This indirect tactic seeks to obtain something from another person engaged in the interaction. Usually the passive person avoids unpleasant or risky situations by hedging or using apologetic language. The ultimate consequence of this behavior may be anxiety and frustration, which can culminate in a later aggressive outburst.

Aggressive Behavior: Getting one's needs met without taking into consideration the right and needs of others.

Although individuals behaving in an aggressive manner may indeed be standing up for legitimate rights, they do so in a fashion that violates the rights of others. Aggressive behavior is an inappropriate outburst or hostile overreaction to some situation. While aggressive behavior may effectively achieve a goal, in the long run others feel resentment and alienation. Although sometimes effective, and therefore self-enhancing, aggressive behavior is usually impulsive and leads to feelings of guilt. In short, friendship and respect may be sacrificed to satisfy immediate needs.

Assertive Behavior: Expressing one's rights and needs while taking into consideration the rights and needs of others.

The assertive individual is emotionally honest and direct, stands up for legitimate rights, but concurrently takes into consideration the rights and needs of others. This individual may be persistent in situations where other are not willing to accept this choice of behavior. Additionally, being assertive respects others' rights to deny requests. Offering and being able to accept compromise is an important assertive skill. The long-run consequences of assertive behavior are confidence and self-respect. In the process of meeting one's needs, if one respects the rights of others, the consequence is generally mutually enhancing, and relationships become freer and more honest.

to each other and to staff. In fact, staff at the state hospital observe that regressed chronic patients are especially fond of the games, and frequently request the opportunity to play.

Other mental health facilities have adapted the games to their service needs. Some centers not only use the games with patients, but for staff development as well. Community Colleges have incorporated the communication series into their Associate degree training programs for Human Service Workers with assistance from the Career Education for Mental Health Workers Project. State Mental Retardation trainers use the games for providing their personnel with continuing education.

The wide range of settings that are already making use of games reflects the flexibility of this innovative technique. This technology has received favorable responses from treatment and training personnel in these varied settings. Research studies are measuring long-term treatment effectiveness, as well as cost efficiency. The potential impact of game technology on state mental health systems is immense. Psychotherapeutic games appear to help prepare hospitalized patients for community care, and may contribute to their successfully remaining in the community. The training of mental health workers with one or two years of undergraduate education in these gaming techniques could substantially increase their effectiveness with minimal funding increments.

REFERENCES

1. Boocock SS: Experimental study of learning effects of two games with simulated environments, in Boocock SS, Schild ED (Eds): Simulation Games in Learning. Beverly Hills, Calif., Sage, 1968
2. Uresky M: Management game: Experiment in reality, in Simulation and Games in Learning. Beverly Hills, Calif., Sage, 1968
3. Huizinga J: Homo Ludens: Study of Plan Element in Culture. Boston, Beacon Press, 1955
4. Adams DM: Simulation Games: Approach to Learning. Worthington Oh., Charles A. Jones Publishing Co., 1973
5. Gordon T: Parent Effectiveness Training. New York, Ritis H. Wyden, 1970
6. Ivey AE: Microcounseling and Media Therapy: State of Art. Counselor Educ Supervision 13:172–183, 1974
7. Egan G: Skilled Helper. Monterey, Calif., Brooks-Cole, 1975
8. Gelatt HD: Decision making, conceptual frame of reference for counseling. J Counseling Psychol 9:240–245, 1962
9. D'Zurilla TJ, Goldfried MR: Problem solving and behavior modification. J Abnorm Psychol 73:107–126, 1971
10. Osborn AF: Applied Imagination: Principles and Procedures of Creative Problem-Solving (3rd ed). New York, Scribner's, 1963
11. Mahoney MJ: Cognition and Behavior Modification. Cambridge, Mass., Ballinger Publishing Co., 1974
12. Manis M: Introduction to Cognitive Psychology. Belmont, Calif., Wadsworth Publishing Co., 1971
13. Davis GA: Strategies for stimulating solutions: Attribute listing, morphological synthesis, and idea checklists, in Psychology of Problem Solving, Theory and Practice. New York, Basic Books, 1973
14. Emmons ML, Alberti RE: Your Perfect Right, San Luis Obispo, Calif., Impact, 1970

15. Palmer J: How to Say What You Want. Tampa, Fla. Florida Mental Health Institute, 1979
16. Alberti RE: Assertiveness: Innovations, Applications, Issues. San Luis Obispo, Calif., Impact, 1977
17. Gordon RE, Gordon KK, Gunther M: The Split-Level Trap. New York, B. Geis Assoc., 1961, pp. 276–284, 360
18. Cameron BA, Ferrandino JJ, Marlowe HA, et al (Eds): Introduction to Assertive Skills Training, Tampa, Fla., Florida Mental Health Institute, 1979

PART B

Improving Morale and Performance of Staff

Visitors have commented on the enthusiasm of staff and the warmth between professionals, paraprofessionals (MHWs), and patients in the modular treatment and peer management and support programs described here. They observe that many patients seem to be proud of their status rather than ashamed of being residents of a mental institution. "How do you establish this atmosphere of pride?" they ask. "How did you develop mutual respect and cooperation between professionals and MHWs, and get them to work together and accomplish so much in an atmosphere of harmony?" Answers to these questions will be provided in this section. Details of professional, paraprofessional, patient, student, family, and administrative relationships will be considered in the context of the management system utilized.

Previous chapters have alluded to matrix management and to training of staff. These subjects as well as staff motivation and cooperation will be developed more fully here. Since education and training are used purposefully to motivate staff and stimulate performance, and matrix management is used to enable staff harmoniously and cooperatively to conduct psychoeducation and training, these three subjects—staff motivation, matrix management, and training and education—are included together in this section.

MANPOWER PROBLEMS IN THE PUBLIC MENTAL HEALTH SECTOR

Harmony does not always prevail in facilities introducing skill-building and peer-management approaches. In the early years in the present setting, many people left their jobs and obtained employment elsewhere because of

125

the conflict between staff—between psychologists, nurses, and physicians, in particular. Only after reorganization and establishment of a matrix management approach, with a policy of involving all staff as fully as possible in the creative activity of the research and training facility, has the high level of conflict and other staff problems subsided.

Nationally, psychiatry is suffering from conflict and demoralization in the public mental health sector, related in part to the efforts at reorganizing mental institutions that began in the 1960s. State mental hospitals are severely understaffed; 50 percent of physicians are foreign medical school graduates; the situation, Doyle[1] says, is worsening. Now the foreign-born physicians are under attack; their jobs are in jeopardy. Because many have difficulty in communicating with native-born American patients, public mental health administrators may overlook the fact that most of these physicians provide medical care of high quality. In the community mental health centers, the numbers of full-time equivalent positions for psychiatrists is also decreasing. This decline is related to dissatisfaction with pay scales, to conflict between professionals, and to what Doyle calls an "anti-medical bias" in many CMHCs.

According to the Harvard Case Report, morale generally is low in the public human service sector.[2] Management has come under critical review. A recently published (July, 1979) comprehensive district management review[2] cites a variety of programmatic shortcomings.

The study also criticized "management style" . . . asserting that it was reactive rather than preventive, and made clear that this reactive style stemmed partly from inadequate definitions of roles and poor communication . . . A survey of 51 staff members indicated:

"Uncertainty regarding scope of authority, responsibility, and accountability were consistently referenced as problems. Role ambiguity was most apparent in relationships between district program supervisors and network personnel. Neither group seemed certain who was specifically responsible and accountable for selected elements of program operation and quality control. Concern was often expressed in terms of . . . too many managerial levels or generalist supervisors who were not making good decisions due to lack of program expertise and knowledge." (pp 24, 25)

Professionals trained in providing mental health services, Liberman[3] reports, are being overwhelmed by poorly informed, undertrained clinical staff; an unhealthy rivalry has developed between state hospitals and CMHCs in many states. He calls attention to the bureaucratic strangulation and over-regulation that is stifling initiative and effective operation in the public mental health sector.

Relentless internal and external pressures are producing rapid changes in the numbers of psychiatric hospitals, their staffing patterns, goals, patient populations, length of stay and treatments, and readmission rates. According to Fierman,[4] the free-standing, isolated state hospital is clearly marked for extinction, and is receiving neither professional support from organized psychiatry nor political support from state governments. State mental hospital patients are being returned to community living, frequently without planning and without sufficient or appropriate community facilities to carry out proper aftercare. Psychiatry itself is under attack as a legitimate medical specialty, and the lack of agreement among its own ranks as to what constitutes quality psychiatric treatment leaves the future of the psychiatric hospital even more vulnerable.

Some facilities must not only cope with these national problems, they must also deal with special local ones. In the fast-growing areas in the nation, such as the one where these studies were conducted, the state hospitals are overcrowded; there is a waiting list for admission. Some states attract mentally ill legal offenders, which increases the need for residential facilities to care for and guard potentially dangerous forensic patients.[5] Research and training centers in these locations are often pressured to admit increasing numbers of residential patients in order to relieve the overcrowding at the state hospitals and to reduce waiting lists. This pressure puts emphasis on meeting custodial service demands at the expense of ongoing research and training programs.

INTEGRATING SYSTEMS OF MANAGEMENT AND EDUCATION

Soon after work on the program described here was begun in 1975, the role and task differences of MHWs were assessed.[6] The study concluded that MHWs can and do deliver many therapeutic services effectively and with high morale. In certain agencies with limited funds, small staff, and a large work load, personnel work closely and harmoniously together. In these agencies, some of the staff attend formal classes and continue their educations toward academic degrees. These observations encouraged the use of MHWs to the fullest extent possible, and suggested ways to do so. Chapter 8 will describe how this was done in a manner that received full support from mental health professionals. It offers a description of how paraprofessional MHWs are motivated to conduct assessment and treatment of patients in preplanned projects, each of which addresses a major assessed mental health need. Professionals organize and manage service programs, develop the assessment and treatment modules, and supervise the paraprofessionals, utilizing project orientation and management by objectives. They also carry out research and training, and hold down costs by using the same service personnel to perform treatment, evaluative research, and training.

The employment of matrix management to harmonize the efforts of bio-

128

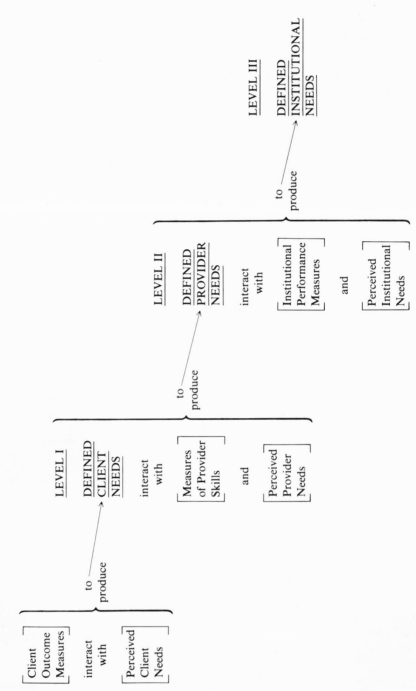

FIG. B-1. A needs assessment model for mental health continuing education.

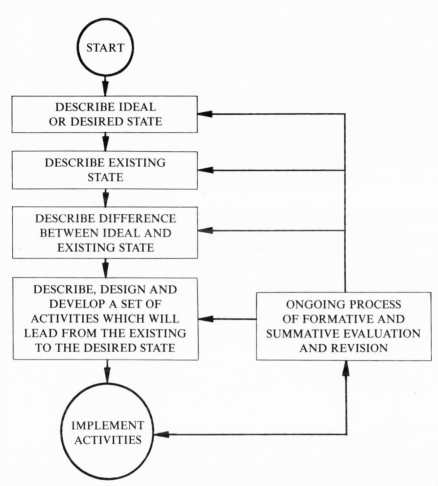

FIG. B-2. Model for developing a new treatment, educational, or management program, and for improving it on the basis of continual performance evaluation.[8] This four-step model generates prescriptive statements for meeting unmet needs that instructional designers, program planners, and treatment innovators address.

medical and psychoeducational staff is shown in Chapter 9. This management system combines the best features of specialty and multidisciplinary team organizations. In it, staff can perform a large amount of creative work with good morale.

Chapter 10 describes how training and dissemination are conducted. Matriculated students, the patients themselves, their families, and currently employed personnel are taught to carry out effective management and treatment innovations. Training, educational, and research endeavors of the service delivery systems are integrated with those of the university and college systems.

A task force led by Cordes[7] has developed the model shown in Figure B-1 for performing needs assessment and evaluation for continuing education in mental health. This work was conducted under the auspices of the Southern Regional Education Board, and was supported by a grant from the National Institute of Mental Health. The model considers the needs of patients and clients for improved services, the needs of treatment staff for further education and training, and the needs of institutions, agencies, and other organizations for service delivery.

All programs—educational, treatment, and management—are continually evaluated and upgraded. Cordes et al.[8] have also developed a model that describes this feedback process (see Figure B-2).

In the state mental institutions, for example, a primary need is for deinstitutionalization. Patients, then, require training in skills that permit them to function successfully in the community; staff need education that both prepares them to train the patients and also provides them with abilities to conduct community-based services, if they wish. The sections that follow address all three of these sets of needs. They show how continuing assessment and evaluation modifies and improves the programs.

REFERENCES

1. Doyle BB: Psychiatrists in varied settings: Toward the 80's. Syllabus and Scientific Proceedings, 132nd Annual Meeting, APA, Chicago, Ill., 1979
2. Whitman D: Reorganization of Florida's human service agency, in Kennedy School of Governemnt, Case Program, C95-80-040. Cambridge, Mass., Harvard University, 1980
3. Liberman D: The rise and fall of the community mental health center. Psychiatr Opinion 16:31–37, 1979
4. Fierman LB: The psychiatric hospital of the future. Psychiatr Opinion 16:15–21, 1979
5. Gordon RE, Webb S: The orbiting psychiatric patient. J Florida Med Assoc 62:21–25, 1975
6. Slater A, Gordon KK, Gordon RE: Role differences of mental health workers: Observations of four sites, in Nash KB, Lifton N, Smith SE (Eds): The Paraprofessional: Selected Readings. The Yale Monograph on Paraprofessionalism. New Haven, Conn., Advocate Press, Inc., 1978, pp 3–11
7. Cordes D, Roberts R, Gordon R, et al: Needs, Assessment, and Evaluation. Atlanta, Georgia, Southern Regional Education Board, 1978

8
Motivating Paraprofessional Staff

The use of MHWs in therapeutic and other mental health activities has remained controversial. At many state hospitals and community mental health centers an attitude prevails that MHWs are not capable of providing any therapeutic services to patients.[1] However, Christensen et al.[2] propose "that paraprofessional therapists be employed to apply well-specified treatment procedures under supervision with clients who have been screened and referred by professionals." They report that "MHWs are equally or more effective than professionals in treating a variety of clients . . . when the effective components of a treatment method have been well defined (e.g. progressive relaxation training, systematic desensitization, training of parents in operant techniques for child management)."

Despite this controversy about the capabilities of MHWs, they have been utilized in a systematic manner in the research and training (R & T) facility's treatment, research, training, and dissemination programs. The following steps were followed to create a high quality, effective, inexpensive treatment program where professionals, MHWs, and patients work together harmoniously and efficiently:

A clear mission statement *was developed to provide staff with an overall goal—a unified sense of purpose to which they could dedicate their efforts.*

Portions of this chapter appeared originally in Gordon RE, Goldstein NS, Gordon KK, et al: The Role of Paraprofessional Mental Health Workers in Family Therapy (Monograph Series No. 1, Report No. 3. New York, National Education Center for Paraprofessionals in Mental Health, 1979), and are reprinted with permission from the Center for Advanced Study in Education, New Human Services Institute.

A project orientation *was established, where each modestly-sized project itself had predefined goals and objectives, evaluated the patient's progress in the projects, and provided continuing feedback on findings to project staff.*

Creative clinical research and training (R&T) professionals, *whose characteristics are those of "bridge persons," were employed to be project directors. They were assigned to develop, administer, and evaluate programs, produce training manuals, teach students and staff, and supervise MHWs in their service activities.*

A learning environment *was maintained, in which MHWs, families, and patients could consider themselves to be both students and peer teachers; sc structured as to minimize dependence of patients and families upon staff and of MHWs upon professionals, in order to maximize each person's potential achievement.*

MHWs were taught to present life skills and self-medication training modules *to groups of patients and families in classes, and to serve as models for patients in peer management and support programs. They were assigned to conduct patient assessment.*

A creative atmosphere *was provided where professionals and MHWs together could direct their energies toward innovation, evaluation, training, and dissemination; recognize problems openly; and search for solutions with good humored perseverence, tolerance of frustration, and determination to overcome obstacles.*[3]

Experienced professionals *were selected and placed in key roles as monitors and censors who set limits and defined boundaries for MHW and other staff performance.*

Matrix management *was utilized to promote close cooperation and communication between medical treatment and modular skill-building personnel who have attained different levels of training, and to provide a setting where MHWs and professionals accept responsibilities and leadership roles to the limit of their abilities.*

Financial support *was obtained through writing grant applications for community programs, vocational rehabilitation, deinstitutionalization, and other less restrictive alternatives to residential care.*

This chapter focuses on the actions required for utilizing MHWs to the fullest extent in mental health settings, the variety of roles they can play, their relationship with professionals and patients, and their attitudes toward their work situation.

STEPS REQUIRED IN MOTIVATING STAFF AND FULLY UTILIZING MHWs

Clarification of Mission

A treatment facility that intends to train and utilize MHWs and to do research and training must clearly state these as policies. An important step is to develop an appropriate mission statement that elucidates a tripartite service-research-training mission and emphasizes the role of MHWs in it. Effective performance depends not only on the validity of an organization's goals, but on the degree to which its goals and the personal goals of each employee can be integrated.[4]

Many conflicting demands, both internal and external, vie for allocation of resources: keeping patient beds filled; establishing a treatment program for deviant adolescents; training state hospital staff in activities therapy; providing management training for community mental health centers; and, in private settings, making a profit. To respond intelligently, it is first necessary to examine needs, resources, expectations, and limitations.

What resources are available? A state hospital staffing pattern with 274 direct service positions provides no R&T support staff. These staffing limitations and a mandate to treat 370 patients require that, to fulfill service, research, and training, priorities must be set for meeting demands. Research must be limited to evaluating innovative management and treatment services, and training devoted to teaching personnel to perform the effective new treatments developed. Service priorities are determined by assessing catchment area needs, the nature of the facilities available, and the capabilities of staff.

In settings where maintenance of a high census is emphasized, there are incentives to keep patients longer, and to provide custodial treatment rather than to develop effective new approaches that result in rapid turnover of patients or keep them in the community. This basic conflict increases when empty beds result in threats to cut staff or funding, or to close a facility— problems that threaten staff security in many hospitals. If hospitals are to be encouraged to deinstitutionalize more patients, this disincentive needs to be removed.

In settings where medical schools run mental health research and training centers, the focus usually is on educating medical students and psychiatric residents, while training for others assumes a secondary role. Medical school research is determined by the interests of faculty, but not necessarily by the service needs of the public mental health system. These R&T centers often perform basic research in the biology and sociology of mental illness rather than applied treatment-related research.

Given the nature of state hospital control and staffing, it becomes clear why the mission statement reads, "The mission is to provide—through innovative utilization of resources—multidisciplinary staff training, applied evaluative research, and quality mental health treatment and rehabilitative services." To perform research, training, and quality treatment functions without a special research support staff, management must be innovative in the use of its MHWs and its limited numbers of professionals. Training is multidisciplinary and is not focused primarily on a special group such as medical or nursing students. Research is directed toward evaluating applied, service-related problems, not toward a special interest of an individual professional or student. The mission statement contributes greatly to morale; it provides direction to staff's efforts. They feel that they are participating in an important enterprise that benefits patients everywhere. The mission statement plus a three-year utilization plan of goals and objectives provide stability of programs. The utilization plan provides a schedule for implementing new projects one at a time, allowing time for researchers to design a series of innovative projects. It restricts diversion of resources from meeting short-term crises[5] and rules out indiscriminant admission of all 370 patients in one large contingent.

Modular treatment and peer management and support create psychiatric production lines analogous to those in industry, where unskilled and semiskilled workers, both patients and staff, perform many simple tasks that together produce large quantities of a highly complicated end-product. Management must therefore be continuously concerned with worker morale, lest MHWs get bogged down in the routine of their jobs, become frustrated by the shifting political forces that pull them to and fro, lose sight of the goals and outcome of their effort, and develop staff "burnout."[6] Repeated emphasis on the importance of the mission and the efforts to fulfill it, with feedback from measured progress in its achievement, both with individual patients and with entire projects, keeps MHW and professional staff motivated and enthusiastic about their work, and helps counteract frustration and anxiety. Project Orientation provides a management approach that meets these objectives.

Project Orientation

All treatment is conducted in projects, each of which provides care to patients in a predetermined age range. The R&T facility was reorganized to conduct these projects in three program sections—Children and Adolescents, Adults, and Gerontology; a fourth section—Health Services—provides medical and nursing direction and care. Project orientation is important to the performance of evaluation and training as well as service; it also serves to boost morale. Filley et al.[7] describe six characteristics of a project:

First, it has a definite operational objective, such as placing a manned satellite in a specified orbit on a particular date within certain budgetary constraints or, in the mental health field, developing a new residential treatment program for chronic mental patients to reduce recidivism and improve their quality of life in the community. Second, a project is more concerned with completing its work in a given period than it is with money costs. Third, one or more interest groups support the project; the projects connected with manned space flight were initiated and supported by both President Kennedy and the Congress; the mental health projects described here are supported by the legislature, the human services administrative structure, and citizens' groups such as the Mental Health Association. Fourth, the longer a project continues, the greater the investment and cost of failure or abandonment, a feature that the R&T center director used to preserve the research and training capabilities of successful projects in spite of the system's emphasis on treating more and more residential patients. Fifth, projects require interdependence among distinct professional specialties. Sixth, and finally, a project typically addresses problems that are new or different from the prior experience of an organization.

The characteristics that should be present in a project group for it to be effective, according to Galbraith,[8] are as follows: reward for participation of its members; line personnel who will be accountable for implementing joint decisions and plans; specialists, including lower level personnel who are familiar with technical details, from all departments that are significantly involved with the work of the project group; authority for project participants to commit their departments to carrying out project group decisions; influence based on knowledge and information rather than upon position in the hierarchy (group members will come from different levels in the organization, and status differences should not interfere with teamwork); project activities built into the regular process of the organization (in a mental health facility the innovation, evaluation, and training should not interfere with treatment services to the community); resolution of conflicts by group problem-solving rather than by force or compromise; participants selected for their skills in developing teamwork and joint effort, and for their ability to deal with interpersonal issues; and leadership provided by an integrator, who manages the process of group activities rather than imposes his own decisions on the project group.

GOALS AND OBJECTIVES

The first characteristic of a project, as noted above, is that it has a definite operational objective. The same can be said about a treatment and training module and many other educational, management, medical, and psychotherapeutic treatment techniques that set goals and objectives in advance to integrate and give direction to organizational and individual preparations. The following procedures all contain written statements of goals and objectives, measure and monitor progress, and provide feedback for upgrading programs on the basis of the assessments:

The Mission Statement and Utilization Plan provide goals, directions, and a schedule for implementing programs, restrict diversion of resources to meet multiple short-term crises, distribute responsibility among individual project directors in an orderly manner, direct their efforts toward achieving the goals, and review performance toward the objectives.[9,10]

The Problem Oriented Record Approach provides treatment objectives and plans for each problem on the patient's list, and follows up on the treatment plan through the use of numbered and titled progress notes for each problem.

The Modular Course in Goal Setting and the Peer Managed Token Economy Program help patients reintegrate their lives, thoughts, and conduct by setting both long-term and short-term goals, planning the steps leading toward these goals, providing feedback on performance, persevering, and completing each step along the way.

The Project Orientation Technique defines in advance the specific innovative objective(s) for each treatment, training, and research project, and evaluates and reports on progress.

The Goal Attainment Scaling System makes scales to show attainment for each of several major goals related to the patient's problems toward which each individual strives.

The Program Evaluation and Review Techniques plan the development of each project in advance, show the sequence and relative stages of completion, and provide feedback on progress.

The Matrix Management Method accomplishes superordinate R&T center goals by reinforcing cross-project, cross-program, and cross-discipline cooperation and creativity.

The Peer Management and Support Program structures staffing patterns and organizes treatment responsibilities so that patient leadership, management, and support are reinforced both by the staff and by the patient group. Information on assessed progress is fed back to patients and staff to motivate effort.

In all of these, goals and objectives are set forth to the fullest possible extent in quantifiable terms; progress is measured and achievement is evaluated as to effectiveness, productivity, and efficiency; results are fed back to staff both to motivate performance and to assist program modification and improvement.

Project orientation organizes staff into small working groups of 10–25 persons in which professionals and MHWs together set therapeutic goals, form personal ties, evaluate outcomes, provide project-related training, and develop the kinds of harmonious team relationships observed in the closely knit agencies studied in the Role and Task Differences research mentioned earlier. A moderate amount of interproject and interprogram competition also is encouraged, as long as it remains friendly and helps motivate efforts. In facilities that do not have a project orientation, staff are frequently shifted from one area to another; this makes it difficult for staff to establish close ties and loyalties and easy for them to become demoralized. MHWs experience some of this kind of upheaval when projects are actually discontinued or are threatened with dissolution.

Project staff jointly sponsor activities such as workshops with staff from other agencies. They cooperate in joint programs with Youth Services, Aging and Adult Services, Retardation, Social and Economic Services, and Vocational Rehabilitation. Professional and MHW personnel in these agencies work closely with R&T center staff in patient treatment and family counseling, and participate with them in research and training. Funding for such programs is often provided by special grants obtained by teams of R&T and MHW staff. These collaborations result in improved services to patients—Aging and Adult Services helps them to find homes in the community, for example, and Vocational Rehabilitation helps them obtain jobs. Successful collaboration in these demonstrations contributes to morale and security of staff in the cooperating agencies. The R&T center gains much needed support from these other programs in its constant struggle not to be diverted from its mission.

Selection of Project Directors and Coordinators

Program and project directors, coordinators, and managers are selected from staff who may be described as "bridge people" or "gatekeepers" having the following characteristics:[11]

They have contributed to at least one discipline, and sometimes to two, or even three disciplines.

They seek active involvement in diverse kinds of problem solving and cope rather than agonize in the face of obstacles.

They communicate openly, thus helping solve problems as well as reward accomplishments.

They are challenged by adversity and meet it with good humor and greater effort.

They have a wide range of interests.

They are cosmopolites with multiple connections to various societies—scientific, social, and cultural.

They tend to be good listeners, empathetic and accepting, able to generate enthusiasm. They encourage their peers, being optimistic and persistent.

They readily accept suggestions from others, and are both critical and trustful.

They are generally good salesmen of ideas and projects.

They are generally sufficiently self-assured to admit ignorance in discussion with colleagues in other disciplines.

They are not afraid to reveal their faults, a fact that makes them accessible as models to MHWs.

They are responsive to patients' needs and pressures.

They like to act as consultants, being enthusiastic about the work of others.

They are flexible and operate well in an open system.

Project coordinators, directors, and managers are the leaders in project development and administration, in evaluation and research, and in training and dissemination. The performance and morale of MHWs is determined in large part by the quality of their supervision by the director and coordinator of their project.

Establishment of a Learning Environment

The skills- and supports-building approach to therapy provides an atmosphere conducive to learning by patients, families, and staff: Patients and families learn to communicate, to solve problems, to cope. MHWs learn to teach patients and families, to assess progress, and to train and disseminate. MHWs, families, and patients are both students and teachers of others. Everyone, including the professional, is in a skills-building continuum; those with more ability teach those with less.

Everyone attends skills-building classes: Those for professionals and supervisors emphasize leadership, management, and continuing professional education. MHWs are taught to emphasize positive reinforcement for each step of improving a skill—reinforcement by word of praise, pat on the shoulder or hug, and by smiling expression. There is none of the depersonalization found in facilities where mental patients must sit or lie around in gray hospital gowns, or worse, must be strapped into beds or tied in chairs while staff parade about in starched white uniforms.

MHWs are encouraged to continue their formal education as well as to attend conferences, in-service training sessions, and continuing education workshops for the state's service delivery personnel. University faculty and students utilize the treatment facility as a field training station. Students are hired half-time (at $4000 a year) to assist with evaluations that are an integral part of research on the effectiveness of innovations. Support of learning is, without doubt, a major contributor to rapport between MHWs and professionals; loss of funding for student MHWs, which occurs periodically as a result of state budget cuts, is a major source of worry. Although staffing patterns and pay scales divide personnel into two categories—25 percent professionals and 75 percent MHWs—many of the latter accept this division because they consider themselves as students training to be professionals.

Utilization of MHWs

Twenty years ago we proposed that mental hospitals affiliate with colleges and with vocational training, recreational, and rehabilitation centers, where skills and supports-building programs can readily be developed.[12] The location of treatment facilities on university campuses provides the kind of setting contemplated.

Although the level of education and experience required for employment and the salaries received by MHWs are modest, the R&T facility attracts students and other bright young people. They seek MHW jobs because they can work in an atmosphere which supports innovation, creativity, and personal growth; perceive opportunities for achievement; gain recognition; perform interesting work; learn treatment skills; and assume important responsibilities. The recognition that produces good feelings about their jobs does not come only from their supervisors, but also from peers, families, and patients.[13]

An urban location makes it possible not only to attract bright MHWs but also for them to become family therapists. Families of local patients can attend daily or weekly sessions, which they could not do if the treatment center were located many miles away in the country. Staff turnover is fast for MHWs. Trained personnel are in demand; after gaining experience and furthering their education they are recruited by other mental health and human services facilities.

MHWs are selected not only for interpersonal and cognitive skills; some are hired because they have special abilities in music, gardening, writing, sports, etc., skills that can be used in modular treatment and statewide staff training. Since the staffing pattern does not provide positions for music therapists, writers, etc., MHWs who have additional skills are utilized in the modular treatment program, where they assume special training positions in addition to their other treatment functions. Management of this dual responsibility is discussed in the sections on Matrix Management.

Development of a Creative Atmosphere

Creative performance in writing manuals, preparing grant proposals, disseminating, and managing is fostered by example, written and verbal reinforcement, and promotion (sometimes with additional pay) to more responsible positions. MHW staff and students participate with R&T professionals in writing training manuals (some of which appear in the Appendix), grant proposals, and scientific reports, and in presenting papers at workshops as well as at scientific meetings.

Frequently central administrators will balk at sending students and MHW-authors to read papers on their innovations at national scientific meetings. They will limit travel only to senior professionals and administrators, who may belong to the organization holding the conference, but often may have contributed nothing to the research enterprise. Thus, in essence, a different behavior than that encouraged here is reinforced—"joining," not creating. When this occurs, assistance is sought from university colleagues who share the academic values of the R&T professionals. They use travel funds in the grants that they and R&T staff have jointly obtained.

Creativity cannot be forced; but it can be modeled, shaped, and reinforced. An environment conducive to creativity can be provided where a critical mass of staff selected for their high level of past creative performance—professionals, paraprofessionals, and students—are brought together and mutually stimulate and inspire each other's innovation.

Pride in creativity helps generate perseverance despite adversity. Staff receive recognition and respect of peers and colleagues at scientific meetings and training workshops, which helps them remain tolerant.

Open communication is stressed. MHWs who are also students are stimulated by ideas from their classes, their teachers, and their readings. They recognize applications to problems in their jobs; their ideas are welcomed, and after review, are often incorporated into projects, grant proposals, and training materials, both for patients and for professional and paraprofessional manpower training. Patients themselves, especially in the community network development (CND), contribute creative ideas that are welcomed and implemented when possible. Project orientation, emphasis on creativity, and support for learning provide an environment that armors MHWs against "burnout."[6] Despite their low salaries, MHWs' morale is maintained by the respect they receive from their professional colleagues, who also serve as their teachers, by their confidence in their ability to learn and be creative, by the feedback they obtain on the assessed progress of the patients they treat, and by the challenge of filling varied roles in the matrix organization. This reinforcement of creativity is quite at variance with customary practice in many organizations where top administrators regularly take the ideas and written work products of their subordinates and others, publish them or use them in speeches as if they were their own original ideas, and never give credit to the true authors and researchers. This practice damages morale among professionals, MHWs, and students, and stifles motivation for creativity among researchers.

Supervision by Standard-Bearers

The preceding sections have emphasized features that motivate high levels of performance and close working relationships between and among staff and patients. There are, however, definite risks in placing MHWs in therapeutic roles, or in charge of ungovernable children or seriously disturbed mental patients in a mental institution, without providing excellent professional backup and experienced administrative surveillance.

Moreover, since creative persons are constantly reaching out to and beyond traditional boundaries, they too need a system of constraints to protect them and their patients from their going too far. For these reasons, experienced professionals—older physicians, nurses, pharmacists, administrators, and researchers—are placed in key roles in a matrix organization. They monitor, survey, review, censor, and assure the quality of the program; they are held accountable for all medico-legal decisions. This medico-legal control is touched on briefly in the next section and is described more fully in Chapter 9.

Matrix Management

In many projects a staff member must fill two role assignments, one as a member of a treatment team with a job such as social worker, nurse, psychologist, or rehabilitation therapist, all under the medico-legal responsibility of the physician, and another in the modular training and evaluative research organization. Assignments are based on individual competencies and preferences, and on availability. Night staff, for instance, will help score assessment data collected by day staff MHWs in modular treatment and training. Rather than sit around bored when patients are sleeping, they perform necessary analyses.

In the matrix scheme everyone holds important responsibilities: a MHW on the night shift with writing ability will serve as an editor of a training manual; another on the day shift with musical talent will supervise leisure skills training. On some projects almost all staff fill a modular training function and also perform traditional duties.[7,8,14] Job descriptions provide specific delineations of duties on which staff performance is graded and reinforced.

Financial Support for Change

The role of the mental hospital is changing. Decreasingly it is serving as custodian for mental patients; increasingly it is preparing patients and staff for living in the community. A treatment facility that is budgeted and admin-

istered like a residential state hospital must obtain grant support to supplement its funding in order to provide leadership in guiding this change. The
Infant Stimulation Project, for example, is a primary prevention project sponsored by Retardation, not Mental Health. Although a project which fills an
important niche in the developmental sequence of the 12 age-related demonstration programs, it could not have been conducted if it were not funded by
a grant.

MHWs need preparation for tomorrow's mental health services. Professionals, aided by MHWs who provide ideas, library work, and literary assistance, write grant proposals aimed at giving this preparation. As described
in previous sections of this report, the thrust of this grant writing is toward
community programs: less restrictive alternatives to residential care, vocational rehabilitation, deinstitutionalization, collaboration with community
agencies, training and dissemination, and prevention. Grant proposals serve
other vital purposes: they provide travel funds for presenting reports at scientific meetings, and salaries for staff and MHW students whose jobs are
threatened; they help maintain the integrity of important projects and other
activities that are in danger of being eliminated.

EVALUATION

Motivation and morale have been assessed by measuring efficiency and
ward atmosphere. The efficiency of service delivery is borne out by a survey
that estimated the percentage of time spent by staff at various duties as obtained from questionnaires from a stratified sample of 64 treatment personnel. Responses showed that, in addition to providing significantly more
effective treatment (see Chapters 2 and 3) to more than twice as large a percentage of patients as the comparable public mental hospitals each year (see
Chapter 9), staff devote more than half (53%) of their time to R&T activities
(1) helping invent, develop, and apply treatment innovations; (2) helping
collect data and evaluate the effectiveness of new treatments; and (3) helping
conduct training and dissemination both in workshops locally and in consultations and on-site demonstrations at the state hospitals and CMHCs. In other words, they spent less than half their time at work for accomplishing all
the traditional psychiatric routines such as escorting patients, cleaning, medicating, writing nursing notes, etc. The challenge of innovating treatment
methods, and the satisfaction derived from actively contributing to measured
improvements in patients' performance and to training and dissemination
provides the motivation that encourages staff to accomplish more than twice
as much as called for in their job descriptions.

The ward atmosphere scale developed by Moos[15] was administered at th

R&T facility by Amuso and Archer.[16] Figure 8-1 shows that the treatment project combines features of both a Therapeutic Community and a Relationship-Oriented program as reported by Price and Moos[17] on the basis of their cluster analysis of 160 psychiatric wards drawn from state hospitals, Veterans Administration Hospitals, and community and private hospitals. Specifically, high patient involvement in program planning and open expression of feelings, including anger and aggression, are characteristics of Therapeutic Communities. Like Relationship-Oriented programs, there is emphasis on clarity of program in the R&T treatment project. The R&T project also contains features common to both treatment and relationship programs—patients are encouraged and supported by staff and other patients, staff control is de-emphasized, and there is concern for the personal problems of patients.

This figure graphically illustrates that patients perceive the treatment program to emphasize both a high quality relationship between staff and patients, as well as a strong therapeutic orientation.

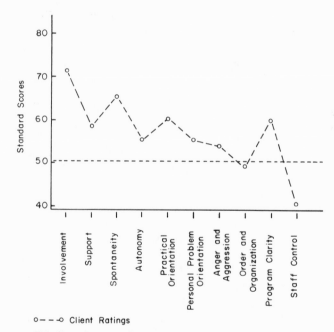

o— — —o Client Ratings

This figure is prepared from data collected by Archer.

Fig. 8-1. Ward atmosphere scale profile for a residential adult project, summer 1979. (From Price RH, Moos RH: Toward a taxonomy of inpatient treatment environments. J Abnorm Psychol 3:181–188, 1975.)

DISCUSSION

The Harvard Case Report describes attitudes of service workers else-where in the state's public human services system.[18]

Few staff workers feel that good work is ever rewarded. . . . Workers no longer have input into the changes which are going to be made. The workers used to feel more valuable. Now not a week passes that we don't hear if we don't get this done, disciplinary action will be taken. . . . No matter how good you are the administration never says thank you. . . . (pp. 43–44).

Talbott[5] points out that in state institutions management by crisis is the order of the day. Administrators are constantly forced to choose between two or more undesirable alternatives. The mission statement, utilization plan, and project orientation provide long-term goals and objectives that reduce management by crisis. It probably would not have been possible to protect the integrity of the Community Network Development (CND), for example, if it were not organized as a project. The fact that it had goals, objectives, a research design, an evaluation plan, and a program of training and dissemination gave it a strength that helped it endure repeated crises. We could point to the funds and time already invested, and could ask did they want to throw away all that effort and expense when early results were pointing to possible success of the project.

In his model for the management of innovation and change, "A Victory," Davis[3] emphasizes open communication. Both creativity and matrix management require free and open communication of ideas, knowledge, information, and plans—sharing, evaluating, criticizing at many levels—before decision and action. Communication from patients and MHWs to top management, as well as between staff of different projects and programs, contributes to treatment innovation. Open communication is a cornerstone of academic freedom,[19] but many public mental health administrators do not generally share these academic values. Usually they resist change, resent questions, do not welcome challenge, and block communication except that which endorses the status quo. "Someone who has a plum of a position can hardly help preferring to maintain the status quo."[3]

Paul[20] has written about the disincentives in funding and the abrupt layoffs, hiring freezes and the like, which damage staff morale. Despite these, the R&T facility has kept staff motivated by a variety of strategies. These include clearly establishing its creative, innovative treatment mission and reinforcing staff for fulfilling it. Other public mental health programs might do the same. Become affiliated with educational institutions. Hire clinical researchers and students to perform both the ordinary service routines and also research and training. Put patients to work helping each other. An example has been set how to do it.

Deinstitutionalizing Staff

As part of the national effort to "deinstitutionalize" patients, public mental hospital staff must also be deinstitutionalized along with the patients, so that staff do not have a vested interest in maintaining the institutional status quo. Behavioral and psychoeducational treatment approaches such as those utilized in the R&T center require physicians, nurses, social workers, and MHWs to practice techniques that they are ill-trained to perform. As pointed out previously, they have not been taught to conceptualize a mental health problem as a deficit in skills that can be treated by training and education—by skills building; nor have they learned to use matrix management to perform both medical treatment and psychoeducational skill building, utilizing a staff of MHWs. With training, professionals and MHWs at the public mental hospitals can learn to help their residential psychiatric patients build the skills needed for successful community living, and patients' families to aid in therapy. Once deinstitutionalization of patients *and staff* has taken place, MHWs and other staff can then utilize these same training approaches when working with community patients and their families.

The main problem to be dealt with in deinstitutionalizing MHWs is how to change attitudes of the professional, supervisory, and administrative people in charge, as well as the attitudes of MHWs themselves, about the role of the MHW. Well-developed social caste systems exist in the public mental hospitals. For example, MHW students in the education program described in a later chapter have been derided by their nonstudent fellow workers for trying to "better" themselves through education. They are told, "It's not what you know but who you know that gets you ahead." Experience with public mental hospital MHWs has shown that training alone will not bring about change.

The crux of the problem is how to deal with the depersonalization and the control-oriented programs, which are primarily found in Veterans Administration and state hospitals.[17] Not only has the patient been depersonalized, but so has the MHW. Better educated, higher paid administrative and professional staff have never expected much from MHWs. Until recently, the role of the MHW has been seen as strictly custodial. However, MHWs who are well-adjusted in their personal life not only have a great deal to offer to the patient, they probably are in a good position to offer help and have the patient and family accept it because they often belong to the same socioeconomic class as the typical patient in a state mental institution.[21-24] To begin to move toward deinstitutionalization, it is first necessary to recognize that many MHWs possess valuable knowledge and skills, and that it is worthwhile to give them the behavioral tools to share these abilities with patients and patients' families. It is also necessary to provide incentives to the workers for taking training.

REFERENCES

1. Slater A, Gordon KK, Gordon R: Role differences of mental health workers: Observations of four sites, in Nash KB, Lifton N, Smith SE (Eds): The Paraprofessional: Selected Readings. The Yale Monograph on Paraprofessionalism. New Haven, Conn., Advocate Press, Inc., 1978, pp 3–11
2. Christensen A, Miller WR, Munoz RF: Paraprofessionals, partners, peers, paraphernalia, and print: Expanding mental health service delivery. Professional Psychology 9:249–270, 1978
3. Davis HR: Management of innovation and change in mental health services. Hosp Community Psychiatry 9:649–658, 1978
4. Hughes CL: Goal-Setting: Key to Individual and Organizational Effectiveness. New York, American Management Association, 1965
5. Talbott, JA: The Death of the Asylum: A Critical Study of State Hospital Management Services, and Care. New York, Grune & Stratton, 1978
6. Podbielski S: "Burn-out": A Growing problem for new professionals? The New Professional 1:4, 1979
7. Filley AC, House RJ, Kerr S: Managerial Process and Organizational Behavior (ed 2). Glenview, Ill., Scott, Foresman, 1976
8. Galbraith JE: Matrix organizational designs. Business Horizons 14:29–48, 1971
9. Odiorne GS: Management Decisions by Objectives. Englewood Cliffs, N.J., Prentice-Hall, 1969
10. Odiorne GS: Management by Objectives. New York, Pitman Publishing Corp., 1965
11. Blake SP: Managing for Responsive Research and Development. San Francisco, Freeman, 1978
12. Gordon RE, Gordon KK, Gunther M: The Split-Level Trap. New York, B. Geis, 1961
13. Herzbert F: Work and the Nature of Man. Scranton, Pa., World (Crowell), 1966
14. Tytler K: Making matrix management work. Training 15:78, 1978
15. Moos R: Ward Atmosphere Scale Manual. Palo Alto, Ca., Consulting Psychologists Press, 1974
16. Amuso KF, Archer RP: Ward atmosphere: A comparison between staff and client ratings. Presented at the South Eastern Psychological Assn., Annual Meeting, Washington, D.C., 1980
17. Price RH, Moos RH: Toward a taxonomy of inpatient treatment environments. J Abnorm Psychol 3:181–188, 1975
18. Whitman D: Reorganization of Florida's Human Services Agency. Kennedy School of Government Case Programs, C95-80-040. Cambridge, Mass., Harvard University, 1980
19. Machlup F: On some misconceptions concerning academic freedom. AAUP Bulletin 41, 1955
20. Paul GL: The implementation of effective treatment programs for chronic mental patients: Obstacles and recommendations, in Talbott A (Ed): The Chronic Mental Patient. Washington, American Psychiatric Assoc, 1978
21. Hallowitz E, Riessman F: The role of the indigenous nonprofessional in a community mental health neighborhood service center program. Am J Orthopsychiatry 37:766–778, 1967
22. Riessman F: What is the relation between poverty and mental health? Psychiatr Res Reports 21:35–54, 1967
23. Riessman F: Strategies and suggestions for training nonprofessionals. Community Ment Health J 3:103–110, 1967
24. Riessman F, Hallowitz E: The neighborhood service center: An innovation in preventive psychiatry. Am J Psychiatry 123:1408–1413, 1967

9
Using Matrix Management to Harmonize Medical, Nursing, and Psychoeducational Treatments

Ten years ago I (R.E.G.) obtained a federal grant and led a project team of engineers, physicians, computer scientists, and statisticians that established a psychiatrically oriented automated multiphasic health testing and service center.[1-3] A member of the Department of Psychiatry, I was assigned to the Office of the Dean of the College of Medicine to launch the center; meanwhile, my colleagues and I continued to teach and hold other responsibilities in our specialty departments. With the dean's administrative support for the multiphasic health center, we were able to draw upon resources from many departments throughout the College of Medicine that, under ordinary circumstances, were not available to members of our departments—from Radiology, the Clinical Laboratory, and Pulmonary Medicine, for example. Upon establishing the center and completing our assignment, my colleagues and I all returned full-time to our home bases in Psychiatry and other departments of the University. This experience introduced me to matrix management, in which I was reporting to two bosses (the Dean and the Psychiatry Chairman), and was responsible for carrying out two different jobs.

This experience and some study of matrix management influenced the development of the mental health research and training (R&T) center. Here, as in the multiphasic testing center, professionals from a wide variety of disciplines need to work together to establish programs and to carry them out

Portions of the present chapter were previously published in a public document by the Florida Mental Health Institute, Tampa, Fla., 1979.

harmoniously. But there was great disharmony and conflict between professionals; morale was particularly low among physicians and nurses. Yet these biomedical professionals were essential to the care of mental patients, even in a center that was developing new psychoeducational treatments. The following case example illustrates what can happen when a psychiatric emergency occurs in such psychiatric treatment facilities.

Illustrative Case Example—"Homicidal Maniac"

"Dr Perez, come to the treatment unit immediately! They just brought in a homicidal maniac! We can't handle him!"

The physician had no difficulty spotting the "homicidal maniac" standing in the center of a circle of nurses and MHWs, brandishing a wooden cane with both hands over his head. Pushed by anxious staff to the inside of the circle, the doctor stood face to face with the patient, a grey haired, short, stocky man of about sixty. The patient's face was flushed and gleamed with moisture; his breath was rapid; his eye pupils were dilated; the collar of his white shirt and the armpits of his gray suit jacket were stained with sweat; his hands holding the cane were shaking; a drop fell from his brow onto his gray tie as he said rapidly to the doctor, "Watch out, they're firing rays at me through the windows. You might get hit."

The first task in the psychiatric rehabilitation of mental patients is to give them a psychiatric and physical medical work-up, and to begin appropriate medical therapy.[4-6] Nevertheless, since the 1960s the medical manpower situation in public mental hospitals and community mental health centers (CMHCs) has deteriorated.[7] This chapter discusses how matrix management combats this deterioration. It shows how it integrates the mental health service, research, and training efforts of medical and psychoeducational professionals and paraprofessionals. Several different management techniques are presented with the advantages and disadvantages of each. These pages provide examples and an evaluation of the effectiveness of integration under matrix management, and report evidence of the success of the overall program.

ORGANIZATIONAL CHANGE IN PUBLIC MENTAL INSTITUTIONS

The development of new psychotropic medications in the 1950s led to dramatic changes in the clinical care of mental patients. The rapid growth of CMHCs in the 1960s set the stage for deinstitutionalization—the trend of the 1970s. The transition from hospital to community care has resulted not only in shorter hospitalization, however, but also in much higher rates of rehospitalization for chronic mental patients.

Dissatisfaction with the care of patients under public mental hospitals' hierarchical psychiatric and nursing leadership has led nationally to efforts at reorganizing these facilities. In order to introduce more effective modern management techniques and to give behavioral, habilitative, and rehabilitative professionals a louder voice in the treatment of patients, new multidisciplinary team approaches have been developed. This chapter will consider three styles of management organization: (1) by professional specialty, (2) by multidisciplinary treatment unit, and (3) by matrix management, which seeks to combine the best features of the first two.

Organization by Professional Specialty

Traditionally, most public mental institutions have been organized functionally in departments according to professional specialty: Psychiatry, Nursing, Social Services, Psychology. Usually a physician is in charge of a patient treatment unit; he has day-to-day functional direction, although not line authority over the nurses, psychologists, and social workers on the unit. The latter are assigned to the ward or unit, but they report to their respective department heads, the Directors of Nursing, Psychology, and Social Service. Most lower level personnel (psychiatric aides) are supervised by the Nursing Department.

Organization by Treatment Unit: A Multidisciplinary Team Approach

In the late 1960s a movement began to reorganize mental institutions into goal-oriented Multidisciplinary Team Units to which patients were assigned on the basis of age, geographical home residence, or treatment program. The manager or director of these units, who exercises line authority over the treatment team, is selected on the basis of administrative ability, not membership in a particular profession (see Figure 9-1). Physicians and nurses are unlikely to have gained experience or training in management or behavioral therapies; leadership of the team, therefore, is no longer their sole province. Professional standards for members of each discipline are set and monitored by standards specialists instead of department heads in Nursing, Clinical Social Services, Psychology, and Rehabilitation Therapy. Standards specialists hold no executive line authority over treatment unit personnel.

In many R&T facilities like the present one initially, R&T professionals are clustered in two or more additional sections that are entirely independent of the treatment organization—the Research and Evaluation Section and the Training and Education Section (see Figure 9-1). Neither of these sections

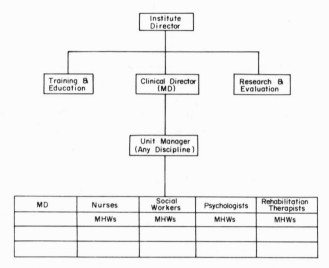

Fig. 9-1. Multidisciplinary team organization under a unit manager. Note that physicians and nurses report to a unit manager, who need not be a licensed professional. Also observe that neither research nor training professionals had any treatment responsibility in the R&T center in its initial organizational plan.

carry any clinical responsibilities. Each goes its separate way. Its personnel conduct activities of interest to themselves without regard to the assessed clinical patient treatment needs of the mental health system. As described previously, an internal reorganization placed all R&T professionals on treatment projects where these professionals were given direct clinical treatment, administrative, research, and training responsibilities, and were held accountable for the consequences of their decisions and actions.

Matrix Organization

A third approach, matrix organization, has been utilized in the present R&T center since its reorganization, As described by Shull,[8] matrix structure is a planned combination of professional specialty departments and goal-oriented multidisciplinary treatment unit styles of management that attempts to maximize the advantages in each and minimize their inherent disadvantages. The matrix may be permanent in nature or may contain temporary projects that continue until project goals are completed.[9]

This form of organization is well suited to settings that need to combine members of specialties into projects. In the typical matrix organization, individuals are members of specialty departments (e.g., nursing, medicine, psychology), but they are also assigned on a full- or part-time basis to projects. Personnel have two bosses, one a member of the specialty department and the other the leader of the project.

Under matrix organization, when a project is terminated, personnel return to their specialty departments, where they maintain employment and resume full-time work. Morale is thus much better in the matrix type of setting than in projects where personnel lose their jobs when the project ends.

In the R&T facility described here, pharmacists, physicians, and nursing-standards personnel remain in a specialty department—Health Services. The R&T professionals are required to accept responsibility for the effects of their treatment innovations on patients; they must share accountability with the nursing and medical professionals for patient care. Therefore, they are re-

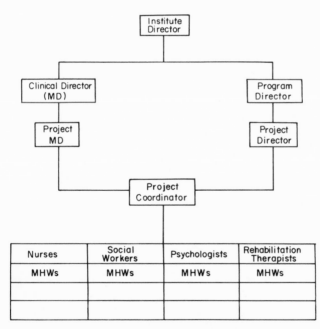

Fig. 9-2. Matrix organization after reorganization at the R&T facility. The treatment unit has been converted to a project with a tripartite mission—treatment, evaluative research, and training and education. Physicians are placed in charge of medical and other specialty services, and research and training personnel are held responsible for psychoeducational services. The project coordinator is shown here as reporting to two lines of authority.

deployed into three patient service areas—the Child/Adolescent, Adult, and Gerontology Programs. Each program is responsible for three to five projects, each led by an R&T professional project director. R&T professionals are responsible for the psychoeducational aspects of clinical treatment, research, and training, as well as for administration of the treatment units.

Treatment units are organized as multidisciplinary teams led by a project coordinator, a bridge person who may be a psychoeducational, medical, or nursing professional. The largest number have been nurses. Project directors exercise line authority for administrative and psychoeducational responsibilities; Health Services manages medical and nursing care and takes responsibility for medico-legal decisions. Every member of the treatment unit staff

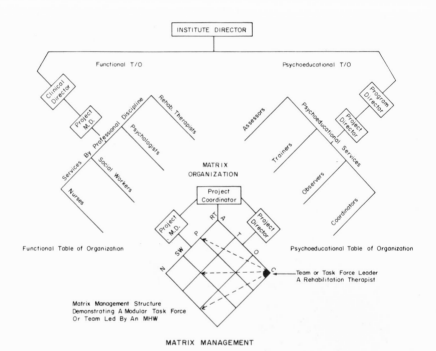

MATRIX MANAGEMENT

Fig. 9-3. Matrix management. In the matrix, the treatment staff on the unit report to the M.D., who is responsible for the patient's medical and other specialty services; the same staff report to the project director, who is in charge of psychoeducational rehabilitative training, research, and education. A project coordinator, a bridge person, provides overall coordination of both treatment and rehabilitation on the unit. Individual modules are taught by teams or task forces led by various staff members with special interests or abilities. In the example provided, a paraprofessional rehabilitation therapist is leader of a team that consists of a professional psychologist, a social worker, and an LPN.

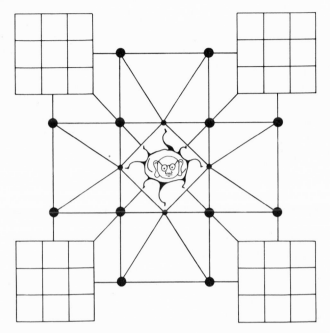

Fig. 9-4. Schematic representation of the matrix network for
the R&T center. The four service areas—health, child/adoles-
cent, adult, and gerontology—are interwoven with the center
director through bridge persons—the clinical director, project
directors, project coordinators, and program directors. This
schema has been adopted by staff and patients at the R&T center as their logo.

thus may have two supervisors, one part of the Health Services chain of command, the other in the project line of authority (see Figures 9-2, 9-3, and 9-
4).

Comment on the Multidisciplinary Unit
System

Numerous advantages of the unit system over the specialty department
system are suggested by Kiger.[10] The unit system provides: continuity of therapy by the same team; consistency, because responsibility can be accurately
assigned; improved communication between staff and patients who have common goals, responsibilities, and identifications; more reliable, meaningful, and
significant feedback; enriched teaching and research; flexibility and opportunity for creative thought and independent activity; more productivity from

staff members and patients; opportunity for the emergence of new leaders from the ranks; enhanced staff/patient relationships; less dependency of patients upon staff, and more upon each other; a more objective attitude toward authority by patients; healthy competition, which enhances morale; greater consultation between units on ideas and techniques; the development of a sense of social responsibility by unit personnel for the patients and the communities from which they come; better working relationships between the unit and the community; and a challenge to the community to develop its own services.

Departments organized by professional specialty, on the other hand, generally are superior to those organized by treatment units in a number of ways: efficiency in the use of resources; ease of measurement of results; preparation of well trained specialists; communication between specialists; and satisfaction with jobs.[11]

Heninger[12] discusses the leadership style in decentralized units. There is less thought and energy devoted to demonstrating "who's boss," more to producing ideas for solving a problem. The best measure of a team leader's skill is ability to draw out staff motivations, screen them, and mold them. The leader's duty is not to have brilliant ideas and to impose them on others, but to cultivate and nourish other people's ideas.

Lewis[13] proposes that the therapeutic team interacts best when the following processes are involved: all staff members communicate openly; they share decision-making; the leader is permissive but has implicit expectations; role definitions are not rigid; and significant feelings are exposed and shared.

Problems with Multidisciplinary Team Unit Management Organization

When an institution is organized into treatment units where nurses and physicians are supervised by nonmedical managers, there may be a greater amount of interdisciplinary conflict than when it is departmentalized into specialties. Furthermore, in the treatment unit organization, accountability is unclear and medico-legal responsibility for the care of patients and for maintenance of proper clinical records often becomes confused. When nonmedical persons exercise decision-making power over medico-legal issues in patient care (admission and discharge of dangerous patients, weekend passes and other home visits, placement on suicidal precautions, etc.), the nursing and medical professionals may be placed in perilous positions of conflict: Physicians or nurses may become legally accountable for decisions of nonphysicians over whom they have no executive control. In the present setting, five administrative levels superior to the position of the treating physician and nurse may be filled by nonmedical personnel. The job responsibilities of these personnel require them to make decisions that affect the treating physician's and nurse's care of mental patients.

Nurses and physicians may not have traditionally received training and education in administration and learning theory, but, on the other hand, staff trained in psychoeducation, management, and rehabilitative therapies often have not received the rigorous discipline and on-the-job training in patient medical care, as well as schooling and experience in ethics and medico-legal issues that characterize the education of most physicians and nurses. Some personnel in public institutions, furthermore, often do not have the dedication to their jobs, sense of responsibility about their work, and respect for patients that are required to provide high quality service. Rapid turnover and/or absenteeism may often be problems with this group. Both to avoid calamities, and to maintain quality, close supervision and monitoring of performance are required.

In some states, only the practices of physicians, nurses, and pharmacists are regulated by law. Although they are state employees, personnel in these biomedical professions who work in the state hospitals are not relieved of legal responsibility and can be held accountable for their own and others' activities; they are liable for malpractice on the grounds of negligence or carelessness for actions of every member of the team. It is only the regulated professional, however, whose license is in jeopardy. Liability can become a problem in a multidisciplinary table of organization. The line authority requires regulated professionals to relinquish critical decision-making responsibilities regarding patient care to unlicensed unit managers who may have had little practical experience. Furthermore, many of the nonregulated psychoeducational and rehabilitative staff in administrative positions may have virtually no knowledge of, background and experience with, nor interest in legal issues.

Team treatment has resulted in a blurring of professional roles in many facilities, Bassuk and Gersen[14] report, and in controversy over the qualifications and training required to treat severely mentally ill patients effectively. Furthermore, Raskin[15] observes that staff dysfunction may develop on units that emphasize open communication, democracy, and role blurring. He points out that, in the presence of crises—suicide, violence, homicidal threats, and medical emergencies such as the example presented earlier in this chapter—those staff members who push most for blurring of roles and democracy reveal their underlying insecurity. He emphasizes that inpatient units require formal administrative principles, and appropriate reinforcement systems directed toward increasing staff skills in working with patients. Confusion and professional dissatisfaction with the multidisciplinary team unit management approach contribute to the psychiatric crises described earlier.

The following list provides examples of some kinds of problems that we observed in facilities operating under multidisciplinary team unit management:

1. A mental patient is sent off the grounds by a unit staff member to obtain a medical consultation without a medical order or an escort.
2. Dangerous patients (for example, an adolescent who had killed her mother and criminal sex offenders) are admitted to an open facility where adequate security cannot be provided; several obtain weapons and menace other patients, staff, and the community; some are returned to their homes without provision for follow-up supervision and control.
3. A junior staff member independently prepares a letter on a patient's condition for use in a court custody hearing without consulting a licensed professional; the professional is blamed.
4. A nonprofessional staff member obtains the Unit Director's support for slapping a child patient as a form of behavior modification. A nurse protests that this procedure is illegal without approval by the Patients' Rights Committee; she is told to mind her own business and tend to her medications.
5. A patient is admitted to a multidisciplinary team treatment unit by special court order. Two weeks later, since she has not responded to treatment, the administrator (who is not a mental health professional) arranges for her transfer to a long-term treatment facility without first obtaining release from the court.
6. A judge wants a representative of a hospital to appear in court to explain a patient's treatment; he subpoenas the physician or occasionally a nurse, not the Unit Director. A patient's attorney decides to sue for malpractice. He picks the physician. In case law in many states, the doctor and nurse are accountable, even though the Unit Director may be in charge. In other states where the Unit System has existed longer, however, Unit Directors are beginning to be called to court.
7. Evening and night staff arrange coverage when they are on duty by friends who are not employees and who are not trained in medical emergency and other procedures.
8. A patient who has made homicidal threats is placed on close observation by the psychiatrist; the Unit Director, nevertheless, permits him to visit the open day room, from which he escapes. The nurse, who was not informed of the Unit Director's action, is held accountable and blamed for the patient's escape.
9. Nursing, medical, and other professional staff are hired by the Unit Director without adequate review of their credentials and interviews with their co-professionals; previous blemishes in their work record are

missed; legal actions ensue when better qualified, overlooked persons file grievances or when it becomes necessary to dismiss the employees.

10. The door to the room where medications are stored on the Unit is kept unlocked and patients on work details who need equipment, which also is stored in the same room, have free unsupervised access. Controlled Substances counts are not prepared nor counted on a regular basis on the unit.

11. Nursing Standards personnel are refused permission to study patients' records, which they plan to monitor, on the grounds that they are not the treating professionals, and their review of the records would invade the patients' right to privacy. When finally they obtain authority, they discover that nursing notes regarding medications given have been whited out and have not been initialed.

12. Turnover of medical and nursing staff is high. Throughout the nation there are shortages of these personnel in public mental health facilities utilizing the multidisciplinary team organization with a nonmedical unit manager.

13. A new psychiatric residential treatment facility is opened under the unit manager system. No policy is formulated regarding patients or staff using alcohol or drugs or bringing firearms or other weapons on the grounds. No training is provided for the management of cardiopulmonary and other medical emergencies. No plan is developed for handling suicidal attempts, elopements, and violence. After the inevitable calamities—including violent death of staff and patients—have occurred, an experienced psychiatrist is finally consulted.

The fourth example above is a problem that requires monitoring by a qualified clinical psychologist in the Psychology Standards Specialist position whose authority to intervene is clearly defined. Likewise, instances can be provided where low income patients are taught handicrafts in Occupational Therapy, such as clay modeling and the use of kiln, which will be of no use to them once they leave the institution and return to their homes; others are sent to reside upon discharge in nursing homes when their level of functioning would have permitted them to live independently. An experienced Rehabilitation Therapy Standards Specialist and a Clinical Social Work Specialist in positions of influence would have helped prevent these ill-considered actions.

Experienced clinicians will recall incidents similar to these that have occurred on units directed by physicians and nurses, but their numbers have increased in facilities where treatment teams are led by nonmedical unit managers. The Harvard Case Report[16] provides other examples of serious problems in the public mental institutions, and other hospitals and institutions. The discussion at the end of this chapter will include some further quotations from that document.

The Continuing Need for the Psychiatrist and Nurse

Despite conflicts, role blurring, and criticisms, psychiatrists and nurses remain essential to the care of patients in mental institutions. Patients still need to be diagnosed and treated with appropriate psychotropic medications and other physiological and biochemical measures. Without these interventions by physicians and nurses to control patients' disturbed behavior and physiological dysfunctioning, psychoeducational and other habilitative and rehabilitative efforts are often of limited benefit. Only after patients become stabilized and their need for medical and nursing care reduced, can skills-building and peer support become primary therapies.

In the case example presented earlier in this chapter, a physician was left facing a "homicidal maniac" who was menacing staff with a cane brandished over his head and talking wildly about rays coming at him.

After speaking to the patient for a few moments, the doctor turned to the head nurse. "Nurse, please bring this homicidal maniac a glass of orange juice." Twenty minutes later the patient was calmly eating a snack with the other elderly mental patients on the unit.

In answer to three simple questions from the doctor, the patient had replied: yes, he was a diabetic; yes, he had taken his insulin that morning; and no, he had missed his breakfast because the van taking him for his first day hospital treatment session had arrived before he had eaten.

This is not an atypical treatment problem.[5] Hall and his colleagues[6] report that many studies have shown that medical illness is the primary cause of at least nine percent of cases presenting as psychiatric disorders. Approximately 60 percent of diagnosed psychiatric patients have physical illnesses in addition to emotional disability; half of these physical problems were unknown either to the patient or the referring physician prior to psychiatric hospital admission.

Elderly people, in particular, tend to show confusion and disorientation as a first sign of infection, pneumonia, heart attack, anemia, dehydration, electrolyte imbalance, and a host of other ills. The elderly are prone to develop mental symptoms as a reaction to drugs that are often prescribed for their common disabilities—diuretics, digitalis, and tranquilizers—at doses that are usually safe in younger adults.

A 74-year-old man was hospitalized because of severe memory loss and confusion, and diagnosed as senile. A check of his medications, however, showed that he had been taking large doses of quinidine ever since a heart attack fifteen years previously. Three days after discontinuing the medication his mind recovered fully.

Cardiovascular, endocrine, infectious, and pulmonary disorders are the most frequent medical causes for psychiatric symptoms. Since it is difficult to distinguish physical disease from functional psychiatric disorders on the basis of psychiatric symptoms alone, a detailed physical examination and laboratory screening are indicated routinely in the initial evaluation of all psychiatric patients.[6]

In order to address these medical care needs of patients, as well as to clarify the roles of medical and nursing professionals and those of R&T professionals, and to create an environment that fosters innovation, matrix management was established in the present settings.

MATRIX MANAGEMENT

Benefits from Matrix Management

Prior to reorganization and the implementation of matrix management, an assessment was made of staff perceptions of the R&T facility and their projections of how it could be improved. A modified Delphi method was used to conduct this assessment. It revealed that staff wanted better communication and more involvement in making policy, creative activity, and decision making. A matrix provides a structure where this can be accomplished. Some of its benefits are as follows:

1. It clarifies the roles of medical and nursing personnel and places them in charge of all medical and medico-legally sensitive areas of patient care.
2. It makes researchers responsible for the consequences of their actions upon patients and staff.
3. It provides an environment that fosters creativity and innovation.
4. It improves communication and gives staff a voice in decision-making processes with respect to creative ideas, new policies, and other matters subject to internal influence; therefore, it motivates staff effort and counteracts staff burnout.
5. As a consequence of the above, it both stimulates staff productivity and provides them with a structure where they do two jobs under two leaders and, as the evaluation section later in this chapter shows, twice as much work.

6. It creates a network that ties together specialty departments and service teams in a well-integrated, interconnected system (see Figure 9-4).

Open Communication

Greenblatt[17] has called attention to the long drawnout lines of communication that characterize the mental health nonsystem. Nothing can be done by facility management about this problem, although colocation helps;[16] but internal communication is enhanced by matrix management. Regular staff meetings, which include both professionals and paraprofessionals, promote communication: daily meetings of psychoeducational project staff and medical/nursing staff resolve issues of joint concern—problems in patient management, suicide, violence, transfer, discharge, accidents, length of patient stay, use of seclusion and/or aversive procedures, inappropriate admissions, medications—as well as programmatic issues—planning, policy changes, problems with other agencies, etc. Weekly meetings of the Director and the Executive Committee of the service and project directors, chief administrators, and health services personnel, which are kept open to all staff, deal with Center policy and facility-wide issues. Weekly service meetings conduct in-service education. Monthly meetings of professionals handle subjects related to each discipline. Paraprofessional MHWs also met for a while, but interest dropped off when their projects became fully developed and up and running. MHWs now attend the daily project and weekly service quality control meetings. Expression of their creative ideas, as well as of their problems are welcomed there, and also through their two lines of administrative supervision—health or project—up to top management. When needed, the director's door is ajar and, of course, the weekly executive committee meetings are also open. The schema shown in Figure 9-4 illustrates the multiple interconnections that facilitate communication in the matrix.

Selection of Service and Project Directors and Project Coordinators in the Matrix

Programs are structured in a manner that fosters creativity by organizing treatment units as multidisciplinary teams, where staff of different specialties are brought under common leadership. Here the matrix is like the multidisciplinary team unit. However, selection of team leaders is vital to success of a project. Strong directors and coordinators are needed who respect the expertise of the personnel of each discipline, and who keep lines of communication open. They need to be "bridge people" who must keep in constant contact with the rest of the treatment team and supervise the management of the crises and other problems that arise daily if not hourly on the unit.

The Psychiatrist and Nurse in Matrix Management

Members of the Health Services Department—psychiatrists, other physicians, pharmacists, and nurses—are given clear, line authority over all decisions in their specialty areas. Psychiatrists and other physicians are supervised medically by their peers, nurses by theirs in their nursing duties. Project coordinators do not exercise line authority over the physicians for professional decisions. Physicians and psychiatrists serve as members of each unit treatment team, but they report to and receive their performance ratings from their own professional superiors—physicians and psychiatrists in the Health Services Department. Clinical pharmacists likewise serve as members of the unit team but report to the Chief of Pharmacy. Junior nurses on each unit report to and are rated by the unit's chief nurse. The chief nurses report to and are rated administratively and on psychosocial performance by the project coordinator; they are also hired, monitored, and rated on nursing performance with the concurrence of the Nursing Standards Specialist, a member of the Health Services Department.

The Office of Health Services has developed standard operating policies and procedures both to provide quality care of patients and to minimize legal risks, which have served as direct guidelines to action. As new research projects and State regulations change, new administrative and treatment team policies are written. Drafts are prepared to comply with the Consolidated Standards for Psychiatric Programs of the Joint Commission on Accreditation of Hospitals, the rules of the Board of Pharmacy, and the Nurse Practice Act; they are then reviewed and modified by the Medical Librarian, a Health Services Committee, the Center Director's Office, and by the involved units.

The Nursing Standards Office helps recruit, select, and monitor the performance of all nurses. It developed nursing policies in the matrix organization, got approval for the matrix structure from professional organizations, developed guidelines for determining clinical privileges for nurses, and obtained accreditation of Continuing Education Courses from the State Nursing Board.

In matters of patients' rights, Nursing Standards first drafts and presents proposed materials to an ad hoc committee that evaluates, makes recommendations, and sends these to the District Legal Counsel for review. Changes are approved before being implemented. This procedure ensures protection of patients' rights, while it protects nurses, physicians, and pharmacists from legal difficulties. The Office of Health Services monitors documentation of the details of patients' unusual actions and verbalizations, medications taken or refused, effects of psychotropic drugs, narcotics counts, medication discrepancies or errors, incident reports, suicide precautions, permission forms for treatment and for research, and matters regarding patients' rights. Health Services directs or serves on Committees on Medical Records, Pharmacy, and Therapeutics, Infection Control, as well as on Human Subjects Research, Patients' Grievances, and Human Rights and Treatment, all of which ensure that patient rights are not violated.

In summary, matrix organization attempts to combine the best features of specialty and multipurpose team organizations. Its format provides each project or task force with the best administration available. By retaining the functional independence of Health Services, however, a higher quality of medical and nursing care is provided; furthermore, the morale of physicians, pharmacists, and nurses, and pride in their work, are higher than it was under multidisciplinary unit team management. There is no diffusion of their medico-legal roles and responsibilities.

Because of the need for a person with maturity and practical knowledge to direct the Nursing Standards office in Health Services, a nurse with over 25 years in state mental and other hospital experience was made Nursing Standards Specialist. She was placed in charge of nurses who had more formal education but less experience. This supervising nurse developed training manuals and training experiences on policies and procedures for dealing with nursing and medical emergencies. Her program, with minor modifications, has stood the test of time. For example, she established a mandatory inservice program of cardiopulmonary resuscitation and training in the Heimlich Maneuver for all direct care personnel. Workshops are conducted by Nursing Standards at least every four months, and mock emergency situations are enacted on individual units to allow practice in response time and team organization, and to reinforce efficient resuscitation measures. This preparation of staff has prevented several critical choking incidents from becoming fatal.

Many MHWs and psychoeducators initially resisted attending CPR and Heimlich maneuver training. But a facility that treats 50–70 elderly mental patients every day will experience an occasional cardiac, pulmonary, or other emergency; younger chronically ill mental patients also will occasionally require resuscitation following suicidal attempts by hanging or asphyxiation. After one or two such crises, where staff were called upon to utilize their emergency skills, staff attitude changed. New staff began attending courses willingly; veterans requested a refresher; psychoeducational professionals no longer resisted sending their staff off the unit to attend class.

EVALUATION

Previous chapters have shown that modular psychoeducational treatment was more than three times as effective as traditional treatment in successfully deinstitutionalizing and reducing rehospitalization of elderly patients; peer management and support in the community network development, along with skill building in residential treatment, reduced adult patients' total number of days of rehospitalization by two-thirds, and hours of outpatient psychiatric treatment by four-fifths as compared to a control group who did not receive peer support in the CND. These were full-scale treatment programs. They were carried out by a state hospital staff who also spent over half their time conducting research, evaluation, training, and dissemination. All these innovations and other accomplishments depended upon a matrix management structure. Matrix management welded together the efforts of professionals and paraprofessionals of a variety of different backgrounds, disciplines, and levels of training in the conduct of these services and evaluations.

Morale of Physicians

The matrix structure produced higher morale among the facility's physicians. Prior to its introduction, 7 of 10 physicians left their positions at the center in a period of less than two years, most of them in an angry mood at being ordered around by nonmedical personnel. During this period no American-born and trained physicians could be recruited to work at the R&T center. Subsequently, after more than two years of matrix management, only 2 of 8 physicians left work at the center, one to enter psychiatric residency and the other to retire from medical practice. Many American-born and educated physicians applied, and five were employed in the period.

Productivity

One board-certified psychiatrist and a cadre of four psychologists established and supervised the service programs described here during a four-year period from 1975 through 1979. Utilizing a traditional state mental hospital staff, which included three Spanish language physicians born and educated in Latin America, and 266 additional service personnel (25% professionals and 75% paraprofessionals), they treated up to 371 patients daily and 972 patients annually. (Three additional physicians joined the rolls of the facility in 1979 when the residential treatment programs for children were expanded.) The mean salary for all patient-service personnel was approximately $10,500 per year.

The daily patient-to-physician ratio of 371/6 (62:1) compares favorably to that at the two state mental hospitals that do not treat forensic patients (whose length of stay is determined in part by the courts). In them, 2282 patients were treated by 42 physicians in 1977–1978 (a ratio of 54:1).

Annual patient turnover was over twice as large (375% to 170% per annum) as that at the state's other public mental hospitals, where patients were treated by traditional methods. Comparing efforts at the R&T center in 1977–1978 with those at the other state mental hospitals as a group, and using the ratio of patients treated per year divided by numbers of staff as a measure of efficiency, the following numbers were obtained: All the state hospitals as a group—2.02; R&T facility—3.25.

In addition to carrying out this clinical treatment of comparatively more patients each year, the R&T center staff also conducted the evaluative research reported here. Moreover, staff offered 55,355 contact hours of statewide training in the fiscal year 1978–1979 to professional, paraprofessional, and other trainees from agencies, colleges, and the community. This level of educational effort is equivalent to providing 154 college students with full-time classroom training for an entire academic year.

DISCUSSION AND CONCLUSIONS

The Harvard Case Report[16] describes services in the public mental hospital and other institutions in the state that are performing under traditional or multidisciplinary team management with a nonmedical unit director or manager. The physicians in these other institutions have the same national and educational backgrounds as those at the R&T facility. They receive the same pay and carry the same patient workloads.

The Case Report looked at one public mental hospital that treats roughly 1000 mentally ill and 80 retarded patients with a staff of 39 psychiatrists:

In 1977 one patient was murdered by three others and three forensic patients raped a school teacher. In 1978, the . . . Sheriff's Department investigated 121 assaults and sexual offenses at the hospital, and in 1979 a County grand jury concluded that the hospital was a "warehouse for the mentally ill," where it was not infrequent for staff members to have sexual relations with mental patients. Of the 39 psychiatrists . . . thirty-four were foreign-born and had severe communication problems. The psychiatrists, who were paid about one-third of what private psychiatrists would be paid, had a workload 3 to 4 times the average workload in a private hospital—each psychiatrist seeing 60 patients, each patient receiving perhaps five minutes of care every other week. . . . Everyone . . . passed responsibility for the state of the institution elsewhere: the director of the hospital deferred to the district administration, who deferred to the Assistant Secretary of Operations, who deferred to the . . . Secretary, who deferred to the Governor, who passed responsibility to the legislature . . . who blamed the judges for placing too many patients in the institution, and so on. As Jack Greener, the hospital's formal clinical director and mental health program supervisor, sarcastically explained, "It's a great system. You can't finger anybody." Dr. James Diodato, former Superintendent . . . commented in a similar vein, "Who's responsible? I don't know who's responsible, and I work here. There are too many layers." (pp. 12, 13).

The Case Report also describes incidents in other institutions. "A horrifying murder . . . resulting from an unsupervised patient (with a history of violence) bludgeoning a profoundly retarded patient to death with a milk crate . . . might have been avoided if 'standard operating procedures' were followed" (p. 30).

Such situations need not prevail. The next chapter describes the changes made in another state mental hospital where an experienced, competent psychiatrist, like those quoted in the above report, was placed in full charge of psychiatric care and held accountable for the medical and medico-legal performance of the doctors and nurses in her charge. Skilled psychoeducators were recruited to implement a full-scale rehabilitative program like that at the R&T facility; they were held responsible for assessing patients' skill deficits and proficiencies, and for supervising the psychoeducational program. Capable bridge persons, drawn largely from the cadre of many excellent nurses and psychoeducators in the institution, managed and coordinated the joint medical treatment and psychosocial rehabilitation programs. Paraprofessionals, many of whom were receiving training in a community college educational course described in the next chapter, provided the bulk of the seven-days-a-week, 8–12 hours-a-day classroom, group, and individual treatments, using the programs described in the chapters of this book.

Everyone was accountable for conducting his piece of the action skillfully. Everyone's performance was continually measured and assessed. No one could pass the buck in his area of competency and responsibility.

Professionals at the institutions backed up the paraprofessionals in the matrix system. Professional societies helped plan, approve, monitor, and improve their own special areas of treatment; through their continuing education programs they updated the competencies of their members.

Matrix management is useful in mental health facilities during periods when they are undergoing rapid change. It provides a structure that promotes innovation yet maintains stability: Regular meetings and close communication between the medical and psychoeducational professionals regarding patient treatment and other issues foster interdisciplinary creativity; continued supervision of sensitive legal areas by experienced nurses and physicians helps protect patients, staff, and facility. There is none of the role diffusion and confusion that is often generated when hospitals are unitized and professionals placed in multidisciplinary teams without experienced health professionals in leadership positions.

A committee of senior officers of the Council of District Branches of the American Psychiatric Association in Florida have studied the matrix organization system developed by the R&T center and compared it to the traditional multidisciplinary team structure, which places mental health professionals under the direction of nonmedical unit managers. After careful study they gave matrix organization their unqualified endorsement. The Council at its next meeting opted to recommend its adoption and implementation in all the state's mental institutions. Some of the hospitals have begun to do so.

Organizational specialists do not recommend continuing a matrix organization indefinitely. Once medical and nursing personnel are fully familiar with psychobehavioral and peer management techniques, and psychoeducational professionals are experienced in avoiding medico-legal hassles, the matrix organization can probably be discontinued in treatment facilities where innovation and creativity are not primary goals.

Automated Multiphasic Health Testing and Services, Medical Manpower Shortages, and Matrix Management

The first paragraphs of this chapter mentioned multiphasic health testing services (AMHTS). With shortages of medical manpower in the public mental health sector, it may be feasible to take another look at its place under matrix management in the psychiatric scheme. AMHTS increases the reach of the psychiatrist, so that a larger number of persons receive a better level of care; it increases the productivity of the physician, increases the economic efficiency of health care services, and increases the overall quality of health care services.[1]

The following tests are performed: (1) general history, including a psychological evaluation; (2) glucose challenge test; (3) chest X-ray; (4) anthropometry; (5) urinalysis; (6) electrocardiogram; (7) blood pressure; (8) cervical Pap smear; (9) audiometry; (10) spirometry; (11) visual tests; (12) blood chemical profile; (13) hematology; and (14) dental panograph.

Appropriate uses include health appraisal, disease detection, diagnostic adjuncts, patient surveillance, and adjuncts to patient management. Industry is now using traveling AMHTS units to screen large numbers of employees in high-risk jobs, where their work exposes them to the effects of toxic substances. Psychiatry can do likewise, since psychiatric patients are also likely to have or develop physical disorders. Further, periodic health assessment of mental patients can be conducted by this technique, which selects out patients for further more detailed examination. Research has pointed to the potential utility of these approaches.[2-3]

REFERENCES

1. Gordon RE: Psychiatric screening through multiphasic health testing. Am J Psychiatry 128:51–55, 1971
2. Gordon RE, Bielen L, Watts AM: Psychiatric screening utilizing automated multiphasic health testing in the VA admission procedure. Am J Psychiatry 130:46–48, 1973
3. Gordon RE, Holzer C, Bielen L, et al: AMHTS and the VA admission procedure, in Davies DF (Ed): Health Evaluation. New York, Intercontinental Medical Book Corp., 1973
4. Gordon RE: The psychiatric emergency, good intentions vs good sense. Consultant 1:34–38, 1962
5. Anderson WH, Kuehnle JC: Strategies for the treatment of acute psychosis. JAMA 229:1884–1889, 1974
6. Hall, CW, Popkin MK, Devaul RA, et al: Physical illness presenting as psychiatric disease. Arc Gen Psychiatry 34:1315–1320, 1978
7. Doyle BB: Psychiatrists in varied settings: Toward the 80's. Syllabus and Scientific Proceedings. 132nd Annual Meeting, APA, 1979
8. Shull FA, Jr.: Matrix structure and project authority for optimizing organizational capacity. Business Monograph No. 1, Business Research Bureau, Carbondale, Ill., Southern Illinois University, 1965
9. Galbraith JP: Matrix organization designs. Business Horizons, 14:29–48, 1971
10. Kiger RS: Adopting the unit plan: I. Processes. Hosp Community Psychiatry 17:207–210, 1966
11. Filley AC, House RJ, Kerr S: Managerial Process and Organizational Behavior. Glenview, Ill., Scott, Foresman and Company, 1976
12. Heninger OP: Adopting the unit plan: II. Perspectives. Hosp Community Psychiatry 17:211–212, 1966
13. Lewis JM: The organizational structure of the therapeutic team. Hosp Community Psychiatry 20:206–208, 1969
14. Bassuk EL, Gerson S: Deinstitutionalization and mental health services. Sci Am 238:46–53, 1978
15. Raskin DE: Staff work dysfunction in a mental health setting: Symptoms and solutions. Hosp Community Psychiatry 26:455–456, 1975
16. Whitman D: Reorganization of Florida's Human Services Agency. Kennedy School of Government Case Program, C95-80-040. Cambridge, Mass., Harvard University, 1980
17. Greenblatt M: Psychopolitics. New York, Grune and Stratton, 1978

Katherine K. Gordon, Arthur L. Slater
Shirley Redcay, Richard E. Gordon

10
Educating and Training Manpower for the Mental Health System

"Not only do I think it's a bad idea for persons with less than a master's degree to move up the career ladder, but I would fight them at every step." So stated a social worker in a large mental health center. Another was less angry: "Why go to college and graduate school for six years, if a high school dropout can do my job?" A psychiatrist was adamant: "I am totally opposed to antiprofessionalism!" These comments were obtained early in 1976 from a study of role and task differences of paraprofessional mental health workers (MHWs), their duties, aspirations, and morale, as well as the attitudes of professional staff toward them.[1]

This study was conducted to determine what roles MHWs were capable of filling in mental health settings. With limited budgets to concentrate on the task of retraining both mental hospital staffs and patients for life and work in the community, it is important to learn what services MHWs can

Portions of this chapter have been condensed from the following previously published materials, with permission:

Slater AL, Gordon KK: Developing a curriculum for human service workers. Career education for mental health workers project. Report No. 6. Tampa, Fla., University of South Florida, 1979.

Slater AL, Gordon KK, Redcay S: Final evaluation report. Career education for mental health workers project, Human Resources Institute. Tampa, Fla., University of South Florida, 1979.

Slater AL, Gordon KK, Redcay S: Human services instructional series (1–8). Tampa, Fla., University of South Florida, 1979.

Slater AL, Gordon KK, Gordon RE: Role differences of mental health workers. Observations of four sites, in Nash KB, Lifton N, Smith SE (Eds): The Paraprofessional: Selected Readings: The Yale Monograph on Paraprofessionalism. New Haven, Conn., Advocate Press, Inc., 1978, pp 3–11.

perform in hospital and community settings, and what training is needed to prepare current and new employees to perform these tasks. This chapter will review the findings of this study, and describe the training program for employees, patients, students, parents, supervisors, and others, based, in part, on its conclusions. It will describe the community college curriculum that was developed for training employees currently working at public mental hospitals.

Traditional professionals are too expensive and too few in number to provide individual therapy for all of those in need. Rusk[2] has forecast that "paraprofessionals will be the general practitioners of the mental health field," and has predicted that professionals will assume new roles as supervisors, consultants, and systems managers. Alley and Blanton[3] have noted that,

Today, about 30 percent of direct community mental health services are provided by paraprofessional staff members, and in some agencies as much as 80 percent of services come from paraprofessionals. This importance is not confined to the sheer weight of their numbers. Paraprofessionals have been crucial to the provision of new and innovative services, which are usually not provided by the traditional professionals.

It is obvious that one way to improve the quality of mental health service delivery is to upgrade the skills and knowledge, the competencies, of the large paraprofessional manpower pool.

Role and Task Differences of Mental Health Workers

Two graduate students in medical anthropology conducted participant observations at four sites, focusing on the following objectives:

1. Determine positions of staff, their different tasks, patterns of work, and associated constraints.
2. Study interaction patterns among staff.
3. Examine why certain patterns of staff utilization, interaction, and constraint exist.
4. Investigate differences in ideology, stated goals, and actual work performed.
5. Learn what staff believes can be done to improve delivery of mental health services.

A state mental hospital was the largest facility studied. Geographically isolated from any major population center, it provides care for about 1200 patients. Its psychiatric aides mostly provide custodial care to patients, following well-established rules and procedures. They feed and bathe patients, escort them to activities, administer oral medications, observe and report behavior and vital signs, make beds, clean the wards, and perform other house-keeping chores. They participate in planned patient treatments only to the extent of occasionally assisting in recording observations of patients, reporting to the nurse in charge who screens and passes on information to the appropriate patient therapist. Charge aides perform the same tasks, but also supervise other aides. All aides are supervised by higher level employees, usually nurses. Aides usually have some high school education, although not all have graduated. They express only the desire for training as Registered Nurses or Licensed Practical Nurses, reflecting the state hospital's orientation, which stresses nursing the ill.

The second site was a large urban center located in a city of 500,000 people, providing all the essential services of a comprehensive community mental health center. Its MHWs do not carry their own caseloads or provide therapy. Primarily they gather information, update forms and charts, prepare prescription and appointment cards, contact absent group members, and close case charts. Both paraprofessionals and professionals feel that supervision is insufficient. The MHWs often feel they are criticized for not being able to handle situations for which they were never properly trained or prepared.

At the urban center the MHW usually has a baccalaureate degree in one of the social sciences. These workers are career-oriented and want to advance in salary, responsibility, and professional status, usually toward a master's degree in social work. The heavy emphasis on professionalism at the urban center leads to the MHWs perceiving themselves as "second class" subprofessionals. The professionals emphasize that the only persons who can assume any real treatment responsibility are those educated to the master's level.

The third study site was a small satellite clinic to the urban center, and the fourth site was a small rural clinic. Due to similarities in the findings, the urban satellite and the fourth site will be discussed together to avoid repetition. Although they infrequently hold administrative positions, MHWs in both the urban satellite and the rural clinic have similar duties to those of professionals. In handling their own caseloads, they perform group, individual, and family counseling. They evaluate walk-in and crisis clients, prepare treatment plans that are submitted for approval to the program coordinator, attend staff meetings, and represent their clinics by speaking to various community groups. The cases assigned to the MHWs are typically aftercare and crisis clients, often requiring visits to the homes of those who cannot come into the clinic. The MHWs are free to schedule their work day around home visits and other out-of-office duties, planning their own hours with the same understanding many professionals have that a forty-hour work week is the minimal expectation.

The MHWs schedule weekly supervisory sessions with their director or program coordinator. The director at the rural clinic stated, "Supervision allows the paraprofessionals to develop their independent capabilities, yet leads to their appreciation for and acceptance of help from professionals with more extensive training and experience." All of the MHWs at the small clinics have had some college education, and several have continued working toward a baccalaureate degree. MHWs at both sites do responsible work, and enjoy the respect of their professional colleagues.

Contrasting Attitudes

In general, the attitudes of MHWs tend to reflect the attitudes of professionals toward them at the different sites studied. At all of the sites, administrative positions tended to be filled by males, and MHW positions tended to be filled by females. Professionals feel that MHWs, particularly the indigenous ones, are best able to empathize with lower-class clients; however, the professionals' fear of being replaced by less highly trained persons is not totally absent in any of these settings.

The overriding attitude at the urban center was one of bitterness about the professional-nonprofessional relationship. The MHWs sense their second-class status and are antagonized by it. They feel they can do the work of professionals and are frustrated because either they are not allowed to do so, or on occasion, when they do take over some professional duties, they are not paid accordingly. The MHWs' lack of self-confidence is also a problem in the urban center. Even though they say they want more responsibility, they may shy away from it when it is offered.

At the state mental hospital, roles and hierarchies are so well-established and so clearly defined that ambition for advancement through any channel except years of experience is not likely. Aides might aspire to join the nursing staff, but this goal can be accomplished only by resigning to obtain full-time Registered Nurse or Licensed Practical Nurse training, which is usually financially impossible. The aides do not even consider taking on duties of case management, treatment planning, and counseling. They are viewed by themselves and others as qualified for only a narrow range of routine custodial-care duties.

Motivation and morale are highest at the urban satellite and the rural clinic. There is an "esprit de corps" rather than a feeling of rigid hierarchy of professionals and nonprofessionals. The directors are confident that MHWs can adequately perform most of the tasks that need to be done at the community mental health clinics, including having full responsibility for a selective case load. The MHWs generally enjoy the use of supervision as a tool that does not leave them feeling as if someone is always looking over their shoulders. Satisfaction with mental health work is evident. All are willing to work long hours and do not abuse their self-set time schedules.

In both of the smaller clinics, good working relationships and extra-office social interaction occur, although residential propinquity and similarity in age, race, personal interests, and church affiliation promote the closest social interaction. In clinical settings where clients come from the surrounding community, indigenous workers express a loyalty to, and concern for their community.

Comment

In observing and contrasting the roles and scope of tasks performed by MHWs, it becomes clear they can deliver many therapeutic services effectively. Smaller scale seems to promote a common sense of purpose in these mental health settings. Mutual recognition of individual ability seems to be another important aspect of working collaboratively and cooperatively.[4] When essential role and task configurations are in keeping with worker competencies, harmony in the workplace and higher productivity are evident. But, when roles and tasks are zealously protected by sophisticates who do not, or will not, recognize ability, harmony and productivity often decline.

The attitudes of professional staff in supervisory positions appear to be one of the most important factors in determining whether MHWs will be encouraged, trained, and supervised to become competent and self-confident in carrying out treatment responsibilities. Education should be directed toward earning a recognized academic degree that will be accepted throughout the health delivery system. Credit hours in a degree program usually are transferable, but hours of orientation and workshop attendance do not necessarily transfer from one job to another.

If MHWs are actively supported in learning to develop skills and to improve their competence, their self-confidence grows, especially when they receive recognition by promotion, and guidance and respect from mental health professionals. Supervisors, too, need training to effectively manage MHWs who have acquired therapeutic skills. Finding that MHWs can and do conduct counseling and carry their own caseloads in settings where they receive professional staff support for doing so, we felt confident in training MHWs, as well as nurses and other employees, in the behavioral principles and competencies needed for conducting treatment and other human services.

The following sections describe a collaboration for upgrading the skills and knowledge of service delivery personnel in the mental health system. This competency-based modular curriculum in human services, which is delivered for academic credit by community colleges to paraprofessional workers at public mental hospitals, can also be used for training other human service workers. The curriculum we developed has been distributed across the country and is available through the Educational Resources Information Center (ERIC) microfilm system (ED 176 098-104).

Our program for training paraprofessionals in human services, described below, serves as one example of the modular approach to training. New employees who are college students or graduates with major areas of specialization in the social and behavioral sciences may require only an inservice training course in behavior management in addition to basic training in medical-nursing care. State hospital MHWs, however, many of whom terminated their formal education in high school, require both basic higher education as well as more extensive training in specific psychosocial rehabilitative competencies.

ASSESSMENT OF EDUCATIONAL NEEDS FOR IMPROVING MENTAL HEALTH SERVICE DELIVERY

We chose to focus the instructional design to meet hospital and community service objectives rather than on work analysis that would reinforce the status quo. A comprehensive list of state supported service programs in each mental health district was compiled from annual plan information. Programs were stratified according to several factors, such as population characteristics of the area, range of services offered, and specialized units. Semistructured interviews were conducted with 43 persons responsible for managing direct service programs to obtain the objectives of each program. The lists of objectives were refined to eliminate duplication, producing 20 service-related statements of program objectives. Five of the objectives were common to the greatest number of mental health service areas: Develop psychosocial evaluations, devise treatment plans, manage and monitor treatment episodes, provide linkage to service resources, and provide psychosocial treatment according to treatment plans. Instructional analysis revealed the need to include a sixth objective: Provide health assessment. These six service objectives were synthesized to produce the overall terminal skill for a human service student in educational programs at the community college level: Develop and implement comprehensive, individualized treatment plans under supervision.

INSTRUCTIONAL DESIGN

Our staff used the systematic instructional design approach developed by Dick and Carey.[5] The major elements in their systems approach model are: (1) identify the instructional goal, 2) analyze instructional content and sequence, (3) identify entry behaviors and characteristics, (4) write behavioral objectives, (5) develop tests, (6) develop the instructional strategy, (7) develop instructional procedures, (8) evaluate, and (9) revise as required.

Gagne and Briggs'[6] hierarchical instructional analysis principles were used to analyze major content areas and suggest instructional sequences. This approach suggests listing instructional goals derived from necessary tasks or functions and then systematically identifying relevant subordinate skills and knowledge. This process produced a hierarchy of the skills and knowledge required for a typical student to become competent in the indicated performance. This approach has several advantages, including: sub-competencies

Table 10-1

Overall instructional design for the competency-based human service modules and human development as originally planned.

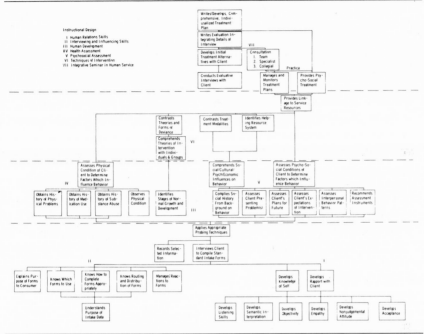

The two introductory level modules, Human Relations Skills and Interviewing and Influencing Skills, prepare the student for the second level Health and Psychosocial Assessment Modules. These, in turn, along with Human Development, set the stage for Techniques of Intervention. The Integrative Seminar in Human Service is the highest level module in the hierarchy.

are clustered to maximize the efficiency of the curriculum, objectives are formulated directly from the hierarchy, and the process lends itself to planning a career-oriented curriculum. Table 10-1 presents the instructional design, as originally conceptualized, for the human service components of the curriculum. The most elementary objectives appear at the bottom of the hierarchy.[7,8]

Competency-Based Module Development

Each of the human service modules is based on learning objectives formulated from the hierarchy identified during instructional analysis. The module goals incorporate the most commonly mentioned service objectives. Each module contains a statement of the goal and seven sections, similar to those described previously for psychoeducational treatment modules: (1) list of behavioral objectives, (2) instructional design, (3) pre-test on module goal, (4) list of materials for the course, (5) instructional procedures for each behavioral objective (including assessment of competency), (6) post-test on module goal, and (7) feedback.

The curriculum emphasizes performance assessment of important competencies rather than rote memorization. This approach recognizes that adult students bring valuable life experience to the learning situation, and encourages the student to be less instructor-dependent and more self-directed. Students are encouraged to learn from each other rather than compete, as each student must be able to reach predetermined performance standards.[7,8]

Curriculum planning must consider necessary content, the characteristics of the target population, college requirements, the instructional environment, and the availability of materials, personnel, facilities, and equipment. Only then can the behavioral objectives, which are the guidelines for developing instruction, be stated for each module. The objectives provide a clear description of what students will learn; they are stated in terms of expected performance. This assumes that knowledge and skills acquired in the learning situation must be translated into competent on-the-job performance in order to improve service to clients.

Each student receives a copy of the module, which outlines all readings, assignments, procedures, and requirements. The students go through the instructional procedures until they can demonstrate competence. Once all behavioral objectives of the module have been met, the student is ready for the post-test, a final assessment of competence in meeting the goal of the module. Feedback from students and instructors is used to improve and update the module as a continuing process (see Fig. B-2).

COMPONENTS OF THE HUMAN SERVICE CURRICULUM

Six competency based modules and four existing community college courses are the major components of this human service curriculum. They provide 32 semester hour credits, and may terminate with a Certificate in Human Service. These credits also may apply toward community college associate degrees if students wish to continue their education. The six modules also can be used for noncredit, inservice, or other educational programs.[9]

The sequential offering of five of the human service modules is recommended. Each of these modules builds upon the knowledge and skills learned in preceding modules. The objectives require increased integration of knowledge and skills as students proceed through the learning hierarchy. The remaining courses are more independent of sequence, although English I precedes English II. Modules were not developed for the four existing community college courses. Currently this human service curriculum is offered in a part-time 5-semester sequence, because the majority of students are public hospital employees who work full time while enrolled.

A brief description of the human service modules and community college courses follows. Compare the content of each course as it finally developed with that shown in Table 10-1 when it was initially conceptualized.

Human Service Modules

Human Relations Skills (3 credits). The focus of this interpersonal skills training seminar is for the student to learn basic communication skills and interpersonal response styles. The student practices techniques of active listening and congruent responding. The use of these skills to develop rapport with clients and to conduct the interview process is stressed (see Table 10-2).

Interviewing and Influencing Skills (3 credits). Basic elements of interviewing, probing techniques, and recording, as practiced in human service programs, are taught. Students conduct a variety of interviews, and receive feedback through videotaped replays and personal interaction (see Table 10-3).

Psychosocial Assessment (3 credits). The student learns to assess psychosocial conditions to determine factors that influence behavior. Skills for the compilation of a social history, presenting problem, and expectations for intervention are taught. Assessment of strengths and weaknesses in interper-

Table 10-2
Instructional design for human relations skills.

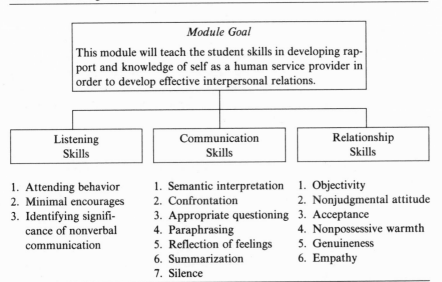

Module Goal
This module will teach the student skills in developing rapport and knowledge of self as a human service provider in order to develop effective interpersonal relations.

Listening Skills	Communication Skills	Relationship Skills
1. Attending behavior	1. Semantic interpretation	1. Objectivity
2. Minimal encourages	2. Confrontation	2. Nonjudgmental attitude
3. Identifying significance of nonverbal communication	3. Appropriate questioning	3. Acceptance
	4. Paraphrasing	4. Nonpossessive warmth
	5. Reflection of feelings	5. Genuineness
	6. Summarization	6. Empathy
	7. Silence	

Table 10-3
Instructional design for interviewing and influencing skills

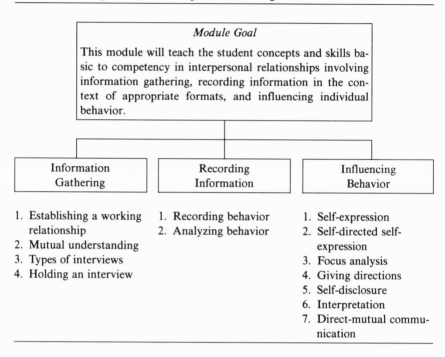

> *Module Goal*
> This module will teach the student concepts and skills basic to competency in interpersonal relationships involving information gathering, recording information in the context of appropriate formats, and influencing individual behavior.

Information Gathering	Recording Information	Influencing Behavior
1. Establishing a working relationship 2. Mutual understanding 3. Types of interviews 4. Holding an interview	1. Recording behavior 2. Analyzing behavior	1. Self-expression 2. Self-directed self-expression 3. Focus analysis 4. Giving directions 5. Self-disclosure 6. Interpretation 7. Direct-mutual communication

sonal behavior through observation, personal interaction, or various types of tests and measures are considered (see Table 10-4).

Techniques of Intervention (4 credits).   Major theories and techniques of intervention are taught, various treatment modalities are contrasted, and factors influencing the decision to use each are discussed. Helping resource systems are identified. Laboratory experience focuses on developing and leading a small group, treatment/rehabilitation plan under individual supervision (see Table 10-5 and Appendix 2).

Integrative Seminar in Human Service (4 credits).   This is a final course for Human Service majors, taken by permission of the instructor only. The student learns to integrate previously acquired skills into a process of developing treatment alternatives with the client. The types and uses of consultation in the managing and monitoring of treatment plans are covered. The student learns to make appropriate referrals, and develops skills in dealing with the community system. Laboratory experience focuses on developing and implementing individualized treatment/rehabilitation plans under team supervision (see Appendix B).

Table 10-4
Instructional design for psychosocial assessment

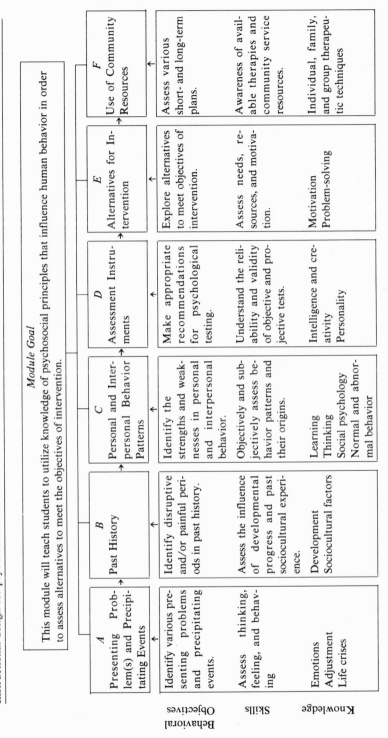

Module Goal

This module will teach students to utilize knowledge of psychosocial principles that influence human behavior in order to assess alternatives to meet the objectives of intervention.

	A Presenting Problem(s) and Precipitating Events	B Past History	C Personal and Interpersonal Behavior Patterns	D Assessment Instruments	E Alternatives for Intervention	F Use of Community Resources
Behavioral Objectives	Identify various presenting problems and precipitating events.	Identify disruptive and/or painful periods in past history.	Identify the strengths and weaknesses in personal and interpersonal behavior.	Make appropriate recommendations for psychological testing.	Explore alternatives to meet objectives of intervention.	Assess various short- and long-term plans.
Skills	Assess thinking, feeling, and behaving	Assess the influence of developmental progress and past sociocultural experience.	Objectively and subjectively assess behavior patterns and their origins.	Understand the reliability and validity of objective and projective tests.	Assess needs, resources, and motivation.	Awareness of available therapies and community service resources.
Knowledge	Emotions Adjustment Life crises	Development Sociocultural factors	Learning Thinking Social psychology Normal and abnormal behavior	Intelligence and creativity Personality	Motivation Problem-solving	Individual, family, and group therapeutic techniques

179

Table 10-5
Techniques of intervention

Module Goal

The student will be able to utilize social service delivery systems and the basic concepts of a variety of intervention techniques. In an experiential laboratory the student will plan and implement an eight-week group experience for a small group of clients/patients.

Behavioral Objectives

- Applies theories and constructs from the various intervention modalities
- Identifies resources and can use the referral process
- Designs, implements, and monitors a structured intervention for a small group

Knowledge Base

- Comprehends theories and techniques of group intervention
- Comprehends theories and techniques of Client-Centered Counseling and Rational-Emotive Therapy
- Comprehends theories and techniques of behavior modification
- Comprehends theories and techniques of family intervention
- Comprehend theories and techniques of crisis intervention

Health Assessment (3 credits). The student learns to assess health factors that may influence behavior. Observation as well as interview skills are stressed. Effects of typical medications and substances are considered. The student learns to recognize signs and symptoms that indicate the need for nursing or medical consultation.

Community College Courses

English I (3 credits). This course helps the student build and strengthen basic skills in written communication. Emphasis is on effective and logical expression.

English II (3 credits). Intensive study of the mechanics of composition emphasizes clear and concise expression of ideas.

Speech (3 credits). Students study the principles and methods of oral communication through speaking and listening.

Human Development (3 credits). Students examine the development of individuals as they move through the various stages of the life cycle from conception until death. Attention is given to the physiological and psychosocial changes that occur. Identification of major needs of individuals at different stages of the life cycle is stressed.

Comment on the Human Service Curriculum

The introductory level modules, "Human Relations Skills" and "Interviewing and Influencing Skills," are based on videotapes and participant manuals developed by Ivey and Gluckstern.[10,11] These teach basic skills in communications and counseling. The Ivey materials were chosen because their behavioral objectives are clearly stated, specific competencies are delineated, and videotapes are utilized to present models and to critique student skill performance.

The second level module, "Psychosocial Assessment," presents general psychological concepts such as learning theory, personality development, social psychology, etc. Students are introduced to the beginning application of these concepts in performing an initial psychosocial assessment. In order to perform effectively, the student uses the skills learned in the preceding two modules.

The third level module, "Techniques of Intervention," presents the major theories and techniques of intervention, with special emphasis on small group approaches. Service resources in the community and procedures for referral are identified. The upper level module in the sequence, "Integrative Seminar in Human Service," helps the student to integrate previously learned knowledge and skills in the process of assessing individual need, developing treatment alternatives, and implementing individualized treatment plans. Students learn appropriate use of supervision, consultation, and service resources. The laboratory experiences of both these upper level modules focus on the development and implementation of treatment plans under both individual and team supervision (see Appendix B).

The module, "Health Assessment," presents knowledge of personal and social health issues as a basis for recognition of symptoms that indicate the need for referral of an individual for nursing or medical consultation. "Human Development," an existing community college course, is introduced early in the curriculum sequence to provide understanding of normal human growth and development as background for identifying deviations. This course covers the entire life span at this introductory level to provide an overall perspective. English I and II and Speech develop essential communication skills. Reading, writing, and composition are necessary skills directly applicable to keeping records and preparing reports in the work situation. Effective verbal expression is also necessary for communication.

This human service curriculum prepares workers to meet service needs such as predischarge preparation of patients, outreach, aftercare, community residential service, and case management.[3] Utilized in isolation from broader manpower development goals, this curriculum can help the individual human service worker in personal development and self-esteem. Its major impact on the delivery of human services is likely to be seriously diminished, however, unless it is part of a comprehensive services and manpower plan. This curriculum equips workers with the competencies to deliver human services, but it requires administrative support and direction if the workers are to be utilized effectively. Professionals who serve in supervisory capacities need to learn to manage human service workers in ways that fully utilize newly acquired competence.

BEHAVIOR MANAGEMENT MODULES

New employees, professionals, MHWs who are being educated in the human service curriculum, parents of child patients, and trainees attending dissemination workshops also receive modularized training in behavior management and skill building. These students are taught the specific modular components of each program area by the staff of the adult, children's, and gerontology programs in separate workshops and courses; but all follow the same modular format, and teach certain basic general principles. Students in each program area learn techniques for treating patients with specific modular components (e.g., listening skills, or self-medication, assertion, problem solving, etc.)[12,13]

These modules present the basic principles and techniques of behavior management for parents of child patients, employees, and students—both those students in academic programs and currently employed personnel who are receiving continuing education. The curriculum provides the trainees with the competencies needed to assist patients in developing, redeveloping, and increasing those adaptive behaviors that ensure them a better quality of life and improve the probabilty of their living in the community successfully. They also teach staff and families techniques for decreasing maladaptive behaviors that result in patients being rejected by society and expelled from community organizations (schools, foster homes, etc.), and being placed in institutions. The curriculum is divided into three parts:

1. *Behavior Management I* emphasizes basic definitions and principles of behavior management: principles of learning; behavior observation; assessment, data collection, and plotting on graphs; behavior analysis; the behavioral approach to treatment, principles of positive reinforcement; and escape and avoidance training.

2. *Behavior Management II* teaches various behavioral training and treatment techniques: prompting; establishing new behaviors by rehearsal, shaping, chaining, backward chaining, and modeling; increasing the occurrence of appropriate behaviors; token programs; as well as techniques to decrease the incidence of inappropriate behavior. Upon completion, the participants have acquired the basic knowledge and skills needed to participate in behavioral treatment programs.

3. *Behavior Management III* teaches different skill and support-building techniques to each project's specific group of families or employees. Staff working with the elderly, for example, learn to use the modules needed by their patients, while those managing the client networks learn about peer management and support procedures. Upon completion, parents know how to reinforce their children's behavior in the home and community, and how to decelerate inappropriate behaviors. Also, staff have acquired the competencies to conduct specific components of programs of modular treatment where they are employed.

The courses are taught to MHWs and other trainees in modules with the same structure that the paraprofessionals and other personnel themselves use in treating and training patients. Each module in the Behavior Management sequence contains a clearly stated psychoeducational goal, behavioral objectives, a list of needed materials (such as readings, films and handouts), an instructional design, pretest, content and procedures, assessments to measure competency, and feedback. Thus, from their earliest experience on joining the treatment team, staff become familiar not only with the content but with the method of the modular psychoeducational approach.

Trainees receive handouts that include a behavioral analysis form with a description of how to use it; materials on plotting data on graphs; a series of exercises that trainees use for practicing what they have learned; a glossary of behavior management principles and techniques (which is included in the Appendix); and a listing of techniques for increasing, decreasing, and establishing behaviors.

EVALUATION OF MODULARIZED TRAINING

Community college instructors provided 8660 hours of career education classes at the state hospitals, and 640 employee-students spent 137,040 hours in accredited classes from 1976 through April, 1979.[8] In addition, 62 of the 87 nurses identified as filling supervisory roles in the state hospital system attended an 8-hour modular inservice training workshop on the Utilization of Trained Mental Health/Human Service Workers.[8,9] Continuing education credits were approved for nurse trainees attending this workshop.

Characteristics of Mental Health
Worker-Trainees

Comparing MHWs who remained in training with those who dropped out, interesting trends emerged. Persons with the following characteristics tended to remain in the program: blacks, more than whites; females, more than males; those with a greater amount of prior education; trainees who were the sole breadwinners in their household, more than trainees from households with more than one breadwinner; persons from households with lower incomes; single, separated, or divorced persons, more than married persons.[8] It appears from these findings that a combination of economic need for better positions and interest in education characterize the persisters.

Mental Health Worker Performance

Supervisors are critical gatekeepers in the public mental hospital. They determine what kind of work staff perform. They shape attitudes toward the organization and toward the work. Since many supervisors are nurses, and the education of nurses in public mental hospital systems is usually limited to a two-year nursing program, they often feel threatened by what a community college paraprofessional training program may do to their own status. A study of supervisors' attitudes was conducted at one hospital site to determine whether or not they considered that their subordinates benefited from academic training. Eighteen MHWs were rated by comparing their performance after training with the performance of fellow workers and with their own preeducation performance. The results are shown in Table 10-6. These positive findings of the benefits of career education are especially convincing. Despite the potential threat the nurses felt, they rated the performance of the 18 graduates in that hospital's program as significantly better than that of other MHWs under their supervision, and improved over their preeducation performance.[8]

Table 10-6
Supervisors' comparisons of employee-students performance after training with that of other supervisees and with their preeducational performance

	Comparison						
	With Other Supervisees				With Preeducational Performance		
Performance Area	Better	Same	Worse	Don't Know	Improved	Not Improved	Don't Know
1. In understanding patients	9	9	—	—	15	2	—
2. In maintaining objectivity	9	9	—	—	15	2	—
3. In demonstrating respect for patients	8	8	1	—	13	3	—
4. In maintaining flexibility	10	8	—	—	15	2	—
5. In utilizing treatment resources	8	10	—	—	14	3	—
6. In developing treatments	7	10	1	—	14	3	—
7. In dealing with patient's family	8	5	1	3	10	3	3
8. In consulting with supervisors	11	6	1	—	13	4	—
9. In writing various reports	10	5	—	3	12	3	2
10. In maintaining attendance	5	10	1	2	8	5	4
Totals	85	80	5	8	129	30	9

N = 18

Table 10-7
Ratings by students of the education they received

Question: Generally speaking, would you say the Human Services Program helped you in:

	Helped a great deal	Helped somewhat	Not very much help	No help at all
interacting with patients?	24	2	—	—
interacting with fellow workers?	22	3	1	—
working with supervisors?	19	2	2	3
dealing with yourself on the job?	23	3	—	—

Question: The following skills have been emphasized in introductory human service courses. How important are they to you in your daily interaction with patients?

	Very important	Somewhat important	Not very important	Not important at all
Listening skills: attending behavior, identifying important nonverbal cues, reinforcing patient self-expression with minimal encouragement.	23	3	—	—
Communication skills: semantic interpretation, use of appropriate questions, accurate paraphrasing.	21	5	—	—
Relationship skills: maintaining a non-judgmental attitude, displaying genuineness and empathy, maintaining an objective point of view with regard to patient problems.	23	3	—	—

Table 10-7 (continued)

Question: You studied the following topics in your human service coursework. How useful have you found these topics in your current job?

	Very useful	Somewhat useful	Not very useful	Not useful at all
Daily nutrition and a well-balanced diet	12	7	6	1
Major types of mental illness	23	2	—	—
The interrelationship between physical and mental health	21	5	—	—
The importance of psychotropic medication	17	6	3	—
Knowledge of the social service delivery systems in your community	13	4	4	5
Techniques of counseling	14	10	2	—
Techniques of behavior modification	18	7	1	—

Question: How would you rate the community college courses that are part of the Human Service program?

	Helped a great deal	Helped somewhat	Not very helpful	No help at all
English I and II	14	7	3	—
Speech	18	5	2	—
Human Development	23	3	—	—

Mental Health Worker Attitudes

The students themselves were very pleased with the education they received. Table 10-7 presents the ratings of 26 students at one training site of what they had learned in response to specific questions.

Unfortunately, change takes place slowly. At the time the students' assessments were taken in April, 1979, treatment at this public mental hospital where they were employed still focused primarily on traditional medical and

Table 10-8
Ratings by students concerning the application of what they learned

Now that you have earned your Human Service certificate, how often in your daily work have you had the opportunity to:

	Very often	Often	Not very often	Not at all
Conduct an evaluative interview?	5	2	8	10
Make appropriate recommendations for psychological testing?	1	2	2	20
Develop treatment alternatives for a patient in your care?	3	3	3	16
Consult with specialists concerning a patient's health or mental disposition?	7	2	5	11
Utilize team treatment?	6	—	2	16
Develop an individualized treatment plan?	5	1	4	15
Manage and monitor treatment plans?	6	4	2	13

custodial care. Further, no students had yet been promoted as a result of improving their competencies, although they have been subsequently. Table 10-8 presents students' responses to a question regarding their use of what they learned.

Follow-up Note

At another major mental hospital, the nearby community college began to provide paraprofessional education in May, 1978. By May, 1980, 35 employees had earned a one-year community college Mental Health Technologist certificate. Presently, 135 employees are enrolled in courses for the summer of 1980. Employee-students usually have taken two courses each semester, and have obtained their certificates in five semesters. They are receiving promotions upon completion of training. At least 15 of the first group of students are continuing to work for an Associate of Arts degree on their own time and at their own expense.

Original plans were to retrain all aides. Administrators now believe that the retraining program is appropriate for about half of their present staff. They realize that many custodial care duties (such as housekeeping, bed-patient care, and escorting) are essential. Those aides who cannot, or will not, be retrained will continue to perform these less technical chores. An important distinction has evolved between custodial care and psychosocial rehabilitation, and a realistic career step has been established for public mental hospital paraprofessional employees.

Statements of professional staff in 1980 contrast markedly with those expressed in 1976 and reported at the beginning of this chapter. A supervisor relates that before training one aide was "just carrying out her duties in a matter-of-fact way." Now "her skills, especially in communicating with both patients and staff, and her sensitivity, have increased twenty-fold. . . . It was the competence she gained in the classroom."

Another supervisor comments about the effects of the training: "People are coming out confident; they behave like professionals. Patients used to say, 'You don't know what you're talking about, you're just an aide!' No more. The patients now accept them as professionals." A psychiatrist asked professional team members to do case histories on the patients; he received no cooperation. He then asked an employee-student to do one; a superior product resulted.

Not all comments are positive, however. Some aides who have not obtained this education view the certificate holders as "uppity." There also is jealousy and antagonism "in practicums when students know more than their supervisors." An administrator captured the essence of the problem: "The supervisors on the units need to learn how to use these people." An answer, of course, is to implement innovative treatment programs, such as those developed at the research and training (R&T) facility. This is being done in a step-by-step manner. The gerontology program, for example, began to be disseminated to a section of the hospital in 1978; and mental health professionals and paraprofessionals there were trained, with the help of Title XX training funds, to conduct modular treatment.

IMPLEMENTING NEW PROGRAMS

An important test of the worth of a training program, or the value of a new treatment technique, or the success of an integrative effort between research, training, and treatment personnel in the mental health system is the ability of trainees to implement new treatments in their own setting. Helen Williams, M.D.,[14] Health Care Services Director at a state hospital, has reported on the successful dissemination of the R&T facility's modular skills-building gerontology program to the state hospital's New Directions Unit. This unit had been established two years previously to reorient to the community those chronically ill elderly mental patients who no longer needed hospitalization and active medical treatment for an acute phase of their mental disorder. Its overall purpose included lessening the shock of returning to the community after a long period of hospitalization.

The patients' average age was 71 years; their average length of stay in the mental hospital had been 24 years. Altogether, the 54-bed unit treated 135 patients in its first two years of existence. Thirty-five to 40 patients have been discharged each year. Only six have returned to the hospital in over two years of operation. Three have died in the community—of natural causes. Follow-up contacts with the former patients indicate that generally they are adjusting well to their community placements.

Prior to implementing the modular skill-enhancement treatment program, the hospital had identified a list of several hundred patients whose medical condition no longer required that they remain in residential treatment. A plan was developed to release at least 50 percent of these patients in six months. Six months went by; nobody had moved out of the institution. Consultation with R&T center personnel was initiated and training of hospital staff begun. Even after the modular program was introduced, staff remained skeptical. The first time several elderly patients were permitted to walk alone on the hospital grounds at night, for example, staff were alarmed. Later, when a group (as part of their training) was allowed to live independently in an apartment complex where many employees made their homes, the hospital staff themselves objected; they did not want patients residing in their neighborhood. Over time this attitude has completely changed. The patients have proved to be good neighbors. The other residents in the apartment complex now accept having them there.

The New Directions Program is satisfactorily fulfilling its original objective: It has already successfully discharged 40 percent of the patients referred for modular treatment. The average period of treatment has been six months. The difference in this hospital's achievement and that during the same time period of its sister institution, whose dismal performance was described in Chapter 9, may be attributed in part to the willingness of administration to provide modular skills-building treatment and train staff to implement it, to turn over medical direction to a perceptive physician—Dr. Williams, to place an experienced educator in charge of the psychoeducational curriculum, and to select skilled bridge persons—a blend of educators and nurses—to coordinate treatment and training in a matrix.

The curriculum itself not only trains patients in activities of daily living and other skills needed for life outside the institution, but also emphasizes self-assertiveness in coping with the legal and other problems that confront elderly persons living in the community.

One patient, who had been at the hospital for 46 years, was successfully placed in a group home in the community. Another, who had given birth to a son in the hospital 38 years previously, had always refused to acknowledge his existence. When she neared the end of her modular treatment program and was about to be discharged, her son was routinely notified of the hospital's release plans. He wrote back from out-of-state indicating that he would like to have her come live with him and his family. A gradual process was begun to acquaint the patient with her disavowed offspring, his wife, and their child. They exchanged pictures, telephone calls, and other communications; six months later the patient joined the family that she had denied for 38 years. Since her discharge she has become an integral member of her son's family.

A third patient had been admitted to the hospital six different times since 1965, and had been released for short periods of time to a succession of foster homes, boarding homes, and adult congregate living facilities. His home community refused to allow him to be placed there again because of the unpleasant experiences they had had with him. His difficulty in communicating, his paranoia, and his psychosomatic complaints made him an undesirable resident in the small community that he called "home." After 15 months of involvement in the New Directions Program's modular training, he was discharged to a community where he was unknown. After nine months he continued to make a satisfactory adjustment with the help of periodic crisis intervention locally.

DISCUSSION

Collaborations between Mental Health Research and Training (R&T) Centers and Academic Institutions

Treatment facilities and academic institutions participate as equal partners in training and education, dividing their responsibilities according to their primary roles. The academic institutions take the lead in teaching formal courses to matriculated students working toward degrees in academic programs; the treatment center assumes primary responsibility for upgrading the skills of currently employed professional and paraprofessional human service workers through continuing education. Treatment facilities sponsor applied research with the academic institutions: Treatment and management innovations, assessment measures, and effectiveness evaluations are developed and disseminated.

College and university faculty often work overtime or summers at the R&T facility to contribute to clinical research and training endeavors. Many R&T employees teach after hours; they teach college and university courses on the academic campus and supervise students in their field placements. Academic faculty are paid for performing clearly defined services at the R&T centers. Their performance is documented by written work products such as training manuals, research grants, and the publications that they author.

Dissemination

Dissemination is carried out in a variety of ways: (1) staff conduct biweekly workshops at the research and training center where they present successful components of the modular treatment program; (2) they provide monthly scheduled workshops in communities throughout the service delivery system; (3) they train matriculated students, as well as workers employed in the service delivery system, at the treatment facility; (4) they offer consultation at community facilities; (5) they assist in the development of formal academic teaching programs and may personally teach a course or section of a course; (6) they assist in the implementation of individual modules, components, or groups of modules at other facilities; and (7) they transfer entire projects, with modifications appropriate to the new setting, into other facilities.

Agencies are thus provided with a wide variety of options from which to choose. These range from a person's attending a single workshop to learn a new treatment skill and to receive continuing education credits if desired, to the staff of an entire section of a mental hospital or community agency being retrained for implementing a new program. Individuals and agencies may shop around, attend workshops, pick and choose among the modules offered, and select those components that they would like to add to their own treatment armamentarium. They may then seek consultation at their own agency and get help in implementing the changes. They may modify their programs gradually or change them all at once.

Fundamental change is, of course, the most difficult. The decision to retrain an entire staff in one large effort requires administrative action that usually must be made at the highest organizational level with the cooperation of funding bodies. Staff must be diverted from service to training, and usually travel must be arranged either for instructors, staff, or both. Decisions are easier in autonomous community agencies like community mental health centers, which are under the direction of local boards, than at public institutions where funding must be provided by the legislature.

CONCLUSIONS ABOUT MODULAR TREATMENT
AND TRAINING

As originally conceptualized, the R & T facility was expected to attract researchers who would join its staff for two to three years, design new treatment techniques, test them, and leave. Staff and space would then be reassigned for new researchers and their research ideas. However, the need to provide continuing treatment to a catchment area's patients, to keep residential beds filled, and to reduce overcrowding at the public hospital serving the area, all combined to make it very difficult to wind down treatment programs and start up new ones.

The modular approach to treatment helps provide an answer to this problem, as well as to training and dissemination. With this approach, changes can be introduced in a step-wise manner. Each new biomedical or psychoeducational innovation can be introduced independently on a treatment project basis, evaluated as to effectiveness and cost, and, if proven useful, implemented in other settings. Rather than tear down entire treatment programs to introduce innovations, with consequent disruption of patient care and damage to staff morale, the modular method introduces changes incrementally. Change takes place gradually and with minimal stress; staff enjoy developing new modules, testing them, and implementing those that are appropriate in the treatment units. Further, long before a project has completed all its investigations, those of its modules that are proving to be useful can be disseminated to other treatment facilities. These new facilities can select components that suit their own programs without themselves going through drastic reorganizations. They can gradually introduce new components, retrain staff, and modify their programs step-by-step.

This issue is of considerable importance because legislatures tend to order change not in stepwise fashion but in major sweeping moves. Such was the case with school integration, with the deinstitutionalization of mental patients, with right-to-treatment legislation, and with reorganization of the R & T facility's parent agency (see Chapter 1). However, there is nothing to prevent an entire program from being introduced all at once, as occurred with the new Santa Rosa Geriatric Facility in Florida, for instance, which implemented the entire R&T center gerontology program. Most facilities prefer to introduce modules incrementally, however.

REFERENCES

1. Slater AL, Gordon KK, Gordon RE: Role differences of mental health workers: Observations of four sites, in Nash KB, Lifton N, Smith SE, (Eds): The paraprofessional: Selected Readings. The Yale Monograph on Paraprofessionalism. New Haven, Conn., Advocate Press, Inc., 1978, pp 3–11
2. Rusk TN: Future changes in mental health care. Hosp Community Psychiatry 23:7–9, 1972
3. Alley S, Blanton J: Paraprofessionals in mental health: An annotated bibliography. Berkeley, Ca., Social Action Research Center, 1978
4. Leininger M: Two strange health tribes: The gurisrun and enicidem in the United States. Hum Org 35:253–261, 1976
5. Dick W, Carey LM: The sytematic design of instruction. Glenview, Ill., Scott Foresman and Co., 1978
6. Gagne RM, Briggs LJ: Principles of instructional design. New York, Holt, Rinebart, & Winston, 1974
7. Slater AL, Gordon KK: Developing a curriculum for human service workers. Career education for mental health workers project. Report No. 6. Tampa, Fla., Human Resources Institute, University of South Florida, 1979
8. Slater AL, Gordon KK, Redcay S: Final evaluation report. Career education for mental health workers project. Tampa, Fla., Human Resources Institute, University of South Florida, 1979
9. Slater AL, Gordon KK, Redcay S: Human services instructional series (1–8). Tampa, Fla., Human Resources Institute, University of South Florida, 1979
10. Ivey AE, Gluckstern NB: Basic Attending Skills. Microtraining Associates, Inc. Box 641, North Amherst, Mass., 1974

11. Ivey AE, Gluckstern NB: Basic Influencing Skills. Microtraining Associates, Inc. Box 641, North Amherst, Mass., 1976
12. Jackson G: Behavior management with the elderly. Gerontology program, Florida Mental Health Institute. Tampa, Fla., Florida Mental Health Institute, 1979
13. Boyd, LA: Behavior Management Training Manual. Child-Adolescent Program, Florida Mental Health Institute. Tampa, Fla., Florida Mental Health Institute, 1979
14. Williams H: Personal communication, 1980

PART C

Introducing Programs of Psychiatric Care for Children and Adolescents

Richard E.Gordon, Philip W. Drash
Joseph W. Evans, L. Adlai Boyd
Katherine K. Gordon

Uncorrected psychiatric disorders in children and adolescents—developmental delay, hyperactivity, schizophrenia, autism, aggressive behaviors, delinquency—have often resulted in lifetime social dependency and the need for periodic residential care in institutions for the mentally ill, the criminal, or the retarded. Presently, the average life-long cost incurred in the United States for institutional care of a severely mentally handicapped person approaches $500,000. If prevention or early intervention could cut the number of such persons requiring residential care in half, the annual savings would be 2.7 billion dollars.[1] Add to this figure the hundreds of millions of dollars spent on special classes for the emotionally handicapped, on correctional facilities for delinquent children, on welfare payments for those whose skill deficiencies or other emotional handicaps interfere with their employment, and on hundreds of other costly social programs to alleviate, treat, and make up for the failures of the emotionally handicapped in this country. It is easy to understand how important it becomes both to prevent and quickly to remediate serious mental and behavior disorders, especially as they occur in children.

Intervention is essential as soon as possible after an emotional or behavioral disorder is diagnosed in a child, even in infancy. Treatment for these disorders includes psychoeducational and support programs for both the parent (or foster parent) and the mentally ill child, and medical programs for the child, as needed. Most modular programs of therapy described here are conducted initially by paraprofessionals and, later, by the families themselves.

195

The treatments that children and adolescents themselves receive, like those for adults and gerontological patients, emphasize the development of effective life skills, a subject that needs greater emphasis in theoretical discussions of the development of children. Peer support becomes increasingly important as children enter adolescence.

Emotionally disturbed children need understanding and compassion, to be sure, and to be well-loved, well-clothed, and well-fed; but they also need to be well-trained, well-stimulated, and well-prepared for the realities of life. Love and training are not incompatible; they are opposite sides of the same coin. Children need to be taught gradually to face responsibility, to develop interpersonal skills, and become inured, in order to face a not so gentle, competitive and demanding world.

> As the child recognizes he must assert himself tactfully, face some hardship, strive, persevere, develop patience, consideration of others, and self-control, he is better prepared to cope with life's stresses. . . . The learning principles by which he can be trained have been demonstrated clearly in the laboratory. They are quite applicable in life (p. 62).[2]

Traditional institutional programs for emotionally or behaviorally disturbed children have produced relatively few positive results in terms of either effectiveness of treatment and/or cost efficiency. Attempts to change institutions for troubled children have often met with frustration. Most institutional programs usually confine children's activities and contacts to members of their own sex, teach them dependency on hospital-like routine, and give them few work skills they can use outside the institution. In essence, traditional institutional programming teaches children to live in a "welfare" system rather than to be as independent and as responsible as possible for their own needs.[3] Institutional programming does not have to follow traditional lines, however. "Buildings don't make an institution, people do!"[4]

The behavioral model, which is beginning to supplement or replace more traditional institutional models, is a two-part system based upon deficiencies and excesses. The model proposes that disturbed or delinquent children (1) have failed to learn appropriate life skills (deficiencies), and (2) have learned a number of maladaptive skills because of lack of instruction, inappropriate modeling, or a history of inadequate reinforcement (excesses). Consequently, the disturbed child displays behaviors that are asocial or antisocial in nature, and that often result in difficulties with parents, peers, teachers, and the community at large. Behavioral approaches emphasize the teaching of skills that enhance successful functioning in society.[3,5-7] The goal of these treatment programs, therefore, is twofold, namely, to establish, through training and instruction, the important behavioral life adjustment skills that the child has not learned, and to suppress or extinguish the negative or antisocial behaviors that the child has learned.[3,8] Once attained, skills will tend to generalize and continue beyond the treatment setting, in part because the natural environment will reinforce them and in part because the program includes training parents, teachers, and others to maintain the reinforcement schedule in the home, the school, and the community.

A second major change is community-based treatment of emotionally disturbed children. In the Scandinavian countries, and more recently in the United States, children are provided treatment in programs within their own communities. They are not removed to institutions some distance away; rather, government-owned hostels, group homes, and semi-independent living units are available for persons in need of treatment.[9] Such a community-based, behavioral treatment system allows the child to learn those skills that are necessary for successful daily functioning. In such programs, children learn social, prevocational, and maintenance skills that are needed for successful living within the very environment in which these skills are demanded. When parents are involved, they learn to maintain the skills that their children have learned, even though they were not able initially to establish them.

Learning positive social skills to supplant negative or maladaptive patterns provides behavioral alternatives for the disturbed child that are important in community adjustment. There is a widespread movement toward community-based treatment, which appears to be less expensive, more effective, and more humane for children in need of mental health, correction, or retardation services. This movement has led to an increased use of foster care.

FOSTER CARE

Foster care, as it was originally developed, was intended to provide a temporary substitute care facility in which a child would reside during periods of severe family crisis (such as illness of parents), or while the child's own home was being strengthened to be able to reaccept him/her.[10] On a national basis, however, there has been a trend not only toward increased use of foster care but also toward its use for children and adolescents with emotional problems requiring special assistance. This changing nature of the foster care population increases the burden both on foster parents and foster care caseworkers, requiring them to be better trained and more skilled. This is particularly the case when children with problems are first placed in foster care as adolescents. Parker[11] found, for example, that while success in foster care was 64 percent for children whose age at placement was under four years, it was only 23 percent for children whose placement age was 11 or over. It appears that many preadolescent and adolescent children are being placed in foster care, but not benefiting from the placement. Further, the Harvard Case Report[12] throws light on another problem in the child-adolescent area. Previous chapters have presented excerpts from this report that described the low morale and poor preparation of service workers in the community treatment agencies. There are also inadequacies in the foster care program.

> Foster parents . . . sometimes abused their . . . wards. Child abuse problems . . . exploded into public view . . . when a . . . man brutally murdered his 3-year-old stepson, who had been returned home . . . (over the warnings of the doctor) after a previous beating, and, after a 17-year-old boy committed suicide following homosexual abuse at the hands of his foster father . . . (p. 29).

Model programs must not only treat children and their families, it appears; they must also train agency staff and disseminate programs for training foster parents and agency staff.

ASSESSMENT OF TREATMENT NEEDS FOR ADOLESCENTS

A research and training center survey[13] of available community services for children and adolescents aged 12 and older conducted in 1976 pointed specifically to multiproblem dependent adolescents as the group for whom an effective treatment program was most needed. Its findings influenced the subsequent development of programs for children and adolescents at the research and training facility. In the survey the following steps were taken:

1. Data on age, race, and sex for all area adolescents in foster care and all adolescent status offenders were gathered from caseworkers;
2. For a sample of 30 adolescents in foster care who were identified by their caseworkers as "needing some type of 24 hour residential care." case records were examined to get data on their problems;
3. The caseworkers of these same 30 adolescents were interviewed to further pinpoint the problems;
4. Information was gathered on the number and age of youngsters residing in foster homes;
5. For a random sample of 50 adolescents in foster care, case records were studied to get data on this type of problem;
6. For a random sample of 100 adolescents in foster care, caseworkers were asked to indicate the types of problems present, the programs and services that they thought would be "most helpful," and the long-term plans for these youngsters;
7. For a random sample of 50 status offenders, case records were studied to determine types of problems and resources available;
8. For a random sample of 100 status offenders, caseworkers were asked to indicate problems present, and programs and services that would be most helpful;

9. Data were obtained from foster parents on types of problems they encounter and the kinds of assistance that would be of greatest benefit to them.

Findings

AGE

The data showed that the peak period for the status offenders was in the 14–16 year age range. The distribution for the sample of foster care adolescents in need of residential placement also showed the heaviest concentration around age 15.

TYPES OF PROBLEMS

The youngsters' case records showed that 70 percent had school problems of some sort; 40 percent had run away from home at least once; 32 percent had been in a correctional facility at some time; 62 percent had been in some other residential facility such as an emergency shelter or mental health facility before coming into foster care.

The ratings of the caseworkers corroborated the above data. The most frequent serious problem selected by caseworkers was learning in school, with behavior in school, noncompliance at home, confused thought processes, and unhappiness or depression close behind. At least one problem was indicated in 59 percent of the cases, and two or more problems for 52 percent. For 20 percent of the sample, five or more problem areas were indicated by their caseworkers.

Taken collectively, these data gathered from case records and caseworkers indicate rather significant emotional and/or other psychiatric problems for from one-third to two-thirds of the 339 adolescents in foster care.

LONG-RANGE PLANS

Foster care caseworkers indicated that they planned foster care until adulthood for 74 of 89 youngsters (83%). This figure illustrates just how far foster care has evolved from a system originally designed as a temporary shelter. One consequence of this change from short-term care to a long-term situation is that foster care has become an expensive financial venture of questionable therapeutic benefit.

STABILITY OF PLACEMENTS IN FOSTER HOMES

One measure of effectiveness that has been used in foster care research has been the stability of placements. Of 49 foster care adolescents, 32 had experienced more than one foster home. For youngsters who had been in two homes, the probability of entering a third home was 69 percent. These very high figures suggest that adolescents who have been in two foster homes should be a target group for interventions.

The chapters that follow describe a community-based, institutional program in which 76 staff assigned to the treatment of children and adolescents in 1979 managed the daily care of 70–75 residential and 45–50 day-treatment patients, and simultaneously performed evaluative research. Annually, the same staff also conducted 3194 contact hours of systematic training and education of agency and institutional staff and foster parents. Since most of the Children's and Adolescent projects have been underway for less than a year, extensive evaluative data on their effectiveness in comparison to controls are not yet available; however, the information collected will be presented. First, we will introduce the adolescent day treatment project in Chapter 11, emphasizing its multifaceted nature. Next, the program for severely disturbed and autistic children will be discussed in Chapter 12, paying particular attention to methods of bringing highly disturbed, violent, antisocial, and idiosyncratic behaviors under control. Finally, the variety of family treatment efforts will be presented in Chapter 13.

REFERENCES

1. Nathan R (Ed): Report to the president: Mental retardation: Century of decision. Washington, D.C., Department of Health, Education and Welfare, 1976, p. 130
2. Gordon RE, Singer M, Gordon KK: Social psychological stress. Arch Gen Psychiatry 4:459, 1961
3. Phillips EL, Phillips EA, Fixsen DL, et al: Behavior shaping works for delinquents. Psychology Today, 7:74–79, 1973
4. Phillips EL: Personal communication to J. Evans
5. Barbee J, Keil EC: Experimental techniques for job interview training for the disadvantaged: Videotape feedback, behavior modification and microcounseling. J Appl Psychol 53:209–213, 1973
6. Clark H, Boyd S, Macrae JA: A classroom program teaching disadvantaged youths to write a biographic information. J Appl Behav Anal 8:67–75, 1975
7. Grinnel RM, Lieberman A: Teaching the mentally retarded job interviewing skills. J Counsel Psychol 24:332–337, 1977
8. Gordon RE, Gordon KK, Gunther M: The Split-Level Trap. New York, B. Geis, 1961
9. Kugel RB, Wolfensberger W (Eds): Changing Patterns in Residential Services for the Retarded. Washington, D.C., President's Committee on the Mentally Retarded, 1969
10. Kadushin A: Child Welfare Services. New York, Macmillan, 1974
11. Parker RA: Decision in Child Care: A Study of Prediction in Fostering. London, George Allen & Unwin Ltd., 1966
12. Whitman D: Reorganization of Florida's human services agency. Kennedy School of Government Case Program, C85-80-040. Cambridge, Mass., Harvard University, 1980
13. Eberly DA: A preliminary survey of services for children in Hillsborough and Manatee counties. HRS District VI Task Force on Adolescents. Unpublished manuscript. Tampa, Fla., Florida Mental Health Institute, 1976

Robert M. Friedman, Judith Quick
Jo Palmer, Edwin Solomon
Richard E. Gordon

11
Enhancing the Skills of
Multiproblem Adolescents

This chapter describes an inexpensive skill-enhancement day treatment program developed for multiproblem dependent adolescents. The program goals are to stabilize the living situations for the adolescents, divert them from psychiatric hospitalization, help them stay out of difficulty with the juvenile justice system, and involve them constructively in education, work, or vocational training. The program combines individualized counseling and skill-enhancement training with modular skill-building efforts. The Adolescent Day Treatment Program (ADTP) described here was developed from two observations of community practices in dealing with teenagers with serious difficulties.

First, it was noted that special education programs for youngsters with school problems, and also independent counseling services for individual teenagers and their parents, are usually available in medium-sized communities. In contrast, however, there are few coordinated programs that integrate under the same auspices educational and counseling services for youngsters with counseling and support services for families. Numerous studies have clearly shown that adolescents' problems typically span more than one setting,[1,2] with family, school, and community difficulties being interrelated. Nevertheless, services for youngsters in most communities are fragmented, with special educational assistance being provided in one setting and family services in another. The system developed here eliminates this fragmentation. It assumes that more effective services will be delivered to youngsters and families through a combination of education, counseling, and family services. Such a combination of services may obviate the need for more restrictive and expensive residential care for many youngsters.

Second, it was seen that communities have been increasingly turning toward the child welfare system for assistance with troubled youth. For example, while the general population of children under age 18 in the United States increased by only 4 percent between 1961 and 1977, the number of children in foster homes increased from 132,000 to about three times as many (394,000) during that same period.[3] Of this group, 48 percent were age 11 or older in 1977. Yet, the effectiveness of foster care for adolescents is particularly questionable.[4]

In addition, the child welfare system is being called upon to assume greater responsibility for children known as "status offenders." This group, composed of youngsters who have repeatedly run away from home; have been "ungovernable," "incorrigible," "unmanageable"; or have been regularly truant from school, has typically been handled within the juvenile justice system. However, the effectiveness and legitimacy of the juvenile justice system as the responsible public agency to deal with these youngsters was questioned during the 1970s .[5-7] In Florida, primary responsibility for status offenders was legally transferred from the juvenile justice system to the child welfare system in 1975.[8]

The survey of available community services and client needs conducted in 1976 pointed specifically to multiproblem dependent adolescents as the group for whom an effective treatment program was most needed.[7] Therefore, these youngsters became the target group for whom the ADTP was developed. This report covers the first 15 months of operation of the program. The description of the ADTP that follows illustrates the synthesis of modular and individualized skill-enhancement training in a program for adolescents having serious behavioral, emotional, and academic difficulties.

ADOLESCENT DAY TREATMENT PROGRAM (ADTP)

Participants

All participants were referred for admission by their social worker from the local child welfare agency. Prospective enrollees attended group and individual orientation sessions with their natural or foster family. The voluntary nature of participation and the research nature of the program were emphasized, and interested students, as well as parents, signed informed consent forms. A total of 50 students attended orientation sessions, of whom eight declined to participate; four were not accepted by the program; and 38 (76%) were accepted. Three of these students ran away between the time of acceptance and admission and did not participate in the program. Only one youngster of the 50 applicants was denied admission because his problems were too demanding to manage within the program. Therefore, the data reported here are essentially on consecutive referrals. Summary descriptive data on the enrollees appear in Table 11-1.

Of the 35 participating youngsters, 16 were in foster homes at the time of entry; there was an average of 6.12 children in these foster homes. Of the 19 youngsters either under foster care supervision or with their natural families under protective services supervision for a status offense, only six were living with both an adult male and female in the home. In only two cases out of the 19 were the natural mother and father still married to each other and living in the home. In 10 instances, only the mother was in the home.

Table 11-1 shows that the adolescents entering the program had experienced severe disruptions in their lives. The group was characterized by multiple changes in living situations (particularly amongst the foster care and foster care supervision youngsters), a long history of behavioral and emotional difficulties, and serious academic deficiencies.

The history of psychiatric hospitalizations in 13 of the 35 participants (37%), the indications of behavior problems, and the frequent placement changes of many of the youngsters suggest that about one-third of these adolescents were at risk for residential psychiatric treatment; some of them clearly would have been hospitalized if low cost facilities were available for adolescents in the surrounding community.

Treatment Program

The treatment program combines individual and group skill-building activities for the adolescents with counseling and support services for their parents. Students attend the program five days a week from 7:45 a.m. to 2:00 p.m. The student schedule is highly structured and similar to a school schedule in organization. (For a detailed treatment description, see Friedman, 1978.[9]) Training for the child welfare staff who deal with problem youngsters is also provided as part of the overall training, dissemination, and prevention effort of ADTP.

A special problem in utilizing a skill-building model with adolescents is that the types of behaviors that may be viewed as appropriate and valued by adults may be seen quite negatively within the peer group where adolescents function. Unless skills can be taught that will be esteemed by other adolescents, the likelihood that they will actually be used beyond the classroom is minimal. In order to deal with these problems, staff sought input from adolescents at the outset of the Adolescent Project as to ways that they would consider appropriate for dealing with difficult situations. The procedures they recommended were built into the program. The next sections describe its content.

Table 11-1

Characteristics of day treatment participants prior to treatment

General Demographics

			n	%	Mean
Males			22	62.9	
Females			13	37.1	
Age (in years)		13	5	14.3	
		14	15	42.9	
		15	7	20.0	
		16	5	14.3	
		17	3	8.6	
Race		Blacks	7	20.0	
		Whites	28	80.0	
Child welfare status	Foster care		16	45.7	
	Foster care, supervision[a]		5	14.3	
	Status offender		14	40.0	

Educational and Intellectual Level

	Mean
IQ[b]	79.7
Mental age (years)[b]	12.0
Chronological age (years)	15.0
Reading (grade level)[c]	4.7
Math (grade level)[d]	5.5

Psychiatric History

	n	%
Prior hospitalization	13	37.1
On psychotropic medications at entry into day treatment	7	20.0
Prior outpatient mental health treatment[e]	20	57.1

Selected Placements Six Months Prior to Placement[f]

	n	%
Psychiatric hospital	7	20.0
Temporary shelter or detention	17	48.8
Foster home	20	57.1

Problem Areas in School[f]

	n	%
Truancy, nonattendance	31	88.6
Disruptive class behavior	25	71.4
Academic warnings and failures	25	71.4
Special education classes	11	31.4
3 or more of above problems	22	62.9
2 or more of above problems	31	88.6
1 or more of above problems	35	100.0

Table 11-1 (continued)

History of Abuse or Neglect[f]	n	%
Physical abuse	12	34.3
Sexual abuse or exploitation	3	8.6
Neglect or abandonment	23	65.7
1 or more of the above	28	80.0

[a]Foster care supervision is a category for youngsters who had been in foster care but are now living with parents under supervision of foster care workers.

[b]Slosson IQ test was used for all but one participant.

[c]Woodcock Reading Test was used for all participants.

[d]Key Math Test was used for all participants.

[e]This only includes outpatient treatment for a two-year period prior to entry into the ADTP.

[f]Child welfare case records were the data source for this information.

Modular Skill Enhancement Classes

Academic Skills. Academic classes are conducted for two periods a day. The primary emphasis is on acquisition of basic skills in reading, writing, and math, although science and social studies are also included. Individuals who have already mastered the basic skills work on practical applications of them, such as reading job applications and calculating budgets. Those who have demonstrated proficiency in functional areas are either given work to prepare them to return to public school, to take the high school equivalency diploma test, or generally to enrich their lives and motivate them.

Social and Vocational Skills. Social skills class is conducted daily. Acquisition of skills is enhanced by active instructional procedures, such as role-playing, behavioral rehearsal, and video-tape feedback of social behaviors. Project staff have developed training modules in areas such as "Using Positive Reinforcement," "Assertiveness," and "Conflict Management." The Careers module is designed to help students acquire the skills to locate jobs, interview for them, and make the necessary arrangements to work rather than to provide actual vocational training. In social skills class, training is provided in such areas as carrying on a conversation, reinforcing others positively, and clarifying and clearly stating views.

Daily Living and Personal Skills. Health education class focuses on personal hygiene, nutrition, diseases, and the whole area of sex and family life education. The students complete assignments that utilize the new knowledge and skills they have gained about good health practices.

Leisure Skills. A class in Leisure and Physical Education, conducted for an hour per day, stresses the development of physical and recreational skills, as well as a general understanding of the functioning of the body. Youngsters participate in group recreational activities, learning both games they can enjoy and the negotiating and sportsmanship skills needed for playing.

Integrative Skills. Values Clarification is taught in class and reinforced in individual and group counseling sessions. The focus here is on assisting students in identifying personal goals, and establishing realistic plans to achieve them.

Peer Network Training

Friends outside of the program who play a significant role in contributing to a client's difficulty, or provide a resource in reducing problems are also involved in training.

Individualized Treatment

In addition to the individual attention that youngsters receive within the classes, they also attend either individual or group counseling sessions every day. These sessions are designed to provide further practice and training in individual and group problem-solving and communication,[10] and to work toward the resolution of specific problems and conflicts not covered in the modular classes. A combination of behavior modification and counseling procedures is employed to help the adolescents with their individual problems.

One of the frequent behavior problems with which staff are confronted is aggressive and defiant behavior. A staff training technique on this topic[11] has been developed, which is used within the ADTP and as part of the program dissemination to other institutions and agencies.

DEALING WITH THE HOSTILE ADOLESCENT

This approach identifies four phases of anger and hostility, and suggests steps that can be taken to intervene at each phase.

Phase 1–Pre-Aggression. To prevent the development of aggressive behavior, a structure with clearly defined behavioral expectations and consequences should be established ahead of time. The sequencing of steps should be considered in planning activity programs, and transition and cooling off time should be built in. Different physical spaces should be consistently utilized for activities, for work, and for privacy, so that adolescents can associate certain spaces with appropriate functions.

Phase 2–Defiant Testing.   There are a number of action steps that workers can take when they notice adolescents testing limits, breaking rules, avoiding contact, and withdrawing from group activities. These include: avoiding eye contact, ignoring minor infractions, diverting the adolescent, *staying on task,* not responding to the limit testing, diverting contact to a neutral ground, allowing the youngster to leave the situation for a brief period, providing alternatives that are incompatible with testing, suggesting invitations with no demands, using humor to lighten the situation, and permitting the adolescent as well as the worker to maintain dignity.

Phase 3–Loud Verbal Aggression.   This verbal behavior is frequently accompanied by rapid speech, intense eye contact, a rigid body posture, and a closing up of physical space between individuals. When these signs are noticed, the worker should try the following actions: keeping affect flat, ignoring verbal content when inappropriate, maintaining eye contact when youngster is quiet, refocusing back to the topic, allowing youngster to leave the situation briefly, using humor if possible, avoiding putdowns, and providing opportunity for de-escalation with all parties maintaining dignity.

Phase 4–Physical Aggression.   Acts like pounding and stamping, throwing or tearing objects, and pushing and shoving usually precede physical aggression against other people. When the anger has escalated to this point, the worker must act to protect self and others, and get help if needed. The worker may wish to move further away, keeping affect flat, avoiding eye contact, terminating talk, and trying to create a chance for a cooling off period.

Reinforcement Program

The entire ADTP is implemented by a staff trained in the use of positive reinforcement. Typically, reinforcements take the forms of words of encouragement, praise for specific acts, attentiveness to requests, and nonverbal indications of approval. This extensive use of positive social reinforcement combined with ignoring minor inappropriate behaviors facilitates the skill acquisition that takes place in the modular classes.

Additionally, students may earn the privilege of participating in special friday reinforcing outings or activities. At each class they earn points for punctuality, completing assignments, positive social behavior, and for individual activities agreed upon between the teacher and the student. For the first four weeks of the program, the teacher assigns the points to each student.

For the rest of the program, students assign their own points, with teachers making changes if they disagree. Those who earn at least 80 percent of their possible points, and attend the program at least three out of five days in a week, participate in a special friday reinforcing activity and receive a certificate of merit, as well. Students who have shown improvement in a class receive further reinforcement by means of notes and phone calls to their parents from staff members to inform the families of the progress.

Report cards are distributed every six weeks. These contain a detailed description of accomplishments both in quantitative terms (number of points earned over the six-week period) and in a qualitative, narrative form. This wide and varied range of feedback from project to home, particularly with its emphasis on providing positive information to parents, not only reinforces student accomplishments but also helps create a constructive relationship for family counseling. (See Chapter 13.)

Family Treatment

Counselors visit each family once a week. When necessary, sessions are conducted in the evening so that working parents can be included. Family counselors discuss the youngster's school performance and home activities during the week. They may also, depending upon the problems and resources of the family, develop behavioral contracts to modify specific problems at home. They try to change maladaptive family interaction patterns, conduct supportive individual sessions with parents, and assist them in obtaining aid from community resources. Family counselors frequently include siblings and other significant persons, such as relatives and friends, in the treatment sessions in an effort to develop a strong, constructive support system.

Foster Parent Training

The format for treatment with foster parents is the same as that with natural parents, but the content of the sessions is often different. In many cases, foster parents have only recently begun to know the youngster. They tend to view their role as a mixture of parent, volunteer, and paraprofessional. Due to shortages of foster homes for adolescents with emotional problems, there often are large numbers of youngsters in each home. The family counselor may therefore provide consultation and training sessions concerning not only the youngster in the ADTP but also the other children in the home. Additional training is provided to foster parents to help them understand the effects upon youngsters of the rejection they have received, not only from their parents but also in many cases from other foster parents. The youngster's behavior is interpreted to the foster parents in the context of his/her history of family disruption, instability, neglect, and abuse; foster parents are taught skills for dealing with the youngsters. These sessions are conducted individually, although the ADTP also assists local child welfare staff in developing and evaluating group training sessions for foster parents.

Duration of Treatment

Youngsters continue in the program as long as they are progressing and working toward goals agreed upon by students, parents, and staff. After a student returns to public school, enters vocational training, or takes a job, the family counselor continues to work with the youngster until he/she is settled into the new situation, and managing satisfactorily both at home and away.

CHILD WELFARE TRAINING AND CONSULTATION

At the same time as Adolescent Project staff are providing direct service to multiproblem dependent adolescents through the ADTP, they conduct training and consultation in collaboration with the child welfare program. These efforts strive to strengthen the overall capability of the child welfare system to deliver effective service to adolescents. They provide both skill- and information-oriented training for caseworkers and supervisors.[12] The training includes an introduction to behavioral principles and an examination of the use of these principles; procedures of intervention in family crises; procedures of ongoing casework intervention with dysfunctional families; training in teaching parents to be more effective at parenting; and training in interpersonal communications, particularly as applicable to relationships with clients. Consultation efforts have been directed at recruiting foster parents and reducing the need for adolescents to enter foster care.[13] The ADTP has also sought to strengthen the child welfare system by serving to promote communication, cooperation, and dissemination of information-sharing on programs for dependent adolescents.[14]

EVALUATION

Program Completion

Of the 35 adolescent participants, 23 (66%) successfully completed at least one cycle of treatment. Of the 12 noncompleters, one moved out of the area, six dropped out of the program, two ran away from their homes, one was asked to leave for noncompliance with rules, one was discontinued be-

Table 11-2
Outcomes of treatment.

General Measures	N	%
Completed Program	23	65.7
Attendance (days)	97	81.7
Points Earned	3180	85.4

Academic Skill Gain[a]	Mean
(Months gain for every month in program)	
Total Reading	1.62
Passage Comprehension	1.58
Total Math	.97

Placement Changes Before and During Program for 23 Completers	Prior to Program	During Program	Change Dif. %	
Foster home placements	27	21	−6	(−22.2)
Temporary shelter, detention	33	27	−6	(−18.2)
Psychiatric hospitalizations	9	2	−7	(−77.8)

Placement Changes Before, During and After Program for 13 Completers	Prior to Program	During Program	After Program	Change Dif.
Foster home placements	13	11	5	−8
Temporary shelter, detention	9	11	8	−1
Psychiatric hospitalization	5	2	0	−5

N = 21. Two completers were unavailable for post-testing.

N = 13. The period of time since the discharge of 10 other completers is too brief in duration for their data to be useful in the present analysis.

cause of poor attendance, and one was committed by the courts to a juvenile training school. Data on the performance of the completers are summarized in Table 11-2.

Attendance

The average attendance for the 23 completers was 81.7 percent. Of these 23, 12 had been labeled "truant" in the public schools, 5 had dropped out of school, and 3 had records of excessive absences. This attendance rate, while low compared to regular public school attendance figures, is extremely high for a group of adolescents in which 20 of 23 had a history of serious attendance problems. Further, this rate of attendance was achieved in a program designed for voluntary participation.

Stability of Living Situation

To determine the effectiveness of the program in stabilizing the living situation of the participants, the number of foster home placements, temporary living situations in publicly supported shelters, and psychiatric hospitalizations during the program were compared to those during a baseline period immediately prior to program entry. The baseline period for each youngster was exactly equivalent to the length of time that he/she spent in the program. The mean enrollment period was 32 weeks, while the range was 13–62 weeks.

The results of this analysis are shown in Table 11-2. There were sizable reductions in foster home placements, temporary placements, and psychiatric hospitalizations. The largest improvement was shown in the reduction from nine psychiatric hospitalizations during the baseline period to only two during the program.

Data on placement changes were also examined for a follow-up period identical to each youngster's length of time in the program. Data were available for analysis on only 13 participants, since 10 completers had not been out of the program long enough for their follow-up data to be available. The average length of time in the program for 13 youngsters for whom follow-up data are available was 25.4 weeks.

As shown in Table 11-2, this analysis showed large improvements in foster home placements and psychiatric hospitalizations. The five foster care youngsters for whom follow-up data are available had 13 different foster home placements during baseline, and only five during the follow-up. The number of psychiatric hospitalizations for the group of 13 was reduced from 5 prior to the program to none during the follow-up period.

Academic Skill Gain

Progress of program completers in academic skills was determined by comparing results of tests immediately upon admission to the program with results at discharge. Both pre- and post-test results were available for 21 of the 23 completers. The average improvement was 1.62 months gain in reading, using the Woodcock Reading Test, and 0.97 months gain in math, using the Key Math Test, for every month in the program. The gains were particularly large for the foster care youngsters. The nine completers for whom test data were available averaged 1.95 months gain in overall reading, 2.15 in reading comprehension, and 1.20 in math, for every month in the program, compared to 1.05 in overall reading, 1.08 in comprehension, and 0.75 in math for the status offenders.

Completers versus Noncompleters

A comparison was made of the 23 completers with the 12 noncompleters to make an initial determination whether the program was proving more effective with particular types of youngsters. The completers and noncompleters were similar with regard to sex, status within the child welfare system, intellectual and academic skill levels, and number of placements in the year immediately prior to the program. However, of the 13 youngsters with at least one prior psychiatric hospitalization, 11 (84.6%) completed the program while only 2 did not.

DISCUSSION

The results of this evaluation of the ADTP, based on 15 months of program operation, are encouraging. The data clearly indicate that the program has enrolled youngsters with serious difficulties in their home or foster home situation, and in the public schools. Despite the seriousness of the participants' problems and skill deficiencies, and despite the histories of nonattendance in the public schools, approximately two-thirds of the enrollees completed the program, and attendance averaged better than 80 percent. Those participants who completed the program have shown sizable academic skill gains, and have begun to settle into stable living situations rather than bouncing from one placement to another. Most notable was the reduction in psychiatric hospitalizations.

Of special importance is the finding that the positive results obtained during the program on placement changes were not only maintained but strengthened after the youngsters were discharged. This finding must be interpreted cautiously, however, since the number of participants for whom follow-up data are presently available is still limited, and the length of the follow-up averages only half a year.

Additional program evaluation needs to focus on the particular features of the ADTP that seem to be of most value. The primary treatment is a combination of modular group-oriented skill enhancement training and individualized counseling and training. This combination appears to meet the varying needs of individual participants in a cost-effective manner. The family counseling and support activities also warrant further evaluation. Caseworkers and parents have indicated that they believe that these are among the most valuable parts of the program.

At this point, however, day treatment that combines modular skill enhancement with individual and family counseling seems to be worth further development from two standpoints. First, it is more intensive, individualized, and family-oriented than the training that typically takes place in public schools, and so serves as an important resource for youngsters whose behavioral and emotional problems do not respond well to public school programs. Especially noteworthy during this period of great concern over the problem of truancy in the public schools is the high rate of attendance in this program by youngsters with serious truancy problems in the public schools.

Second, day treatment retains the main therapeutic elements of residential treatment, while keeping the families actively involved, and keeping the youngster in the community. It is both less restrictive and less expensive than residential psychiatric care. The national trend toward deinstitutionalization and treatment in the least restrictive environment has developed because of observations of problems institutions may foster, including the following:

1. Institutional care may foster dependency, and may be less effective than community care.
2. Youngsters with serious problems, when grouped in residences with each other and with others with severe problems, exert negative peer influence on each other; they tend to worsen each others' conditions and to create the need for control of problematic behavior.
3. The grouping of youngsters who present management problems often results in primary emphasis being placed on the achievement of immediate behavior control rather than on treatment aimed at producing enduring improvement.
4. The removal of youngsters from their home communities makes more difficult the maintenance of family and community ties and the involvement of the family in the treatment program; in time the family may extrude the youngster permanently.
5. Institutional placement tends to give the youngster a negative label, which itself may become a lifelong stigma.
6. Institutional care is expensive and drains resources from cost-effective treatment programs.
7. Institutions often are not accountable to either the community or the individual.

A small percentage of adolescents with serious difficulties, nevertheless, cannot be adequately treated in a community-based day treatment program like the one described: Children with serious problems that represent a danger to themselves or others, and those whose negative reputations require that they be removed in order to gain a fresh start elsewhere, may require specialized residential programs away from their home community.

Day treatment programs such as the one described here would appear to have an important role to play in the continuum of services for emotionally and behaviorally disturbed adolescents. Preventing the need for institutionalization is a complex matter, however, requiring a variety of services,[15] including those outlined below.

Individual and family counseling.   This is the least expensive of the services listed, and may eliminate the need for additional intervention.

Individual and family crisis intervention.   Despite the fact that programs that work with families at a point of crisis can keep the families together and strengthen them,[16,17] such programs are inadequately funded.

Day treatment.   As shown by the current study, day treatment can be very effective in preventing the need for more costly services. Yet, serious system disincentives prevent the development of day treatment programs. For example, private insurance companies will typically pay for residential psychiatric treatment, and not for day treatment. Similarly, state agencies frequently have purchase of service budgets that are far greater for residential treatment than day treatment.

Foster care.   This is the least expensive of all out-of-home operations. Yet foster care programs have rarely been given the resources needed to work with difficult populations, such as adolescents with behavior problems. The large caseloads that caseworkers carry, the lack of training they receive, the small payments families receive, the lack of training provided for foster parents, and the large number of children placed per home all interfere with the effectiveness of foster care.

Therapeutic foster care.   Such programs, in which the foster parents receive special training and services, and possibly an extra stipend for care of particularly difficult youngsters, are substantially less costly than residential care.[4]

Group living homes and half-way houses.   These small, community-based programs can be responsive to local needs, and operate on either a five- or seven-day a week schedule.

Child care and residential treatment centers.   Community-based group child care and residential treatment centers are less expensive than residential psychiatric care, since they operate more on psychosocial models than medical ones. Funding for the programs is usually inadequate to encourage the development of quality services and expansion of programs.

The existence of a continuum of community services, such as those listed above, permits relatively nonintrusive and inexpensive interventions to be tried before the more restrictive and costly ones are used. It also permits the development of a differentiated service program, in which problems and assets of youngsters can be matched with particular programs rather than having to choose programs by default. The present chapter has concentrated on day treatment as an important and often overlooked element of that continuum.

The ADTP focused on youngsters being served within the child welfare system. Mental health professionals have typically been only peripherally involved in this system,[14] despite the large number of youngsters served within it. The project represents a model not only for direct service, but for combining that service with research and consultation efforts aimed at modifying the overall system from which the direct service clients come. These research and consultation efforts are presently being expanded into a statewide assessment of the foster care system through a federal grant to the state child welfare agency.

REFERENCES

1. Elliott DS, Voss HL: Delinquency and Dropout. Lexington, Mass., D. C. Health & Co., 1974
2. Friedman RM, Wolfe D, Lardieri S, et al (Eds): Programs for Dependent Adolescents: Issues, Problems, Alternatives—Proceedings of a Conference. Tampa, Fla., Florida Mental Health Institute, 1978
3. Shyne AW, Schroeder AG: National Study of Social Services to Children and Their Families. Washington, D.C., United States Children's Bureau, Department of Health, Education and Welfare, 1978
4. Friedman RM, Ziegler C: Therapeutic foster homes: An alternative residential model for emotionally disturbed children and youth. Presented at the Southeastern Psychological Association Meeting, Washington, D.C., 1980
5. Bazelon D: Beyond control of the juvenile court. Juvenile Court Judges Journal 21:42–50, 1970
6. National Council on Crime and Delinquency: Jurisdiction over status offenses should be removed from the juvenile court. Crime and Delinquency 21:97–99, 1975
7. Eberly DA: A preliminary survey of services for children in Hillsborough and Manatee Counties. Tampa, Fla., HRS District VI Task Force on Adolescents, 1976
8. Gilman D: Status offense jurisdiction: Change without reform. Crime and Delinquency 22:48–51, 1979
9. Friedman RM: Summary report of first cycle of Adolescent Project Day Treatment Program. Unpublished manuscript. Tampa, Fla., Florida Mental Health Institute, 1978
10. Palmer JC: Adolescent target behaviors and prescriptive intervention for building social skills within the group process. Presented at Southeastern Psychological Association, New Orleans, March 1979
11. Quick J, Smith G: Dealing with the hostile adolescent: The escalation continuum, in Friedman R, Wolfe S, Lardieri, et al (Eds): Programs for Dependent Adolescents: Issues, Problems, Alternatives—Proceedings of a Conference. Tampa, Fla., Florida Mental Health Institute, 1978
12. Friedman RM, Lardieri S, Murphy R, et al: Training of child welfare staff: Statistical summary of participants and outcomes. Unpublished manuscript. Tampa, Fla., Florida Mental Health Institute, 1979

13. Friedman RM, Lardieri S, McNair D, et al: Foster care for adolescents: Problem or solution? Presented at the American Psychological Association Meeting, New York, 1979
14. Friedman RM, Quick J, Lardieri S: The child welfare system: A rarely used but highly important area for involvement of psychologists. Presented at the Southeastern Psychological Association Meeting, Washington, D.C., 1980
15. Friedman RM: Preventing the need for institutionalization, in Friedman RM, Wolfe S, Lardieri, et al (Eds): Programs for Dependent Adolescents: Issues, Problems, Alternatives—Proceedings of a Conference. Tampa, Fla., Florida Mental Health Institute, 1978
16. Baron R, Feeney F: Juvenile diversion through family counseling. Washington, D.C., U.S. Department of Justice, 1976
17. Kinney J: Homebuilders: An in home crisis intervention program. Children Today 7(35):15–17, 1978

Richard E. Gordon, Philip W. Drash
Joseph Evans, L. Adlai Boyd

12
Improving the Behavior of Severely Emotionally Disturbed and Autistic Children

Residential children's programs treat some of the most difficult of all psychiatric populations. Nevertheless, severely disturbed autistic and physically violent children benefit from modular treatment in group settings that is combined with individualized programs fit to each child's specific needs.[1]

GENERAL PROGRAM STRUCTURE

A modular skill-building program is combined with an individualized educational program and treatment plan. These are based on behavioral assessments and parent reports. One staff person is assigned as primary therapist for two children and their families. Each child's parent(s) or foster parent(s) also participate(s) in a biweekly home training session in which modeling and immediate feedback takes place.

The program emphasizes procedural consistency and quantitative data evaluation. Detailed treatment and assessment procedures are distributed to all treatment and supervisory personnel. All treatment procedures contain a recording section where data are graphed and evaluated. Revision of treatment procedures is based on evaluation of the data. Each child is also assessed every six months on the Functional Behavior Checklist,[2,3] which measures 22 areas of basic skills, and/or the Woodcock Reading Readiness Test and the Key Math Test. After discharge, each child is assessed at least once every six months in the first year. Extensive objective data from home, school, and community, as well as verbal reports of progress from parents are gathered. In addition, follow-up consultation is provided upon request.

Participants

Many children diagnosed as autistic do not talk, do not understand language, have no self-help skills, and are functionally mentally retarded. Others are echolalic, incontinent, self-abusive, destructive, and inappropriate in their behavior. They and other severely disturbed predelinquent children, aged 3 to 12 years, are treated in an intensive residential five-day, four-night a week program. To be admitted for treatment, the children's problems must be so severe that they cannot function in the community (home, school, or other agency).

The children in the autistic group show extreme social withdrawal, frequent repetitive movements and self-stimulation, low tolerance to environmental change, and severe tantrums, aggression, or self-abuse. Predelinquents exhibit frequent physical aggression, verbal abuse, noncompliance, negative teasing, tantrums, or running away.

The boy–girl ratio is about 8:1.5. More than 60 percent of the children have either a step-parent, only a single parent, or foster parents.

Life Skill Training: A Comprehensive Curriculum

The teaching programs are characterized by five basic features: (1) a clear definition of the teaching stimulus, the target behavior, and the consequence for the pupil; (2) the systematic delivery of contingent rewards such as tokens, edibles, and praise for good listening and correct responses; (3) a consistent interaction pattern between the teacher/therapist and the pupil; (4) objective written evaluation of pupil progress by the teacher, usually in the form of trial-to-trial performance on a day by day basis; and (5) written procedures specifying the teaching conditions and steps.

The repertoire of behaviors taught is described in the following sections.

ACTIVITIES OF DAILY LIVING

All children receive training in all basic self-help skills that they do not have. Training includes combing hair, brushing teeth, buttoning, and tying shoelaces. Toilet training is provided for those who need it.

SOCIAL-INTERPERSONAL SKILLS

Social graces, greeting and conversation, sensitivity, and cultural awareness are taught when appropriate. The interaction procedure described in Chapter 6 is used.

ACADEMIC SKILLS TRAINING

Autistic children receive training in the following categories: following instruction; vocal imitation for those who are nonverbal; training in receptive and expressive prepositions; verbal imitation training; training in reducing echolalia for those with the problem; training in answering questions involving logical relationships and daily activities; training in counting beads; training in identifying numbers; training in addition, subtraction, and money counting; picture naming and conversation training; listening to stories; and playing group games.

RECREATIONAL SKILLS

This training takes place in the evening and on biweekly field trips. It includes training in activities such as swimming, cooperative play on the playground, playing at the beach or park, and in going shopping.

SURVIVAL SKILLS

A combination of strategies are employed to reduce unacceptable or inappropriate behavior that would cause children to be excluded from school or other community-based activities (smearing feces, head-banging, screaming, physical violence, self-exposure, etc.). These include token rewards and fines, overcorrection, differential reinforcement of other behavior, and time-out from positive reinforcement. Medication is prescribed when necessary. The training for each child is individualized according to the type of behavior and the child's needs and responses.

All training sessions are broken down into trial-to-trial teaching, and each trial is recorded by the therapist. The percentage of correct trials is plotted daily on graphs.

Dealing with physical violence and aggression.   These have been identified as the primary behaviors that cause children to be placed permanently in residential centers. As long as a child is not violent or aggressive, parents can maintain him in a home setting, but once the child becomes violent the parents can no longer cope. Once placed in a residential setting, aggression and physical violence continue to be the most difficult problems confronting the staff.

Children can gain intrinsic pleasure and personal satisfaction from physical violence and destructiveness, from losing their temper and beating someone. Aggressive outbursts by their very nature almost invariably receive attention from parents, peers, and staff. Bullies get obedience from persons smaller than themselves; they enjoy ordering others around. Bullying often gets reinforced by the attention of others. Analysis of a child's aggressive behavior, therefore, includes identifying not only the antecedents, but also the attention-gaining consequences that help maintain aggressive behavior.

Staff encounter many problems in working with aggressive children and their families in their homes. They must find positive reinforcers there, and help parents gain control over the reinforcers and use them with their child. However, monitoring food consumption, for example, or access to the outdoors, while desirable, is often extremely difficult in the home. It is especially hard for parents to control autistic "self-injurious" behaviors, such as head-banging. Further, utilizing an effective punisher, such as a time-out empty room, often requires space that parents do not have. Also, neighbors may complain or suspect child abuse when the child has tantrums in the time-out room. Therefore, applying prescribed consequences makes physical and psychological demands on the parents or teachers that they sometimes are unable to meet. Effective punishers may not be available in certain settings such as churches or shopping centers, or, if used, may provoke negative responses from observers. Positive reinforcers like swimming will depend on the weather and the availability of swimming facilities.

Using differential reinforcement of other behaviors to control aggression and other disruptive behaviors. One of the more effective techniques of dealing with aggression and disruptive behavior is to differentially reinforce other acceptable behaviors such as reading quietly or watching television. Any positive behaviors that are incompatible with aggression receive praise, physical approval, gestures (e.g., pats on back), tasty snacks, and favorite activities (e.g., bike riding and swimming).

Using aversive procedures to reduce aggression and disruptive behavior. Aversive procedures are used sparingly, and are always reviewed and approved by the Human Rights Committee prior to implementation. This committee continues to monitor the use of these procedures. In addition to time-out, examples of aversive procedures that have been used include: For screaming or disrupting class, the teacher holds the child's hands for up to two minutes. Aggression toward other children is managed by blocking vision for 30 seconds with a helmet. Spitting results in blindfolding with a ski mask. Frequent self-abusive behaviors (head banging, slapping, hand biting, etc.) are treated with two drops of apple cider vinegar applied to the children's mouths through a plastic bottle with a sponge cap (a stamp moistener) upon each occurrence. All occurrences of self-abuse are recorded and plotted on a graph for each child.

Using token rewards and fines in the training program. Over the years token reinforcement systems have proven to be a highly effective component of any behavior management or educational program. A token system is established by first giving the patients a number of free tokens in the beginning of training. After each training session patients are taken to a gift shop where, if they want something, they purchase it by giving the trainer a token. If the patient wishes more, the trainer continues to charge him tokens. After a period of time, tokens are no longer given freely. Instead, each patient must earn tokens by performing a list of tasks specified for him. He loses tokens and thus privileges when he emits a specified undesirable behavior.

Predelinquent children earn star-tokens for every half hour of good behavior and/or good work, and spend them on free play, recess, toy rentals, and edibles. In addition, inappropriate behaviors (aggression, tantrums, running away) are targeted, and performance of one is followed by loss of a star-token and/or by sit-out in the corner for two minutes if the child has no tokens. If he does not sit out properly, he is sent to a quiet room (time-out) for a minimum of two minutes. Thereafter, he has to be quiet for fifteen seconds or stay for a maximum of twenty minutes if not quiet. For serious aggression and running away from the unit, the children lose their activity privileges for that evening.

The children receive frequent, contingent praise and attention for all good behavior and good work, in addition to receiving tokens. At the end of each week, the earnings for each day by each child are tallied, and the children who have earned at least 90 percent of all possible tokens receive special treats (e.g., going out for lunch with a staff member).

Autistic children who can speak only one or two words receive poker chips as the reinforcing medium in their token system. The children earn tokens by performing specifically defined self-help and play skills, and by making correct trials in training sessions—in language, math, motor imitation, or compliance with instructions. Tokens are used to purchase soft drinks, pieces of fruit, or candy, toy rentals, and other activities. The children lose earned tokens when they are aggressive toward others or deliberately throw their tokens away. Children can also have their meals delayed, but cannot lose a meal.

Using Psychotropic Medications

In addition to the psychoeducational treatment program, which is based primarily on contingency management, many of the children also receive psychotropic medications. These medications assist in reducing the frequency of aggressive and other destructive actions, and help the children become more amenable to the behavioral treatments (see Figure 2-1).

Human Rights

All programs and procedures, especially those using restraint or aversive procedures, are approved by the Human Rights and Treatment Review Committees. At their discretion the Committees may seek review and approval by the Program Director, who may present them to the Institute Director, if necessary.

RESULTS WITH AUTISTIC CHILDREN

Results obtained previously with this program[4] illustrate dramatically how effective psychoeducational treatment can be with very seriously disturbed autistic children. A group of 12 youngsters in a modular day treatment class obtained an average improvement score of 11.91 on the Hung Functional Behavior Checklist. In comparison, matched groups of autistic children in three control groups achieved an average score of only 3.18 (p < .01).

The most striking difference occurred between results achieved with the day treatment approach and those accomplished in a traditional residential treatment program in which seven matched controls improved by only 2 points. Modular day treatment was more than five times as effective as traditional residential care. Comparing costs of the two programs produced the following figures for treating one child for one year:

Modular day treatment—less than $7,000

Residential treatment—more than $40,000

The cost of modular day treatment was about one sixth of that of traditional residential care.

SUMMARY

The foregoing pages have focused on the management of more serious behaviors in these difficult-to-treat young patients. Chapter 5 described the standardized interaction procedures used to train children's psychosocial skills and the instruments used to measure their progress in treatment (proficiency gauges). In Chapter 13 we shall present the programs of family therapy that round out the main components of the treatment program for children with chronic mental illness.

REFERENCES

1. Hung D: Program Description of the Children's Intensive Residential Treatment Project. Tampa, Fla., Florida Mental Health Institute, 1979
2. Hung DW: A Training Manual for the Functional Behavior Checklist. Tampa, Fla., Florida Mental Health Institute, 1979
3. Hung D: A Functional Teaching Manual for Children with Learning Handicaps and/or Behavioral Problems. Research Report, Metropolitan-Toronto School Board, March 1979
4. Hung, DW: New Directions in the Teaching of Autistic Children: Evaluation of a Functional Teaching Manual. Research Report Submitted to the Ontario Ministry of Education, Ontario, Canada, 1977

Richard E. Gordon, Philip W. Drash
L. Adlai Boyd, Joseph W. Evans
Robert M. Friedman, Nancy Goldstein
Katherine K. Gordon

13

Training Families to Manage Children's Behavior

THE INTERACTIVE SYSTEMS MODEL OF FAMILY BEHAVIOR

The family is an interactive environment. A child is born into a family system and inevitably changes the system as he or she becomes part of it. Each family member develops a characteristic role or set of roles in the family system; behaviors are shaped by, modeled after, and maintained by reinforcement from other family members. The exchange system of reinforcers between parent and child is not a closed system. The parenting role is also reinforced from the outside. Grandparents of the infant and parents' peers are observing and judging, giving advice, compliments, and criticism. The young parent is sometimes very self-conscious or worried about being a good parent, doing the right thing for the child.

Although a child models much of its behavior after that of parents and siblings, each individual exhibits a wide range of creative or idiosyncratic behavior. A child that has any physiological abnormality or limitation may exhibit highly original behavior, may be unusually inactive, or may not respond to the ordinary reinforcers that have successfully selected and shaped adaptive behaviors in other children in the same family. Even behavior that may

Portions of this chapter were previously published in Gordon R, Goldstein N, Gordon K, et al: The role of paraprofessional mental health workers in family therapy (National Education Center for Paraprofessionals in Mental Health, National Institute of Mental Health, Paraprofessional Manpower Development Branch, Monograph Series No. 1, Report No. 3, May, 1979), and are reprinted with permission.

be maladaptive has usually been reinforced by family members in some way. Other family members may be reinforced, in turn, by this undesirable behavior.

It is important to keep in mind that at all times the "helpless" baby has some real input in determining the course of the relationship: The baby may be fussy because of an immature digestive system; the baby may be good and passive because of some underlying physiological problem that will retard its development; the baby may be more at one end or the other of the normal activity continuum—very active or very placid—and this may be one of the child's enduring characteristics. Even the physical attractiveness or unattractiveness of the infant has an effect on the relationship.

During infancy, many of the reinforcers exchanged between mother and child meet primary biological needs. The baby's nuzzling and crying are rewarded by sensations of pleasure and relief of breast engorgement. The infant very quickly learns the power of its cry in shaping its parents' behavior. Parents are rewarded by the infant's ceasing to cry in the middle of the night and going to sleep. They attend to the infant's needs in order to obtain peace.

As the infant matures, it has a wider behavior repertoire, and can do more things that are reinforcing to the parent. The child can smile, show affection, stop soiling its diapers, be entertaining and amusing. Social reinforcers from the parent become more important to the child, although primary reinforcers are still powerful. The child learns how to give social reinforcers back to the parents.

As the child grows, he or she acquires an increasing number of behaviors that are rewarding or punishing to the parent; these play an increasing role in shaping a wider range of parental behavior. Although outside social factors continue to be important to the parent, there are more rewards and punishments intrinsic to the parent–child relationship. The child, gaining awareness of other parent–child relationships and making comparisons, will copy other children's good and bad behavior in order to get parents to shape up.

When the child enters adolescence, social reinforcement from peers becomes more important to the youngster. Parents, too, may find more social reinforcement for acting in other roles outside the family. The adolescent now has a number of material reinforcements to offer the parent, however, because he or she has many skills and capabilities, considerable physical strength, and boundless energy. The adolescent is still dependent to some extent on parents for the basic necessities of life at this point, and for some of the niceties as well—such as car transportation, spending allowance, assistance in projects, etc. There is a potential for a growing fairness in exchanges of goods and services between parents and the adolescent. Social reinforcements such as attention, approval, interest, and affection become more meaningful. An adolescent's opinions may also carry more weight in family conferences.

The following sections will illustrate a continuum of effectiveness of intervention that is related in part to the age of the child. Parents of infants who are at risk for developing emotional or mental problems can fairly easily be trained to give the infants special learning experiences that serve to prevent later difficulty. When the mother–child relationship is very young, neither one has to unlearn much undesirable behavior. Parent Training in Infant Stimulation is the only primary prevention project at the research and training center, and is supported by Developmental Disabilities, not Mental Health.

One of the important gaps in the mental health system occurs in primary prevention. It is very difficult to document the effectiveness of preventive programs, because high risk individuals are not given a diagnosis of illness, and funding usually is tied to treatment of mental illness by governmental agencies and private insurance companies. The mental health system is hard pressed to meet the treatment needs of the mentally ill, so preventive programs, unless separately funded, often get put aside and/or are not well evaluated.

The outlook for secondary prevention efforts with preschool children in the age range of 2 to 5 years who are beginning to develop behavior problems appears fairly optimistic. Parents and foster parents of children in this age group and up through preadolescence learn many effective approaches for reshaping their children's behavior, including the use of positive and negative reinforcement, techniques for reducing aggression, and contingency management. Training Parents of Noncompliant Child Patients, Retraining Predelinquent Children in a Teaching Family, and Using Token Economies in the Home, deal with children in this age group and their families.

As children grow into adolescence, the process of change becomes more complicated. It becomes necessary for adolescents themselves to understand behavior management. Unlike young children, adolescents are in a position to bargain. "I will do this, if you will do that." Good communication and negotiation skills are needed in addition to principles of behavior management.

Since adolescents' problems often develop in homes where the parents themselves have problems, it becomes necessary to provide increasing amounts of individual and marital counseling, as well as crisis intervention, to other members of teenagers' families. Furthermore, because adolescents are increasingly influenced by people outside the home, as are adult patients, it becomes important to pay increasing attention to the development of support groups in the community at large. The section on Training Parents and Foster Parents of Multiproblem Adolescents is concerned with these problems.

TEACHING PARENTS TO STIMULATE THEIR INFANTS

Rationale

Infants at risk for developmental delay usually go through the same processes of sequential learning and development as a normal child, but their rate of development may be slower. Slow development in one area may profoundly delay normal development in other areas. For example, a delay in learning to talk may affect the child's ability to socialize with other children, thus compounding the child's problems and putting him/her even further behind peers.

When a child falls far behind his age-mates in skill acquisition, adults and other children in his social environment may respond to him in various harmful or crippling ways—from doing too much to help him, on the one hand, to ignoring his needs completely, on the other. A retarded or an autistic child affects relationships within his family profoundly, putting stress on the marriage relationship and causing problems with siblings.

Furthermore, a child who experiences little success may stop trying to learn. If a child at risk can be helped to learn as quickly and fully as possible at each stage of development, he/she will have a better chance of growing up with the skills needed to live an independent and rewarding life.

Infants with Down's Syndrome, hydrocephaly, cerebral palsy, or evidence of brain damage who are given much stimulation—who are touched and held often, who are spoken to, and who are presented with various objects to look at, feel, and hold—develop more rapidly and fully than infants not given these learning opportunities. An enriched learning environment brings the developmental rate of infants at risk closer to that of normal children. The earlier this kind of training begins, the better the outcome. With early skills training, an infant at risk may not fall behind his age-mates at all; or a handicapped child may be helped to function at a high enough level to live a rewarding life.

MHWs train parents of infants who are at risk for retarded mental development. Stimulation helps the infant learn receptive and expressive language, and visual perceptual-motor, gross-motor, fine-motor and personal social skills.

MHWs from the Project visit the home to interview the parents and to assess the infant's physical and behavioral strengths and weaknesses. They also assess the parents' acceptance of their child's condition, the nature of mother–child interactions, and cognitive skills of both parents. Team members set up short-term and long-term behavioral goals for the infant based on the assessment, and devise a program of stimulation exercises to help the infant attain these goals. For approximately two months, a Project MHW teaches stimulation exercises to the parents in the home. Contracts between Project and parents ensure that parents carry through on the program.

The infant's development is tracked and charted. After two months, the child usually has progressed sufficiently for home visits to be decreased to one per month.

Within the first month of home training, parents begin to attend weekly small-group (8–10) parents' modular training sessions conducted by MHWs. The classes have three components: (1) didactic sessions in child development for parents; (2) stimulation demonstrations and parent–child group practice of exercises; and (3) problem-solving discussions and relaxation training for parents.

This primary prevention project illustrates many important issues related to the mission of a mental health facility and the role and utilization of MHWs, discussed in Chapter 8.

TRAINING PARENTS OF NONCOMPLIANT CHILDREN

Uncontrollable children who are behaviorally disordered and/or developmentally delayed in acquiring language, social, or cognitive skills are treated in a residential program designed to bring the child's behavior under control—specifically under parental control. The approach is psychoeducational, and the primary student in this effort is the parent, usually the mother, who learns to teach her child more rewarding behavior.[1] Parents are in a position to extinguish or reinforce the myriad behaviors of their children. Their knowledge of and skill at using basic principles of learning are often the critical variables for success.

Uncontrollable preschool children and older children who have been excluded from school and/or reassigned to special classes are treated, and so are their parents or foster parents. The project provides early intervention for preschool children to prevent more serious maladjustment at later ages, and remedial intervention for school-age children. It continues and extends Drash's pilot work[2] with hyperactive and noncompliant children.

The five-day-a-week structure of this residential program minimizes dependence of patients and families upon staff. Families, patients, and staff all benefit from this approach. Staff are able to provide weekday skills-building services to patients and families at the research and training center, and weekend consultation in the patients' homes helping families carry on treatment programs while the patient is at home for the weekend.

It is essential that these very difficult problem children return home every weekend, and that their families be required to continue to cope with their behavior there. Parents of children, and other patients who are very disruptive of family life, experience a tremendous sense of relief when the burden of keeping the patient at home is removed. Unless the treatment plan includes compulsory home-care each weekend, families frequently resist the eventual return of the patient to the home after an extended period of total hospitalization. After experiencing the relief of not caring for the child, the family may abandon the patient or consign him permanently to a residential facility.

Assessments

Pretreatment assessments are made of both parents or foster parents and their child. Direct observations in three settings set baselines of parent–child interactions: (1) in the treatment facility; (2) in the home; and (3) in a community location where the child was most uncontrollable such as the school, the supermarket, the playground, etc.

Four instruments are used to measure progress in treatment:

1. The Louisville Behavior Checklist: Using this checklist, parents report their child's behavior on a variety of scales, which can be compared with normative data.
2. Drash Individual Compliance Behavior Checklist: This structured checklist records observations of the behavior and the consequences administered by parents. It provides frequencies and percentages of compliance, noncompliance, reinforcement, punishment, shaping, and prompting.
3. Drash Group Compliance Behavior Observation Checklist: This checklist assesses a single child's behavior in a group classroom situation.
4. Parent Training Academic Evaluation Form: This written examination tests cognitive understanding of behavior principles. It contains 41 questions, including true-false, multiple choice, and matching items.

Training Program

The child is admitted into an age-appropriate modular psychoeducational class where the educational-behavioral treatment program is individually selected to suit the needs determined by the preassessments. The educational component meets state and federal requirements for these children. The classroom also gives staff an opportunity to deal directly with each child's behavior in a highly structured and controlled setting.

Simultaneous with the child's beginning the remedial psychoeducational program, one or both parents are required (upon penalty of discharge) to participate in the complete range of parent training activities. Each parent is enrolled in a nine-week seminar that teaches specific principles, procedures, techniques, and action steps for the successful behavior management and proper stimulation of children to be applied at home and in the community.

Parents learn the vocabulary, constructs, and theory supporting behavior management. After parents score 80 percent on a post-test on the content of the course, the skill development training phase begins.

Each parent's skills have been preassessed. Parent–child interaction is again directly observed, and repeated measures are taken of their behaviors and interactions. After each training phase, all of the proficiency measures but the written test are repeated in order to determine readiness for the next training phase. Predetermined criteria have been set; movement from one phase to another, skipping phases, and ultimate discharge depends upon "passing" each measure.

The following examples illustrate some of the content that parents are taught in classes, which are usually conducted by paraprofessional mental health workers.*

LEARNING BY DOING

It is difficult to learn any skill without "going through the motions." Repeated practice is necessary for learning words, ideas, and other behaviors. It is not enough only to expose children and their families to the correct information; they must practice the skills; the more times they practice them correctly, the better they will learn them.

PROMPTING DESIRED BEHAVIOR

A *prompt* is any event (coming before the behavior) that encourages a child to do or say a particular thing. Prompts may vary in how *directive* they are and in how *complete* they are. Families are taught to use the least amount of prompt required to get the desired behavior. As learning progresses, less and less assistance should be given. Help should be withdrawn slowly, however. This process of gradually withdrawing assistance is called *fading a prompt*. The following prompts are listed in order, with the most directive first:

Physically putting a child through a motion. Taking a child's hand and placing it on the object for him to locate. An example of an incomplete prompt would be taking the child's hand, moving it in the desired direction, and letting go of his hand, permitting him to complete the motion himself.

Modeling. Acting out or demonstrating the desired behavior. A model is very effective when the model receives lots of praise. Modeling shows the child what he should do, and it also suggests that he, too, will get praise by copying the model.

*From Gordon R, Goldstein N, Gordon K, et al: The role of paraprofessional mental health workers in family therapy. National Education Center for Paraprofessionals in Mental Health, National Institute of Mental Health, Paraprofessional Manpower Development Branch, Monograph Series No. 1, Report No. 3, May, 1979, pp. 16, 17.

Verbal Prompts. Telling the child exactly what to do. There is a fine line be-tween verbal prompting and modeling verbal behavior. For example, if a mother is prompting her son to say his name by pronouncing it first for him, she is actually *modeling* the behavior for him; however, if she gives him a "hint" by pronouncing only the first syllable or letter of his name, she is giving him a verbal prompt.

PROVIDING CONSEQUENCES FOR BEHAVIOR

A consequence is an event that *follows* a behavior, and that appears to be a result of that behavior. A consequence may be pleasant and rewarding or unpleasant and punishing. People tend to repeat behaviors that are followed by rewarding conse-quences. They usually do not repeat behaviors that have unpleasant consequences or that appear to have no consequence at all.

Families learn to reward those behaviors to be repeated and ignore those to be eliminated or discontinued (any kind of attention, including scolding, may be reward-ing to some children).

The testing room is set up to resemble a sitting room in a house, complete with couches, chairs, a coffee table, lamps, toys, etc. Observations are made from an ad-jacent room through a one-way mirror; the observer instructs the parents by means of a microphone. Measurements are taken of the parent's use of behavior management techniques and the child's compliance or noncompliance. Using a standardized obser-vation format, observations are taken as the parent responds to four different tasks: (1) interact freely with your child; (2) teach the child a task; (3) play a game with your child; and (4) give the child commands. No other instructions are given the par-ent or child. These measures indicate the degree and effectiveness of parents' use of contingencies, antecedents, and consequences to behavior.

When parents do not perform to criteria, they receive "Bug-in-Ear" training; the parent trainer provides immediate, direct, individual instruction and feedback to the parent by means of a wireless radio receiver worn in the ear of the parent. The parent trainer, observing through a one-way vision mirror (or in the home or community from a short distance away), speaks to the parent through a portable microphone. The child and parent can be both seen and heard by the parent trainer, while only the par-ent can hear the feedback and instructions of the parent trainer. Parents are dis-charged once testing demonstrates that they perform proficiently in all three settings—home, treatment facility, and community—and that their cognitive knowl-edge is adequate. If measurements of the child's progress indicate satisfactory im-provement, the child also may be discharged.

Behavioral measures are repeated in the home and community settings at inter-vals of 1, 3, 6, 10, and 16 months after discharge. If child or parent performance slips, remedial action is taken immediately on site, a practice that ensures maintenance of gains by both child and parent. In these ways, the program helps the child's parent learn to become the child's primary therapist. Finally, a staff member accompanies each child to day or public school, and helps the teacher there to employ the behav-ioral procedures that were most effective with the child.

Evaluation

Early findings can be reported on a few treated children and their parents, but no data are available on controls; some comparison figures are also presented. The mean Parent–Child percentile rank improved on the Behar Preschool Behavior Questionnaire on total Disturbed Behavior from 65 pretreatment to 99 post-treatment. On the Drash Individual and Group Compliance Behavior Checklists, children's mean after-treatment compliance with parental demands in the home was 71 percent; in the clinic it was 77.5 percent; and in the classroom it was 99.5 percent. In contrast, only 38.6 percent compliance was observed in a group of five hyperactive preschool children who had not yet received treatment in the project. Finally, trained parents scored 77.5 percent on the Drash Compliance Checklist, as compared to 35 percent for untrained parents.[1]

RETRAINING PREDELINQUENT CHILDREN
THROUGH THE TEACHING FAMILY MODEL

Children who get into serious trouble with the law often show predelinquent or socially maladjusted behaviors—running away, truancy, minor theft, ungovernability, and disruptive activity at school. In contrast to the psychotic or autistic child who often withdraws, the socially maladjusted child displays behaviors that are antisocial, aggressive, and poorly controlled. The child usually is two-to-three years behind academically; bullies other children and may steal from them; disobeys adult direction; responds negatively to criticism; speaks rudely and/or abusively to adults, and cannot be trusted to tell the truth to an adult; damages property and shoplifts, and may have appeared in juvenile court. When a child gets this far out of hand, a parent may have very little real control over the child's life outside the home. Even with training in more effective parenting techniques, working parents or parents with their own problems may be unable to find the time and energy to do what is necessary to get the child back under control.

When a child has exhausted the available community social services, such as individual counseling, family therapy, and school remediation, a different home situation may be called for. Placement in a foster home often does not help, however: The typical foster parent has not been adequately trained to teach children new, prosocial behaviors. If children are belligerent and continue to get into trouble outside the home, they may be shunted from one foster home to another, their behavior getting worse with each successive move. (Some children have been in as many as 25 foster homes.) What is needed is a group home with a set of trained, full-time surrogate parents who can retrain the child in social skills and coordinate the efforts of other adults in the child's life.

The Teaching-Family Model

The Teaching-Family Model is based on the Achievement Place Project of child care developed at the University of Kansas. This model has been subjected to both procedural and program evaluation, and has proven to be effective in both a community-based program setting as well as in a private institutional program.[3,4] Numerous publications have resulted from the systematic evaluation of this model. Specifically, research has been conducted in the Teaching-Family Model regarding modification of disturbed youngsters' classroom behaviors,[5] articulation errors,[6] self-government behaviors,[7] maintenance behaviors,[8] negotiations of conflict situations,[9] academic behavior problems,[10] conversation skills,[11] vocational behaviors,[12] improved school grades and reduced truancy,[13] and autistic-like behaviors.

Studies have also indicated success of the Teaching-Family Model in effecting a lower grade of recidivism in children served by the program.[3,4,14] The Teaching-Family Model has been demonstrated to be not only an effective human service delivery program, but one that, as with all quality human service programs, is in need of continued development and research.

The present program, the Family-Teaching Project, extends the findings of the Family-Teaching Model by experimentally investigating the applicability of this model to a public institutional setting, the viability of teaching procedures in a community-based program that is on the grounds of an institution, and the dissemination capacity of such a model to other institutions and child-care facilities.

Recent application of a community-based behavioral model to an institutional setting has proved to be successful with adolescent youths at Boys Town, Nebraska. Youths served in this program live in individual cottages that closely resemble family-style living in the greater surrounding community. The staff in these programs, known as Teaching-Parents, function as surrogate parents and provide the treatment necessary for their "Family" of eight youngsters. The youngsters utilize, as much as possible, surrounding community resources for school, employment, and generalization of skills to the natural environment. This approach has proven effective in increasing cost efficiency, decreasing absenteeism, decreasing runaway behavior, increasing satisfaction on the part of the youngsters served, decreasing amounts of vandalism, and increasing social skills.[3]

This community-based behavioral skills-building model can be adapted to public and private institutional settings. The model is also appropriate for children of younger ages. It provides a program that can be used in group home facilities in the community, and in other treatment facilities for emotionally disturbed, predelinquent, and/or retarded citizens. The skills building model solves many cost-efficiency problems for institutional programming; it creates an entirely new concept in the child-care field.

MHWs as Family Teachers

Each group home houses eight socially maladjusted children between the ages of 6 and 14 and a Teaching-Parent couple, who may have their own children. The treatment program, based on a model developed at the University of Kansas, uses a token economy to modify antisocial behavior. The teaching family is trained to reward appropriate behavior with praise as well as points; ignore and extinguish unacceptable activities; give criticism, suggestions, and directions in a nonconfronting, enthusiastic, and positive way; explain why certain behaviors result in unpleasant or disappointing consequences (for example, pouting, sulking, or turning away from criticism makes an adult in authority—a judge, policeman, or teacher—angry and punishing); give specific directions for doing a better job, acknowledging the part of the job that was done adequately or well.

Teaching parents receive instruction in behavior management techniques, group programming, and individual counseling, as well as in ways to communicate with children—how to express affection, sympathy, concern; how to provide support and reassurance. They are supervised on the job for a period of one year, and their skills are regularly evaluated by trainers, by the children themselves, and also by social workers and school teachers involved with the children.

The National Teaching Family Association, with its headquarters at the University of Kansas, has been created to maintain high performance standards for teaching parents or family teachers. This is a certifying organization that now has approximately 200 certified members; NTFA is going about establishing Family Teachers as a new profession. The Teaching Family model has been used successfully with orphans, "emotionally disturbed" children, and retarded children and adults in a total of 125 group homes nationwide.

Token Economy in the Treatment Facility

When the children first come into the group home, they are given many simple tasks and much social reinforcement for performing them. They are put on a token economy of points. In the beginning, they trade their points daily for privileges. After they thoroughly understand the point system, they are taken off it and graduate to a merit system. The idea is to have the children perform for social reinforcement rather than for material rewards as soon as possible. Eventually, as the children's behavior improves, they are moved up to a "homeward bound" system, where they spend increasing amounts of time at home. After a child returns home to live there full-time, teaching parents maintain contact with child and parents, and continue in a counseling role.

Advantages of the Family Teaching Model

Savings in costs. The small staff, minimal administration, and reduced costs for housekeeping, laundering, food purchases, and maintenance all serve to keep expenses down. The cost of replicating the Family Teaching project in other settings is estimated at 27 to 35 dollars a day. Since the youngsters attend public schools, academic costs are also minimized.

Legal benefits. Teaching parents live, vacation, and work with their clients like any other family. Thus they provide a least restrictive environment for children or youths who cannot reside in their own homes. The program offers a normalized alternative to institutionalization.

Accountability. Teaching parents, with their structured, well-developed curriculum and small number of staff, provide more consistent and responsible care for the clients than does the amorphous multidisciplinary "team."

TRAINING PARENTS AND FOSTER PARENTS OF MULTIPROBLEM ADOLESCENTS

Rationale

The Adolescent Day Treatment Project serves youngsters between the ages of 12 and 18 with serious behavioral and/or emotional problems. A major focus on this project has been on adolescents adjudicated as "dependent." These dependent youths include those who have been placed in foster homes because of abuse, neglect, or abandonment by parents, and also those who live in their own home but have repeatedly run away, been truant, or are beyond the control of their parents. Without special interventions, these adolescents are likely to encounter increasingly serious difficulties, not only within the child welfare and educational system, but also with the juvenile and mental hospital systems. One-third of adolescents were hospitalized in psychiatric facilities prior to entry into the Project.[15] (See Chapter 11.)

The MHWs provide a coordinated set of special educational and individual counseling services for youngsters, plus family counseling and support activities. This integration of services is particularly needed with the youngsters served, since they and their parents typically have a history of poor follow-through with community services.

MHWs help youngsters acquire the practical, social, academic, and pre-vocational skills needed for effective functioning in the community. This skill building takes place in a setting that maximizes opportunities for youngsters to succeed through an individualized, noncompetitive program with a heavy emphasis on positive reinforcement for even small amounts of progress.

Parent Training by MHWs

Stabilizing and strengthening a youth's living situation is one of the primary goals of the program, and parents must agree to participate in weekly family counseling sessions, and to keep the program staff informed of significant home developments.

Parents of these youngsters are accustomed to receiving negative reports about them from teachers, counselors, etc. This kind of unpleasantness has oftentimes contributed to parent–child conflict, while discouraging parents from engaging in any intervention program. Staff attempt to keep parents closely informed about their child's progress in the program, and to emphasize positive accomplishments as much as possible. MHW teachers strive to send at least two positive notes home per week with each child, or to make two phone calls with positive news each week. Report cards detailing student performance and progress in each program area are sent home every six weeks. No grades are assigned. Rather, the report cards state the percentage of possible points that students have earned during the marking period in each class and the percentage of days they have been present. Comments from teachers and counseling staff focus primarily on positive behaviors and achievement, although areas in need of improvement are mentioned. The work covered in each class during the marking period is indicated. This feedback from project to home, which emphasizes positive information to parents, reinforces student accomplishments and contributes to the development of a trusting relationship between staff and families; it eases the way for MHW family counselors to work with the families.

MHWs receive training in family interviewing and counseling, using the simulated family interviews, modeling by staff, and video-taped feedback or role-played situation. This procedure helps counselors to focus on behaviors of all family members, rather than just the identified client. In addition, weekly supervision-training sessions are conducted to review the progress and problems encountered with each family.

Home Visits

Since many of the parents have no transportation, and large numbers of kids live at home or at a long distance, MHW counselors go out to the family once per week to conduct family sessions. This is a costly procedure, but more effective than dealing with the high percentage of missed sessions that results with this population of parents when sessions are held away from the home. Sessions may be held in the evening to include working parents. A strong emphasis is placed on including both parents, if at all possible. Family counselors discuss the youngster's school performance and home activities during the week. The specific interventions that they utilize depend upon the particular problems, needs, and resources of the family. They may, for example, develop behavioral contracts to modify specific problems at home, or even construct a token economy system when there are multiple behavior problems. MHW counselors may conduct individual supportive counseling sessions with parents, particularly for ventilation and clarification of issues and feelings. Conjoint family sessions are conducted in which the counselors intervene to try to change maladaptive patterns of family interaction that are contributing to the youngster's problem. Specific training in communication and problem-solving skills, as well as in positive reinforcement, are also conducted as needed. Family counselors frequently include siblings and other significant persons such as extended family and friends in the treatment sessions in an effort to develop a strong and constructive support system for the family.

Foster Parent Training

The same individualized format is used for treatment with foster parents as with natural parents, but the issues dealt with often differ. In many cases, foster parents have only recently begun to know the youngster. They tend to view their role as a mixture of parent, volunteer, and paraprofessional. Due to shortages of foster homes for adolescents with emotional problems, the foster home may have several youngsters in it. The family counselor may therefore provide consultation and training sessions concerning not only the youngster in the Project but also the other children in the home. Additional training is provided to foster parents to help them understand the effects upon youngsters of the rejection they received, not only from their parents but also, in many cases, from other foster parents. The behavior of the youngster is interpreted to the foster parents in the context of his/her history of family disruptions, instability, neglect, and abuse; foster parents are taught skills for dealing with youngsters with such histories.

COMMENT ON FAMILY TRAINING

Many remedial educational/behavioral children's programs are content to change behavior in the treatment setting and hope that changes will generalize to other settings. The projects described in this chapter consider the job only partially completed when a child makes progress in the facility classroom or other treatment setting. They make certain that treatment gains are maintained in the natural setting by a systematic sequence of training of both child and parent in both home and community, as well as in the treatment facility. Training in all these settings prepares the parent–child dyad to respond appropriately to cues and other stimuli in the natural environment. This chapter has presented a variety of strategies for training parents and foster parents of children of different ages and with different types of problems.

REFERENCES

1. Drash PW, Stolberg AL, Bostow BE: Does hyperactivity mean noncompliance? Modifying noncompliant behavior of children diagnosed as hyperactive. Tampa, Fla., Florida Mental Health Institute Publication, 1979
2. Drash PW: Treatment of hyperactivity in the two-year-old child. Pediatr Psychol 3:17–20, 1975
3. Evans JH, Dowd TP, Schneider K, et al: Evaluation of the boys' town youth care department. Boys' Town, Nebraska. Father Flanagan's Boys Home Publication, 1976
4. Kirigin KA, Fixsen DL, Wolf MM: An evaluation of fourteen community based programs in Kansas. The final report to the Kansas Department of Social and Rehabilitative Services, Topeka, Ka., 1974
5. Bailey JS, Wolf MM, Phillips EL: Home-based reinforcement and the modification of predelinquent classroom behavior. J Appl Behav Anal 3:223–233, 1970
6. Bailey JS, Timbers GD, Phillips EL, et al: Modification of articulation errors of predelinquents by their peers. J Appl Behav Anal 4:265–281, 1971
7. Fixsen DL, Phillips EL, Wolf MM: Achievement place: Experiments in self-government with predelinquents. Ment Health Dig 5:38–46, 1973
8. Phillips EL, Phillips EA, Fixsen DL, et al: Achievement place: Modification of behavior of predelinquent boys with token economy. J Appl Behav Anal 4:35–39, 1971
9. Kifer RE, Lewis MA, Green DR, et al: Training predelinquent youths and their parents to negotiate conflict situations. J Appl Behav Anal 7:357–364, 1974
10. Kirigin KA, Phillips EL, Timbers GD, et al: Achievement place: The modification of academic behavior problems of youths in a group home setting, in Etzel BC, LeBlanc JM, Baer DM (Eds): New Developments in Behavioral Research: Theory, Method and Application. Hillsdale, N.J., Earlbaum Associates, 1977, pp 473–487
11. Minkin N, Braukman CJ, Minkin BL, et al: The social validation and training of conversation skills. J Appl Behav Anal 9:127–140, 1976
12. Ayala HE, Minkin M, Phillips EL, et al: Achievement place: The training and analysis of vocational behavior. J Appl Behav Anal (in press)
13. Maloney DM, Maloney KB, Timbers GD: Improved school grades and reduced truancy: Preliminary program evaluation report no. 1 from the Bringing It All Back Home group home project for youths in trouble. Western Carolina Center Papers and Reports 5, No. 2, 1975
14. Phillips EL, Phillips EA, Fixsen DL, et al: Behavior shaping works for delinquents. Psychology Today (June 1973) pp 73–79
15. Friedman RM; The summary report of first cycle of adolescent project day treatment program. (Unpublished manuscript.) Tampa, Fla., Florida Mental Health Institute, 1978

PART D

Programming for Psychiatric Care of Chronically Ill Adult Mental Patients

The treatment programs for chronically ill adult mental patients described here, and in the previous chapters on children's programs and subsequent ones on gerontology programs, link institutional and community components in a fashion that Feldman, et al.[1] have shown to be significantly more successful than nonintegrated services. Further, the adult programs provide ties between professional aftercare and self-help that go beyond most traditional community support projects (see Figure 2-1). A unique conceptualization of adjustment and rehabilitation characterizes these treatment projects. This section will briefly describe this theoretical model of adjustment; the subsequent chapter will detail the projects' components.

Stresses, Models, Training, Skills, and Supports

Mental patients have usually experienced many stresses in their lives. As children many were sensitized by loss of a parent, breakup of family, illness, and other hurts. In later life they are pressurized by the death of loved ones,

---

Portions of this section appeared originally in Edmunson ED, Bedell JR, Archer RP, et al: Integrating skill-building and peer support: The Early Intervention and Community Network Development projects (in Slotnik R, Jeger A [Eds]: Community Mental Health: A Behavioral-Ecological Perspective. New York, Plenum Press, 1980) and Edmunson ED, Bedell JR, Gordon RE: Bridging the gap between self-help and professional aftercare (in Gartner A, Riessman F [Eds]: Mental Health and the Self-Help Revolution. New York, Human Science Press, in press), and are reprinted with permission.

personal divorce or separation, financial troubles, loss of support groups, legal problems, and the like. Highly sensitized and pressurized, they are especially vulnerable to life's crises. Acute phases of their illnesses are often brought on by precipitators—new crises that, along with their past and present stresses, overburden their ability to cope.[2] Holmes and Rahe have quantified many of the pressurizers and precipitators into Life Crisis Units.[3]

Mental patients also have received inadequate preparation in coping. People learn the skills needed for effective functioning in life from their family in the home, from teachers and fellow students in the school, from employers and fellow employees on the job, and from friends in organizations and in social and leisure activities.

Many parents of mental patients were unable to provide good role models and adequate training. Patients often quit school and failed to obtain either the formal knowledge that gives them control and direction of their lives, or the training in behavioral skills such as setting goals and persevering in their attainment. Both of these—lack of knowledge and lack of skills—are related to poor mental health and to poor response to psychiatric treatment. In addition, mental patients often fail to keep jobs, do not generally belong to organizations, and have few friends, most of whom are not especially skillful.[2,4,5]

The psychiatric treatment described here provides patients with: (1) psychotropic medications and other physiologic treatments that calm their abnormal physiologic functioning, disturbed thinking, and other behavioral abnormalities; (2) dynamic insight and (3) behavioral treatments that desensitize and extinguish abnormal responses; (4) social supports; (5) skill-building in areas where the patients are poorly prepared; (6) family therapy; (7) recreational activities and training; and (8) assistance from community agencies. (See Figure 2-7.) Patients must receive skill training if they are to benefit fully from treatment. With it they gain greater personal control over their lives and reduce their stresses to more endurable levels. To these last they must become inured.[5]

A Behavioral-Ecological Conceptualization of Adjustment

According to a model of the adjustment process developed by Edmunson,[6] the ability to cope with the debilitating effect of stress is central to successful adjustment. When a problematic life event occurs, whether it be of major significance, such as the loss of a job, or relatively minor, as in the breakdown of a car, the individual's normal pattern of functioning is interrupted. The amount of stress the individual experiences as a result of any particular event depends on a number of factors; i.e., the nature of the event, the quantity of stress to which the person is subjected, the individual's personality structure and past experience with similar problems, and how well the person has become inured to hardship. Whatever the nature or amount of stress experienced, the individual must make use of personal coping skills and knowledge to effect a resolution. Those who have been educated and trained to use their intelligence in facing, coping, and solving life's problems do better than falterers, quitters, and drop-outs.[5,6]

Problem-solving involves several discrete steps, as shown before in Chapter 7: recognition or awareness, definition, alternatives generation, and, finally, decision-making or action. Adjustment can fail at several points in this process. The individual may be unable to define the problem in a rational and complete way, or he may not be able to identify appropriate action alternatives. Adjustment may also fail if the individual lacks the skills or knowledge to personally implement his solution or to ask for appropriate assistance.[7,8]

It becomes apparent that problem resolution and adjustment may fail as a result of skill deficits. The individual under stress must have an accurate assessment of his problem and its potential solutions, and he must also have the skills to implement the solution, either through his own efforts or through obtaining the help of others. If the individual's skills are not adequate to deal with the problem, or if the nature of the problem is such that external help is necessary to its solution, then the next factor in the adjustment process comes into play, namely, the individual's external resources and support systems.

The external resources or supports that are potentially available for help in solving life's problems may be broadly categorized into two groups: natural support systems and professional support systems. The natural support system is composed of family, close friends, neighbors, co-workers, and other community groups or individuals. The professional support system is composed of individuals and agencies who exist specifically to provide counseling or social services. An individual may initially seek help from either of these sources, depending upon past success or failure. The individual may be unable to obtain external aid for several reasons: a natural or professional support system may be unavailable, the individual may not seek assistance because he does not perceive the system as willing or able to help, and the natural or professional support system, even when requested to intervene, may be unwilling or unable to respond to the need.

Thus, at least three factors are involved in successful resolution of problematic life events: (1) the adequacy of personal, social, and living skills; (2) the adequacy of external resources and supports, whether they be natural or professional; and (3) the modifiability of the social environment (whether the stresses can be reduced either by the individual's own efforts or by the efforts of persons in the support network).[8]

If, for example, no free legal assistance were available to Suella, she might have lost her child permanently; her rehabilitation would possibly have been more difficult.

Mental patients' deficiencies in personal skills have been well documented,[2,9,10] as have their gaps in community support and other resources.[11] Research evidence suggests that the natural helping provided by an individual's social network provides protection against a wide range of physical and emotional problems.[11-17] Community supports appear to be a critical factor in keeping former mental patients out of the hospital.[8,18] A growing body of literature also documents the inadequacy of the typical mental patient's support system.[19-22] Assisting mental patients to improve their natural support system provides a powerful clinical intervention.[2]

Family Therapy in the Treatment of the Chronically Ill Adult Mental Patient

Interactions between family members of adults are very difficult to change. The goal in the case of the adult is to involve families (often reinvolve families) so that the home environment becomes more of a sanctuary in which the patients may improve or maintain their gains from treatment. The family learns the tools for maintaining a reinforcing, supportive environment to continue long-range rehabilitative efforts within the home rather than in an institutional setting. Work with families of adults also emphasizes the development of community support systems.

When personal coping skills and family supports are not adequate, mental patients must turn to the professional establishment for assistance. Unfortunately, this support system often fails to meet their needs as well. At the very best, mental patients are doomed to the frustration of trying to get help from bureaucratic institutions that operate slowly, have confusing criteria for providing service, and do not coordinate with each other to meet their needs. This lack of integrated service delivery has been identified as a major problem in serving the mental health population.[23]

MODULAR SKILL BUILDING FOR CHRONICALLY ILL ADULT MENTAL PATIENTS

Chronically ill adult mental patients require psychoeducational programs that are related to their degree of psychosocial impairment. Programs for younger, less impaired adults seek to intervene early in the patient's residential treatment experience, reducing the need for future and repeated hospitalization. Rather than simply provide a physical and pharmacological "refuge" from life stresses, the treatment involves patients in an active, time-limited regimen designed to increase personal coping skills and independence. An intensive modular training program develops patients' skills in a variety of areas, and behavioral therapy techniques are used to decrease the occurrence of maladaptive behaviors.

During residence, all patients participate in structured modular skill-building groups. The focus of these groups is on acquiring positive adaptive skills, rather than just exploring individual failures and psychopathology. Each psychoeducational skill-building class combines the didactic presentation of relevant information with experiential exercises to facilitate skill acquisition and generalization.[24] The patient attends groups in the dual role of client and student. Participants are encouraged to take an active stance in asking questions, performing "homework" assignments, and relating the skill training to their own life situations. Skill training programs are designed with strong attention to behavioral and educational principles, including sequential learning, immediate feedback, successive approximation, and stimulus and response generalization. Modular skill training is provided in a variety of functional skill areas.

Patients who have been hospitalized repeatedly and for long periods in mental institutions often require training in activities of daily living. Custodial treatment in an institution can produce isolation, alienation, lack of motivation, dependency, and loss of basic social skills. These chronic patients are also less likely to have families available, so their treatment must prepare them to live with an alternative family or in a congregate living facility. They require, in addition to their medical needs, housing and income maintenance, as well as skill-building in communication, human interaction, the use of leisure, and basic coping techniques for dealing with modern life. Many middle-aged chronic patients have lost virtually all contact with life outside the institution. A transitional program offers them habilitation and rehabilitation services.

Adult patients who can be released from traditional treatment units in state hospitals, both those whose assessments indicate that they are heading toward jobs and those moving toward a boarding home or alternative living track, need training in skills to help them cope with problems, increase their ability to reduce stress, restore their competency, and increase the quality of their lives. The program is designed to extend the length of time that graduates successfully spend back in the community. Categories of skills are differentiated, as in other programs, into the basic incremental steps necessary for mastery. Treatment includes preassessment, instruction as indicated by the assessment, and postassessment.

Brief descriptions of skill-enhancement modules for adult patients follow. Patients who have skills in these activities may skip some or all of this training.

Activities of Daily Living

Basic maintenance skills (ADL I).   Basic skills include purchasing groceries, comparing food costs, planning nutritious menus, cooking and preparing meals, housekeeping, using the laundromat, and budgeting.

Skills necessary for community contact (ADL II).   At the next level, skill training includes finding out about transportation, using the telephone and directory, using the newspaper for shopping, leisure, and work information, and identifying and using service organizations.

Skills necessary for community living (ADL III).   Preparation for discharge requires information on a variety of housing sources, on setting up a household (furnishings, utilities, relationships with neighbors); shopping; establishing working relationships with community service organizations; making social contacts and keeping them; keeping a job and what to do if fired; car pooling, bus riding, getting transportation from a co-worker, acquaintance, or friend; developing a support system in the community; budgeting, using banks, and obtaining credit.

Personal and Social Skills

Problem solving.   This training includes the steps described in Chapter 7. In Recognition Training patients acknowledge problems, accept responsibility for them, and establish priorities for dealing with them. In Definition Training they learn to break problems down into component parts and establish a goal-oriented approach to solving them. Generation of Alternatives Training teaches different methods of developing possible solutions to problems. Finally, in Decision Training, alternative solutions are evaluated and the best is selected.[7] (See Appendix 1.)

Relaxation training.   Utilizing lectures, audio-visual work, group discussion, fantasy, and exercises, staff teach self-help and relaxation. Relaxation training teaches the patient to relax at will and to counteract the effects of stress by reciprocal inhibition.[25]

Assertion training.   Assertion skills training helps patients learn to differentiate between passive, assertive, and aggressive behaviors. They learn to accomplish their goals in a direct, tactful manner, to shunt destructive anger into constructive thought and reasoning, and to develop respect for themselves and others.

Negotiation training.   Many Americans, both patients and normals, lack skill in negotiation. They do not know how to ask questions and gain the information they need to make a good bargain because they have had little example in their early home life. As a result, those who have not learned to negotiate skillfully face frustration as they proceed through life, because they come out on the short end of many deals. They rightfully feel that people are getting the better of them. They may wrongfully conclude, however, that people are out to get them; they do not realize that they simply are not well trained negotiators.

In Negotiation Training, classes divide up into couples, without regard to sex. Each couple is instructed to develop a "Relationship Contract" dealing with routine chores—cleaning the kitchen, scrubbing the bathroom—and simulated ones—picking up the children from school, staying out late after work. The pair compromise, make deals, and learn to come to satisfactory agreements.

Sex role training.   This module addresses many of the sexual topics that confuse psychiatric patients and interfere with their establishing lasting interpersonal relationships. The program seeks to accomplish many of the same therapeutic benefits that Suella's group therapist had attempted, and which had embarrassed and confused her. However, the content of the modular psychoeducational classes is presented in a manner that is designed to avoid shock and to facilitate understanding and gradual extinction.

Sex role awareness improves understanding of the different training men and women have traditionally received in their upbringing. *Love and committed relationships* explores patients' attitudes about loving relationships and the place of sex in their value hierarchy.

Sexuality education presents didactic training on sexual anatomy and physiology, as well as on birth control and venereal disease; it explores patients' fears, anxieties, and misinformation on these subjects. *Sexual myths and fallacies* covers common beliefs that are untrue and interfere with normal, happy, loving relationships. *Sexual values clarification* is concerned with a number of controversial issues, such as homosexuality, nude dancing in public; living together and sexual activity before marriage; it helps patients to examine their own values, to recognize where theirs fit on a continuum with those of others, and to reassess theirs if they no longer appear to be relevant to the realities of their life. *Vocabulary desensitization* teaches patients the sex language of science, of childhood, of the street, and of common communication; it helps them overcome anxiety and embarrassment in talking and thinking about the subject.

Personal health care.   In addition to self-medication training, patients learn about nutrition, preventing sickness, and getting medical, psychiatric, and dental help.

Vocational Skills

Vocational training combines community on-the-job experience and skills training. Patients are placed in community jobs for which they need no job reference, no job interview, nor any other entrance employment requirement. In their psychoeducational classes they learn how to participate in a job interview, how to fill out a job application, how to groom themselves, how to look for a job, and how to keep a job. Finally, they meet on a regular basis with other employed patients to discuss problems of working, and to offer each other advice and support.

Integrative Skills

Patients receive a brief course in what a goal is, how to set a goal, and how to plan in order to reach a goal. They are then required to set both long-term goals (concerned with their community living plans) and weekly goals (steps leading toward long-term goals). The weekly goals are broken down into planning steps with target dates for the completion of each step. Initially, staff facilitate the goal-setting process by strongly reinforcing every step a patient takes in the direction of completing a goal. Later, patients learn self-reinforcement—they themselves pair a reward with each movement toward a goal. Gradually, patients learn step-by-step to prepare and plan in advance, to integrate their efforts in pursuit of increasingly distant goals, and to persist patiently and persevere in attaining them.[26]

COMMUNITY SUPPORTS

Froland et al.[27] have identified five emerging forms of collaboration between natural and professional helping systems. Three of these models have potential applications with aftercare patients: the Personal Network model, the Volunteer Linking model, and the Mutual Aid Network model.

In the Personal Network approach, the professional attempts to strengthen or modify the existing personal support network of an individual client. This model has limited application within deinstitutionalization programs, however. Frequently, the mental health client's network is small. Even family members may have abandoned the patient, or, if they remain an active part of the support system, they may be involved in pathological interactions with the patient. Working to change this impoverished and pathological system may be too difficult and time-consuming to be practical with a public aftercare system.

The Volunteer Linking model has similar practical limitations. In this approach, the professional staff take a directive role, attempting to create a supportive network for an individual client by linking him/her to volunteer helpers or other individuals in the client's natural environment. Again, there are serious logistical problems, since the volunteers recruited for integration into a client's network may not remain over time unless there is substantial professional support and monitoring.

The most efficient model for use with aftercare clients would appear to be what Froland et al.[27] have termed the Mutual Aid Network. Within this model, the professional focuses on a client population experiencing similar problems and either collaborates with an existing self-help group or alternatively creates a network among a group of clients. This was the approach initiated effectively with new mothers, and elaborated much more fully in the Community Network Development (CND).[6,12] Experience with antenatal class groups and with CND illustrates how a mutual aid network can be effective in reducing both emotional distress after a critical life change experience and hospital recidivism among mental patients. Long-term benefits four to six years later were demonstrated with the former group. The CND structure also provides research evidence that rehabilitation can be accomplished as a result of a partnership between formal, professional helping systems and informal, natural helping systems.

CND affirms that mental health clients have strengths and abilities that enable them to take an active part not only in their own rehabilitation, but in the rehabilitation of their peers as well. The type of helping provided by a peer is more personal, spontaneous, flexible, and enduring than the help that can be provided by a professional. Self-help or mutual aid activities that exist outside the realm of professional influence have proven they may fail to link with professional systems of care, or even assume an than the help that can be provided by a professional. Self-help or mutual aid activities that exist outside the realm of professional influence have proven susceptible to a variety of ills, however. They may lack sufficient structure and organization, they may fail to link with professional systems of care, or even assume an antiprofessional stance, and they may over time develop undesirable dogma and norms. Gartner and Riessman point out, as reported by McNett,[28] that self-help can be used as a political argument against support for professional services. Those who join these groups may be diverted from seeking appropriate professional services when needed. And self-help groups can foster dependency by encouraging group members to believe they can stay healthy only by staying in the group. Riessman and Gartner, who founded and co-direct the National Self-Help Clearinghouse at the City University of New York, have been strong supporters and publicists for the CND approach.

CND's development was guided by the belief that a self-help or mutual aid program for aftercare clients would be most effective if it were structured and supervised by professionals. Ideally, this partnership should allow both professionals and natural helpers to complement each other's efforts. Natural helpers would be allowed to function within the network, maintaining their special characteristics and unique helping roles. Professional staff would be responsible for tasks that require high levels of training, knowledge or professional expertise. The description of CND's staffing pattern and role assignments will illustrate the programmatic structure that evolved in an attempt to implement these goals.

The chapter that follows describes a comprehensive rehabilitation program for adult psychiatric patients. It assists them in each step of the adjustment process. The program trains patients in problem-solving and other psychosocial skills; it helps them develop peer support and natural support systems in the community; it provides them with professional and paraprofessional assistance and backup support after they leave residential treatment.

REFERENCES

1. Feldman PS, Sadtler TM, Lipman R: Phasing down state hospitals: Integrated versus non-integrated services. Hosp Community Psychiatry 30:327,1979
2. Gordon RE, Gordon KK, Gunther M: The Split-Level Trap. New York, B. Geis & Co., 1961
3. Holmes TH, Rahe RH: The Social Readjustment Rating Scale. J Psychosom Res 11:213–218, 1967
4. Gordon RE, Singer MG, Gordon KK; The stress of obtaining a higher education. J Med Soc NJ 59:608–614, 1962
5. Gordon RE: Sociodynamics and psychotherapy. AMA Arch Neurol Psychiat 81:486–503, 1959
6. Edmunson ED, Bedell JR, Archer RP: Integrating skill building and peer support: The Early Intervention and Community Network Development Projects, in Slotnik R, Jeger A (Eds): Community Mental Health: A Behavioral-Ecological Perspective. New York, Plenum Press, 1980
7. D'Zurilla TJ, Goldfried MR: Problem solving and behavior modification. J Abnorm Psychol 73:107–126, 1971
8. Gordon RE, Singer M, Gordon KK: Social psychological stress. Arch Gen Psychiatry 4:459, 1961
9. Anthony WA, Margules A: Towards improving the efficacy of psychiatric rehabilitation: A skills training approach. Rehabil Psychology 21:101–105, 1974
10. Lamb HR: An educational model for teaching living skills to long-term patients. Hosp Commun Psychiatry 27:875–879, 1976
11. Gordon RE: Prevention of Postpartum Emotional Difficulties. Ann Arbor, Mich., University Microfilms, 1961
12. Gordon RE, Kapostins EE, Gordon KK: Factors in postpartum emotional adjustment. Obstet Gynecol 25:158–166, 1965

13. Gore S: The effect of social support in moderating the health consequences of unemployment. J Health Soc Behav 19:157–165, 1978
14. Nuckolls KB, Cassel J, Kaplan BH: Psychosocial assets, life crisis and the prognosis of pregnancy, Am J Epidemiol 95:431–441, 1972
15. Miller PMC, Ingham JG: Friends, confidantes, and symptoms. Soc Psychiatry 11:51–58, 1976
16. Brown GW, Bhrolchain MM, Harris T: Social class and psychiatric disturbance among women in an urban population. Sociology 9:225–254, 1975
17. Medalil JH, Goldbourt U: Angina pectoris among 10,000 men, II. Am J Med 60:910–921, 1976
18. Byers ES, Cohen SH: Predicting patient outcome: The contribution of prehospital, inhospital, and posthospital factors. Hosp Commun Psychiatry 30:327, 1979
19. Tolsdorf CC: Social networks, support and coping: An exploratory study. Family Process 16:407–418, 1976
20. Pattison EM: Clinical social systems interventions. Psychiatry Dig 38:25–33, 1977
21. Hammer M, Makiesky-Barrow S, Gutwirth L: Social networks and schizophrenia. Schizophrenia Bull 4:522–545, 1978
22. Sokolovsky J, Cohen C, Berger D, et al: Personal networks of ex-mental patients in a Manhattan SRO hotel. Hum Org 37:5–15, 1978
23. Turner J, Ten Hoor W: The NIMH community support program: Pilot approach to a needed social reform. Schizophrenia Bull 4:319–348, 1978
24. Bedell JR, Weathers R: A psychoeducational model of skill training: Therapist and game facilitated applications, in Upper D, Ross SM (Eds): Behavioral Group Therapy: An Annual Review. Champaign, Ill. Research Press, (in press)
25. Gordon RE: Counseling for modern environmental stress. Consultant 10:4–6, 1962
26. Gordon RE, Singer MG, Gordon KK: Social psychological stress. Arch Gen Psychiatry 4:459, 1961
27. Froland C, Pancoast DL, Chapman NJ, et al: Professional partnerships with informal helpers: Emerging forms. Paper presented at American Psychological Association, September 4, 1979
28. McNett I, Made for each other. APA Monitor, 10, 12, 1 and 2, 1979

Eileen D. Edmunson, Jeffrey R. Bedell
Robert P. Archer, Richard E. Gordon

14

Integrating Skills-Building, Peer Supports, and Aftercare for Adult Mental Patients

The Adult Programs are a comprehensive and interrelated service system designed to meet the needs of chronic psychiatric patients from the point of entering residential treatment until long after their return to community life. They include three residential and three community projects for adult psychiatric patients. Innovative residential treatment programs are represented by the Intensive Residential Treatment Project (IRT), the Early Intervention Project (EIP), and the Psychosocial Reentry Project (PREP). The daycare, boarding home, and community aftercare programs include the Junction Prevocational Skills Project, the Adult Congregate Living Facility (ACLF) Project, and the Community Network Development (CND) Project, respectively. Each program has been designed with consideration of cost effectiveness and dissemination to other public mental health settings. The reader may wish to review the information presented in Figure 2-1 and the discussion regarding treatment programming related to that figure while considering these programs.

INTENSIVE RESIDENTIAL TREATMENT PROJECT (IRT)

Over the last decade, mental health management has moved strongly toward insuring that the civil rights of patients are preserved, providing treatment in the least restrictive environment, and reducing the rolls of large state mental institutions. In tune with these national trends, a system of mental health treatment has evolved that includes receiving centers for the acutely

251

mentally ill, crisis stabilization units (CSU), and the state mental hospitals. A major function of the crisis stabilization units and the receiving centers is to make it unnecessary to relocate mental patients in the restrictive environment of the rural state hospital. The crisis stabilization units and receiving centers provide an important community-based mental health service that has helped to stem the flow of patients from their local communities to the state hospital.

Presently, however, there is an increasing awareness that the crisis stabilization units and the receiving centers are only partially effective in deinstitutionalization. Many mental health patients continue to be referred to the state hospitals, and repeated admissions to the receiving centers and subsequent transfer to the state hospitals has established a "revolving door" system of mental health for many individuals. For example, in the catchment area served by the research and training (R&T) facility discussed in this book, over 600 mental health patients were transported from receiving centers to the state hospital during the 12 months prior to September 1979. This substantial number of individuals represents an inability of the receiving centers in these communities to return their patients to a level of functioning that would prevent state hospitalization. Thus, it seems that for a large number of individuals, the current system of treatment is ineffective, or only partially effective.

A wide variety of reasons have been given to explain the continued need for sending patients to the state hospitals from the receiving centers. Although it is not possible to identify with any great certainty the specific programmatic issues that would rectify this situation, "alternatives" to treatment programs that send patients from their local community to the state hospital are being sought. One such alternative is the Intensive Residential Treatment Unit (IRT). Although no specific program components were required, the goal of the IRT was to provide residential non-state-hospital treatment, and to address the needs of the population of patients who spend 30 days or less in the state hospital before being discharged and returned to the community. The IRT attempts to develop a service linkage available to mental health patients who had been provided all available assistance (e.g., crisis stabilization at a CSU and short-term hospital treatment at a residential unit of a receiving center), and for whom no further treatment was possible except at the state mental hospital. In essence, the IRT is a new service link for those patients who have failed to respond to the existing public mental health programs located in the community.

Treatment Program Description

The treatment program on the IRT project is divided into three general areas: (1) admission, (2) unit treatment, and (3) discharge. In each of these functional areas of treatment, a team has been established to specialize in one of these areas while at the same time interrelating with other components of the project.

The majority of the staff and resources on the IRT Project are committed to the operation of the residential treatment unit. This unit provides a short-term treatment experience (average length of stay 30 days) in an attempt to rehabilitate clients who would be referred to a state hospital to a level where they can make a minimal adjustment in the community. Treatment, therefore, is oriented toward restoring patients to their premorbid level of functioning and, in addition, to providing minimal amounts of social skills training to facilitate community adjustment. Clients involved in the IRT who cannot be rehabilitated to this minimal community adjustment level within approximately 30 days may be referred to other residential R&T facility projects for additional rehabilitation and skill training as offered by the Early Intervention Project (EIP) and Psychosocial Rehabilitation Entry Project (PREP).

Once a community placement is made for these patients, continued rehabilitation of IRT clients is assumed by community oriented R&T center projects including Junction Day Treatment and Community Network Development (CND) programs, in addition to the aftercare programs available at each community mental health center in the geographical area.

The IRT program is designed to establish a nonhospital program. The psychosocially oriented interdisciplinary team approach to treatment used on the unit constitutes a very active program involving psychological, social, and psychiatric therapies. The residential treatment program is designed in such a way as to provide a maximal stabilization and skill training experience, which may be modularized to facilitate wide dissemination of this program. To facilitate dissemination, a structured schedule of activities for the residential program has been developed. A brief description of the treatment goals, the schedule of the unit, and the content of the program will be presented.

Clients being treated on the IRT unit represent a heterogeneous group functioning within a wide range of psychological development. Because of the number of patients (32) and the potential for disruptive behavior on the unit, a well planned schedule of daily activities addressing the needs of each client is an important component of the IRT treatment unit. The daily schedule of client activities on the IRT treatment unit is present in Table 14-1. There are five major components of treatment broadly scheduled: (1) medications, (2) individual counseling and case management, (3) skill training groups, (4) activity therapy sessions, and (5) recreational activities.

Medications are prescribed and administered as needed. Every attempt is made to achieve self-medication and use of a single daily dose regimen. Individual counseling and case management are scheduled during three hours of each day across the day and evening shifts. During these times, clients meet with their treatment coordinator to deal with individual problems, case management, and rehabilitation issues. In addition to individual therapy,

Table 14-1

Weekly schedule of activities on the adult intensive residential treatment unit (IRT). (This level of programming structure is similar to that used with all adult, child, and elderly patients.)

Time	Monday	Tuesday	Wednesday	Thursday	Friday	Saturday	Sunday
6:30							Wake Up (Optional)
7:00	Wake up	→	→	→	→		
7:30	Medication	→	→	→	→		
8:15	Breakfast	→	→	→	→		
9:00	Get ready for day Room clean up	→	→	Client/Staff Community Mtg.	Free Time		
9:30	Exercise	→	→	→	→		
10:00	Activity Therapy						
10:30	Recreational Activity					→	Rec. Act./Outing
11:00	Life Skills Group	Problem-Solving Group	Nutrition Group	Problem-Solving Group	Stress Management	Life Skills Group	Life Skills Group
11:30	Free Time & Individual	→	→	→	→		
12:15	Counseling Sessions						
1:00	Lunch	→	→	→	→		
1:30	Free Time	→	→	→	→		

254

Daily / Weekly Treatment Schedule

Time					
2:00	Activity Therapy →				
2:30	Recreational Activity →				
3:00	Activities of Daily Living Group	Communication Skills Group	Medication Group	Communication Group	Life Skills Group
3:30	Free Time & Individual Counseling Sessions →				Visiting Hours & Free Time →
4:00					Recreational Activity →
4:30					
5:00					
5:30	Medication →				
6:15	Dinner →				
7:30	Visitors →				
8:00	Activity Therapy →				
8:30	Recreational Activity →				
9:00	Family Therapy	Assertion Group	Life Skills Group	Assertion Group	Peer Support Systems Group / Leisure Skills
9:30	Relaxation Exercise →				
10:00	Medication →				
11:00	Bedtime →				Bedtime (Optional) →

7:30–8:30 Client/Staff Communication Meeting

there are three 90 minute group activity sessions scheduled daily across the day and evening shifts. During each of these 90 minute sessions, there are three concurrent therapeutic and rehabilitative activities. The concurrent activities include (1) a skill training group, (2) an activity therapy session, and (3) a recreational activity. Each of these three activities is designed to provide a rehabilitative experience for from 6–12 individuals at a time. The sessions are arrayed in such a way as to provide a relevant activity for individuals at each of three levels of psychological functioning. Recreational activities are designed for individuals operating at low levels of functioning, where basic reality orientation, self and group awareness, and low performance demands are an appropriate level of focus. The activity therapy sessions require a somewhat higher level of functioning; they are oriented toward developing awareness of clients' strengths and weaknesses, the development of self-awareness. The highest level of rehabilitative activity is offered during the skill-training group sessions, in which basic psychosocial skills are trained and rehearsed according to psychoeducational methods of treatment.

Each skill-training session, activity therapy group, and recreational activity in this program is designed to obtain certain specified treatment objectives that are oriented toward rehabilitating the clients to a minimal level of community adjustment potential. The series of activities operates on a two-week cycle. During a two-week period, no single session is repeated. In this manner, the weekly program (Monday through Friday) contains 15 different skill-training groups, 15 activity therapy sessions, and 15 recreational activities. The weekend program, which allows lots more time for visiting hours and more unstructured time, contains four additional sessions in each of these three different areas. Thus, there are 38 independent treatment modules in each of the three areas of activity. At the end of the two-week cycle, the program repeats, and this repetition recurs every two weeks thereafter.

Employing the above schedule of activities, it is possible for the IRT client who stays on the unit for 30 days to experience a full range of activities that may be uniquely tailored to his individual needs. Treatment is individualized for each patient by way of medication monitoring, individual counseling, case management, and reviews of progress in the team meetings. The group activities are also individually tailored to a large degree. For example, take a client who enters the IRT in a psychotic state with a low level of adaptive functioning. During his/her initial week or two on the IRT treatment unit, this individual may primarily be managed with medications and be involved in individual counseling and recreational activities. As the client makes progress, his medications are adjusted and he continues to engage in individual counseling sessions, but he begins to participate more frequently in activity therapy sessions that are at a slightly higher level of functioning than the recreational activities. Case management is modified to meet current treatment needs. As the client progresses during the middle range of his/her stay on the unit, he tends to be less involved in simple recreational activities and more involved in activity therapies, and he begins to enter the skill training groups. Toward the end of the client's 30-day stay, when case management activities focus on discharge, he mainly receives skill-training, with little participation in either activity therapies or recreational activities. Medications continue to be adjusted, and single daily dose and self-medication are implemented, if possible. (See Figure 2-1.)

During this client's month-long stay on the IRT unit, the schedule of group activities is repeated twice. Due to the fact, however, that the client progressed from a low level of functioning toward a higher level and to discharge, he was engaged in a different portion of the available group program during his first two weeks of treatment as compared to the latter two weeks. Although the program repeated during the time this client was on the unit, he experienced a full array of constantly differing activities and therapy sessions that were commensurate with his level of functioning and rehabilitative progress.

Clients who stay on the IRT unit for two weeks or less experience only one iteration of the program. Because of the variety of the program, they can have an experience similar to that illustrated with the above 30-day client. Those clients who stay longer than 30 days also experience a continually different program. Due to the structure of this program, clients may stay on the IRT up to six weeks without repeating a major group activity; individual work is continually modified to meet current treatment needs. Clients may repeat specific aspects of the program that were difficult initially or where an increased therapeutic effect would be obtained by the repetition.

Another important aspect of the IRT treatment unit is the daily team meeting. During these meetings, shift report occurs, and patient progress and individual treatment plans are discussed. Members from the Intake Team, the Discharge Team, as well as the Treatment Unit Team are present at these meetings. This interdisciplinary staff meeting includes representatives of psychiatry, psychology, social work, rehabilitation therapy, and the treatment unit staff. Within this structure, an interdisciplinary broad-based discussion of individual client progress occurs on a daily basis.

In addition to the daily team meeting, each shift has a staff meeting once a week, and there is a once-a-week "across shifts" meeting. This meeting deals exclusively with staff issues. This combination of treatment meetings and staff meetings greatly facilitates communication and treatment planning for clients and good working relationships among staff.

Evaluation of IRT

A preliminary evaluation of the IRT was conducted on the first 58 patients admitted and treated on the program after it opened in January 1980. This evaluation indicated that significant improvements in psychological functioning and potential for community adjustment occurred during treatment; these gains were maintained on an average of three months postdischarge. Gains, however, were from a level where the individual could not function in most life areas to a level of borderline functioning where community living is possible, but with difficulty.

The data on the amount of rehospitalization and use of community treatment after discharge from IRT are consistent with this finding. Almost all the patients utilized some outpatient, day treatment, or inpatient service subsequent to discharge. Twenty-one of 32 patients tracked required some residential care in the three months since discharge. Although this indicates a high rate of relapse, it is also important to note that only seven of the 32 clients required admission to a state psychiatric hospital. However, *all* patients treated by IRT would have been sent to a state hospital from the mental health center where they were being treated if the IRT were not available. Thus, community resources were more actively used by these patients in lieu of institutional care.

The evaluation of the IRT project suggests that patients can be diverted from state hospital treatment by an intensive short-term program. The need for treatment continues in the community, however. Programs such as Community Network Development and the Junction, described later in this chapter, are used to fulfill this treatment need.

THE EARLY INTERVENTION PROJECT (EIP)

Modern authors have frequently noted that the process of residential psychiatric treatment often carries major countertherapeutic effects. In particular, emphasis has been placed on the tendency of patients to become socialized into an institutional setting that discourages their own active involvement in their treatment. Faced with an irresponsive system, patients are said to become passive, dependent, compliant, and withdrawn.[1] Goffman[2] has described psychiatric hospitals as functioning to "institutionalize" the patient, and fostering the permanent adoption of a "sick role." Once the patient has learned to accept the hospital as providing for all needs, this institutional dependency renders the task of community readjustment much more difficult. Thus, patients tend to return to residential care again and again—the "revolving-door phenomenon"—whenever substantial stress is encountered in their community placements. This revolving-door syndrome is clearly reflected in the findings of a study of state psychiatric hospitals in Florida.[3] During the fiscal year 1975–1976, 53 percent of patients admitted to the state psychiatric hospitals had received prior residential care in this health care system; 72 percent of total readmissions reported two or more prior admissions and 22 percent reported five or more. Given that these rehospitalization statistics do not include admissions to hospitals other than the four state-maintained facilities, it is probable that these figures are conservative in reflecting total numbers of psychiatric hospitalizations.

The Early Intervention Project (EIP) was created in 1977 to serve as a model of residential treatment that provides intensive residential treatment to psychiatric clients, while minimizing the development of institutional dependency. The project seeks to intervene early in the psychiatric patients' experience with hospitalization, and to decrease the necessity for future readmissions. As described by Archer et al.,[4] EIP provides a model for time-limited residential treatment, and fills a programming void between crisis stabilization short-term treatment units and long-term hospitalization programs. Approximately 66 percent of EIP patients receive psychotic diagnoses at admission and 75 percent of clients are on psychoactive medications. Most clients have been hospitalized at least once prior to EIP admission, but total residential treatment prior to EIP is restricted to not more than 120 days.

The Early Intervention Project facilitates patients' independence, self-esteem, and competence in several ways. Treatment is limited for all clients to nine weeks. Thus patients entering treatment have a positive expectancy of change occurring during this period and a certain knowledge of treatment duration. This may be compared to the average length of stay of 864 days for state hospital patients.[3] Further, patients return to their home or community placements each weekend to allow for a continuation of community relationships and functions while in treatment. Finally, the patient is required to take an active role in the behavioral and social skills treatment components of the EIP program.

Clients in the EIP participate in a series of social and personal skills-building groups that combine didactic with experiential instruction methods. Communication skills are provided in a twelve-session format that includes emphasis on self-disclosure, feedback, paraphrasing, and accurate reflection techniques. A thirteen session assertion skills program is offered, which stresses the conceptual and behavioral distinctions between passivity, assertion, and aggression, and includes programmed exercises to practice assertion skills in simulated exercises. Other highly structured groups are provided in areas including problem-solving skills, relaxation skills, sexuality information, anxiety and depression, management techniques, and nutrition and medication awareness. Each skill group encourages the participant to adopt an active student role rather than the traditional and passive "patient" stance. Indeed, educational rather than medical terminology is fostered, e.g., patients participate in "courses" rather than "therapy" groups and are "graduated," rather than "released" or "discharged" following completion of the program. The effectiveness of the skill-building groups has been shown in a series of investigations by Archer, Bedell, Amuso, and Marlowe.[4-6] Archer et al.[5] demonstrated that patients' expectancy of exercising personal control over life events increased, and trait anxiety levels decreased, as a function of skill group participation. Bedell et al.[6] reported that participation in six weeks of problem-solving training produced significant increases in clients' knowledge concerning problem solving techniques and their performance in actual problem situations (see Chapter 2).

A second major treatment component designed to actively involve the patient is based upon behavioral techniques. Comprehensive reviews have supported the effectiveness of behavioral programs in residential treatment, particularly as employed in token economics.[7-9] The EIP employs a traditional token economy program during the client's first six weeks of treatment. During the first days following a client's admission, a staff member is designated to work with each patient in developing a series of behaviors to be targeted for change. The therapist and client collaborate in this task, with the client assuming major responsibility for identifying broad problem areas, and the therapist for defining these areas into observable behavioral units. Staff consistently monitor and reinforce behaviors, and staff and clients meet weekly to revise or modify targets as needed. Reinforcement points are exchangeable for a variety of goods in a ward "store" or for social privileges on the unit. During weeks seven through nine of EIP, treatment procedures change as patient groups enter the peer managed token economy program. Patient groups meet daily during this last stage of EIP to perform peer reviews of each individual's behaviors, and to determine general behavioral targets for the group. Each client assumes a specific role in maintaining the token economy program (TEP), from chairing the daily meetings to recording patients' behaviors and dispensing reinforcement points. Professional staff have a very limited and circumscribed consultant role in the peer managed TEP to insure it remains peer controlled. Interestingly, staff consultants have frequently voiced initial anxieties over the clients' ability to handle TEP tasks, and have found it difficult to avoid becoming overinvolved. After some experience in the consultant role, however, staff reservations have inevitably subsided and been replaced by respect for the clients' competence and abilities in making their own decisions. The peer managed token economy serves to foster clients' self-reliance, to reduce dependency on professional staff, and to provide a transitional stage to community reentry. Evaluation of the peer managed economy by Bedell and Archer[10] demonstrates its effectiveness in fostering and maintaining adaptive behaviors. Patients show significant gains during this treatment segment not only in modifying specifically targeted behaviors, but also in improving general ratings of social adequacy and community adjustment potential (see Chapter 2).

In summary, the Early Intervention Project provides an intensive residential treatment experience that seeks to support and foster clients' psychosocial development without creating countertherapeutic institutional dependencies. Employing a combination of skills-training and behavioral techniques, the patients assume an active and responsible role in their own treatment. Outcome data indicate that at six months follow-up, 72 percent of EIP clients have not required rehospitalization. When EIP treatment is linked to CND referrals for aftercare, 82.5 percent of clients are not rehospitalized at ten-month follow-ups. Although many models of residential treatment are clearly needed to meet the varied needs of mental health clients, it is suggested that the EIP provides a viable example of one approach to time-limited residential care.

PSYCHOSOCIAL REHABILITATION ENTRY
PROJECT (PREP)

The Psychosocial Rehabilitation Entry Project (PREP) deals with the chronically and repeatedly hospitalized mental patient who has grown dependent upon the state mental hospital and is involved in the "revolving door" pattern of adjustment. As the name implies, this program is designed to use psychosocial techniques to rehabilitate the chronic patient for reentry into the community. Much of this program is based on the work of Fairweather.[11]

Over the past decade, a number of treatment strategies have been developed for utilization with the chronic mental patient. Although these programs have sometimes suggested successful outcomes, there is limited evidence that any long-term improvements in community adjustment have been demonstrated. Meanwhile, readmission rates nationally continue to be approximately 50 percent within six months, and 75 percent within 18 months, of discharge.

Several explanations regarding the failure of hospital programs to change community behaviors have been offered. One that has particular appeal suggests that the mental hospital represents a low stress, supportive environment where staff inadvertantly teach dependency. The community, which is the alternative residence for these chronically disturbed individuals, is a relatively high-stress environment, where one can easily become isolated and ignored by others, and where support and compassion may be hard to find. Thus, chronic patients seek out the shelter of the institution, and manipulate staff in such a way as to prolong their stay in the hospital.

The dilemma for mental patients is that they have learned to adjust to the social environment of the hospital by being dependent and compliant and by avoiding stress. All these behaviors are antithetical to those needed in the social environment of the community. Being in the hospital, therefore, leads, in the long run, to poorer community adjustment.

The problem then becomes how to develop a social environment in the hospital that will permit chronic patients to assume a more active, independent role that facilitates their adjustment to community life after leaving the hospital. To solve this problem, groups of chronic mental patients are formed to operate, as much as possible, independently from staff control. The use of these groups was based on studies with noninstitutionalized people that found that belonging to such a group greatly enhanced the adaptive behavior of individual members.

Description of Small Group Program

The Small Group Program was modeled after the Fairweather Small Group Program.[11] The intent of the Small Group Program is to create, within an institutional setting, a social environment consistent with that of community living. Four requirements must be met to establish this environment: (1) groups must be "autonomous" in the sense that they must solve problems and make decisions with no staff present; (2) a communication system must be established that allows staff to present problems to client groups without involving staff in the small group decision processes; (3) the task set for the group must be related to solving behavioral problems of group members, managing day-to-day living problems, working on the unit, and discharge planning; and (4) the system of reward and punishment must be applied to the group as a whole. This system involves weekly cash allowances and pass times.

Clients admitted to Small Group, with the exception of initial introduction and interview by staff, receive orientation to the program by members of the group. Clients are admitted to a four-tier system that requires progressively increased responsibility with increases in rewards.

The Step Level System

The resident entering the group begins Step 1 and must comply with the rules set forth by the staff, which in Step 1 are as follows: The client must get up on time, arrive at meals on time, shave daily, put soiled clothes in the correct place, dress suitably, maintain personal cleanliness, get to all appointments on time, which includes meetings with his group and with staff. The client must handle complaints about group members during group discussion, greet and introduce new members to the group, and in general attempt to make them feel welcome in the group and on the unit. After being on Step Level 1 for a week, the client is eligible to be promoted to Step Level 2.

The standards to be met for promotion to Step Level 2 were established both by staff and clients. The minimum standards accepted by staff are that the person can not have above 15 notes; these notes include both written notes and what are referred to as matrix notes. Matrix notes are counts kept on each client for breaking basic unit rules. Before the weekly staff/client meeting, the clients meet in their group to determine recommendations for

Step Levels of each member of the group. The clients recommend promotion to the next step level, demotion to a lower step level, or maintenance on that same step level for each client.

After the staff/client meeting, the staff meet to review the recommendations made by the group. The staff make decisions regarding the whole group, not individuals in the group. The staff review each recommendation made, and state if the recommendation is acceptable to the staff or not acceptable. If the staff determine that there are too many wrong recommendations by the clients for that week, the staff can either freeze the group at the current step levels, demote the whole group, or, if the clients behave in an acceptable problem-solving way, the staff can accept the package of recommendations made by the group. In addition, staff review other aspects of the clients' activities that week, including the number of notes received by the group as a whole, and number of recommendations and actions made by the group that are acceptable to the staff. If a client meets the requirements established by the staff and by the group members, he is advanced to Step Level 2.

In Step Level 2, the client fulfills all the requirements of Step Level 1, plus has a satisfactory work performance on all assigned tasks; the client has to be attentive at meetings, on time for all assignments, and is graded in his performance of tasks as "poor," "fair," or "good." In addition, the client has the responsibility to make an appointment with the Vocational Rehabilitation Counselor. When the resident meets all the requirements of Step 1 and Step 2, he is advanced to Step 3.

Step 3 is considered as a predischarge planning step. In Step 3, the resident begins to make his plans as to when he expects to be released from residential treatment and what he will be doing after discharge. These plans include such things as going to school, finding a job, and determining where he will be living upon discharge. Plans are submitted to the unit social worker for approval before the client is eligible for promotion to Step 4. In addition to complying to the above requirements, the client also meets all the requirements of Step Levels 1, 2, and 3, and is expected to be more responsible within his group and to assume more duties in assisting other clients who are on lower step levels. If a client meets these requirements to the satisfaction of both his group and the staff, he is recommended by the group for advancement to Step 4.

The requirements of Step 4 include compliance with the duties of the previous steps, plus the client is expected to initiate plans for the future. Example: If the client had made plans to find a job on being discharged, he is expected to make an effort to locate and interview for jobs. During this step level, the client receives predischarge leaves of absence to help initiate his plans. At the beginning of Step 4, the client is expected to turn in final discharge plans to be approved by the social worker. If the plans are acceptable to the social worker, they are presented to the staff and to the unit director for final approval. Once the plans are accepted, the client is expected to be actively involved in carrying out his discharge plans. In addition, the client is expected to be involved actively within his group, and to be involved in providing leadership for his group. During this stage, the client can be excused from afternoon work assignments, if actively involved in initiating his plans.

If at any time an individual commits an infraction of the rules set forth by the staff and by his group, the group discusses the infraction and recommends appropriate corrective action. In addition, the group is responsible to make sure that these actions are carried out.

As a person is promoted from one step level to another, not only is he expected to assume additional responsibility, both for himself and for his fellow group members, he is also given additional privileges. On Step Level 1, he is allowed a one-day pass per week, from 8 a.m. to 11 p.m., plus 10 dollars spending money from his work fund. In Step 2, he is allowed two one-day passes, from 8 a.m. to 11 p.m., plus 15 dollars spending money. In Step Level 3, he is allowed an overnight pass every weekend, from 8 a.m. Saturday to 11 p.m. Sunday, plus 20 dollars spending money. In Step 4, the client can have all the weekly passes desired, plus a weekend pass, from Friday at 3 p.m. to Sunday, 11 p.m., and 25 dollars spending money. In addition, a member at Step Level 4 is allowed additional money and leave of absence time, providing that this is approved both by the group and by the staff.

The client's assigned group is responsible as a unit for its individual members. Each group is required to meet once a day during the week to deal with notes submitted by staff regarding individual and group behavior. These notes are written by the staff to communicate to the group daily problems that the group needs to deal with in their meetings. Notes are written by staff both to present problems and to provide information for the group. Once a week, the staff meet with each group to review the previous week's activities. This meeting includes reviewing all notes, actions taken by the group, and staff reaction to notes. The group also submits to the staff their recommendations for step level changes, money, passes, and departure plans.

Immediately after this meeting, the staff meet to review the group's recommendations and actions regarding their rationality and appropriateness in dealing with the previous week's activities. The staff then determine whether or not the group's behavior and actions in correcting problems are appropriate. Staff reaction is, as mentioned before, to the whole group rather than to individuals.

Staff role with the client group is that of a consultant. Any staff member can be summoned to present factual information requested by the group. Staff cannot make decisions for either the group or individuals. If a client requests a staff member to solve a personal problem, the client is referred back to his group, and a note is sent to the group informing them of the client's improper behavior.

The formal structure of the small group is designed as much to control staff behavior as to shape group members' performance. The staff are involved with clients on a social basis within the structure of the program. The client's group can and do initiate action on group members without staff prompting. For any emergencies or crisis situations requiring immediate action, staff can and do intervene; but, staff turns over responsibility to the group as soon as possible.

Evaluation of PREP

The PREP program was evaluated,[4] and the results compared to those obtained in the original demonstration of the small group program conducted by Fairweather.

There were two differences between the two groups of subjects studied. In the Fairweather research, the clients were all ex-military personnel being treated at a Veterans Administration Hospital; all were males. In the PREP study, only 48 percent were male, and only 17 percent had prior military service. Also, the PREP subjects had fewer days of hospitalization prior to the study, although the PREP subjects had a larger number of hospital admissions. On most other demographic variables such as age, education, marital status, and employment history, the treatment groups were comparable.

The recidivism rates for the PREP study were approximately the same as those found by Fairweather. At the six-month follow-up period, 32 percent of the PREP patients had been hospitalized, and 41 percent were rehospitalized by 18 months postdischarge. The generality of the small group program appears to be valid for this replication conducted on a different patient group by a different staff, approximately 15 years later in time.

The continued high level of recidivism observed with these patients suggests that continued community aftercare and support are necessary to close the revolving door. Programs described later in this chapter, such as Community Network Development and Adult Congregate Living Facility Project, when used in conjunction with programs such as PREP, may be effective in further reducing rehospitalization.

THE JUNCTION PREVOCATIONAL SKILLS PROJECT

Among the behavioral deficits frequently found in chronic emotionally disturbed clients, perhaps the most basic and fundamental to community adjustment are prevocational and employability skills. Anthony[12] has estimated that only 20–30 percent of patients released from residential psychiatric treatment obtain competitive full-time employment. Harrington and Wilkins[13] and

Peretti[14] have identified vocational maladjustment as a major factor precipitating psychiatric rehospitalization. Neuhring and Thayer's[3] comprehensive community follow-up on over 400 patients released from Florida psychiatric hospitals during fiscal years 1975–1976 found that within six months of discharge, one-third of these patients were rehospitalized within the state system. Interview data indicated that unemployment and employment problems served as major contributors to rehospitalization. Specifically, they found that fully 87 percent of expatients were unemployed at six-month follow-up, and that 70 percent had not been employed *at any time* since hospital release. Further, among rehospitalized patients, none were employed at the time of their readmission. The need for comprehensive vocational rehabilitation programs for psychiatrically disabled adults has been stressed by Bean and Beard, Goldstein et al.,[15] Steele,[16] Safier,[17] and others. Results of a national survey of mental health providers and administrators also supports the call for prevocational services.[18] Analyses revealed that nearly half of all respondents rated employment seeking and job retention skills among the five most important skill-training areas for chronic psychiatric patients.

The Junction program attempts to address the employment skill deficits of chronic psychiatric patients by didactic and experiential skills training in general preemployment and/or prevocational areas. The training emphasis is not on preparation for a specific occupation, but on general skills-training in areas necessary to seek and maintain employment across a variety of fields. The program may be divided into three components: (1) the Work Resource Center, (2) the Work Adjustment Station, and (3) placement in full-time or transitional employment.

Work Resource Center

The Work Resource Center is the entry level component of the Junction. Following intake evaluation, clients receive three to six weeks of training in work readiness and general life skills. The Work Resource Center is a highly structured five-day-a-week day-treatment program designed to improve the general community adjustment level and prevocational behaviors and skills of participants. Each client receives instruction in daily-living skills including personal hygiene, money management, agency assistance, nutrition, use of public transportation, and other community resources. Additionally, clients are provided with intensive training in job-hunting skills and career planning. Each participant is also evaluated daily by staff members in ten prevocational behavioral skills areas, with systematic feedback and review provided to each client. The prevocational behaviors selected for evaluation include: (1) punctuality, (2) attendance, (3) transportation planning, (4) appearance, (5) medication self-monitoring, (6) peer volunteer and interpersonal communication, (7) group interactions and socialization, (8) response to supervision, (9) attention to assignments, and (10) utilization of free time. Resource Center staff also provide supportive case-management services stressing awareness of the client's total life needs. When the client has reached a functional level of employment readiness as determined by daily ratings and course work evaluations, he or she is placed in the Junction's Work Adjustment component.

Work Adjustment Station

The Work Adjustment Station provides clients with a "real work" environment in which to test and refine the skills they have acquired in the Work Resource Center. In the Work Adjustment Station clients operate and maintain a food service "snack bar." The purpose of training is *not* to train clients for food service jobs, however, but rather to prepare them for common work place stresses and requirements. Again, clients are evaluated daily in quantity of work, quality of work, job safety, care of equipment, response to supervision, and ability to deal with customers. Staff members coordinate job assignments, maintain financial records, and promote the business in the community. Day-to-day business decisions and internal employee organization, however, are done by clients. In peer-managed "business meetings" clients are encouraged and supported by professional staff, who allow them to progress at their own pace. A monetary incentive program is used to reinforce appropriate work behaviors. Based upon clients' daily ratings, they receive between 10 cents and one dollar hourly wages. When the clients reach job readiness, as determined by a mutual staff and client decision based upon results of daily evaluations, they enter the vocational placement services.

Vocational Placement

Vocational Placement staff attempt to locate a job appropriate for each client, to facilitate clients' entrance into employment, and to follow-up on their employment problems. Recently, through a federal grant awarded to Attainment of Tampa, Inc., a nonprofit corporation, a transitional employment program has been added to Junction's job placement services. Transitional or 20-hour-week jobs are identified with community settings that can be utilized by the emotionally disabled employees. The staff member accompanies all transitional employment clients to their first days of work, remains on the job with them through initial training, and provides on-the-job-site support as necessary. Thus, the Junction places its clients in either part-time or full-time competitive employment positions, based upon the individual client's skill level and stress tolerance and a careful coordination of client and employer needs.

In total, the Junction Prevocational Skills Project offers a comprehensive plan for the vocational rehabilitation of the chronically emotionally disabled

adult. The program provides a structured curriculum of daily-living and prevocational skills training, direct "real life" opportunities to further develop
these skills, and eventual placement into competitive employment. By providing extensive skills training before attempting job placements, the Junction
seeks to reduce the likelihood that the clients will fail in their employment
situation. Flexibility of programming is encouraged, and clients may return
to prior treatment components if additional training appears beneficial. Further, the speed with which individual clients may complete any stage of the
Junction experience is based directly upon their individual needs and abilities.
As clients are admitted to the Junction, their vocational planning is also coordinated with the state Department of Vocational Rehabilitation, which
monitors the client's progress throughout the program. The Junction is still
in the initial stage of operation; however, its first few clients have been successfully placed in a variety of competitive employment positions. Future follow-up evaluations will clarify how the Junction can serve as a viable and
effective model of prevocational training that enables clients to maintain gainful and rewarding employment.

THE COMMUNITY NETWORK DEVELOPMENT
PROJECT (CND)

As President Carter's Commission on Mental Health recently noted, social networks and support systems are essential to an individual's community
adjustment. The lack of a natural support system among mental health clients
appears to be a prime cause of rehospitalization and dependency on the social
service system. To address this natural support system gap, the Community
Network Development Project (CND) was developed.

CND is a community treatment program whose goal is to promote independent living and to prevent hospitalization by creating a community support system. It is our contention that this community support system must
be composed of natural as well as professional helpers. Although professionals must attempt to make their service provision more responsive to client
needs, these efforts in and of themselves will never be sufficient. Professional
support systems will never be able to provide either the quantity or the type
of support that can be provided by natural support systems. An effort must
be made to help the mental health client develop a natural support system
composed of peers that can respond with immediacy and personal concern
to his/her problem. The CND project fosters the development of a peer support system whereby former mental health clients who reside in the community form a helping network for each other and provide each other with
emotional, instrumental, and recreational support in their daily lives.

There are at least two levels to the CND support system: (1) the formal support system that is provided by the structured CND program and (2) the informal or natural support system that develops among CND members as a result of their participation in CND. For example, the CND program itself may offer a supportive function to its members (e.g., a trip to the beach); however, although a type of recreational support is being provided, it is nonetheless different than the more informal process by which one CND member calls another during the week to arrange a trip to the movies. CND believes that there is a need for support activities at both the formal and informal level. However, the informal support systems that develop among CND members are of more ultimate value to the individual members than the structured support that can be provided by our program. Thus, an attempt was made to design all CND programs and activities in a way that would promote and develop peer involvement and support. The resulting philosophy, organization, and activities of the CND project will be described in the remainder of this section.

Philosophy

There are four basic assumptions that have guided the development of CND's program. First, CND assumes that members are capable and responsible and can, therefore, take an active part in the design and implementation of treatment programs. Unfortunately, the abilities and strengths of mental health clients are usually not recognized by their families, friends, or society in general. As a result, clients begin to feel that they are incapable and are, therefore, undeserving of status and respect as human beings. This results in a further loss of self-esteem, energy, and motivation to overcome problems. It becomes, in effect, a self-fulfilling prophecy. CND, on the other hand, assumes that clients are capable of helping themselves and of helping each other. CND incorporates this assumption into the program in several ways. First of all, participants in CND are viewed as "members" of a club or organization, because the term "member" does not imply the "one down" status that the term "client" implies. A client is someone who always *receives* help. A member is someone who can help others as well as receive help. As would be the case in any club or organization, members are seen as valuable resources and potential contributors to CND programs. In fact, members are encouraged to assume as much responsibility for the development and operation of CND projects as possible.

CND projects are centered in the community whenever possible, because this "normalizes" members' experience in CND, helping them move away from client or patient status. Centering CND activities in the community also helps members become aware of resources and support that exist outside of mental health settings.

The CND project is also founded on the belief that the long-term support needs of mental health clients should be centered or directed toward peers rather than toward professional staff. Peer relationships are more similar to friendships than the formal relationship of client and therapist. Peers can provide a responsive and personal source of both emotional and instrumental support for each other. Peer relationships are more continuous than client-therapist relationships, and are more likely to end gradually. When a client no longer needs therapy or when he needs to be rehospitalized, his relationship with peers does not necessarily change, as it probably does with a professional therapist. Professional staff, because of manpower shortages and role definitions, cannot provide the same type of indefinite, flexible support that peers can provide.

Finally, CND activities are grounded in the belief that structure and aggressive outreach is essential in the "networking" of members. Although no program can force or guarantee the development of friendships, CND maximizes members' opportunities to do so in several ways. First of all, CND creates an ongoing series of structured events and activities in which members can socialize and work. Furthermore, instead of waiting for members to contact their peers, "drop in," or come to activities on their own, CND members actively reach out to other members, contacting them regularly to see how they are, telling them about upcoming activities, and helping them arrange transportation to activities. Since individuals who need social support the most may be the least likely to seek it, CND's active outreach involves many at-risk members who would otherwise not participate.

Membership

CND's membership ranges between 100 and 125 individuals. Almost all members have a history of psychiatric hospitalization and 60–70 percent have been diagnosed as psychotic. Members range in age from 18 to 55, with most members in their 20s or 30s. Only those individuals in need of close supervision or who have a primary diagnosis of OBS, alcoholism, drug abuse or retardation are barred from membership. CND's membership is, therefore, heterogeneous, with high and low functioning members at a variety of age levels.

The CND program operates within four geographical areas, each approximately the size of a mental health center catchment area. The factors that determine how many separate CND "areas" or groups are created are (1) geographical size and (2) number of members. A CND survey indicated that members usually will not travel more than thirty minutes to see a friend. Since transportation is a problem for so many mental health clients, CND chose to keep areas geographically small so that contact between members is facilitated.

Size of membership is also an important factor in determining how large a geographical area should be. CND's areas are still developing, and it is not yet clear how large an area can become before it should be subdivided. Currently, the smallest area contains 15 members and the largest area contains 50 members.

Staffing Pattern

There are three categories of paid positions in CND. Staff Area Managers (SAMS) are full-time professional positions, and are usually filled by mental health counselors who have some degree of experience in mental health. Community Area Managers (CAMS) are part-time paraprofessional positions and are filled with CND members, all of whom are former mental patients. Member-Leader positions are also filled with CND ex-patient members. The Member-Leader position is also part-time, with the number of hours worked per week varying in accordance with the needs of the program. Other CND members who donate their time to the CND project without pay are called Member Volunteers.

The CAM is responsible for planning the agenda for weekly area meetings, providing transportation to meetings for members who need it, presiding over the meetings, and acting as a facilitator to develop interaction between group members. At times, CAMs facilitate "Goal Planning" or problem-solving with members who request the group's help with a personal problem. Additional responsibilities of the CAM include helping the entire CND network with activities such as the CND Newsletter, network meetings, fund-raising projects, and major social activities.

Because they are or have been mental health clients themselves, CAMs are sensitive to the needs of the other members, relating to them in ways professionals cannot. Because CAMs have been able to deal successfully with many of the members' problems, they also serve as good role models for the rest of the members.

CAMs are chosen on the basis of their maturity, adjustment, and social skills. They receive formal training and orientation in ethics, medication and side effects, crisis intervention, listening skills, and community resources. A Peer Leader's manual is given to each CAM, providing step-by-step instruction and information for dealing with the most frequent problems that arise in an area. In addition, on-going training, supervision, and support are provided by the SAM.

The role of the professional staff in the CND program is considerably different from traditional mental health roles. Instead of acting primarily as therapists, CND professional staff are more involved in supervising activities, developing programs, consulting with member groups to promote self-help and peer support, conducting research on new treatment methods, and disseminating the results of research.

A SAM is assigned to supervise each geographical area. Since the CAM is the main communications link between the members and the SAM, the SAM tries to insure that all communications from the members are channeled through the CAM. The SAM acts as consultant and resource person to the members in the area, maintaining contact with them by attending area meetings with the CAM, and by receiving reports from the CAM.

The SAM is responsible for hiring, training, and supervising the CAM. The amount of supervision and guidance a CAM needs from a SAM varies according to the ability of the CAM. The SAM and CAM meet regularly to discuss interactions with members and work out details for the area meetings. At these meetings the CAM's activities are reviewed and any Goal-Planning that may have been done with group members during the week is discussed. These meetings give the SAM a chance to assist the CAM in solving any other problems that may have arisen. Based on the CAM's reports and the SAM's observations, the SAM maintains records on all the members of the area.

In situations where members need help beyond the CAM's expertise, the SAM may directly intervene and handle a situation himself. The SAM is also actively involved in developing aspects of the CND program in expanding community resources.

Above all else, the SAM's role is to promote peer support and peer counseling, rather than to intervene directly. His/her primary activities are supervising the CAM and developing programs and resources that can then be turned over to the CAMs and to the membership.

Member Leaders and Member Volunteers work for CND, assuming responsibility for tasks on an as-needed basis. Their duties include transporting members to meetings and appointments, doing office work, writing and visiting CND members, participating in CND workshops and demonstrations, organizing fund raising activities, etc.

Members of CND also assume duties that are an important part of the network. For example, members submit articles to the Newsletter, make presentations to area meetings, give other members rides to the area meetings, etc. Some of the older members serve as "buddies" to the new members to help them become oriented to CND. Members' involvement differs from Member Leaders' and Member Volunteers' in that they do not have permanent responsibility for an activity or duty.

Activities and Services

CND provides its membership with a broad range of social and educational experiences. Since the expressed needs and wishes of members are the basis of all program planning, the exact agenda of CND events and projects varies across time. The area and network meetings, however, are the core structure around which all other CND activities are built.

Members in each geographical areas get together regularly for Area Meetings. These meetings are held weekly at a location chosen by the members. Members without transportation are picked up by another member, a CAM, or a SAM. Most meetings are social or recreational in nature (e.g., outings to the movies, restaurants, covered dish dinners, picnics). On other occasions members may plan an educational meeting (e.g., trip to a museum, visiting speaker, CPR training). Occasionally fund-raising meetings are held. These events allow members to raise funds for more expensive recreational activities (e.g., trips to Disney World). Fund-raising events that have taken place so far include car washes, disco dances, bake sales, garage sales, etc. Occasionally area meetings are used to help a member solve a problem or plan personal goals. This activity only takes place at the request of a member, however.

Once a month members from all four areas meet together in a network meeting. The network meeting allows members from all areas to maintain contact. Network meetings also are used for planning of overall network goals or projects. Awards are given at each network meeting to the "Member of the Month," the CND member who has contributed the most to the network in the prior month. Since the network meetings typically involve 50–75 people, social and recreational events of larger scale are frequently planned, including beach parties, talent shows, bingo games, holiday parties, etc.

The CND project provides a variety of other services and activities to its members. A Membership Directory allows members to contact each other between meetings for support or socializing. A monthly newsletter keeps members informed about area activities and other members, as well as provides useful information and an opportunity for self-expression. Community Living Skills courses are available for members who need information and skills to equip them for community life (e.g., managing a household, money management, how to find a place to live). A community resource file provides members with an up-to-date file of agencies and programs available to serve them. Advocacy efforts by the CAM or SAM are provided when needed services are inaccessible to members. Crisis support is available from CAMs or, when warranted, from SAMs. Other specialty services are provided on an as-needed basis. For example, CND, at the request of several members in one area, helped to start a cooperative house for members who wanted to leave their families' home but felt inadequate to handle a totally independent living environment.

ATTAINMENT OF TAMPA

The creation of Attainment of Tampa is, perhaps, the most extensive program development activity of CND. Over the course of several years, CND members have identified a number of needs that could not be met within the restrictions of most mental health agencies. (For example, the need for a low interest member-loan fund became apparent.) In order to address a variety of unmet member needs, CND cooperated with the Mental Health Association and several other service agencies to establish a nonprofit corporation, Attainment of Tampa. Attainment exists to advocate for mental health clients and to foster or sponsor the development of resources and services to meet members' needs. Its articles of incorporation establish it as a partnership between mental health consumers, professionals, and other community members; ex-patient-consumers fill half of the positions of Attainments' board of directors. Projects currently under development include the initiation of a member-loan fund, a satellite apartment, and a transitional employment program. Most CND members have become members of Attainment, and several have assumed leadership roles on the board of directors or on special project task forces. One hopes that this fledgling attempt at true consumer involvement in planning and providing services for mental health clients will be successful and will extend and eventually supplant the services offered by CND.

Effectiveness of CND

As described in Chapter 3, clients were randomly assigned to two groups during their last two weeks of residence on the Early Intervention Project. Upon discharge, clients in the control group were referred only to traditional aftercare services (e.g., community mental health centers, VR), while clients in the experimental group were also given a referral to the CND program. Ten months later, clients from both groups were interviewed in the community in order to determine the extent to which both groups had required further mental health treatment. Only 40 days of rehospitalization were reported within the CND group, while the non-CND group reported a total of 136 days of rehospitalization during the same period. The CND group reported a total of 201 hours of outpatient contact within the 10 month follow-up period, while non-CND groups reported a total of 1158 hours (p < .01).

A special follow-up study of previous CAMs or Member Leaders was also undertaken in order to determine the stresses or benefits of these leadership roles on mental health clients. As reported in Edmunson et al.,[19] mental health clients who took leadership roles within CND do not describe these roles as stressful, but to the contrary, indicate that their job was a positive, growth-producing experience for them. Objective indices (rehospitalization rates, employment status) tend to substantiate these findings.

Dissemination

Although the CND treatment program is nontraditional, it has begun to be accepted widely throughout the state as well as elsewhere. Based on early reports of follow-up results, the state mental health program office has incorporated the social network concept into their deinstitutionalization plans.

Two of the state's three deinstitutionalization pilot projects have a social network component. CND has provided extensive training and consultation to Boley Manor, the psychosocial program in urban St. Petersburg. Under this deinstitutionalization plan, Boley is responsible for developing three areas during the first year of their deinstitutionalization grant. At this time, Boley is ahead of schedule, with three areas operating successfully. Boley's success with their social network has caused other mental health agencies to become interested in social networks. A social network is now planned for all three catchment areas served by the local Comprehensive Community Mental Health Center.

The Human Resource Institute of Volusia County, another deinstitutionalization project site, is also developing a social network. Since Volusia County includes rural and urban areas, implementing a CND program should provide invaluable information about the adaptations that are necessary in differing community settings. Our experience to date suggests that the CND can operate effectively within community mental health settings.

Cost-Effectiveness

Accurate cost-effectiveness data are difficult to obtain on the R&T center's CND project. Since R&T center staff time is used in research, program development, and training, as well as in clinical service, CND's staffing pattern far exceeds that which would be necessary to implement the project in a community setting. Therefore, it is more meaningful to consider the staffing and cost of Boley Manor's network.

In Boley's network one half-time professional SAM is hired at 7000 dollars per year. Three half-time CAM positions are funded at a total cost of 9000 dollars. Additional administrative and operational costs bring the total budget of this program to 22,562 dollars. In its original budget proposal, Boley projected a cost per client per year of 564 dollars. Actual cost data solely on the social network component of Boley's program is not yet available. Information on the total cost of all components of Boley's social program (which includes a drop-in social club as well as a network) is available, however. Based on expenses for the month of January, Boley spent a total of 1.44 dollars per client day for social programming.

ADULT CONGREGATE LIVING FACILITIES (ACLF) PROJECT

Over the past 20 years, boarding homes have increasingly been used as community residence and care facilities for the chronic psychiatric client. Changes in legal requirements placing or retaining individuals in state hospitals, and the emerging philosophy of deinstitutionalization have combined to increase the utilization of boarding homes as placements for mental health clients. Unfortunately, this shift of psychiatric clients to "less restrictive" community settings has often occurred without adequate professional planning and support. As a result, boarding homes, and indeed the whole concept of deinstitutionalization, have received a considerable amount of criticism. The news media, lawmakers, and concerned community residents have all expressed concern about the quality of life of the boarding home residents. At times, this media criticism of mental health "ghettos" has threatened to undermine the entire deinstitutionalization effort. The major descriptive references to boarding homes in the professional literature also characterize them as settings in which the "lives of the residents are less rich than they were in the hospital and in which retreat from the world is even more possible,"[20] and as providing a milieu that perpetuates a low level of functioning.[21]

Given these conditions, it is hardly surprising to find that mental clients placed in a boarding home situation are at risk of rehospitalization. Constantine[22] in his six months follow-up study of 400 clients discharged from Florida state hospitals, documents that of all discharged patients living in a variety of situations, those residing in boarding homes were the most likely to be readmitted to the state hospitals. Pryce[23] and Wing and Brown[24] argue that an increase in symptoms resulting in readmission to a state hospital is frequently found in a boarding home milieu. It is apparent that the quality of support and rehabilitative services provided to the boarding home client must be improved before this "at risk" group can be successfully and humanely maintained in the community.

The renovation of the boarding homes into viable community residences for psychiatric clients would also benefit the deinstitutionalization process in other ways. Datel et al[25] in their analysis of the SID Project in Virginia found that inadequacy or unavailability of housing was a primary reason for clients remaining in an institution long after their clinical need for hospitalization had subsided; thus, the creation of adequate boarding home environments for psychiatric clients would enable more rapid placement of discharged inpatients who are merely waiting for adequate housing, and help to decrease the high recidivism rate that is endemic in boarding home residents.

The ACLF project was created to address the need for adequate boarding homes and for a cost-effective, clinically effective model for intervention with ACLFs. The ACLF project was charged with the responsibility of improving quality of life and reducing recidivism rates within three target boarding homes. The project has also been assigned the tasks of evaluating the impact of its interventions and developing and conducting training for other service providers throughout the state.

Preliminary Needs Survey

In 1978, the Junction Project conducted a needs assessment in order to determine what problems existed in the utilization of boarding homes as placements for psychiatric clients. Concurrently, a review of the literature was conducted to identify national issues and programs that relate to the role of boarding homes in deinstitutionalization. Interviews were conducted with a number of individuals and agencies that interact with boarding homes.

The needs of the boarding home client fell into two main categories: (1) improved quality of life for those clients living in the boarding home whose level of functioning is such that this environment is appropriate for them on a long-term basis, and (2) rehabilitation opportunities for those residents for whom the boarding home may simply be a step toward more independent living.

The needs of the boarding home operators fell into two main categories: (1) training, and (2) crisis support. Many training needs were identified. First of all, operators needed training in using community resources. Training was also needed in understanding the typical course of psychiatric illness, understanding psychotropic medications and their side effects, understanding various concepts of rehabilitation, and in setting realistic expectations for psychiatric clients. Training in basic helping skills was also needed, including training in problem-solving, communication skills, dealing with problem behavior, etc. Furthermore, operators felt they needed more consultation and crisis support from professionals when an individual client's behavior became problematic.

A number of "systems needs" were also identified. One primary problem centered around the failure of the various agencies and individuals involved with boarding homes to communicate with each other, clearly define their own roles, and coordinate their service delivery. For example, social workers and aftercare workers at times worked not only in isolation, but actually at cross purposes with each other. A number of boarding home operators also identified "double binds" that are placed upon them by current legislation and bureaucratic structures. In some of these areas, more investigation and organized effort to bring about system change seem warranted.

Pilot Project Phase

The first six months of the project was designed as a pilot phase. During this time period, ACLF staff were to obtain experience within the three target homes and to pilot evaluation instruments and training and intervention techniques. The staffing pattern, characteristics of target homes, and intervention model developed during this phase will be described in this section.

CHARACTERISTICS OF CLIENTS AND TARGET
HOMES

The three targeted boarding homes that were served in the pilot phase were selected on the following criteria: (1) acceptance of state funded clients, (2) underutilization of available bed space, (3) lack of already existing program agreements with another service agency, (4) current licensure, and (5) willingness to sign an agreement to work with the ACLF Project.

The three target homes differed considerably. Home A was operated in a lovely old hotel. It is within walking distance of stores, churches, recreational facilities, transportation, and state and local agency offices. Its operator and three full-time staff manage a 30-bed facility. Residents, a mixture of private residents, winter tourists, and state mental health clients, range in age from 20 to 80.

Home B exists in an old motel. Residents range in age from 22 to 80. Most residents are mental health clients, and many are physically disabled as well. Two full-time and two part-time staff operate this 39-bed facility. Community services and stores are within easy walking distance.

Home C is an old single story building, designed as a nursing home. It is located in a low income area with easy access to the bus line, but not to stores, churches, etc. All residents are over 45, with most 65 and over. Almost all are state clients with multiple physical and emotional handicaps. Five full-time staff operate this 20-bed facility.

GOALS AND OBJECTIVES

The activities of the ACLF project fall into three basic categories: (1) *Provision of Services* to Residents; (2) *Training and Consultation* with operators, service providers and policy-makers; and (3) *Evaluation* of the project's success in achieving its stated objectives. Specific objectives in each area will be described.

Service provision goals. The primary goal of the ACLF project is to reduce the return of mental health clients to state or other hospital settings. In order to accomplish this goal, the ACLF project must improve the quality of life of residents in boarding homes and create a network of needed community services to support the resident and the operator. Specifically, the ACLF project has attempted (1) to insure that ACLF residents are being served by the recreational, vocational, and rehabilitative programs in the community; (2) to insure the delivery of health and medication services to ACLF residents; (3) to insure that the ACLF operator has adequate procedures and backup support in the area of crisis intervention; (4) to stimulate the development of additional services that are needed but are not presently available in the community (e.g., transportation).

Two project staff were assigned to each ACLF during the six month pilot phase. In establishing their relationship with the operator and in developing programs for the home, project staff were reminded that they are working in the ACLF by agreement. The ACLF is a private business and operators are only required to provide room, board, and personal care. Although project staff were encouraged to do whatever was necessary to deliver needed services to ACLF residents, it was not the intention of the project to create another agency, duplicate services, or create a closed system or total care institution. Therefore, in establishing programming opportunities or providing service, the staff were instructed to prioritize solutions in the following manner: (1) assist the residents in finding appropriate rehabilitative, social, recreational, and vocational activities *away from their place of residence;* (2) arrange for *existing services* to be brought into the home for those residents who are unable to go out for them; (3) provide the needed service themselves.

Given this philosophy of intervention, the problem-solving sequence followed when service needs arose was to (1) identify any existing person or agencies that is delivering the service and make appropriate linkages, (2) identify and stimulate any person or agency that could deliver the service, (3) provide the service themselves while attempting to stimulate another person or agency to take over the task and evaluating whether the task is a real service gap that should become integrated temporarily or permanently into their role.

If, for example, several of the residents need assistance with daily living skills, the staff would contact a community program offering skills-training classes and arrange for attendance of the residents, or arrange to have a living-skills instructor conduct classes in the home, or design and conduct a skills program in the home for the residents while attempting to stimulate or identify another agency or individual to take over this function. If this problem-solving sequence was followed and no other resource for meeting this service need could be found, ACLF staff would then evaluate the importance of this service to determine whether it should become a permanent part of their role.

Training and consultation goals. The training goals and objectives of the ACLF project were to assess the training needs of ACLF residents, operators, service providers and policy makers; to develop training programs and materials for use in training residents and operators; to provide training and consultation to service agencies who work with ACLFs; and to provide information and consultation to policy makers who determine funding levels, licensure requirements, and service programs for ACLFs.

Observation showed that operators needed training in such areas as home management, recordkeeping, use of community resources, crisis intervention, active listening, understanding psychiatric diagnosis, and the use and side-effects of psychotropic medication. Service providers would benefit from training in the psychosocial and medical needs of ACLF residents, the effective use of community resources, case management concepts, and the role of ACLFs in deinstitutionalization. Consultation is also needed to help service providers clarify their roles and overlapping responsibilities in providing services to this group.

Residents themselves need training in basic life skills (e.g., grooming) and in proper use of medication. Having identified these training needs, the ACLF project is currently developing training materials and procedures for pilot testing and subsequent statewide dissemination.

EVALUATION

The primary evaluation objectives during the first phase of the ACLF project were to pilot and refine data collection procedures that could subsequently be used to (1) obtain a comprehensive demographic description of ACLF residents; (2) document the amount of movement in and out of the home, including recidivism rates; (3) document the services needed by and the services provided to ACLF clients in order to determine service gaps, etc.; and (4) to assess the home environment in order to determine changes in the home as a result of project interventions.

The data collection procedures and instruments piloted and selected during the first phase of the project are presented in Table 14-2.

PROJECT FINDINGS

A complete description of the ACLF project and its outcome is available, and may be obtained from the authors. A brief summary of these findings will be presented in this section.

Resident needs. Project staff were successful in significantly increasing the number of services provided to residents of the three targeted ACLFs. Contrary to many service providers' preconceptions about resident needs, however, the lack of mental health services was not high on the hierarchy of resident needs.

The most pressing problems of ACLF residents were medical and physical. Many residents suffered from chronic dental and medical problems, a lack of needed prosthetic devices, etc. These basic needs had to be addressed before any other intervention was possible. Furthermore, a small study in one home discovered that *none* of that home's residents were taking their medications properly. Since boarding home operators are not licensed medical staff, they are forbidden by law to supervise resident medications. Residents were typically too confused or indifferent to maintain their medication properly, however. Therefore, training in self-medication became a priority for ACLF training efforts.

A serious lack of social and recreational opportunities was also noted. These needs were addressed through referral to outside programs (e.g., CND) and through in-house activities led by volunteers.

Finally, the need for a strong case-manager/advocate for residents became apparent. The residents of ACLFs are frequently indigent, have multiple disabilities, and often have no family or friends to act as their advocate. The provision of case management services for ACLF residents was critical to the success of the project, and case management activities consumed the majority of staff time. In one fairly typical case, an ACLF staff member spent four hours on the phone and contacted 15 agencies in order to get one resident evaluated for prosthetic limbs. The enormous fragmentation and in-

Table 14-2
ACLF Data Collection Instruments

Instrument	Information Obtained	Decision-Making Relevance/ Policy Application
ACLF Resident Census and Status Form	Arrivals and departures: places/dates. Identifies State clients and physical/mental health status.	Tracking of all residents in ACLF's. Verification of recidivism. Establishing proportions of disabilities. Planning for levels of care and services required.
ACLF Resident Assessment	Basic demographics. Clinical information, e.g. history of psychiatric treatment. Physical and behavioral levels of functioning.	Providing comprehensive picture of ACLF population characteristics. Determining levels of care and projecting proportions of population requiring each level. Planning resource allocation. Assessing amount of attention required for physical vs. behavioral needs.
ACLF Resident Utilization of Services	Categories of services used per month. Quantities of services provided (in hours). Providers.	Describing quantities and kinds of services used by this population. Identifying providers. Establishing patterns of use. Projecting major areas of use for resource allocation. Tracking use of services and treatment follow-thru. Clarifying case management task and time.
Environmental Deprivation Scale	Estimate of quality of life. Degree of environmental support for adaptive behavior.	Planning treatment, i.e. targeting major areas in resident's life requiring attention. Evaluating program effectiveness. Predicting recidivism.
MEAP: Multiphasic Environmental Assessment Procedure	Environmental assessment of a facility including: physical features, policy resources, program resources, resident characteristics, staff characteristics, social environment.	Developing accurate ACLF descriptions and referral procedures for residents. Determining facility characteristics requiring changes, and monitoring changes (involves administrator, staff, and residents in planning process, thereby facilitating change).

accessability of services make case-management/advocacy an essential service for this population.

Operator needs. As anticipated, operators did not have an adequate understanding of psychiatric illness, medication, etc. Other unexpected needs arose during the course of the project, however. ACLFs are frequently family businesses and each operator in our three target homes needed training/consultation in budgeting, business management, nutrition, etc. In many cases the quality of life in the home was negatively affected by the operator's lack of organization and planning.

Operators frequently deal with crisis situations and need training in crisis management. However, on the occasions when a client's acting-out behavior can not be contained, crisis stabilization services are needed.

This service is ostensibly provided by mental health centers, but the criteria for admission exclude acting out clients, most of whom are not sufficiently dangerous to warrant involuntary commitment. In these situations the operator is left with a volatile client but no professional help.

System needs. The gaps, blocks, and fragmentation of the current human service system are staggering. The multiple needs of ACLF residents made it necessary for project staff to grapple daily with a broad cross-section of service agencies. Not only are needed services scarce and inaccessible, but, to complicate the problems further, service agencies and staff are frequently competitive. Even though ACLF resident needs were not being met, other agencies involved with this population became threatened and resentful when the ACLF project began to enter their "turf."

Conclusion. Both objective and subjective data point to the need for greater involvement with ACLF operators and residents. Our experience indicates that a case-management/advocate model can be effective in providing needed services to ACLF residents. In the next phase of the project, we will attempt to "give away" the various activities and roles of the ACLF staff to other agencies and individuals. If this is possible, their intervention can begin in a second generation of target homes.

DISCUSSION

The program outlined in this chapter was designed to provide comprehensive services for adult psychiatric clients. The locked Intensive Residential Treatment unit serves to stabilize patients who did not respond to brief treatment (1 to 15 days) in the community inpatient units. Two other residential treatment units, the Early Intervention Project and the Psychosocial Rehabilitation Entry Project, offer extensive skill-training to prepare patients for community life. Both residential programs emphasize self-help and peer support activities, and foster independence and interdependence rather than dependence on professional services. Community programs for adults provide for the vocational, social support, housing, and social service needs of patients. The Junction Day Treatment program teaches work skills and assists patients in finding appropriate work placements; the Adult Congregate Living Facilities Project helps psychiatric residents of boarding homes to obtain benefits and services, as well as needed social and recreational opportunities. The Community Network Development Project provides social and recreational activities for patients in other community settings, and attempts to develop helping networks among patients.

REFERENCES

1. Paul G: Chronic mental patients: Current status–future directions. Psychol Bull 71:81–94, 1969
2. Goffman E: Asylums. Garden City, N.Y., Doubleday and Company, 1961
3. Nuehring E, Thayer J: From hospital to community: A six month follow-up study of 400 clients discharged from Florida State Hospital and South Florida State Hospital. Report to the Mental Health Program Office, Department of Health and Rehabilitative Services, Tallahassee, Fla., 1977
4. Archer RP, Amuso K, Bedell JR: Time-limited residential treatment: Issues and evaluation. Hosp Community Psychiatry (in press)
5. Archer RP, Bedell JR, Amuso K: Interrelationships and changes of locus of control and trait anxiety among residential psychiatric inpatients. Soc Behav Personality (in press)
6. Bedell JR, Archer RP, Marlowe HA: A description and evaluation of a problem-solving skills training program, in Upper D, Ross S (Eds): Behavioral Group Therapy: An Annual Review, vol. 2. Champaign, Ill., Research Press, 1980, pp 3–36
7. Ayllan T, Azrin NH: The Token Economy: A Motivational System for Therapy and Rehabilitation. New York, Appleton-Century-Crofts, 1968
8. Carson GG, Hersen M, Eisler RM: Token economy programs in the treatment of hospitalized adult psychiatric patients. J Nerv Ment Disorders 155:193–204, 1972
9. Kazdin AE: The Token Economy. New York, Plenum Press, 1977
10. Bedell JR, Archer RP: Peer managed token economies: Evaluation and description. J Clin Psychol (in press)
11. Fairweather GW (Ed): Social Psychology in Treating Mental Illness. New York, John Wiley and Sons, 1964
12. Anthony WA: Psychological rehabilitation: A concept in need of a method. Am Psychologist 32:658–662, 1977
13. Harrington C, Wilkins ML: Treating social symptoms of mental illness. Hosp Community 17:136–139, 1966
14. Peretti PO: Precipitating factors of readmission of psychiatric patients. Commun Ment Health J 10:89–92, 1974
15. Goldstein AP, Spraffrin RP, Gershaw NJ: Structured learning therapy: Training for community living. Psychotherapy: Theory, Research, and Practice 13:374-377, 1976

16. Steele RL: Humanistic psychology and rehabilitation programs in mental hospitals. Am J Occup Ther 30:358–361, 1976

17. Safier D: Using an education model in a sheltered workshop program. Ment Hyg 54:140, 1970

18. Messina JJ: Meeting the needs of the chronic emotionally disabled adult in the community. Report from the Florida Mental Health Institute. Tampa, Fla., March, 1979

19. Edmunson ED, Bedell JR, Gordon RE: Bridging the gap between self-help and professional aftercare, in Gartner A, Riessman F (Eds): New York, Human Services Press, (in press)

20. Lamb HR, Guertzel V: The demise of the state hospital—a premature obituary? Arch Gen Psychiatry 26:489–495, 1972

21. May PRA: Adopting new models for continuity of care: What are the needs? Hospital Commun Psychiatry 26:519–601, 1975

22. Constantine RJ: From hospital to community: A six month follow-up study of 400 clients discharged from Florida State Hospital and South Florida State Hospital. Tallahassee, Fla., Mental Health Program Office, Department of Health and Rehabilitative Services, 1978

23. Pryce JG: The effects of social change in chronic schizophrenics. Psychological Med 7:127–139, 1977

24. Wing JK, Brown GW: Institutionalism and Schizophrenia. London, Cambridge University Press, 1970

25. Datel WE, Murphy JG, Pollack PL: Outcome in a deinstitutionalization program employing service integration methodology. J Oper Psychiatry 9:6–18, 1978

PART E

Programming for Treatment of Chronically Ill Elderly Mental Patients

Innovative treatment programs for deinstitutionalizing elderly mental patients deserve high priority in states where large numbers of the patients residing in state mental hospitals are over 65 years of age. In the mental hospital serving the region where the research and training (R&T) center discussed here is located, 34 percent of the more than 1200 patients are elderly.[1] The gerontology projects, therefore, were among the first to be launched. They have been in existence the longest of all those described here, having begun in December, 1975. They have the most complete data on assessments, effectiveness, and long-term outcomes.

The gerontology programs hold special interest, because they were the first to offer a day hospital component aimed at reducing hospitalization of older patients, along with a residential component designed for deinstitutionalization. However, as with every other project that utilized staff for treating patients who were not in residence, the gerontology project received a good deal of political criticism in its early stages. Funding for facilities with beds is often linked to keeping the beds filled, not for keeping patients in the community. Performance is measured by bedcount not effectiveness of treatment. The day treatment component has been repeatedly threatened with being cut back or shut down; periodically it has been required to surrender staff to new residential projects that were being started up.

Initially designed by Bates,[2,3] the modular program for the elderly originally called only for the treatment of residential patients. However, a survey of community needs and resources turned up tangible local support for day treatment as an alternative to hospitalization of mentally disturbed elderly persons, such as the elderly diabetic whose case was described briefly in

Chapter 9. Community agencies offered to provide transportation of patients to and from the R&T facility each day (an essential requirement for a day treatment program), as well as additional treatment staff, if the program could be conducted for patients in both residential and day treatment.

We welcomed this opportunity to form ties between the state R&T facility and community agencies, and to obtain additional resources in the pursuit of community programs. Permission was obtained to proceed in this joint venture, contracts were written to bind the agencies together (an essential step in the crisis-oriented public mental health field), and the project plan was modified to include day treatment.

Early studies had shown that social and behavioral techniques used to augment dynamic psychotherapy were successful with elderly patients, as well as with those in other age groups. More than twice as many older patients responded satisfactorily to a combined approach as did to dynamic psychotherapy alone.[4] The elderly did not respond nearly so well as did younger patients, however.[5] Office practice could not provide these patients with the training in leisure and other skills they required. More than any other age group, they continued to require hospital care. But hospitals did not provide modular skills training at that time. A program to develop modules for use in training the elderly, therefore, offered much promise.

Early findings with patients ten months after discharge were reported in Chapter 2. These promising findings, tangible local support, and successful dissemination of the entire gerontology project into three major, politically conspicuous public mental hospitals have resulted in the program's receiving wide acceptance, and have kept the day treatment component alive.

TREATMENT ENVIRONMENTS

Patterson and Jackson[6] have sought to create a therapeutic environment in this program. They have developed a useful classification of treatment environments that clarifies their goals and compares the program with others. They suggest that the following definitions provide an unambiguous and accurate description of current environmental approaches with the elderly:

The Prosthetic Environment assists patients with physical disabilities. In it, artificial limbs, walkers, canes, wheelchairs, hearing aids, grab-bars, etc. enable patients to perform activities that cannot occur without these devices.

The Training Environment uses learning principles to establish or reestablish behaviors. These are maintained by providing supportive antecedents and reinforcers in the training setting.

The Therapeutic Environment offers a training program in which learned behaviors are generalized to the outside world. There they are maintained by naturally occurring events.

The Custodial Environment provides protective, medically oriented nursing care for the prevention and treatment of diseases; it offers no systematic behavioral treatment. This type of environment, which is appropriate for the patient who needs intensive and extensive nursing care, can be combined with any other approach for increased effectiveness.

Many infirm elderly patients require Training Environments in institutions and nursing homes. When needed, appropriate medical care and prosthetics are included. For physically active elderly mental patients a Therapeutic Environment is the ideal situation to strive for. Unfortunately, when programs fail to provide for the generalization and maintenance of behavior in the natural environment, they qualify as only Training Environments. The gerontology program described here fills this gap; it incorporates behavioral treatment and maintenance components in a coordinated manner to provide a true Therapeutic Environment. The chapter that follows also describes the evaluation and dissemination aspects of this gerontology program.

REFERENCES

1. Slater A, Gordon K, Patterson R, et al: Deinstitutionalizing the elderly in Florida's state mental hospitals: Assessing the problems. Monograph Series No. 2. Tampa, Fla., Human Resources Institute, University of South Florida, 1978
2. Bates HD: Proposal for a gerontological assessment, treatment and training project at the Florida Mental Health Institute, Tampa, Fla., Florida Mental Health Institute, July, 1975
3. Bates HD (Ed): Gerontology project staff training manual and workbook. Tampa, Fla., Florida Mental Health Institute, December, 1975
4. Gordon RE: Sociodynamics and psychotherapy. AMA Arch Neurol Psychiatry 81: 486–503, 1959
5. Gordon RE, Singer M, Gordon KK: Social psychological stress. Arch Gen Psychiatry 4: 459, 1961
6. Patterson RL, Jackson GM: Behavior modification with the elderly, in Hersen M, Eisler RM, Miller PM, et al (Eds): Progress in Behavior Modification, Vol. 7. New York, Academic Press, 80

15
Treating Chronically Ill Elderly Mental Patients with Skill-Enhancing Modules and Placing Them in the Community

Patterson and Jackson[1] recently reviewed the literature on behavior management with the elderly. The approaches they described utilize individualized behavior modification techniques or token economies that reinforce a variety of behaviors, but may or may not teach specific target behaviors. Neither approach, as a rule, trains patients in the variety of skills needed for successful life in a noninstitutional environment. Mental hospitals and nursing homes that care for elderly patients usually do not employ experts to implement behavioral treatments. The following section describes a comprehensive approach that is broad in scope, easily learned, and inexpensive. This program has received a letter of commendation from the State, which recommends that it be used as a model for transfer to all public mental hospitals and community programs for the elderly. Our own observations of gerontology programs for the mentally ill in other states, as well as comments of visitors from out of state, suggest that many geriatric programs nationally can benefit from adopting components of the modular psychoeducational approach developed

Portions of this chapter were previously published in Gordon R, Patterson R, Bates H, et al: Modular treatment and training, in Slater A, Bowmen L (Eds): Career Education for Mental Health Workers Project (Monograph Series No. 2, Report No. 2, Tampa, Fla., Human Resources Institute, College of Social and Behavioral Sciences, University of South Florida, April, 1979), and are reprinted with permission.

by the R&T center's Gerontology Program. The description that follows highlights components of the program; more detail can be found in staff publications and presentations.[2-21]

A MODULAR PSYCHOEDUCATIONAL TREATMENT PROGRAM FOR BUILDING SKILLS WITH ELDERLY MENTAL PATIENTS

Isolation, improper use of medications, excessive anxiety, confusion, and financial trouble act singly and together to reduce independence of elderly persons and contribute to their institutionalization. Many elderly patients have developed patterns of extreme dependence. They are unable to perform simple, daily living tasks associated with personal hygiene or meal preparation; they have become disoriented as to self, place, and time. Many suffer from excessive tension or loss of self esteem. Some display socially unacceptable behavior such as exposing themselves, striking others, or constantly complaining. Modular psychoeducation for enhancing skills, combined with medical care and individual treatment to correct specific behavioral abnormalities, comprise the program for elderly patients. All patients' treatments are selected to fit their specific needs.[2]

Survival Skills

Disorientation and unacceptable behavior prevent many patients from functioning outside an institution such as a mental hospital or nursing home. Therefore, training for deinstitutionalization must be directed at their gaining personal control over these activities.[2] Patients' placements after treatment depend heavily on their amount of information about themselves and their medications, and the degree of control they gain over their unacceptable behavior.

Personal Information Training. All patients are assessed to establish their orientation to time, place, and person. Those who have lost their orientation receive training in classes with other patients. Patients who fail to pass the orientation test after training will require placement in sheltered care facilities after discharge.

Medication Information Training. The proper use of psychotropic medications relieves unacceptable behavior in many patients. However, failure to continue to take medications once discharged from the hospital and improper use of medication (in the case of elderly patients in particular) are important contributors to hospitalization and to recidivism. Medication Information Training modules teach patients to be responsible for their own medications. They learn drug classification, therapeutic effects (reasons for a given medication), dosage, frequency of administration, side effects, and drug interactions and precautions. As they progress, they receive increasing responsibility for administering their own medications in preparation for independent living.

Daily Living Skills

Activities of daily living are taught on three levels:

Activities of Daily Living I (ADL I).   Patients learn to take care of their personal hygienic requirements: bathing, oral hygiene, nail care, and eating. For example, many elderly patients do not use a knife efficiently; they fail to cut up foods, especially meats, into small slices. An attempt to swallow large pieces can lead to choking, an important cause of death among the elderly, which is often confused with an acute heart attack. Patients are taught to take time enough while eating to cut their food into small portions. All patients receive this level of training regardless of anticipated post-treatment living situations.

Activities of Daily Living II (ADL II).   Patients whose assessments indicate that they will be placed in sheltered care facilities learn to care for their clothes and rooms, to manage funds and make change, to choose foods and follow diets, to take care of their laundry, and to use the telephone.

Activities of Daily Living III (ADL III).   Those who ultimately will be living independently learn how to budget time and money, and to utilize community resources such as bus systems and health services. They receive training to select nutritious diets and prepare meals, and to keep their homes clean and safe.

Personal and Social Skills

These modules teach patients conversation skills, effective communication of pleasure and displeasure, and problem solving.

Communication Skills.   Teaching hospitalized psychiatric patients to communicate effectively helps prevent recidivism. Patients learn to improve their relationships with other people. Most are "social dropouts" who have failed to maintain adequate contact with others. Patients practice using their words, bodies, and voices to express thoughts, feelings, needs, and information clearly and effectively. This training helps overcome the apathy frequently found in elderly patients.[2]

Problem Solving. Patients are shown how to integrate their skills in solving their personal problems. Using the problem-solving approach described in Chapters 7 and 14, they learn to deal with actual situations in their own lives. As their skill and self-confidence increase, they are encouraged to tackle increasingly more difficult tasks. Rather than depend on professionals, patients learn to cope by themselves. Success in problem-solving helps build independence and self-confidence.

In a therapeutic environment, adult and elderly patients become proficient in solving their own problems outside the institution.[3] Consumer satisfaction and other follow-up data show that patients appreciate this training, which prepares them for community living.

Leisure Skills

Elderly patients usually have access to a great deal of unstructured time; however, few programs teach leisure activities to the elderly. At the R&T center patients are trained in inexpensive, readily accessible activities that they can do alone (reading, listening to music, sewing), in small groups (playing cards and other games), and in large groups (dancing, playing bingo). Patients learn to use community resources such as recreation centers for senior citizens.[2] They learn simple crafts using common household tools with readily available materials. Patients from higher income groups can be taught pottery making, which requires expensive materials and a kiln, or jewelry-making. Lower income persons can gain satisfaction from learning to use construction paper, playing cards, and yarn—items that most households can afford.

Current Events Training. Patients read the newspaper each day and practice their communication skills by discussing current events. They interact with each other in response to television news. They learn to participate actively, rather than merely listen passively.

Integrative Skills

Patients learn to reintegrate their thinking about themselves, their lives, feelings, and behavior.

Self-Esteem Training. Patients reassess themselves and begin to develop an awareness of their positive attributes. They keep personal files of their positive characteristics and how well they use them in their daily living. They report in class and discuss the items in their files.[2]

Anxiety Management and Relaxation Training. A module teaches patients to be aware of muscle tensions in various parts of their bodies, and to relax these tensions deliberately. This treatment assists them in overcoming insomnia and other tension-related problems.[2] Another module helps patients to restructure their thinking and to relieve unfounded and unjustified anxiety by means of Rational Emotive Therapy.

PLACEMENT

Since boarding home and foster home operators, like foster parents of child patients, are often reluctant to keep an improperly placed patient who causes them trouble, it is important that social workers carefully match patients with placements. Inadequate performance in ADL I and in Survival Skills points to the need for a supportive, sheltered living situation. At the other extreme, patients without physical problems should not be placed in nursing homes when they can be trained to reside in less restrictive alternatives. It is also important that operators of these homes be taught how to reinforce patients positively in order to help maintain the effective new psychosocial skills the patients have learned.

ILLUSTRATIVE CASE HISTORY—MARGARET M

The following example illustrates the combined use of modular skill-building, individual behavior management, and family training in the treatment of an elderly invalid.

Margaret M, a 62-year-old married patient, arrived on the gerontology unit in a wheelchair. She had been increasingly confined to the chair for the five years prior to admission, ever since her husband, Peter, had a heart attack and retired from work to remain full-time at home. Margaret had become depressed, increasingly feeble, and socially isolated. She ate less and less, and her weight dropped from 130 pounds to 82 pounds on admission. Eating created quite a problem for both Margaret and Peter, since he provided the motor power for her wheelchair. She felt compelled to go to the toilet after each meal, as well as whenever she ate or drank anything between meals. Since she also wanted to visit the toilet at least three times each hour and several times during the night, Margaret's daily routine was fairly well circumscribed.

Margaret's psychiatric hospitalization was precipitated by Peter's developing a viral respiratory infection. He had to call the social welfare agency to assist with Margaret's care while he was confined to bed. The social service workers who visited their home recognized the psychiatric nature of Margaret's problem and arranged for her to receive residential care; Peter was admitted to day care along with her in order to help with her management, as well as to learn how to treat her when she returned home.

Following her assessment testing, Margaret was assigned to classes in activities of daily living, communications, assertion, leisure, and self-esteem training, as well as depression management. Her husband attended these psychoeducational classes with her. Since she responded to few of the usual positive reinforcers (food, affectionate pats, etc.), her treatment plan employed the Premack Principle to train her in self-help and self-assertion. Going to the bathroom was an activity that she performed with high frequency; it was used to reinforce other more desirable activities: First, her use of the bathroom was increasingly made contingent upon her decreased use of the wheelchair. Margaret was reinforced by being permitted to go to the bathroom more than once an hour when she herself used increasingly greater personal effort to propel her wheelchair there rather than requiring others to push her. Next, after she had mastered wheeling herself to the bathroom, and elsewhere about the unit, she was gradually trained to use a walker and give up the wheelchair. The next step was for her to learn that she could walk alone to the bathroom without the walker. The following step in this particular sequence was for Margaret to attend all activities without wheelchair, walker, or any other crutch except her husband as a companion. The final step and target goal was for her to attend activities alone, without her husband along.

Meanwhile, Margaret attended her classes, where she received strong positive reinforcement for grooming herself increasingly on her own—washing her face, combing her hair, and even bathing without her husband's assistance. Her progress in activities of daily living (ADL I) is charted on her proficiency gauge in Chapter 5, Figure 5-1. She was assigned as part of her leisure training to work with the plant and flower collection on the unit, a favorite of many patients of low income who can easily obtain clippings or seeds from a friend, some dirt, and an old pot. She received praise for cutting and arranging flowers around the unit, for displaying them to visitors and guests, and for expressing appropriate remarks, "I like pretty flowers and making arrangements to show them off. Do you?" In self-esteem training she learned to reassess her own worth and began to make positive statements about herself.

Group discussions, as well as individual sessions with her primary therapist and her husband, brought out that Margaret was an orphan who had married Peter when she was 16. They had had no children; their whole lives had been wrapped up in each other. After his heart attack they had discontinued sexual activity. Her worry about Peter, her fear about what would happen to him, and then to herself if he died, and their restricted lives led to her depression. Peter had become increasingly attentive and devoted as Margaret became more and more of an invalid; his retirement provided him with the time and incentive to devote himself fully to reinforcing her sickliness.

Praise and encouragement for eating produced an increase in Margaret's weight to 110 pounds; she and Peter could see her weight improve each week, since it and all her other target behaviors were measured and plotted on graphs in her chart where she and her therapists could follow her progress. Margaret began to play bingo with the other patients. She and Peter entered a checkers tournament, and learned a few fox trot steps to favorite old tunes. As Margaret became increasingly involved with and interested in her program of activities and classes, her bathroom compulsion gradually subsided.

Differential reinforcement of these competing behaviors resulted, after two months of treatment, in Margaret's needing to visit the bathroom only once every two to three hours, a goal that staff considered to be within the range of normal for patients of her age. Her assessments on standardized global rating scales and proficiency gauges measured her overall progress (see Figures 6-1 and 6-2).

Meanwhile, Peter learned along with Margaret what he had been doing that had reinforced her sick, dependent behavior, and what now to do to maintain her more competent, independent conduct back in their home life outside the institution. Peter also came to realize that his own life style contributed to Margaret's problems. After retirement, he had little to interest him besides his wife. For most of his life he had compulsively devoted himself to getting ahead on his job. His ambition, drive, and single-mindedness—qualities that won him praise and success at work—reduced his adaptability to retirement. Instead of his and Margaret's devoting themselves to common leisure activities, they concentrated on her illness. In treatment, their programs of training in a variety of leisure and other skills diversified their interests, and provided them with healthy outlets for their energies.

EVALUATION

During the period when R. Gordon served as director of the R&T facility, approximately 130–150 patients were admitted to the Gerontology Program each year, about half to residential and half to day treatment. Most residential patients were diagnosed as psychotic, and had had between two and three previous hospitalizations totaling between one and two years of inpatient treatments. Day treatment patients had fewer prior hospitalizations, but had remained in hospitals for nearly as many months. The residential group of mental patients consisted largely of the chronically hospitalized; the day treatment group were patients who presented a high risk of becoming institutionalized.

Treatment Outcome

Outcome data from a quasi-experiment with elderly patients indicated that 77 percent of these residential patients undergoing modular treatment were discharged to and remained in nonistitutional community settings for one year or longer; only 24 percent of patients treated in the traditional public mental hospital program were discharged to and stayed in the community for the same period, less than one-third the percentage of those in the modular program.[1]

Efforts by Gerontology staff with all the patients in the program produced similar results. They placed between 75 percent and 80 percent of all residential patients treated, and more than 90 percent of day treatment patients, in community settings in boarding and foster homes, with their family or spouse, or in independent homes.

The standardized global rating scales (NOSIE-30, CAP, and SABRS) and 7 of 10 staff-developed scales indicate that both the residential and the day treatment patients made significant improvements, often within the first

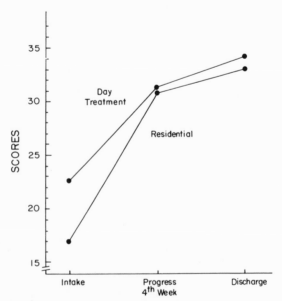

Fig. 15-1. Assessment of communication skill acquisition. Data presented were collected from 116 elderly mental patients who were trained to communicate pleasure.

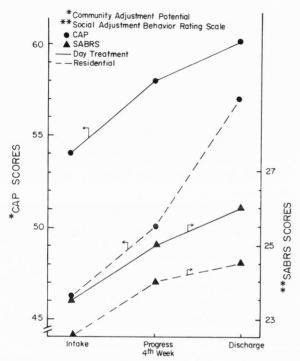

Fig. 15-2.   Assessment of readiness for community living. Data presented were collected from 133 elderly mental patients on the SABRS and CAP scales.

four weeks of modular treatment. These patients continued to make progress until discharge, as shown in Figures 15-1 and 15-2. Initial test results with day treatment patients on admission were consistently higher than those for residential patients, but on many scales the residential patients' scores continued to improve with further treatment, so that at discharge residential patients' scores approach those of day treatment patients.

Figures 15-1 and 15-2 present graphs that are adapted from materials developed by Eberly[14] and the Gerontology Program staff. Figure 15-1 illustrates improvements in scores of patients who received communication training in expressing pleasure; improvements in scores on the Community Adjustment Potential (CAP) (readiness for discharge) and Social Adjustment Behavior Rating Scales (SABRS) (overall social adjustment) appear in Figure 15-2. Except for the residential patients' CAP scores, these graphs show that patient progress follows a typical learning curve pattern and most learning takes place in the first four weeks of treatment. Patients also made significant increases on three subscales of the NOSIE-30: Social Interest, Retardation, and Irritability.

Increased irritability may not be considered an improvement, but, as noted by Price and Moos,[22] treatment environments that emphasize "open expression of feelings, active preparation for patient release, and concern with the personal problems of patients" are usually associated with patients' expression of anger. The three NOSIE-30 scales considered as a group indicate that the patients are becoming more active in general, and are communicating and expressing themselves more. These behaviors are in marked contrast to the lethargy, apathy, and depression frequently found with psychogeriatric patients and which characterize many units of mental institutions where chronically ill mental patients reside.

Consumer Satisfaction after Discharge

Follow-up data indicate that three months after discharge patients treated in the residential program and their families and friends were satisfied with the treatment program. For example, on a scale from one to five, where one is the most favorable response and five the least favorable, patients gave these average satisfaction scores:

With living situation	1.47
With social involvement	2.62
With treatment program	2.07
With preparation for community life	2.08

Reports from families and friends confirmed the patients' favorable self-ratings.[21]

Correlations Between Progress and Outcome Measures

Intercorrelations between scales were reported in Chapter 6. These pointed to the validity and reliability of the staff-developed Proficiency Gauges. However, data are not yet available on the correlations between recidivism, quality of life in the community, and scores on Proficiency Gauges and global psychosocial rating scales.

DISCUSSION

The Harvard Case Report has noted a lack of boarding homes for the elderly resulting from community indifference or opposition, or to outmoded program practices.[23] To fill this gap the R&T facility's gerontology program developed a program for the mentally ill elderly that prepared them for successful lives in those community boarding and foster homes that were available. Because patients and placements are properly matched and square pegs are not fitted in round holes, the community has accepted these mental patients who are being deinstitutionalized from the state's mental hospitals. Discharged patients are placed in settings that are suitable to their assessed level of functioning.

Baseline data are obtained and progress is tested at every step, utilizing both comprehensive psychosocial rating scales and modular proficiency gauges. Follow-up assessments measure consumer satisfaction and maintenance of treatment gains in the community. Community social service personnel who work with the aged are trained, not only so they can help the R&T facility's discharged patients, but also so they can better assist their other clients. The program evaluates its own activities, and trains staff of gerontology programs throughout the state; it has disseminated successful modules, as well as the program as a whole.

The Gerontology Programs director, Roger L. Patterson, is editing a book on the project to which staff members and university faculty are contributing chapters. The reader who would like to learn further details about the treatment program and its evaluative findings is urged to read Patterson's book when it is published.

REFERENCES

1. Patterson RL, Jackson G: Behavior modification with the elderly, in Hersen M (Ed): Progress in Behavior Modification. New York, Academic Press, 1980 (in press)
2. Gordon R, Patterson R, Bates H, et al: Modular treatment and training, in Slater A, Bowman L (Eds): Career Education for Mental Health Workers Project. Monograph Series No. 2, Report No. 2. Tampa, Fla., University of South Florida, Human Resources Institute, College of Social and Behavioral Sciences, April, 1979
3. Patterson R, Smith G, Goodale P, et al: Three procedures for improving communication skills among elderly mental health clients. Presented at the Nova Behavioral Conference on Aging. Port St. Lucie, Fla., May, 1978
4. Patterson RL: Re-education for community life: The role of the Florida Mental Health Institute Gerontology Program, in Bell WG (Ed): Returning the Institutionalized Elderly to the Community. Proceedings of a Training Institute. Tallahassee, Fla., Florida State University, 1979
5. Slater A, Gordon K, Patterson R, et al: Deinstitutionalizing the Elderly in Florida's State Mental Hospitals: Assessing the Problems. Monograph No. 2. Tampa, Fla., Human Resources Institute, University of South Florida, Tampa, 1978
6. Johnson RJ, Frallicciardi V, Patterson RL: A multiple baseline evaluation of a reality orientation classroom. Presented at the 23rd annual convention of the Southeastern Psychological Association, Hollywood, Fla., 1977
7. Patterson R, Smith G, Goodale P, et al: Improving communication skills in psychogeriatric clients. Presented at the 29th annual meeting of the Southeastern Psychological Association, Atlanta, Ga., March, 1978
8. Patterson R, Dee C, Smith G, et al: Measuring communications effectiveness in elderly mental health clients. Presented at the 29th annual meeting of the Southeastern Psychological Association, Atlanta, Ga., March, 1978

9. Gordon RE, Patterson RL, Bates H, et al: Modular treatment and training. Presented at the Florida Psychiatric Society Annual Meeting, Ft. Lauderdale, Fla., April, 1978

10. Gordon RE, Patterson R, Eberly D, et al: Modular treatment of psychiatric patients, in Masserman J (Ed): Current Psychiatric Therapies., vol. 19. New York, Grune and Stratton, (in press)

11. Patterson R, Jackson G: A modular treatment approach to skills enhancement with psychogeriatric clients. Presented at the Nova Behavioral Conference on Aging. Port St. Lucie, Fla., May, 1978

12. Patterson R, Eberly D, O'Sullivan M: Re-education for community life: The role of the Florida Mental Health Institute Gerontology Program. Presented at: Returning the Institutionalized Elderly to the Community, a Training Institute held at Orlando, Fla., January 29–31, 1979

13. Patterson R, Penner L, Eberly D, et al: Behavioral assessments of intellectual competence, conversation skills, and personal hygiene skills of elderly persons. Poster session presented at the 2nd Annual Nova University Behavioral Conference on Aging, Ft. Lauderdale, Fla., January, 1980

14. Eberly D: Evaluation programs for the enhancement of the quality of life of elderly mental health clients. Poster session presented at the 2nd Annual Nova Behavioral Conference on Aging, January 25, 1980

15. O'Sullivan M, Eberly D, Patterson R: The Gerontology Program at FMHI. Presented at the Geriatric Psychiatric Conference, Tampa, Fla., Tampa VA Hospital, May 9, 1980

16. Patterson RL, Eberly Penner L: A three year evaluation of a skills enhancement program for elderly mental health clients. Presented at the 26th Annual Meeting of the Southeastern Psychological Association, March, 1980

17. Patterson RL, O'Sullivan M, Eberly D, et al: Helping elderly mental health clients by skills enhancement: A total treatment program. paper submitted at the Southeastern Psychological Association Annual Meeting, New Orleans, La., March, 1979

18. O'Sullivan M, Patterson RL, Eberly D, et al: Presentation to Mental Health Program Office Advisory Council, FMHI, Tampa, Fla., August 28, 1979

19. Patterson RL: Personal communications, 1979, 1980

20. General Descriptive Information. Gerontology Program, FMHI, Tampa, Fla., 1979

21. Gordon RE, Goldstein N, Gordon K, et al: The role of paraprofessional mental health workers in family therapy. Monograph Series No. 1, Report No. 3, National Education Center for Paraprofessionals in Mental Health, National Institute of Mental Health. New York, New Human Services Institute, May, 1979

22. Price RH, Moos RH: Toward a taxonomy of inpatient treatment environments. J Abnorm Psychol 84:181–188, 1975

23. Whitman D: Reorganization of Florida's Human Services Agency. Kennedy School of Government Case Program, C95-80-040, Cambridge, Mass., Harvard University 1980

Richard E. Gordon
Katherine K. Gordon
Carolyn J. Hursch

16

Integrating Systems of Psychiatric Services for the Chronically Ill Mental Patient

Psychiatry is entering a new era. The first revolution, led by Pinel, freed "madmen and madwomen from their chains."[1] The second, the psychoanalytic enlightenment of the early 1900s, "released them from mental bondage"; it moved psychiatry into the private practitioner's office.[1] Psychodynamic treatment offered help to neurotics and patients with moderate character disorders, but it was of less use with the chronically ill mental patient. In our own experience in the early 1950s, a psychiatrist or other psychotherapist using psychodynamic methods could treat fewer than 40 new patients each year, about one-fourth to one-third of referrals.[2] About one-third of our patients required mental hospital and/or electroconvulsive therapy; the remainder were not taken into treatment because the costs outweighed the potential benefits. These experiences frustrated us and many colleagues. Psychoanalytic insights, on the other hand, which stemmed largely from clinical observations of patients, impacted psychology, education, and the social sciences, and have greatly influenced thinking about human behavior.

The psychopharmacologic breakthroughs of the midcentury provided opportunities for community treatment not only of neurotics but also of psychotics; they diverted many of the latter from lengthy institutional care and paved the way for severely ill chronic mental patients to leave the mental institution; but they did not improve the quality of these patients' existence in the community. Improvements in medications, sponsored by pharmacology and chemistry, brought psychiatry closer to traditional medicine in treatment and theory.

Behavior management, skills-building, peer support, and quantitative, evaluative techniques, new developments from psychology, education, statistics, and social and computer sciences, when combined with psychopharmacologic treatment and dynamic therapy, offered chronically ill patients the promise of a more normal life outside the institution. Further, using these combined therapies, we could treat three to four times as many new patients each year in individual sessions as we did with dynamic therapy alone; we could also evaluate results quantitatively.[2] In addition, we could provide preventive training to between 150 and 250 at-risk persons each year in psychoeducational classes. We now found our work far more satisfying than previously, especially since feedback from the evaluations showed that both our therapeutic and preventive efforts were largely successful.

New management techniques now provide psychiatry with an organizational structure that connects treatments—psychodynamic, medical and pharmacological, behavioral and skill-enhancing, and peer management—into a harmonious whole. Together with modular psychoeducational techniques, structured peer support, and standardized assessment and evaluation instruments, they create an integrated system, a regularly interacting, interdependent group of techniques that form a unified pattern of psychiatric treatment, care, and evaluation. Using this system in collaboration with professional colleagues, we could train and direct a staff composed largely of paraprofessionals, and could effectively treat and evaluate the care of nearly 1000 new patients each year. With this orderly system providing a process where great numbers of chronically ill mental patients are deinstitutionalized and established in comfortable lives in the community, professional and paraprofessional job satisfaction was high; staff "burnout" was not a problem. Possibly these new skills-enhancing, supports-building, evaluative, and management techniques will help improve the treatment of other medical patients with chronic illnesses, as well as help upgrade the care of other persons in need of social, rehabilitative, and other human services.

Previous chapters have shown how to create this exciting problem-solving system in mental health, where professionals, paraprofessionals, patients, families, other human service workers, and students join in finding ways to close the numerous gaps in today's treatment programs. This last chapter will summarize the solutions proposed, and will suggest how the proposals apply to systematic deinstitutionalization of the chronically ill mental patient, to comprehensive manpower development planning, and to investigating disincentives in other public health and human services. The Harvard Case Report concluded that co-location helps communication between service programs within each district, but outside the district, communication still needs improvement. Elsewhere, gaps and conflicts continued, and quality of service did not get noticeably better. Calamities still occurred. Evaluation did not get done. Morale remained low. The troubles generally were longstanding in nature and predated reorganization.[3]

CLOSING THE GAPS

This section reviews some of the gaps and conflicts in the current mental health nonsystem and what the programs described in this book do about them, beginning with the needs of and services to patients and clients.

Deficiencies and other gaps in patients' psychosocial and other life skills. Train patients' skills in modular psychoeducational fashion and utilize paraprofessionals to deliver each predetermined, standardized training package under professional supervision.

Defects in patients' family and community support groups. Establish structured patient-led peer support networks with professional and paraprofessional backup for consultation, training, evaluation, and feedback.

Discontinuities between hospital and community programs. Structure programs so that patients' skills are established and enhanced in the treatment setting, and maintained after discharge. Self-medication training and the single daily-dose regimen aid patients in continuing to take their medications after they leave the hospital. The peer support CND helps maintain skills of adult patients, and family and foster parent training accomplish this with children and adolescents.

Gaps in treatment of the individual patient. Combine skill-enhancing modules, behavior therapy, family therapy, peer support in the community, and proper use of psychotropics with dynamic psychotherapies as illustrated in the case histories shown.

Separate programs of formal schooling, psychoeducation, and family therapy for children with problems. Combine all these in one coordinated program like that demonstrated in the adolescent day treatment and family teaching projects.

Disintegration and lack of cooperation between mental health and a variety of other human service agencies. Establish combined programs with aging, vocational rehabilitation, retardation, public health, and youth services, for example, as well as with social welfare agencies, HUD, children's protective services, the school systems, legal aid, and other organizations. Efforts to integrate all these under one large umbrella agency are steps in the right direction, but they need people who are trained and experienced in the variety of services being rendered and in quantitative evaluative methods. Agreements and contractual responsiblilities need to be spelled out clearly, yet revised periodically in a standard way in the light of experience, innovation, and feedback from evaluation. Change should take place slowly, planfully, but steadily, and in step-by-step fashion.

Continuation of ineffective programs. Train treatment staff to make standardized assessments and to evaluate the effectiveness of programs while in the process of providing service to clients. Project orientation and the modular approach facilitate assessment, evaluation, and feedback, and thus the continuous upgrading of treatment.

Lack of cooperation and/or open conflict between patient peer groups and professional service providers: Develop structured linkages like the Community Network Development, which combine both into one unified, mutually beneficial program.

Separation between the public and private sectors in the care of the chronic mental patient. Forge links between these two sectors in the comprehensive care of the patient. Private practitioners now refer their private patients to the public R&T institution for day or residential psychoeducational skills and supports-building. Chronic and other patients who receive this training become more amenable to dynamic insight-giving and behavioral approaches, which they receive from the private practitioners after they return to the community. Gaps between the private and public sectors, and also between behavioral and psychodynamically oriented therapists, are closed when working patients obtain the full benefit of both kinds of treatment.

Traumatization of patients' children by institutionalization of patients. Use peer support groups to close gaps in shattered families; they support patients and keep them from lengthy rehospitalizations. They can bring to an end the traumatization that results from separation from and loss of parents and other loved ones, and that sensitizes the child to mental illness and other problems.

Gaps in the preparation of foster parents and group home managers. Provide training in programs like the teaching family, the Junction, and the Adult Congregate Living Project. Preparation in the teaching family will itself possibly accomplish a similar purpose to that of peer support groups in reducing the perpetuation of human misery from generation to generation.

Child abuses, deaths, and other calamities. Place standard bearers—professionals with proven experience in client and patient care—in strategic positions where they supervise treatment, monitor quality of care, and uphold ethical and medico-legal principles. Matrix management has provided a means to accomplish this and at the same time maintain good administration of the R&T center.

The management techniques and educational procedures that corrected problems and improved the quality of the mental health system are now reviewed with consideration of whether they might work elsewhere:

Staff burnout and deterioration of morale. Create a clear mission statement with goals and objectives where all staff provide input and with which they can identify; welcome staff ideas and reward their inventiveness; treat paraprofessional staff as if they were professionals in the making; evaluate performance and provide feedback to staff; reinforce effort and initiative; reduce rule by fiat and fear; operate openly, not secretly.

Knowledge gaps among both professionals and paraprofessionals. Use the competency-based modular approach to training. Develop a manpower training program and make it an integral part of the total program. (This will be elaborated more fully later in this chapter.)

Conflicts between academic and mental health educational sectors. Spell out the specific roles of each, and encourage collaboration in projects that conduct treatment innovations, evaluative research, education, training, and dissemination. Rather than compete for funding from only one public source, cooperate in obtaining grant proposals from many sources to further common activities.

Lack of program and progress evaluation. Establish systematic methods of measuring client and staff performance, and assess programs and progress continuously. Employ management personnel to fill key administrative positions who are trained programmatically and quantitatively. Train all staff to assess patient progress as part of their service routine in a manner similar to that described here.

Poor communication, antagonisms, and gaps between different treating professions. Use matrix management for bringing together personnel with different educational backgrounds and perspectives in projects, programs, and networks, and for applying their skills and knowledge creatively and harmoniously in the service of the client. Put "bridge persons" in charge—professionals who have proven creative ability, evaluative training, skill in communicating, and experience in working collaboratively across professional ranks. Many important inventions occurred as a result of the cross-fertilization of ideas that ensued from this step at the R &T center: Single bedtime dose self-medication training for patients, standardized proficiency gauges to

measure progress in treatment, modular psychoeducational treatment to enhance patients' skills, and structured peer support networks in the Community Network Development are some examples.

The next section will demonstrate how some of these integrating forces
apply in a plan for the systematic and orderly deinstitutionalization of chronically ill mental patients.

A SYSTEMATIC APPROACH TO
DEINSTITUTIONALIZATION

The deinstitutionalization of large numbers of public mental hospital patients can become a complicated and costly process. This is particularly true
since the public mental hospital population is heterogeneous, and different
types of community support will be needed by different subgroups.[4] For example, deinstitutionalizing the elderly mental hospital resident may necessi-
tate the construction of more nursing and boarding home facilities,
particularly since chronic medical difficulties often occur in this population.
The needs of the younger, less severely ill patient will differ considerably, involving, for example, the development of group homes, supervised apartments, graduated employment opportunities, etc. If the deinstitutionalization
process is to proceed in an orderly and efficient fashion, however, effort must
be made to assess carefully in advance and set priorities as to the needs of
these various groups, since the funds available are limited.

Deinstitutionalization involves much more than the physical transfer of
patients from large mental institutions to smaller community settings. It implies the creation of a range of community treatment alternatives that allows
each individual patient to function in the least restrictive setting possible. In
these days of great taxpayer concern about public spending, it also seems prudent first to establish programs requiring the least spending before developing
more costly ones. With these two goals in mind, the following policy suggestions can be made:

1. Place a priority on the training and retraining of current professional and
    paraprofessional mental health and social service workers. De-emphasize
    their tendency to "do for" patients, and stress their learning to help pa-
    tients to help themselves. Retrain public mental hospital personnel to
    provide community treatment and support. Other targets for training and
    consultation include boarding home operators, vocational rehabilitation
    counselors, etc. By upgrading and retraining current mental health and
    other human service workers, many community treatment programs can
    be staffed without new hiring.

2. Skill-training, peer management, and peer support approaches that emphasize self-help and mutual help should be treatment "themes" of the deinstitutionalization process. As these studies have indicated, skill-training and peer management approaches can be effective with chronic patients. The use of peer support and peer management technologies promotes independence and creates a less restrictive environment than exists within more traditional staff-intensive programs. These types of programs are also cost-efficient, since peer management and peer support approaches can be applied throughout the entire range of treatment settings, including residential programs, day treatment programs, boarding homes, cooperative living facilities, etc.

3. Fund the development of the least restrictive community programs and placements first. Then, as unmet needs become more evident, invest effort and resources in more restrictive "institutional" services. By proceeding in this fashion, program development and expenditures will occur in an ordered fashion, as a result of clearly felt treatment needs. Besides eliminating the possibility of overbuilding or overdeveloping programs, mental health professionals may find that it is possible to maintain many patients in a less restrictive environment than they might have believed possible. For example, if a well-developed system of cooperative and supervised apartments is created within a community, there may be a lesser need for new boarding homes and half-way houses than planners would have anticipated.

4. The public mental hospital population is actually composed of a number of distinct subpopulations. The deinstitutionalization process should begin with those subgroups that will require the fewest new community services, and should then progress to include more problematic groups. For example, a recent GAP report[5] stated that 10–15 percent of chronic state hospital patients are in need of highly structured care. This percentage may be higher in states where great numbers of patients have drifted in from out-of-state. These patients have few friends, relatives, or other ties to their adopted community.[6] Many have serious physical illnesses, as well as chronic mental disorders that limit their ability to function outside of a hospital, nursing home, or other institution. Efforts to sustain these individuals in the community should not be made until the deinstitutionalization of those requiring less extensive care has been accomplished. In some percentage of these cases true deinstitutionalization may not be a viable concept, and the benefits of moving these individuals back to the community should be carefully weighed against the cost.

The retraining of mental health and other human service personnel in the deinstitutionalization plan should be part of a larger integrated manpower development strategy. Previous chapters have provided information and ideas that suggest the nature of this strategy. It can be incorporated in a state or national overall manpower development plan. Legislation can be aimed at providing incentives for its implementation. The approach proposed here indicates the training and education required for professional and paraprofessional personnel.

A MANPOWER DEVELOPMENT PLAN

Students in the mental health professions learn to fill new managerial roles in addition to their traditional ones, and to serve as supervisors of paraprofessional mental health workers (MHWs) and as consultants to them. Those who have received stipends, scholarships, or other forms of reimbursement from public sources while obtaining their education and training pay back their debt by accepting work assignments in the public mental health sector for equivalent periods.

HMWs, both those presently working in the public mental institutions and new students in academic programs, learn techniques for psychosocial rehabilitation and assessment, including, in particular, behavior management and the modular psychoeducational treatment approach. This training, which should itself be modular in form, prepares both new and long-term mental hospital employees for community work, since both hospital patients and those residing in the community benefit from appropriate skill-building and support-building training.

Social service workers currently employed in the service delivery system learn to overcome the fragmentation that presently exists in the mental health system and to coordinate a wide range of community services, including housing, legal aid, income maintenance, health, foster home care, transportation, food and nutrition, and the like, providing assistance to the patient-run community support network development (CND) in cooperation with MHW staff area managers. They also learn to apply modular treatments in the care of their clients, both mental patients and others requiring human services.

Adult patients receive training in peer management, and serve as client area managers and member leaders in the CND. They receive backup support from MHWs, who in turn, are backed up by professionals when problems arise beyond their competence to handle. This approach is cost-efficient, and, as has been shown, an effective means of maintaining many adult, chronically ill, formerly hospitalized, mental patients in lives of high quality in the community.

Members of patients' family network—parents, foster parents, spouses, and other family members—learn to become therapists and supports for each other and for their child and adult patient relatives.

All personnel—professonals, patients, families, paraprofessionals, and students—are encouraged to participate in the creative development of better treatment, management, and assessment modularized procedures. All training and educational activites are conducted simultaneously, since they are interrelated. Everyone receives assessments prior to beginning training, and all are guided to learn roles that suit their special interests, resources, and abilities. Progress in learning is reassessed regularly, and training is completed when a predetermined level of competency or proficiency is reached. Professionals and students who are interested and capable can also learn to become program administrators and evaluators.

Matriculated college students receive training to be part-time or full-time MHWs, and to participate in treatment and assessment, in evaluative research, and in training to the extent that they are capable.

Current employees receive inservice training in behavior management and the modular treatment approach, and are also encouraged to continue their formal education; they are helped to attend part-time classes for academic credit in order to increase their competency in their jobs, to advance their careers, to enhance their morale, and to stimulate their creativity.

Professionals in the service facilities, independently, or in collaboration with colleagues at academic institutions, apply for research and training grants to develop service innovations and new assessment instruments, to train students, and to disseminate knowledge throughout the treatment system.

There is no need to engage in wholesale firings of staff to implement this manpower plan. Continuing education is now becoming mandatory for most practitioners; continuing employment is now based on annual performance evaluations. The changing demands of a professional or paraprofessional job can be spelled out clearly; accredited training in the new techniques can be offered; and levels of competency can be measured. Personnel who wish to continue to contribute to the evolving mental health treatment system can be expected to obtain appropriate continuing education. Their new skills will evolve with their patients' treatment needs.

REMOVING DISINCENTIVES IN OTHER HEALTH
AND HUMAN SERVICES

Disincentives and fragmentation also drive up costs and disintegrate treatment programs in other sectors of the health and human services besides mental health. These too require innovation and change. Many changes affecting mental health that we recommended and predicted twenty years ago subsequently have come to pass. Most important has been the women's movement. *The Split-Level Trap,*[7] which was a best seller in 1961, urged women to improve their mental health by becoming more productive economically, preparing for careers, diversifying their interests, developing job skills, joining mutual support organizations, and preparing to swap roles with men when necessary. In it, we predicted that men's and women's roles "will undoubtedly become more and more interchangeable." *The Blight on the Ivy*[8] proposed that girls and women go on with higher education and not quit and drop out of college.

Today women are participating in ever greater numbers in the labor force; their dedication to work not only contributes to their improved mental health, but the two-income family helps dampen the excessive boom-and-bust swings of the business cycle. Less serious economic depressions mean fewer hospitalizations of chronically ill mental patients.

Couples are now holding down the size of their families. They are not overloading the schools and other community resources for children as they did in the post-1950s, which contributed so much to delinquency and other problems with children and youth. Social organizations and community recreation and adult education centers, where people can learn social leisure skills in classes and put them into practice, have proliferated. Community support organizations, particularly those for women and high-risk groups—new mothers, displaced homemakers, parents without partners, former mental patients, and the retired and the elderly—are flourishing. They are teaching their members to be assertive, to communicate better, and to solve problems, and are providing them with mutual support.

But major problems remain in the health and human services sector of American society; problems that the nation can ill afford. They can be corrected. Paramount among these are the disincentives and fragmentation that parallels that described in mental health. For instance, current methods of compensation often hurt the sick and injured.[9] Just like mental patients, many patients with physical illness—hypertension, diabetes, etc.—must enter the hospital and/or remain ill to receive insurance, pensions, compensation, and the like; and just like mental patients, they can be made more dependent and sicker when their illness is reinforced. Present social welfare practices, in many instances, are rewarding "Active Dependency"—*not* working and *not* getting well. Rather than encourage self-support and peer support, these features of the current system emphasize keeping patients in nursing homes, not in home health care, training patients to be compliant, not self-reliant. The health system itself drives up the costs of health care—debilitation is fostered; rehabilitation penalized. Persons who receive transfer payments (social security disability benefits, veterans' benefits, aid for dependent children, etc.) are discouraged from developing independence; as soon as they become self-sufficient, they lose benefits. Many public services provide endless handouts rather than a helping hand.

Rather than continue to foster this present counterproductive system, which is straining the nation's finances, professonals and public officials should receive support and assistance for trying to find solutions. Modular health educational classes, like psychoeducational ones, and peer support for patients with many chronic physical illnesses, will provide some of the answers. Just as they prevented at-risk groups of college students and new mothers from developing problems, and aided patients with chronic mental illness, they will help many persons with chronic physical illness. The first chapter mentioned classes for patients who suffered heart attacks. In these, patients learn to control their weight, to curb their smoking, and to exercise. They also can be taught by behavioral methods to relax, and to make whatever other behavioral changes that evaluative research shows would improve their health and reduce their chances of future heart attacks.

Health insurance policies could provide incentives for practicing good health habits and correcting unhealthy ones. They could follow the example of auto insurance carriers, which charge higher premiums to drivers with poor accident records, and which reduce charges to persons who attend driver education courses. Health policies could charge more to smokers, heavy drinkers, and overeaters; they could reduce premiums to graduates of psychoeducational classes who successfully complete a course and break their unhealthy habit. Peer support groups like Alcoholics Anonymous and Weight Watchers would not only help their members stay healthier, they would be helping them keep down their insurance costs!

The CND peer-support model can be used with patients with chronic physical ills just as well as it has with chronic mental disorders. Networks of hypertensive, arthritic, cardiac, asthmatic, and other patients can provide members with mutual emotional, informational, leisure, instructional, and other supports. There is every reason to believe, based upon experience with mental patients, that psychoeducation and peer support will cut costs and improve the health of patients with chronic physical illness, especially where features related to life style and habits play a part in the illness.

A few years ago we proposed a plan for motivating pensioned patients to seek rehabilitation when their disabilities contained behavioral components.[6] This proposal will be restated here with slight modification: Continue disabled patients' pensions, but replace the all or nothing system with a new one where the schedule of payments is graded. Disabled pensioned patients would receive a greater total amount of pay and compensation for progressing in job and other skills-training. Gainful employment would result in still greater income. Patients would pay taxes on their earnings, however. As they earn more and more, they ultimately contribute in taxes as much as or more than they receive in pensions.

Since many insurers are reluctant to provide insurance for high-risk disabled workers, employers are hesitant to hire them. Therefore, provide a special form of workmen's compensation insurance guaranteed by the federal government so that employers who hire disabled employees can conform to state laws.

The patients' supplemental allowances are administered with their rehabilitation care, so that they clearly recognize that rewards are contingent upon making progress and upon fulfilling each phase of the rehabilitation plan.

HOPE FOR THE FUTURE

The programs for the chronic mental patient described here are now up and going; professionals and others can implement them in their own settings with confidence, knowing that they (in most cases) have been evaluated and shown to be effective. The main struggle is now in the past, and many of the principle designers of the projects have moved on to new ventures. Many projects and programs are now operating under the direction of second or third generation leadership. This fact in itself speaks favorably about the adaptability of the modular and peer support approaches.

Unless a major calamity occurs—a nuclear war or major economic depression, for instance—hospitalized mental patients may become as much a rarity in America in the next decade as hospitalized tuberculous and epileptic patients are today. Present mental patients will learn to help each other in community peer support groups. Further, few Americans need become chronically mentally ill in the future, once every child and adult has facilities and modules available to learn effective psychosocial skills in modular psychoeducational classes taught in school by elementary, high school, and college teachers. Fewer people will develop chronic life habit-related physical illnesses, either, because most will know how to communicate effectively, to assert themselves sensibly, to solve personal problems, and to keep their appetites for food, alcohol, drugs, and tobacco under control.

Based on experience in the treatment of aggressive, violent children and youngsters, there is reason to hope that delinquency, crimes of passion, and criminal offenses by the mentally ill will abate. All these may be preventable and treatable with skills-building, behavior management, and peer support techniques, combined as needed with medical and psychodynamic approaches. But first, disincentives and fragmentation in their programs need to be ended. Again, Suella's case provides an illustrative example. Suella was sent back to the mental hospital by the staff of the psychiatric clinic for her third admission when they became alarmed that she might harm her daughter during an acute psychotic state. Professionals have sought continually to uphold patients' dignity, to protect their moral and constitutional rights, and to avoid unwarranted hospitalization. But society retains through its laws and courts the authority to protect its members and to admit patients to mental institutions, even against their will, when they are likely to harm themselves or others. Suppose now that the clinic staff had not sent Suella to the hospital; suppose that, instead, Suella had at that time gone into the bay to purify herself and had taken Mary Ellen with her; and suppose that Mary Ellen had drowned. Then Suella would have been sent to a forensic mental hospital for mentally disordered offenders. She would have been able to benefit just as well at the forensic hospital from a program of combined psychoeducational, medical, peer support, and psychodynamic therapy as she did at the R&T facility. But what incentive would she have to cooperate? What use would it have been for her, and for other patients who today are in the nation's forensic hospitals, to gain personal control over their violent or other antisocial behavior, when the consequence would be for them to be sent from the forensic facility to prison when they show signs of improving?

Mental Health Service Delivery in Criminal Justice Systems

Crime statistics for all communities in the United States, large and small, show a marked increase over the past decade and a half. Public officials have met this challenge mostly by building bigger jails and prisons, which only a few years later are filled to overcrowding.

Close examination of these jail populations reveals that in every setting a large proportion (estimated from 10–50 percent) of the inmates have severe psychiatric problems. Mentally disordered offenders are found in the entire range of crimes from minor misdemeanors to first-degree felonies.

It has been argued that anyone justifiably convicted of a crime has a mental health problem. Certainly most jail inmates exhibit the same inability to sustain themselves independently in the community as that displayed by the typical chronic patient in a mental health institution. Most chronic offenders and chronic mental patients share similar gaps in their psychosocial skills.

Some authors suggest that the current shift of mental health patients from hospitals to jails is due to a legislative change described as "criminalization of mentally ill behavior."[10] Regardless of causes, the situation does exist throughout the criminal justice system at the present time, and current law states that jail inmates must be given access to medical care including mental health services.[11]

Therefore, one of the most pressing problems now confronting jail administrators is the question of how to satisfy both the judicial requirements of a law enforcement facility, and at the same time fulfill the mental health requirements. Embedded within this problem is the fact that mental health delivery systems are anxious to leave the most disturbed patients within the jail, while overburdened jail systems demand that these obvious mental cases be shipped elsewhere, since they require the most expensive jail time and space. In other words, a highly disturbed inmate who presents a danger to himself and/or others cannot legally be incarcerated in such a way that he may commit suicide or murder. His entrance to the jail system may have been on a simple charge like disturbing the peace; yet he needs not only maximum security to keep him there, but constant supervision by jail personnel in order to protect him and the other inmates. To refer him to the local mental health center, with its backlog of cases, may be of little help if he cannot be seen immediately. Most mental health centers operate with a large outpatient capacity, but a very limited inpatient facility. They do not like to treat the criminal, because he will disrupt ongoing programs, and he will require more security than they normally provide. To commit him to a secure, long-term mental hospital takes time-consuming legal procedures. So, the inmate may remain in jail, under maximum security, for a month or two, in a pretrial status, simply because of his need for mental health services that are not immediately available.

To combat this problem, many criminal justice systems are incorporating mental health services. Some of these consist of personnel from the local mental health center who spend a few hours a week in the jail. Some are permanent units housed in the law enforcement facility. Some systems are building psychiatric units within their jail system to drain off the large percentage of inmates who would be placed within a secure mental health facility if such were available on short notice.

During his incarceration, the inmate, whether adjudged in need of mental health care or not, goes through some type of rehabilitation. The extent and focus of this treatment varies widely across the country, and is dependent upon the resources of the community and, in some cases, upon whether or not the facility has been forced by a recent lawsuit to provide such services.

But "rehabilitation" has become a very negative concept with the public who must receive this former inmate back into the community. Most rehabilitative programs are concerned only with jail behavior. They traditionally are devoid of follow-up treatment and evaluation, and have been offered on a meager budget. They have had little effect on the recidivism rate. The same unfortunates appear in the jails again and again on minor charges, to be processed through their six-month to one-year terms, and then are sent back out again with the same basic inadequacies and skills gaps with which they entered the criminal justice system the previous year. Periodically, such a recipient of "revolving door justice" commits a shocking crime in the community to which he has recently been released, thus reinforcing public distrust of the "rehabilitation" he received while incarcerated. But, in fact, he may have received nothing but a minimum of medications and counseling, which enabled him to adjust only to life inside, rather than outside the penal institution. In many cases, not even this succeeded, and he becomes another jail suicide.

Hope lies in the skills and supports-building methods described here. Some criminal justice systems are finally being forced to the conclusion that the only alternative to larger and larger jails is to teach the vast flood of itinerants, who continually re-enter the system, the basic psychosocial skills necessary to live a reasonably rewarding and competent life outside. The methods elucidated in this book are completely applicable to criminal justice systems at all levels. Even the state prison, with its two-, five-, and ten-year inmates, must at some time inculcate the skill-building techniques explained in preceding chapters if it is to release these people back into society. It is not surprising that disaster sometimes results when a man whose life has been totally proscribed for ten years is given 100 dollars and a new suit of clothes, and turned out into a community with which he had lost touch. He could not find a lawful place in it for himself ten years earlier when he was familiar with it. Now his readjustment is complicated by his loss of skills during his institutional residence and by the community's rejection of released criminals.

As for the recidivism problem of petty miscreants in county and city jails, these people are unable to adjust to society because they lack basic skills; they failed to learn them in their early years of life, and they are not taught them in adulthood. Even in the most enlightened communities, the local jails contain an amazing amount of basic illiteracy, as well as deficits in more complicated problem-solving and other coping activities.

At the same time, it is mandatory that, as demanded by the Brunswik lens model, and as exemplified in the studies discussed in previous chapters, follow-up be conducted in order to be certain that the skill-building and other mental health treatment has had the desired effect, or, in Brunswik's terms, that the "distal variable" of successful community adjustment has been achieved.

A chief reason that "rehabilitation" has fallen into bad repute is that the results of the techniques employed are not checked out after the recipient returns to society. Textbook applications of therapeutic approaches may work on the mildly disturbed patient who continues to live in the community while undergoing therapy; whether or not these same procedures will work on an institutionalized offender or patient must be tested, retested, and then changed to accommodate the fact that the unstructured world outside bears little resemblance to the controlled world within—either the mental hospital or the county jail.

True, follow-up may be time-consuming and expensive; but recidivism is even more so since, besides forcing the expansion of the jail system to meet the needs of the increasing population, it incurs an incalculable cost in human life.

The skill-building methods described in preceding pages, with follow-up for perfecting procedures, may provide a budgetary answer to the problem of overcrowded and unmanageable jail populations. In fact, such methods offer a major hope for rescuing overworked county and state officials from the self-defeating alternative of polluting the landscape with ever-enlarging containment facilities.

As this book has shown, however, despite disincentives and fragmentation in the current mental health and forensic systems, effective prevention, treatment, and rehabilitation can be developed for the most difficult-to-treat group—the chronically ill mental patient. There is every reason to feel confident that the 1980s will see great improvements in closing the gaps in programs of prevention, treatment, and rehabilitation for chronic mental patients and other persons who require human and health services for chronic problems.

REFERENCES

1. Greenblatt M: Foreword, in DiMascio A, Goldberg HL (Eds): Emotional Disorders: An Outline Guide to Diagnosis and Pharmacological Treatment. Oradell, N. J., Medical Economics Co., 1977
2. Gordon RE: Sociodynamics and psychotherapy. AMA Arch Neurol Psychiatry 81: 486–503, 1959
3. Whitman D: Reorganization of Florida's Human Services Agency, Kennedy School of Government Case Program, C95-80-040. Cambridge, Mass., Harvard University, 1980
4. Gordon RE, Edmunson E, Bedell JR, et al: Utilizing peer management and support to reduce rehabilitation of mental patients. Report No. 7. Tampa, Fla., Human Resources Institute, University of South Florida, 1979
5. The chronic mental patient in the community. Group for the Advancement of Psychiatry 10:102, 1978
6. Gordon RE, Webb S: The orbiting psychiatric patient. Florida Med Assoc 62: 21–25, 1975
7. Gordon RE, Gordon KK, Gunther M: The Split Level Trap. New York, B. Geis and Associates, 1961
8. Gordon RE, Gordon KK: The Blight On the Ivy. Englewood Cliffs, N. J., Prentice Hall, 1963
9. Gordon RE, Lyons H, Muniz C, et al: Can compensation hurt the sick and injured: The active dependency syndrome. J Florida Med Assoc 60: 36–39, 1973
10. Whitmer GE: From hospitals to jails. Am J Orthopsychiatry 50: 65–75, 1980
11. Singer RG: Providing mental health services to jail inmates—legal perspectives. Prepared for the Special National Workshop on Mental Health Services in Local Jails, Baltimore Md., Sept 27–29, 1978

PART F

Appendixes

The Appendix contains three sections. Appendix 1 presents a manual on problem-solving that is used in the modular skill-building treatment of adult mental patients. This manual illustrates the content and procedures in the modular approach, as well as includes a staff-developed proficiency test for measuring patients' performance in solving problems and their progress in treatment.

Appendix 2 describes the laboratory experience of the Techniques of Intervention course that state hospital mental health worker employee students attend as part of their community college curriculum. This description, which is taken from a module developed for the course by Malchon, shows how modules spell out what is expected of both teachers and students in the training sessions.

A glossary of behavioral terms and descriptions of their use appears in Appendix 3.

Appendix 1
Manual on Problem-Solving

SESSION ONE

Symbolic Self-Disclosure: An Introductory Exercise
by Valerie S. Reed, M.A.

OBJECTIVES

1. To give group members the opportunity to become better acquainted with both the facilitators and with the other workshop participants.
2. To give each individual the opportunity to begin to self-disclose in an informal, relaxed setting.

MATERIALS

None.

TIME

20 minutes.

Appendix 1 was developed by the Department of Health and Rehabilitative Services, Florida Mental Health Institute, Adult Programs Department (Problem-Solving Skills Training: Didactic Sessions, Vol. 1). It is edited by Valerie S. Reed, M.A., Herbert A. Marlowe, Jr., Ed.S., and Joseph J. Ferrandino, Ph.D., with contributions by Judith L. Amour, B.A., Robert P. Archer, Ph.D., Jeffrey R. Bedell, Ph.D., Deborah Black, B.A., Patricia L. Cameron, B.A., Steven Harris, M.A., Herbert A. Marlowe, Jr., Ed.S., Frank Reyes, B.A., Valerie Reed, M.A., and Linda Williams, M.A.

PROCESS

Ask participants to find some material object or personal possession which they feel best symbolizes their character (ring, shoe, key, etc.). Participants then identify the object, present it to the group, then introduce themselves symbolically in relation to that object and indicate how it represents their personality, style of behavior, mode of functioning, physical characteristics, etc.

Introduction to Problem-Solving: Its Role-Value

PRESENTATION TYPE

1. Lecture and Assessment

OBJECTIVE

1. To delineate the value and need for using the problem-solving model.

MATERIALS

1. Chalkboard and chalk
2. Permanent Problem-Solving Steps Chart (depicting problem-solving model), Session 4 Part 3

TIME

10 Minutes

PROCESS

Lecture on the objective of this group.

SAMPLE LECTURE: The purpose of this first lecture is to introduce you to our problem-solving model which is on this chart (point to problem-solving steps chart). This model will aid you in solving your personal problems in a step-by-step manner by giving you an outline to structure your problem-solving process. In this and following group meetings, I will focus on explaining and teaching you each step of our problem-solving model and giving you practice at using these skills. In addition, this group will give you an opportunity to participate in problem-solving exercises to give you some idea of what it is like to work on a problem that is not your own, or a simulated problem. Through working with these simulated problems you should be able to try out problem-solving skills that can later be used to solve personal problems. Therefore, the problem-solving program will be set up like this:

1. You will be given several lectures on the problem-solving model, its value and definition.
2. You will watch and participate in exercises which demonstrate problem-solving skills.

3. You will participate in exercises which help you practice problem-solving skills.
4. You will be given homework to encourage skill practice outside of group.
5. You will be given the opportunity to share your own ideas and methods of problem-solving and to give feedback about the group expertise.

This program was designed to help you build on your own existing skills. Although it might seem difficult at times, I would hope that you would try your best to get involved in learning and in practicing the skills. I think that you will find that it is as exciting and educational as you make it.

Introduction to Problem-Solving Theory and Didactic
by Valerie S. Reed, M.A., Steven Harris, M.A., and Herbert A. Marlowe, Jr., Ed.S.

OBJECTIVES

To delineate the value and need for using the problem-solving model. Also to familiarize participants with the structure and intent of the four-stage problem-solving model.

TIME

15 Minutes

MATERIALS

Problem-Solving Steps Chart (Session 4, Part 3)

PROCESS

Deliver lecture covering four-step problem-solving model. A sample lecture follows.

The Problem-solving Model was developed in order to provide psychiatric clients with a conceptual framework for working through their personal problems. This model provides an organized structure consisting of a four-step process for systematically identifying, evaluating, and resolving problems. There are several reasons for teaching this technique: First, the problem-solving model introduces a *system* that can be applied to any problem situation. It is analogous to being given a tool box full of tools with instructions on how and when to use each tool. As with most tools, whether you use them skillfully or not is left up to your own judgment. However, it is assumed that with knowledge and practice will come comfort and familiarity with the process. Second, the problem-solving procedure strives toward a goal of *proficiency* by emphasizing skill practice and group interaction while applying the process. As such, clients are encouraged to generalize these techniques beyond the therapeutic environment. They are urged to use them with family, friends, or other individuals and groups that can provide feedback, as part of an active "homework" program. It is also important to note that the model can be used independently, without needing feedback. The third reason has to do with the concept of *choice*. Many people feel locked in by a particular problem they are experiencing. They do not realize that they have created this feeling of helplessness by ignoring or failing to recognize their sense of choice. Often we can broaden their awareness by increasing the amount of information available to them, thus increasing their options. For example, if you found it very expensive to maintain your car, you might continue investing in it with no relief. On the other hand, if you are aware of other options (if you had more information, for instance that it might be cheaper to sell or trade in your car for another model) a choice situation is created. In effect, there are alternatives to living with a costly car. Fourth, the problem-solving model attempts to *eliminate the experience of being so overwhelmed with problems* that there is no place to start. Teaching clients to simplify and prioritize problems minimizes confusion and maximizes problem-solving ease. Last, problem-solving as we teach it represents a continuous dynamic process. What we mean by this is that although the model is structured, it is not absolute. It is flexible in the sense that it can be modified or adapted to meet your own personal or professional needs. An error or mistake that occurs while engaged in the process is a temporary situation. Decisions are not irreversible. Re-evaluation is always acceptable.

The Problem-Solving Model consists of four basic steps: Problem Recognition, Problem Definition, Alternatives Generation, and Decision.[1] Since problem-solving is a cognitive process these steps are necessarily sequential. In other words, they proceed in a logical progression. Problem Recognition is further broken down into four component substeps which are, acknowledging the problem, identifying the problem, accepting responsibility for the problem, and prioritizing. To acknowledge a problem is to become aware of or face up to a problem you think you might have. This process is stimulated by focusing attention on symptoms or events leading up to a problem situation. Identifying the problem simply represents the process of isolating or targeting specific problem areas. A helpful strategy for identifying problems is to analyze the context in which problem manifestations such as symptoms and events occur. Accepting responsibility for that problem is important in solving it independently. Clients are taught to take responsibility for their problems by using "I language" and language of volition ("won't" instead of "can't"). The last substep of the problem recognition process is the first step to actively working through your problems. Prioritizing problems means to sequence them in order of importance. As such, clients are given several suggested criteria to aid them in determining which problems to work on first.

The second major step of the Problem-Solving Model is called Problem Definition. Problem Definition can also be referred to as operationalizing your problem. To operationalize a problem, you must first break it down into workable units and, second, state it in such a way that it appears solvable. Breaking a problem down involves taking a large complex problem and partitioning it into a series of smaller, more discrete problems. For example, some questions you might ask yourself in breaking a problem down are, "Is money involved? Travel? Other people?, etc." Taking these individual elements of a problem and dealing with them separately should lead to solving the original problem. However, first, each of these component problems must be resolved independently. It is important to keep a definite goal in mind when operationalizing a problem. This goal will give you something to work toward. Stating the problem in "how to. . . ." format is a simple method for identifying and defining your problematic goal. For example, if your problem centered around marital difficulties it might be stated as: "How to resolve my marital conflicts."

The third stage of the Problem-Solving Model is identified as Alternatives Generation. At this point, you are taught how to think up possible problem solutions. It is the most creative of all the steps, as you will be encouraged to share your own subjective methods of alternatives generation in addition to learning how to apply ours. There are five methods proposed for generating alternative solutions and these are: brainstorming, making up an idea checklist, changing your frame of reference, taking a solution from a similar problem, and problem diagramming.[2-5]

The final step of the Problem-Solving Model is, of course, *decision.* This step is comprised of two processes: an analysis of alternative solutions generated in the previous step and choice of the most suitable solution. In an effort to teach these skills, ranking possible solutions as a function of their feasibility and hints on making a rational decision are emphasized.

Each of these steps will be examined in more detail as the group progresses. You will also be given the chance to apply these techniques to simulated problems in practice situations and eventually to problem areas in your own lives.

Problem-Solving Performance Test

PRESENTATION TYPE

1. Assessment

OBJECTIVE

1. To evaluate clients' problem-solving skill level before treatment—a behavioral pretest measurement.

MATERIALS

1. John's Story (1 per client) (Session 4, Part 1)
2. Answer sheets (1 per client) (Session 4, Part 2)
3. Pencils

TIME

50 minutes

PROCESS

1. Pass out materials
2. Read instructions

SAMPLE INSTRUCTIONS: This is a story about a man named John who has problems. I would like you to listen carefully to this story and read along with me. After I am finished reading, you should answer the questions on the answer sheet in the space provided. These questions refer to John's problems that were stated in his story. In answering these questions, use your knowledge of the problem-solving model that we have discussed in group. I realize that you have had little experience in working with this model, so try your best to answer these questions as clearly and accurately as you can. You are not expected to answer all questions correctly.

3. Answer questions.
4. After group has completed the assessment, collect the answer sheets and return them to the data collector.

Problem Recognition (acknowledging, identifying, and accepting the problem)

PRESENTATION TYPE

1. Didactic and demonstration exercises

MATERIALS

1. Permanent Problem-Solving Steps Chart (model) (Session 4, Part 3)
2. Problem Recognition exercise (Session 4, Part 4)
3. Responsibility Accepting exercise (Session 4, Part 5)
4. Paper, Pencils
5. Chalkboard, Chalk

TIME

One hour

PROCESS

1. Lecture on the objective of this section.

SAMPLE LECTURE: The purpose of this group is to begin breaking down the problem-solving model and discussing each step in more detail. In this first lecture you will learn about problem-recognition, the first step of the problem-solving model. You will also be given the opportunity to apply the skills you learn in group exercises.

2. Lecture on the problem recognition process of acknowledging the existence of the problem.

SAMPLE LECTURE: As I mentioned previously, the first step of the problem-solving model is problem recognition. There are four sub-steps to problem recognition and these are: (1) acknowledging the existence of the problem, (2) identifying the problem, (3) accepting personal responsibility for the problem, and (4) establishing priorities. I will describe each of these substeps more thoroughly as we go along.

To acknowledge the existence of a problem means to face up to or look at more closely a problem that you may think you might have. Many people go through life upset by a problem they didn't even know they had. For example, someone whose marriage is falling apart may not be aware of any difficulty. Also, people sometimes avoid looking at a problem that is staring them right in the face, especially when it might cause fear, insecurity or some other negative emotion. For example, an alcoholic who turns to drinking in order to escape from personal problems.

There are two methods of acknowledging an existing problem or problems. One way is to become aware of behavior changes that might indicate a problem. We call these behavior changes "symptoms." Some examples of symptoms are: escaping through turning to drugs or alcohol; personality changes such as becoming shy or withdrawn around people; not accepting responsibility such as, being late for work, or not taking care of yourself; rationalizing your behavior, such as, telling people you can't help yourself; becoming preoccupied by spending most of your time thinking about yourself and not considering others, etc. These are just some of the symptoms that might indicate a problem.

Another method of acknowledging the existence of a problem is to look at the events or actions leading up to that problem. For example, you may have noticed that you have gotten very tense in the last six months, but you don't know why. If you go back and look at the events of the last six months more carefully you may be able to identify several things that contributed to this tension: you had an affair with another person; you changed jobs; you left your wife or husband; or you became very close with a new group of friends.

Both of these methods (becoming aware of behavior changes, of symptoms, and looking at past events) are simply means of acknowledging that a problem exists. They are not problems in themselves. However, once you acknowledge that you have a problem you can go on to the next step: identifying the problem. It is not necessarily true that all problems that are faced can be solved, but a problem will never be solved until it is faced.

3.   Conduct problem acknowledging exercise.

Setting up.   Maintain participants in the large group. Pass out problem recognition exercise to each group member.

Procedure.   Read the Problem Recognition Exercise (Session 4, Part 5) to the group as they read along with you. Have them verbally describe the symptoms and events leading up to problems that Evelyn has. Write down their descriptions on a flip chart in two columns labeled "symptoms" and "events." Prompt and discuss these responses as a group. Positively reinforce all appropriate responses, making sure that all responses are either symptons or events and *not* problems. The following is the key to this exercise:

Symptoms	**Events**
Excessive drinking	Oversleeping
Neglected health	Blaming others
Disorganized	Absentmindedness
Rationalizes behavior	Late for appointments
Irresponsible	Doesn't eat regularly
Neglecting appearance	
Incompetent	

4.   Lecture on identifying the problem.

SAMPLE LECTURE: The most important thing to remember when identifying problems, is to remember to separate "manifestations" of existing problems such as the symptoms and events described earlier from the actual problem. Sometimes a symptom becomes so extreme that it becomes a problem in and of itself. Such is the case with the problem drinker. However, you must keep in mind that there is probably something bothering you that has caused you to allow your drinking to get out of control. For example, marriage problems or problems on the job can lead to excessive drinking. The best way to tell the difference between an actual problem and an event or a symptom of a problem is to try and ask yourself the reason for the behavior or the situation. If you can identify a reason, then what you are working with is probably a manifestation rather than a problem. For instance, you can always ask yourself what is the reason for your drinking, or what is the reason for your lack of responsibility. On the other hand, if you cannot identify the reason for your behavior or your situation you are probably dealing with a problem. Some examples of problems might be that you are unhappy with your marital relationship, you are unhappy with your job, you have trouble maintaining interpersonal relationships, etc. Once a problem is identified you can go about looking for a solution.

5.   Conduct the problem identification exercises.

Setting up.   Maintain participants in a large group. Make sure everyone still has the problem recognition exercise sheet.

Procedure.   Have participants verbally identify problems in the Problem-Solving Recognition Exercise. Write their responses down on the flip chart. These are in this exercise.

1.   She is very disorganized.
2.   She has a poor family relationship.
   a.   marital
   b.   children
3.   She drives others away with her complaining and sarcasm

6.   Lecture on accepting responsibility for the problem.

SAMPLE LECTURE: Accepting responsibility for your problems is very important. Your problems belong to you. When you blame others, or outside factors for your problems, you are not accepting the problem as your own. By doing this, you are giving up your power to take action and solve the problem. For example, if you blame your inability to get a job on the national unemployment problem, how can you possibly solve your problem. You are blaming economics or the government. However, if you were to say that you don't have a job because you haven't been looking around enough, you are taking responsibility for your problem and you can do something about it. If you take the attitude that you are responsible for your problems, you are taking control of your life and its outcome. Another example of not owning up to a problem is shown by Hank, who blames others for not coming to visit. As long as Hank looks at the situation this way he will continue to be lonely. But he can take responsibility for this situation by saying, "I'm lonely because I haven't tried to make any new friends and I haven't gone to visit any of my old friends." If Hank accepts this statement of the situation he can do something about his problem, and change the situation.

7.   Conduct responsibility accepting exercise at this point.

Setting up.   Maintain participants in a large group. Pass out responsibility accepting handouts. Make sure everyone has a pencil.

Procedure.   Have participants read through exercises and complete them by checking off those statements that suggest they are accepting personal responsibility. Process the exercise (See Session 4, Part 5, Responsibility Accepting Exercise).

8.   Lecture on establishing priorities.

SAMPLE LECTURE: The next step in problem recognition is deciding what order to work on your problems. This is called prioritizing your problems. There are several ways to decide which problems should come first. The *first* question you should ask yourself is whether or not the problem is under control. If you are dealing with problems over which you have no control, you are wasting your time. For example, suppose that when you go to the grocery store, the prices are so high that you cannot afford to buy all the food that you need. If you decide to work on "how to get the prices lowered," you are working on a problem that is out of your control. If you can see that the problem you are working on is not under your control you should put it aside and work on one that is more solvable.

A *second* way to establish priorities is to first work on pressing problems, and especially crisis situations. The reason for doing this is that until you have gotten your pressing problems out of the way, you probably won't be able to concentrate on any other problems. You would be wrapped up thinking about your crisis situation and may not be able to make very good decisions. Once you have solved the pressing problems, you will be more likely to be relaxed in solving further problems.

A *third* thing to keep in mind while establishing priorities is to begin working on a problem that is less difficult than others. For example, it is easier to work out a problem that involves only two people than one that involves an entire family and friends. The reason for choosing a less difficult problem, is that if you choose a very difficult problem and fail to solve it, you will probably have a much harder time facing future problems. On the other hand, if you choose a fairly easy problem to work with, your success at solving it will make you more confident in your problem-solving ability and give you a good start at dealing with future problems.

A *final* thing to keep in mind is to work on problems that will make your situation better. It is not a good idea to work first on problems that create new problems. For example, I have decided to leave my job because I am not happy with it; if I leave my job, I will lose my salary; if I lose my salary, I will not be able to support myself; if I am not able to support myself, my life will be very difficult. It is easy to see that, if you leave work, each of these successive problems will build up. Therefore it might be better to try and work on those problems at work that will not create new problems. For instance trying to change your working conditions by speaking to your boss, or trying to establish better relationships with other staff members. Until you have solved your most difficult and confusing problems, you should try to avoid creating new problems. However, if you feel that this is the most logical way of dealing with your problem, you should wait until you feel more confident in your problem-solving ability before you make such a move.

SESSION TWO

Problem Definition: Breaking down your problem and making goal-directed "How to . . ." statements (Session 4, Parts 6 and 7)

PRESENTATION TYPE

Lecture and demonstration exercises.

OBJECTIVES

To familiarize participants with the process of breaking down a problem and stating it in such a way that it is solvable. Also to demonstrate these skills in order to enhance awareness of how they can be applied.

MATERIALS

1. "How to . . ." problem list (Session 4, Parts 6 and 7)
2. Problem break-down list (Session 4, Part 8)
3. Pencils
4. Paper

TIME

2.5 hours.

PROCESS

1. Lecture on the purpose of problem definition.

SAMPLE LECTURE: The purpose of this session is to teach you how to *define* or *break-down* your problems so they are solvable in a step-by-step manner.

2. Lecture on breaking down your problems.

SAMPLE LECTURE: The second step of the problem-solving model is called problem definition (*point it out on the P.S. Steps Chart*). To define a problem is to break it down into parts. Often a problem is so large that it may be made up of several smaller problems.

In order to solve a problem, we must break it down into its simplest parts (time, money, people, transportation factors, etc.). If you break your problem down, you can look at each of these parts separately and see how they add up to the whole. On the other hand, if you try to tackle the problem as a whole, it may seem overwhelming, or impossible to solve. Once broken down into parts, the problem should be less difficult and confusing.

The process of breaking down your problem involves two steps: First you list the elements or parts of your problem; these may include time, people, money, transportation, etc. Second, you prioritize these smaller problems in order of their importance. Once the series of smaller problems has been solved, the main problem is taken care of.

3. Conduct problem break-down exercise.

Setting up.   Maintain participants in large group. Distribute the "How to" problem list to participants.

Procedure.   Tell each participant to select a problem from the list. Once the problem is selected each person should read his or her problem to his or her partner. After this, participants should privately complete their problem breakdown lists, by checking "yes" to those questions that apply to their problem and "no" to those questions that do not apply to their problem. Every one should be ready to share his or her responses with the group.

4. Lecture on the purpose and method of making positive problem statements.

SAMPLE LECTURE: The way we state our problems has a lot to do with how we view them. For example, if I say my problem is "being broke all of the time" I am focusing on how bad the problem is. On the other hand, if I say my problem is "how to budget my money" I am focusing on a positive side of my problem. If I sound more positive in stating my problem, I will probably feel more positive about dealing with the problem.

5. Conduct the exercise on making problem statements positive.

Setting up.   Maintain participants in a large group. The facilitator should act as a spokesman directing a problem statement to each participant.

Procedure.   Make a statement to each large group member individually. Have the participant restate the problem so it sounds positive.

SAMPLE STATEMENTS:
1. How to stop being lonely.
2. How to stop failing in school.
3. How to quit losing jobs.
4. How to stop losing my money.
5. How to stop being late for appointments.

6. How to not criticize others.
7. How to stop eating so much.
8. How to stop letting others take advantage of me.
9. How not to avoid responsibility.
10. How to quit being lazy.
11. How to stop downgrading myself.
12. How not to be so disorganized.
13. How to stop losing my temper.
14. How not to miss group.

6. Lecture on the purpose and method of making "how to . . ." statements.

SAMPLE LECTURE: In general, a problem arises because we aren't getting something we need or want. Another name for a need or want is a *goal*. Therefore, a problem can be stated in terms of a goal. To do this, we use goal-directed "How to . . ." statements. For example, say you ran out of gas. Your need or *goal* would be more gasoline. Therefore, your statement of the problem would be "How to get more gasoline." So, you can see the value of recognizing your goal before stating your problem. If you were just to state your problem as "being out of gas" that would not give you a goal to shoot for. However, making a goal-directed "how to . . ." statement gives you a place to start.
The "how to . . ." statement should name a specific goal rather than a general idea. For example, "How to stop arguing with my wife" is better than "How to improve relations with my wife." Arguing is a specific, observable behavior, whereas relations is a very vague, general concept. Another thing to remember is that the "how to . . ." statement should deal with tangible needs or wants, rather than intangible ideas or process. Here are some examples of poor "how to . . ." statements:
"how to make a decision"
"how to figure out what I want"
"how to be happy"
Here are some examples of good "how to . . ." statements
"how to find a job"
"how to meet new people"
"how to stay on a diet"

7. Conduct exercise on making "how to . . ." statements.

Setting up.   The group should be divided into triads. Give each participant a copy of the "how to . . ." problem list, along with paper and pencil.

Procedure.   Each triad should be told to read through the problem list and write a "how to . . ." statement for each of the problems listed. After this is completed (10 minutes) the group should come back together for discussion. The facilitator should select certain terms from the "how to . . ." problem list and ask for examples of "how to . . ." statements. Any appropriate "how to . . ." statements should be reinforced by the facilitator.

SESSION THREE

Alternatives Generation

PRESENTATION TYPE

Lecture and demonstration.

OBJECTIVE

The purpose of this lecture is to introduce participants to the alternatives generation step of the problem-solving model. In particular, it will focus on five different methods of generating alternatives.

MATERIALS

1. Chalkboard and chalk
2. Problem-solving Steps Chart
3. Problem Diagram (Session 4, Part 9)
4. Pencil and paper for each participant

TIME

2.5 hours.

PROCESS

1. Lecture on the objective of this session.

SAMPLE LECTURE: The purpose of this lecture is to introduce you to the alternatives generation step of the problem-solving model. In particular, I will be teaching you five different methods of generating alternative solutions to problems. You will also be given the opportunity to practice using these methods by doing exercises like we have done in past groups.

2. Lecture on the purpose of generating different alternative solutions and the first method of alternatives generation, "brainstorming."

SAMPLE LECTURE: You have now learned to recognize your problem and to define it so that it is in a more workable form. Now, you are going to use your creativity and come up with some ideas about alternative solutions to your problems. This process of generating alternative solutions is Step #3 of our problem-solving model (*point it out on the chart*). We are giving you five methods so that you can pick the best course of action for working with your own problem. However, if you have any suggestions of your own about how to generate alternative solutions you can also bring these up in our group.

It is important to have several different solutions to a given problem. The reason for this is because the first solution that comes to your mind may not be the best. It is likely that when solving a problem, you may either act too fast by taking the first solution that comes to mind, or you might be so disorganized in your approach, that the more you try, the more confused you get. Hopefully, by giving you these methods to work by, you will avoid these common mistakes in solving your own problems. Therefore, you can use either one or several of these alternatives generation techniques.

The first method we will talk about is called *brainstorming*. Brainstorming is best done in a group, but it can be done individually. When you use brainstorming, you think up, say out loud, write down solutions or activities without stopping to think about how good or bad the idea is. This approach is probably very different from the way you normally think up alternative solutions. Normally, participants would think up one solution, decide how good or bad it is, and then either use it or think up a new solution depending upon how well they like it. By doing this, you make two mistakes: First of all you usually accept the first alternative solution that you like without comparing it to other good solutions that you have not yet considered. Second of all, you usually tend to decide too quickly how well you like an alternative, therefore sometimes rejecting solutions that might work well had you looked at them more closely. What brainstorming does is to allow you to bring up all your ideas so that you have many alternatives to choose from. By getting all your ideas out into the open first, you can then take the time to compare them to each other, and to decide how well you like them and how well they solve your problem.

In summary, brainstorming has two ground rules. Number one is to say any idea you can think of, and number two is not to decide how good or bad the idea is until after you have come up with all the ideas for solutions that you can think of.

3.   Conduct brainstorming exercise.

Setting up.   Maintain participants in a large group.

Procedure.   The facilitator should pose several problems to the group in "How to . . ." format. The participants should then propose alternative solutions for dealing with the problem as a group. These ideas should be written on the blackboard. The facilitator should keep the group "on target" by not allowing them to judge or evaluate any potential solutions, and any idea should be reinforced no matter how impractical or far fetched. The facilitator should terminate the exercise by pointing out that although some of the ideas appear to be somewhat impractical, had they been eliminated before they were written down, some valuable ideas might have been lost.

Sample problems   (or come up with your own problems)
1.   You want to visit your parents on the weekend but your car is in for repairs.
2.   You need to catch the early bus to get to work on time. When you awake, you notice you have overslept.
3.   Your mother/father is constantly telling you how to run your life.

4.   Lecture on the second method of generating alternative solutions: Changing your frame of reference.

SAMPLE LECTURE: A second method of generating alternative solutions is called "Changing Your Frame of Reference (or point of view)." Very often, people get so bogged down with a problem that they cannot see the many possible alternatives that are open to them. Often you are so busy looking for a complicated solution, that you miss a very simple one. This might be because your solution was not very good to start out with. For example, have you ever tried to connect nine dots like this

5. Exercise on changing your frame of reference.

Setting up. Arrange participants in large group.

Conducting the exercise. Draw a nine dot figure on the board. Tell participants to join all nine dots with four straight lines without lifting their pencil. Have participants try this. (*Hint:* Most people make the faulty assumption that they must stay within the boundaries of the dots. You can now utilize the area outside the dots to do the task.) Allow participants to try again. Demonstrate the solution:

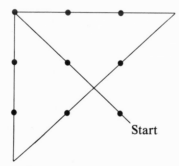

Start

6. Continue lecture on changing frame of reference.

SAMPLE LECTURE: Although this is a very simple problem and probably does not relate to your personal problems it illustrates how the situation can develop when you adopt a poor solution based on faulty assumptions. Many people do this when attempting to solve personal problems. For example, you may give up trying to solve a problem simply because you don't think you can do it. Yet, if you would simply allow yourself to look at the problem from a different point of view, you can actually find a reasonable solution. One way of doing this is to become another person while trying to solve that problem. For example, ask yourself "How would I solve this problem if I were someone else?"

7.   Lecture on adapting a solution from a similar problem:

SAMPLE LECTURE: A fourth method of generating alternative solutions is
to take a solution from a similar problem to fit your problem. It is often the case that
the solution selected by one person in one situation would not apply to another person
in the same situation. However, this solution could be modified, or changed somewhat
to meet the needs of the person and the situation. For example, suppose that you have
been looking for a job, and you have been given the runaround at the employment
agency. You hear that a friend of yours has been having a similar problem at a different agency and he found a solution. This person is somewhat aggressive in your
opinion, and thus demanded to see the director of the employment agency. Upon seeing the director your friend insisted upon some direct answers about job leads. Realizing that you are not an aggressive person, what could you do to solve your
problem?

8.   Conduct exercise on adapting a solution from a similar problem.

Setting up.   Maintain participants in large group.

Procedure.   Ask several people in the group to answer this question:
"Realizing that you are not an aggressive person, what could you do to solve
your problem?"

9.   Continue lecture on adapting a solution from a similar problem.

As you can see, we have come up with a solution to your problem by al-
tering your friend's solution to fit your situation.

10.   Lecture on the fourth method of alternatives generation: writing out an
idea check-list.

SAMPLE LECTURE: A fourth method of generating alternative solutions is
simply for you to write out a list of questions to consider as you think about possible
solutions. This list would vary from person to person and from problem to problem.
Basically, the list should resemble a grocery store list, to stimulate new ideas for solving your problems. For example, a sample list might contain these questions:
   a.   Can I change my behavior?
   b.   Can I change other people's behavior?
   c.   Can I get more money?
   d.   Can I change my living situation?
I will provide you with a sample checklist that will present these question and
others that you can use in coming up with workable solutions to your problems.

11.   Lecture on the fifth method of alternatives generation: making up the
problem diagram.

SAMPLE LECTURE: The fifth and last method of generating alternative solutions is called the "Problem Diagram." The purpose of the problem diagram is to
provide a schematic or concrete representation of the steps involved in solving your
problem. This procedure is analogous to a flow chart which is used by professional

people to organize a step-by-step course of action for solving a work problem or implementing a plan. To use this method you draw a diagram of your problem using symbols to represent different parts of your problem. You might use a stick figure to represent a person, and a dollar sign ($) to represent money. Arrows can be used to indicate direction or sequence of events in solving your problem. Here is an example of a problem diagram on how to solve the problem "How to buy a car." (*Facilitator should draw this on the chalkboard.*)

By shuffling around the steps in the diagram you can come up with a sequence which most successfully meets your needs. You might even think of a new step that was not included, but will aid you in solving your problems. Seeing your problem on paper should help you by providing a more clear and concrete picture so that you can come up with more effective solutions.

12.   Conduct exercise on problem diagram.

Setting up.   Arrange participants in triads. Distribute Problem Diagram Exercise and pencils (Session 4, Part 9).

Procedure.   Have participants read the problem and discuss in their small groups how to draw the arrows to represent the most successful sequence. The group should come up with a consensus about their solution. After they have had time to do this (about 10 minutes) let each group present their solution.

SESSION FOUR

Alternatives Evaluation: Solution

PRESENTATION TYPE

Lecture and group exercises.

OBJECTIVE

To explain the background and application of the alternatives generation step of the problem-solving model and how it fits in. Also to demonstrate some of the skills involved with this process to enhance group awareness.

MATERIALS

1.   Alternatives Evaluation Exercise.
2.   Pencils.
3.   Problem-Solving Steps Chart.

TIME

   2.5 hours.

PROCESS

1.   Lecture on predicting the possible outcomes of each alternative solution.

   SAMPLE LECTURE: The final step of the problem-solving model is that of evaluating alternative solutions. Once you have completed this process, the decision or solution to your problem follows. The basic process of evaluating alternatives consists of five substeps: (1) predicting the possible outcomes of each alternative e.g., what will be the result of choosing a particular alternative; (2) determining the likelihood of each outcome occuring e.g., how probable is it that that outcome will occur; (3) considering the desirability of each outcome e.g., consider the "pros" and "cons"; (4) ranking the alternatives in order of preference; and (5) making your decision. We will discuss each one of these steps in more detail.

   The purpose of predicting possible outcomes is to try and determine in advance what will happen if you choose a given alternative solution. For example, if your problem is "How to end the arguments I am having with my spouse," one alternative might be to seek a divorce. In looking at this alternative, I can see that there might be several different outcomes: My spouse may or may not contest the divorce, the divorce may or may not improve the quality of my life. In predicting the outcome of an alternative, we should try to think of all possible outcomes.

2.   Conduct exercise on predicting possible outcomes.

   Setting up.   Arrange participants in a large group.

   Procedure.   Give the group a problem solution. As a group they should come up with at least four possible alternative outcomes to this solution. (Emphasize both positive and negative outcomes.)

   Sample Problem Solutions.   Problem: "How to improve your job situation."

   Solution 1:   You quit your job.
   Solution 2:   You look for a new job while staying in the old one.
   Solution 3:   You talk to your boss.
   Solution 4:   Leave things as they are.

3.   Lecture on determining the likelihood of each outcome.

   SAMPLE LECTURE: In the next substep, determining the likelihood of each outcome, we are trying to determine whether or not the possible outcomes you have identified will actually occur. For example, using the divorce alternative example we just discussed, I may decide that it is not very likely that my spouse will grant me the divorce without contesting it. Therefore, I would consider the outcome that my wife would allow the divorce to proceed without protest is highly unlikely. This process of determining the likelihood of each outcome should be carried out for each outcome you have listed.

4. Conduct exercise on determining the likelihood of each outcome.

Setting up.   Participants should remain in the large group.

Procedure.   Using the outcomes they generated for the last exercise, the group should look at these outcomes and assign a "0" to those outcomes that are unlikely, a "1" to those solutions that are somewhat likely, and a "2" to those that are very likely. Have each small group share their ratings with the large group.

5. Lecture on Substep #3: Desirability.

SAMPLE LECTURE: Substep #3 calls for us to consider the desirability of the outcomes you have listed. In other words, how do you like or dislike the way things would turn out if you choose a given alternative. In problem-solving language, this could be called examining the "pros" and "cons" of that outcome. Using our divorce example again, I must decide whether or not a court hearing would be desirable. Therefore, I must think about the effect it would have on me, my spouse, my children, etc. All possible outcomes should be examined in this way. In looking at the desirability of each of your outcomes you should ask yourself these questions:
  a. What are the "pros" of this solution? (How does it make me feel good?)
  b. What are the "cons" of this solution? (How does it make me feel bad?)
  c. Does this solution create new problems or new advantages? If so, can the problems be corrected and the advantages used?

6. Conduct desirability exercise.

Setting up.   Have participants remain in a large group.

Procedure.   The group should again look at the outcomes they have listed and discuss their desirability—how much they like or dislike it. They should assign a "+" to those outcomes they like, a "0" to those that are indifferent and a "−" to those that they dislike (undesirable). Have each small group discuss their ratings with the large group.

7. Lecture on ranking outcomes.

SAMPLE LECTURE: Once you have completed the process of determining desirability you are ready to go on to substep #4 of alternatives evaluation. This step calls for ranking the alternatives in order of preference. This step is very much like the prioritizing substep you learned in problem recognition. In ranking our alternatives we should consider all the previous substeps, all possible outcomes, their likelihood or probability, and their desirability. Once you have ranked your alternative solutions you are ready to make your decision.

8. Conduct ranking exercise.

Setting up. Large group.

Procedure. Have group add up the score for their alternative solution by adding those numbers with a plus, subtracting those with a minus, and cancelling those with a zero.

EXAMPLE PROBLEM: How to stop arguing with spouse.

Solution 1: Divorce her

		Probability	desirability
Outcomes:	a. wife will contest the divorce	2	−
	b. wife will accept the divorce	0	+
	c. my situation will improve	2	+
	d. my children will suffer	2	−
	Score	−2	

The large group should prioritize alternatives based on scores (highest score = highest rank).

9. Lecture on decision.

SAMPLE LECTURE: The final step of the evaluation process and the entire problem-solving model is decision. Our decision at this point will determine the consequences (what will happen to us). Although decisions can be reversed or modified, careful selection of the best alternative solution will reduce the need for later changes. In making your decision you should consider several criteria: (1) compare the rankings you have given different alternatives, (2) choose a solution that is in keeping with your own personal values, (3) choose a practical solution with a high probability for success, and (4) choose a solution that will let you move gradually and systematically towards your goal.

10. Concluding lecture.

SAMPLE LECTURE: Although the problem-solving process presented in these sessions is structured, it is not absolute. In other words, it allows you the freedom to use the model in a way that will suit your needs and encourages you to be creative in choosing a course of action. It is designed to provide you with a source of information so that you will have more questions to choose from when making a decision. Thus, it is like being given a tool box, full of tools, with instructions on how and when to use each tool. Whether or not you use these tools skillfully is up to you. Also, the problem-solving model is dynamic or continuous. The skills you learn can be used continually to find solutions. Making an error or mistake is a temporary situation, re-evaluation is always possible. That is why there is an arrow from the alternatives evaluation and decision step back to alternatives generation (point to flow chart). This is to suggest that if something goes wrong during this step (e.g., you are not content with the possible outcomes or you can't live with your decision), you should go back a step and generate some more alternative solutions.

   If you make use of this problem-solving model in solving personal problems I think you will find you are more likely to succeed than if you used a less structured problem-solving method. In other words, you will probably increase your chances for finding a successful problem solution.

SESSION 4 SUPPLEMENT

Part 1: John's Story

John: Hi, I'm John and I'm in a real bind. I've got to make some pretty important decisions in the next few days and I'm just not sure what would be the best decision. You see, I have a wife, Nancy, and an 8-month-old little girl, Janey. We live here in town. We got a pretty good deal on a two bed-room house in a nice neighborhood here. My wife is happy that we've finally settled down and Janey will have a nice place to go to school and grow up in. I'm really glad my wife and little girl are happy now, but, *I'm* not so hap-py at this point in my life. I work as a clerk in a local department store here, and I really hate the job because there's no challenge to it. It's been getting me down pretty bad lately. I feel trapped and depressed a lot of the time. It's really gotten to the point now that I can't leave my problems at work. I stay depressed a lot at home. My wife doesn't seem to understand. She thinks I don't love her anymore because I don't laugh and smile and talk to her much. She even asked if I'm seeing someone on the side. I'm not. I'm not interested in anyone else. It's just that I can't seem to think about anything but my dead-end job. It's *so* boring, and the pay is bad too. My wife—she's an LPN nurse—she makes more money than me—I feel like *she* supports the family, like I'm not pulling my own weight and contributing my fair share to our family. I mean with all the medical bills we have right now I just feel like I really have to make more money. I think maybe I could even adjust to the small amount of money I make. It's just that this job is so unchallenging. Sometimes I get so bored I feel like I'm going to do something crazy. I think I'm pretty smart really, and I just feel like I'm wasting my intelligence and talents on this mindless job. Anyway, things were really getting pretty bad, so I went to talk with my boss to ask about a promotion, just as I've done many other times before. This is what happened. . . .

SCENE I

(John enters room where his boss is sitting at a desk)

John: Mr. Logan, I wanted to speak to you again about a promotion. As I've told you before I've been working here for three years—longer than the majority of workers here. I feel that I know the business better than any-one else in my position, and feel that I deserve a raise and an opportunity for a more challenging managerial position.

Employer: John, we've been over this many times before. As I've told you, I'd like to promote you. I realize you are a hard worker and that you know the business, but I just can't afford to give any raises or promotions at this time.

John: Well, Mr. Logan, if that's the case how come you were able to give your son-in-law a salary raise? He's only been here three months!

Employer: Well, John (*clears throat*) that was an entirely different case. My son-in-law has had a little experience coming to this job. He had worked for me over his Christmas vacation from college. That's a whole different ball game.

John: Well, I now have *three* years of experience compared to the 4 weeks your son-in-law had.

Employer: John (*harsh voice*), like I said, I really want to promote you, but I just can't at this time. With so many people out of work you should be happy you have such a stable job.

(END OF SCENE)

John: Stable! "Stable" isn't the word! It's so stable I think I'm going out of my mind! Anyway, after that conversation with my boss I decided I was going to try and do something else about the problem. So I applied to a number of technical colleges in Computer Programming. I always liked math and machines in high school and I really wanted to go into a computer program. But as it turned out I got married instead and Janey was born shortly after, so I've had to put school aside for awhile. Now that Janey is old enough to have a babysitter I thought that this was a good time for me to get back into things. About a week ago I got a letter in the mail from the best technical school that I applied to. Here's what happened when I told my wife. . . .

SCENE 2

(John enters room opening letter and reading it.)

John: Honey, I've been accepted in Computer Programming at Hale Technical College! They've even given me a scholarship that will pay for my tuition, books and housing! I can't believe it! Hey, look here—they've also offered me a part time job as an assistant coach. I'll be able to send money home for you and Janey! This is like a dream come true!

Wife: You want to go away to school? What's wrong with our local technical school?

John: They don't have the program I want, honey, and besides I got a scholarship from this school.

Wife: But if you go there you'll be gone for weeks at a time—I'll only see you once or twice a month, John—I mean, what's going to happen to our marriage? As it is now you hardly talk to me.

John: But, honey, It's just that I've been so depressed about work. You like your job, so it's hard for you to understand how down a person can feel when he has such a lousy job.

Wife: What about Janey? Who's going to take care of her on the nights I have nursing class? I've got to go to class or I'll lose my nursing license! I shouldn't have to bear total responsibility for Janey—she's your child, too!

John: My mom and dad have told us repeatedly that they would be glad to help us out, babysitting or even lending us money. They love Janey, they'd be glad to babysit on those nights you have class.

Wife: And another thing. We've been planning our cross-country trip for so long. If you go back to school, there's no way we can buy that camper van, let alone take a long trip. It's just not fair to me or Janey!

(END OF SCENE 2)

John: My wife's last remark about our daughter Janey is what really made me stop and think. You see, our infant daughter has a lot of serious allergies, and we've been having a lot of testing and evaluation done on her to find out exactly what the problem is and what can be done about it. Because Janey is so young and has a lot of trouble breathing, with all these allergies she can't really be left alone or with someone inexperienced. My parents are all for me going back to school, and said that they would be glad to help Nancy and Janey out financially as well as by babysitting. Nancy doesn't like to ask for such favors from my parents. I wonder if I would be a real heel to leave my family now?

I had just about made up my mind *not* to go to school until my friend Steve dropped by the house. Steve and I have been close friends for years. Steve has been going to school at Hale Technical College for a year now. Actually he's the one who got me all the information in order to apply to Hale Tech, and he checked into the part-time assistant coaching job for me.

SCENE 3

Steve: Hey John, long time no see!

John: How are you doing, Steve?

Steve: Oh, I'm just home on Easter break. Good to see the wife and kids. Seems like my being away for so long makes us appreciate each other more when we are together. Anyway, John, what do you think? Are you going to be my roommate at Hale Tech this fall? I mean, you did get the scholarship and all, right?

John: Yes, it all looks really appealing Steve, but I just don't know. You know I have responsibilities here—to my wife and Janey.

Steve: So do I, John, and I take them seriously, but I feel that after I get this training I'll be able to finally have an interesting job and be able to take care of my family the way I'd like to. They really deserve the best. John, they've got a great placement service at school—95 percent of last year's graduating class were able to find jobs! I call that pretty promising.

John: Yes, that does sound really good, Steve.

Steve: John, this school is really first-rate. Good teachers—they know their stuff. The facilities and equipment are new, and even the classes are small, so you get a lot of one-to-one attention.

John: Gee, Steve, I just don't know. . . .

(END OF SCENE 3)

John: Well, this gives you an idea of what the problems are that I'm facing now. Maybe you can help me problem-solve and come to some solution to my present problem.

Part 2: John's Story

NAME_____   DATE_____

1. In *one* statement, state John's problem. (Be as specific as possible.)

2. What are the basic elements or factors involved in this problem?

3. What are the factors to John's *disadvantage* in solving the problem? (What blocks, obstacles are preventing him from solving the problem?)

4. What are the factors to John's *advantage* in solving the problem? (What are his resources and supporting or helpful factors?)

5. *List* possible ways to solve John's problems.

6. *Rank* the possible alternative solutions you have listed. (Mark #1 to the left of your *most* desirable and practical solution. Mark #2 to the left of your second most desirable and practical solution, and so on.)

7. Look at the solutions you ranked as #1 and #2. List your reasons for choosing each of these.

Part 3: Problem-Solving Model

PROBLEM RECOGNITION

1. Acknowledge the Problem
2. Identify the Problem
3. Accept the Problem as Your Own Responsibility
4. Establish Priorities for Choosing Problems for your Attention

PROBLEM DEFINITION

1. Break the Problem Down Into Workable Units
2. State the Problem in Such a Way That It Appears Solvable (This should be in the form of a goal-directed "How to . . ." statement.)

ALTERNATIVES GENERATION

1. Brainstorming
2. Change Your Frame of Reference
3. Adapt a Solution from a Similar Problem
4. Make Up An Idea Checklist
5. Problem Diagram

DECISION

1. Evaluate Alternative Solutions
2. Decision

Part 4: Problem Recognition Exercise

IDENTIFY THE PROBLEM AREAS IN THE
FOLLOWING SITUATION:

Evelyn has been having a great deal of difficulty over the last year. She has been trying to identify the problem areas in her life so that she can begin to iron them out and return to a more trouble-free existence. She has asked us to accompany her as she goes about her business on a typical day, and would like us to watch for problem areas we see so that we can discuss them with her.

Well, things seem to start off all wrong. Evelyn oversleeps when her alarm clock goes off at 6:30 a.m. Although she has a very important interview this morning, she stayed up until 3:00 a.m. having, as she puts it, a few drinks. When the alarm went off, she felt her throbbing head and queasy stomach, and just rolled over and went back to sleep. She finally wakes up at 8:30 a.m. She has a half hour to get to her appointment, and she has quite a distance to travel. She rolls out of bed, grumbling that her husband should have awakened her. She thinks to herself, "He never thinks about my needs." Her husband, George, had left for work at 6:15 a.m. as usual. He actually could wait until 6:45 a.m. to leave and still get to work on time, but he likes to get out of the house before Evelyn wakes up.

Evelyn dresses quickly, mumbling to herself, "Now, where did I leave my purse." She looks in several of her usual spots, but can't find it. After looking for five minutes, she finds it under the couch, where she had absentmindedly thrown it the night before. She then finds that her keys are missing. She, of course, blames those "damn kids" for taking her car without asking her. She then notices the keys under a pile of her stockings, where she had dropped them last night on the family-room floor. She runs out of the house, forgetting to lock the door, jumps in her car, and races off to her interview. She arrives 10 minutes late, looking like she just rolled out of bed, which of course we know she had. Her boss, standing at the door when she arrives, says, "another late night, eh?" Evelyn responds sarcastically, "I suppose you're never late for work." He responds, "Not on mornings when I'm meeting with important clients." He notes the time, her appearance, and her sarcasm, and says, "You know, your behavior is beginning to get out of hand." "Well, if you didn't dump so much work on me, I wouldn't be so worn out," she says. He realizes that she's just making excuses. Actually he has been assigning less and less work to her lately. Evelyn goes on into her office, mumbling angrily to the clerk to get her the damn file for this interview. The clerk, annoyed with Evelyn as usual, reminds her that the file is on her desk.

Evelyn's client has now been waiting 15 minutes, and she proceeds to blame her tardiness on her husband and those monsters of hers who are always taking advantage of her. Evelyn then proceeds to give her presentation for the client, who remains unimpressed. When Evelyn realizes that she has not persuaded the client to buy her company's product, she invites him out to lunch to try to make one last sales pitch.

At lunch, Evelyn has her usual four martinis, while her client has one. She begins to slur her words, and then goes on to talk about how she can't get her husband or kids to help her with any of the work at home. Her client tires of listening to her story, makes up an excuse, and leaves. Evelyn thinks about what a rough day it's been and decides to go home early. When she arrives home at 2:00 p.m., she decides to take a short nap.

As usual, when George and the kids get home at 5:00 p.m., they find Evelyn sound asleep in bed. They all pitch in, clean up the empty glasses and piles of clothes lying around, and cook dinner. When they wake Evelyn, she, of course, doesn't feel like eating and goes back to sleep. At 10:00 p.m. that night she wakes up and can't sleep any more. She sits up and wonders "Why didn't George or those damn kids wake me up earlier."

Part 5: Responsibility Accepting Exercise

Which of the following statements shows that the person making the statement is accepting personal responsibility:

1. I can't change; that's just my personality.
2. My parents made me this way.
3. I have been holding all my feelings in and that has gotten me depressed.
4. People are always taking advantage of me.
5. I don't stand up for my rights often enough.
6. My wife makes my life impossible.
7. I have not been paying attention to my wife's feelings, and she has been very angry with me.

8. My boss is too busy to appreciate my work.
9. I have not been trying my best lately, and my work is beginning to show it.
10. My medication is making me sleep all the time.
11. I have not informed my doctor of the side effects my medicine is having.
12. My roommate has no consideration for my feelings, she should know that I can't sleep with the radio on.
13. I need to let my roommate know that her radio is bothering me.
14. That teacher graded my paper unfairly, she's trying to flunk me.
15. I didn't study very hard for that test; I'll have to try harder next time.

Part 6: "How to" Problem List

1. I have so little time. I work every day 8 to 4:30, and then there's so much to do around the house when I get home. And I always like to go out on a date after I get all that stuff done. I just can't stand to sit at home. There's this friend of mine that's leaving. We need to get together for one last time and say our goodbyes. I feel weird about that. That's gonna be no fun.
2. My salary is too low. That paycheck hardly goes anywhere. All those bills of mine have to be paid every time I get my paycheck, and then there's hardly any money left for me to buy groceries or any of the other things I need to buy. Like toilet paper, you know. My budget is just too limiting. And all those old bills won't be paid until the 24th. It's so hard for me to live like this until that day.
3. All my clothes are dirty so I can't go out tonight. Damn, I really want to go out too. Why in the world do my clothes get dirty so fast? I know what it is, I just don't have enough clothes. But I can't afford to buy any more now. When was the last time I washed clothes? Oh Lord, I think it's been three weeks.
4. My mother hasn't written me in a month. Oh, well, her letters only talk about the weather and the cat and the dog anyway.
5. My friend will hardly talk to me on the phone. She seems to always be busy with something. I wish I could catch her when she could talk more. I'm ready to quit trying.
6. I feel depressed. My best friend is leaving town next week. I want to have a going away party, but feel like its too sad an event to celebrate.
7. I've scheduled a conference with my child's teacher and made plans to meet a friend for lunch. I hate dealing with confusion and conflicts.
8. My brother has asked me to work a shift in his store because he wanted to go to the dog races. I don't approve of betting.
9. My spouse wants a vacation this year. I am afraid I may be laid off and don't know what to say.

10. Friends called to cancel, they can't come over for dinner. This is the third time this has happened. I'm lonely.
11. I've been hospitalized for my nerves. My neighbor, noticing I am never home, starts asking me how I can allow my home to look so unkept.
12. My job is boring. I want to earn more so my children can do some things I never could.
13. I feel so dumb. I just started this basic math class, and everyone else can do the problems faster than I can.
14. My job interview is in 15 minutes. I'm so nervous. What if they ask me about the time I spent in the hospital? Maybe I should ask a friend to go with me.
15. My spouse always yells. It drives me crazy. Why don't I just leave? I've never worked before.

Part 7: Handout on Forming "How to . . ." Statements

1. The goal should be stated in positive terms rather than negative, so that the problem will appear soluble rather than impossible (e.g., "How to budget my money" is better than "How to keep from being broke all the time").
2. The statement should name a specific goal rather than a general vague idea (e.g., "How to stop arguing with my wife" is better than "How to improve relations with my wife." "Arguing" is a fairly specific behavior, whereas "relations" is a very vague general concept).
3. The statement should deal with tangible unmet wants, needs, or goals rather than intangible ideas or processes. The following are examples of poor "how to" statements:
    "How to decide whether to _____ or _____."
    "How to figure out what I want."
    "How to deal with ————-."
   The following are examples of good "how to" statements:
    "How to earn the respect of my children."
    "How to cut down on my drinking."
    "How to find a job."
    "How to meet new people."

Part 8: Problem Break-down Question List

YES OR NO
1. Are there family members involved in this problem?
2. Are there friends involved in this problem?
3. Are there positive feelings involved in this problem?

4. Are there negative feelings involved in this problem?
5. Is money involved in this problem (earning it, budgeting it, lending it, borrowing it, etc.)?
6. Is time involved in this problem?
7. Is scheduling time involved in this problem?
8. Is there only one main element involved in this problem?
9. Is this a new problem?
10. Has this problem been brewing for some time?
11. Is your confidence or your pride involved in this problem?
12. Is there an intimate or romantic relationship involved in this problem?
13. Is your work involved in this problem (past, present or future)?
14. Is your age a part of this problem?
15. Are hurt feelings (yours or someone else's) a part of this problem?
16. Is transportation involved in this problem?
17. Is discipline (self or others) involved in this problem?

Part 9: "Problem Diagram"

It is Friday and you have just completed your ninth week at EIP. Your parents are willing to lend you $200 to get you started in your new life. However, they will give you this money only if you can find an apartment and set yourself up on your own. You already own a car, which is also at your parents' house, and you will begin a new job on Monday. There are several things you must do between now and Monday when you start work. Here are some of the things you must do:

1. establish a checking account at the bank
2. go visit your parents and pick up the money and your car
3. arrange for transportation
4. find an apartment and pay the deposit and first month's rent
5. figure out a budget for the $200 so that it will last you until your first pay check at the end of next week
6. buy food
7. move into your apartment
8. arrange for electricity to be turned on

Using the chart below, draw in the route you choose to follow in taking care of this situation. Keep in mind the importance of the sequence (order) of the steps as you draw your route (for example, you cannot establish a checking account without money). Arrows can be used to show direction of movement from step to step.

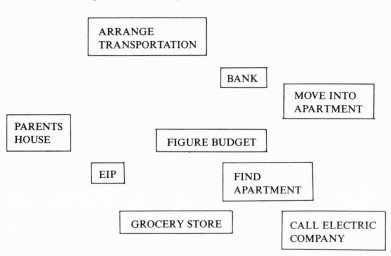

REFERENCES

1. D'Zurilla TJ, Goldfried MR: Problem-solving and behavior modification. J Abnorm Psychology 78:107–126, 1971
2. Osborn AF: Applied Imagination: Principles and Procedures of Creative Problem-Solving (3rd ed). New York, Scribners, 1963
3. Mahoney MJ: Cognition and Behavior Modification. Cambridge, Mass., Ballinger Publishing Co., 1974
4. Manis M: Introduction to Cognitive Psychology. Belmont, Ca., Wadsworth Publishing Co., 1971
5. Davis GA: Psychology of Problem Solving, Theory and Practice. New York, Basic Books, 1973

Margaret Malchon

Appendix 2
Techniques of Intervention
Laboratory Description

Students in the Techniques of Intervention course will be asked to lead an eight-week group of four to eight individuals in weekly meetings dealing with communication skills, problem-solving skills, remotivation, or reality orientation. In order to supervise this laboratory experience, students will be asked to meet one hour a week in groups of three with a group consultant to discuss their group experiences and receive suggestions and criticism from their consultant and peers. Such meetings should help the students improve interpersonal skills; evaluate their own performance in the laboratory task; familiarize themselves with the approaches, problems, and successes of two other students; and offer themselves the chance to discuss problems and necessary changes in group strategies or personal approaches.

Training Objectives

Consultants will be asked to rate the students on a seven point scale (from poor to excellent) on the degree to which they have demonstrated the following skills:

1. Assumes *responsibility* for the routine functioning of the group.
2. Displays *insight* into the group processes and the individual group members' contributions to these processes.

Portions of this section were previously published in Malchon M: Techniques of intervention: Module number 4 (Tampa, Fla., Human Resources Institute, University of South Florida, 1978), and are reprinted with permission.

3. Demonstrates ability to *learn from client/patient contact,* e.g., which methods work and which do not.
4. Demonstrates *creativity* and the ability to modify situations as needed.
5. Displays *motivation* and a desire to learn.
6. Displays *dependability* both as a group leader and as a consultee.
7. Is *open and honest* with the consultant about both problems and successes in the group.
8. Takes constructive *criticism* well.
9. Attends consultation sessions regularly and is punctual.
10. Demonstrates ability to implement the *consultant groups' recommendations.*
11. Consultants' *overall rating* of the students' performance in the practicum assignment.

The Consulting Hour

Before implementation of the group plan, approval will be obtained from the appropriate personnel. The behavioral objectives selected by the student and the appropriateness of the procedures specified to meet these objectives should be of particular concern to the consultant. The consultant should question and comment freely on the plan, pointing out any roadblocks or problems that would hinder the student's efforts.

During the weekly consultations after the groups have been started, the consultant will want to discuss the procedure carried out in the group and its effectiveness. Among the issues that might be discussed are the following: How did the group members respond? Did some participate more readily than others and, if so, what was done or what could be done to bring out the reticent members? Were there any practical problems that need to be resolved before the next meeting, such as getting the patients to the meeting, or the time or place of the meeting? How does the student feel about his performance? Are there any needs for change in the group plan before the next meeting? How did his relationships with the group members differ from his daily interactions with them on an individual basis?

One potential pitfall in the consultation process is the student's anxiety or ambivalence about being evaluated. These feelings might be manifested by the student missing or coming late to consultation appointments, presenting examples of good work only and avoiding discussion of anything that would suggest a need for assistance, or relying too heavily on the consultant for suggestions rather than coming up with his own. In working with this ambivalence the following set of principles and strategies may be helpful:

1. Work hard to get mutual training objectives concretely defined early in the relationship.
2. Listen a lot, as empathically as possible (especially in the early stages of

supervision), with two specific aims: (1) to communicate respect and understanding of the student's feelings and real skills, and (2) to understand the student's particular style in dealing with ambivalence of supervision, if it exists.

3. Give as much positive reinforcement as possible through genuine approval and praise of skills and competencies demonstrated.

4. Do everything possible to help the student have, as much as possible, many successful work experiences; this provides the student a "savings account" of competence, and facilitates facing the problems that come with every job experience.

5. Continuously expect the student to do the best that he or she can within the limits of the laboratory experience; and respectfully point out when this is not the case.

6. Approach the students' mistakes, feelings of inadequacy, and failures to perform as expected as a natural happening and with an expectancy that discussing them will lead to new feelings of competence. It is helpful to share with the students the notion that mistakes are necessary but not sufficient for growth in any experience.

7. Try to be available to students for those extra times when they need support.

8. Whenever the process reaches an impasse, call in a colleague to help as an unbiased third party.

The course instructor will keep in contact with the consultants during the eight weeks of the laboratory experience.

LABORATORY EXPERIENCE RATING SHEET

(To Be Completed by Group Consultant). Please rate the student you have been consulting with on the following items. Going over your ratings with the student during your last consultation sessions will make the ratings a learning experience. Have the student return the rating sheet to the instructor.

		poor						excellent
1.	Assumes *responsibility* for the routine functioning of the group.	1	2	3	4	5	6	7
2.	Displays *insight* into group processes and the individual group members' contributions to these processes.	1	2	3	4	5	6	7
3.	Demonstrates ability to *learn from patient/client contact,* e.g., which methods work and which do not.	1	2	3	4	5	6	7
4.	Demonstrates *creativity* and the ability to modify situations as needed.	1	2	3	4	5	6	7

5. Displays *motivation* and a desire to learn.   1 2 3 4 5 6 7

6. Displays *dependability* both as a group leader and as a consultee.   1 2 3 4 5 6 7

7. Is *open and honest* with the consultant about both problems and successes in the group.   1 2 3 4 5 6 7

8. Takes constructive *criticism* well.   1 2 3 4 5 6 7

9. Demonstrates ability to implement the *consultant group's recommendations.*   1 2 3 4 5 6 7

10. Attended regularly and was punctual at consultation sessions.   1 2 3 4 5 6 7

11. Consultant's overall rating of the student's performance in the laboratory experience assignment.   1 2 3 4 5 6 7

Comments:

L. Adlai Boyd
Richard E. Gordon

Appendix 3
Glossary and Descriptions of Terms

The following list describes and explains basic principles and procedures used to help patients learn and practice appropriate behaviors, even as they learn not to behave in inappropriate, disruptive, hyperactive, noncompliant, and otherwise handicapping, abnormal ways.

Accidental Punishment and Extinction: Just as "accidental" consequences to behavior can be reinforcing, they can also be nonreinforcing or punishing. If Sally, who is withdrawn, ventures out to join an activity spontaneously, and Billy kicks her, she may withdraw even more. Or, if staff happen to be busy, and Henry successfully shares a toy for the first time, and no one notices, accidental extinction of sharing may occur. A planned, "living" environment is necessary to overcome the results of some accidental consequences, because they will always occur, like it or not.

Accidental Reinforcement: An unplanned reinforcement of a behavior that often results in "superstitious behavior" or in the maintenance of undesired behavior.

Antecedent: Environmental event(s) that occur(s) immediately before a behavior.

Assertive Training: A technique whereby clients are taught to assert themselves in an appropriate manner. This is used with those clients who are either withdrawn or aggressive prior to training.

355

Backward Chaining: A process of teaching a complex task by dividing the task into several behaviors that can be chained together. The last behavior in the chain is taught first, followed by the second to the last, etc.

Baseline: An objective record of behavior in measurable terms prior to the implementation of treatment.

Behavior: The specific, measurable, observable acts of an individual.

Behavior Management: The systematic application of learning principles to change behavior.

Chaining: A sequence of behaviors in which one behavior produces the necessary stimulus conditions for the next behavior.

Combinations: Patients need to assimilate new experiences and accommodate themselves to the realities of life. Heavy reinforcement of appropriate behavior, whether spontaneous or prompted, combined with a smattering of negative feedback (e.g., time out) simulate the natural world. Emphasis, of course, is on the positive, but patients must learn through negative consequences as well. Planned reinforcement usually occurs at about a 5:1 ratio of positive to negative consequences.

Consequence: Environmental event(s) that immediately follow(s) a behavior.

Contingency Contracting: A contingency is the relationship between an "if" event and a "then" event, but both must occur, otherwise the patient is not reinforced. "If you take the garbage out, I will give you a cupcake" is an example of a contingency contract.

Correcting: Simple feedback that a behavior is incorrect, along with the correct response, is often all that is necessary to teach the correct response. Staff will say, "No, Johnny, the truck goes in the other cabinet" or "Put your shoe on the other foot." When and if these cues do produce the correct response, positive reinforcement of the correct response should follow on some kind of systematic schedule.

Disapproving—Verbal or Facial: A very mild kind of negative feedback that a behavior is inappropriate or incorrect (a small grimace or a simple statement such as "Mary, do not throw your food on the floor" after she has done so) provides correction, plus mild disapproval. (Always reinforce Mary later, when she is not throwing food.) Stern negative feedback (i.e., "Mary, no pushing!") is used only to interrupt dangerous behavior. Negative attention to behaviors is often a reinforcer, maintaining or increasing the very behavior that the staff tries to stop.

Exclusion Time-out: A procedure in which a client is immediately and temporarily removed from an activity contingent on the occurrence of specified inappropriate behavior. The client is removed from view of the other clients to a bland environment for a brief time.

Extinction: A procedure using time-out from positive reinforcement in which the reinforcer maintaining a behavior is withheld. This results in a decrease in the occurrence of that behavior. If the consequence that has been reinforcing an undesirable behavior (e.g., tantrums) has been adult attention or "giving in" to that behavior, avoid giving attention or giving in. If the reinforcer is disallowed, the behavior will decrease, especially if that behavior has been regularly reinforced in the past. Not all behaviors can be extinguished, since some consequences cannot be identified or controlled. For example, if the reinforcer for hitting is seeing and hearing another child cry, ignoring it will do no good at all, because attention is not the reinforcer. Therefore, other, more direct means of decreasing some behaviors are used in these cases.

Generalization of Behaviors to Other Places and People: New improved behaviors learned in an institution (or decreased inappropriate, handicapping behaviors) do not automatically occur elsewhere, such as in the community and with the family. The desired behaviors must be systematically transferred (generalized) to the home and community. This process may be difficult, especially if whatever may have been reinforcing inappropriate behaviors is still present "out there." Further, new behaviors learned in the institution may not be maintained (reinforced adequately) at home or elsewhere. Antecedents (cues) may be specific to the therapeutic or training environment (a staff person, for example), and not to the real world. For instance, many children learn to stop throwing tantrums in the classroom very shortly after being admitted, but continue at home and elsewhere.

Because there is no automatic generalization of behaviors, it is necessary that programs of prevention and remediation ensure that cues, procedures, consequences, etc., begin with clients while they are in therapy or training, and continue after they are discharged. A way of accomplishing this is to ensure that the parents and other family themselves consistently use successful procedures and principles. The following activities assist generalization of treatment gains to other environments.

1. *Observation:* Family members and others watch and hear the patients in the modular classroom environment and notice the differences between behavior there and elsewhere. Observations usually convince them that the "problem" is not solely in the patients (because they see them behave

correctly and enjoy themselves in the process). Typically, they will say,
"It's not him—it's me!" Then families are strongly motivated to learn behavioral management techniques.
2. *Classes for families:* Families participate in training sessions to learn principles, procedures, and basic language. They learn material contained in
this description, as well as other information important to the implementation, as well as the cognitive understanding, of the behavioral approach
to remediation and prevention of problems. Taking a problem-solving approach, families are soon offering suggestions to each other, as well as
verbally trying out new ideas and ways themselves.
3. *Home visits:* Therapists make home and community visits with the families and clients, doubly ensuring generalization or behavioral gains by
helping apply behavioral procedures more and more consistently and naturally there.

Graduated Guidance: Physical guidance is provided, often an initial
cue, in order to assist the client manually to perform the target behavior. The
least amount of physical prompting necessary is used. Prompting is reduced
as the client begins to exhibit the movement voluntarily. If the desired behavior slows down or stops, the least amount of prompting should be used to restore the behavior at the desired rate.

Intensive Training Program: A training program in excess of one hour
per day in which a client is intensively involved in learning a new behavior
(e.g., a 90-minute daily session on communication).[1]

Matrix Management: In a matrix organization staff report to two lines
of command. As used in the programs described here, the psychoeducational
hierarchy supervised the behavioral, skills-building and peer management
components of treatment, and the medical-nursing leadership controlled the
medical and medicolegal aspects. Bridge persons coordinated the treatment,
research, and training services on each unit.

Modeling: A technique designed to assist a client in developing a new
behavior by reinforcing the client for imitating the appropriate behavior as
demonstrated by a model.

Module: A psychoeducational module is a systematically written, self-
contained unit of treatment that has an integrated theme, provides staff and
patients with information needed to acquire specified knowledge and skills,
and serves as one component of a total therapy program.

Positive Reinforcement: An increase in the occurrence of a behavior as
a result of presenting a pleasurable event or object to the person immediately

following the behavior. Catching a patient doing something useful and rewarding him for it will generally increase the likelihood that the action will be repeated. Nagging or fussing over any unwanted behaviors unfortunately runs a high risk of increasing those very behaviors.

1. *Primary reinforcement:* This involves using food or drink, almost always in tiny amounts, right after a correct, appropriate, or successful behavior occurs. Verbal praise always accompanies this kind of reward so that the praise in association with the food or drink takes on more and more of their rewarding characteristics. It helps to use very small, easily given, and quickly consumed portions (e.g., half a peanut); establish new behaviors by using the primary reinforcer each time the new behavior occurs, until it occurs rather often; use reinforcers less and less often, and unpredictably to maintain new behaviors; use rewards at the end of an activity, or after a long or complex task, or for a long period of good behavior; use them, otherwise, as seldom as possible; and vary the kinds and types of rewards to avoid their losing reinforcing power.

2. *Secondary reinforcement:* This involves using verbal praise, toys, hugs, pats, smiles, activities, tokens—the list of rewards for appropriate behavior is endless. These reinforcers have to be learned. Again, it is best to vary these reinforcers; to use those which are easily and quickly delivered; always to use descriptive praise when giving any of these rewards; to try to "thin out" these rewards by using them less and less often for well-established behaviors; to create new secondary reinforcers by using them at the same time as already proven primary or secondary ones; and not to assume that what works for one person will work for others.

Positive Reinforcement of Other or Incompatible Behaviors: This is one of the most effective positive approaches available for eliminating undesirable or handicapping behaviors. It calls for identifying several behaviors that cannot occur at the same time as an inappropriate behavior. Then, heavily reinforce the patient when his behaviors are appropriate, usually ignoring him when the behaviors are inappropriate. For example, if Mary constantly screams, we "catch her being good" by reinforcing her heavily when she is talking normally: "Oh, Mary, I really like the way you are talking so quietly. I can hear you perfectly!"

Premack Principle ("Grandma's Law"): If one activity occurs more frequently than another, it can be used as an effective reinforcer for the frequently occurring behavior. In other words, the client is persuaded to engage in a typically high frequency activity only after completing the less frequently occurring behavior (e.g. riding a bike only after cleaning one's room). Undesirable behaviors (like running around the room) may be used to reinforce and shape desirable ones (like sitting quietly in a chair). Other reinforcers, used with smaller and smaller amounts of the undesirable reinforcer, can eventually get rid of the unwanted behavior altogether.

Prompting and Fading: Prompting is a procedure whereby a client is assisted in either initiating or completing a behavior. There are various kinds of prompts:

1. *Verbal:* Asking the client to complete the behavior or giving instructions.
2. *Modeling:* Showing the client what to do by demonstrating.
3. *Gesturing:* Pointing or using other gestures to indicate the next step in a behavior.
4. *Occasional physical guidance:* Guiding the client through all aspects of the behavior. To get Janie to clap her hands with the others, say, "Clap your hands, Janie," and actually put her through the claps by holding her hands and clapping them together. Follow by abundant praise. Fade out the prompts by requiring more and more effort by Janie before reinforcing. In this manner, Janie will soon be clapping her hands all by herself on cue.

Psychoeducational Treatment Psychoeducational treatment uses psychobehavioral and educational methods to teach patients personal and social skills. It combines structured educational curricula with lesson plans, didactic teaching, and exercises to facilitate the gaining and application of knowledge about the skills to be learned, and employs psychobehavioral methods—modeling, role rehearsal, practice, and reinforcement—to train the skills. When the modular approach is used, psychoeducation becomes psychoeducational modular treatment and training.

Reinforced Practice: A teaching technique in which the number of opportunities to learn and practice a new behavior is increased to facilitate learning and performance. Density of reinforcement is increased.[1]

Response Cost: Removal of a positive reinforcer immediately following a previously defined inappropriate behavior (e.g., when a client kicks the TV set, the response cost is that the TV is turned off).

Response Generalization: Responding in a different but similar manner to the typical response to a training stimulus.

Seclusion Time-out: A time-out from positive reinforcement procedure in which a client is immediately and temporarily placed in a locked, seclusion time-out room contingent on aggressive and destructive behavior. The room must be free from obstacles, well-lighted, well-vented, and contain an observation window. The client is to be monitored at a minimum of every five minutes while in the seclusion time-out room.

Shaping ("Reinforcement of Successive Approximation"): Developing a new behavior not presently in the client's repertoire by reinforcing successive approximations of that target behavior. (The first behavior reinforced will only slightly resemble the target behavior; however, each succeeding reinforced approximation more closely resembles the target behavior until finally the target behavior occurs and is reinforced.)

Reinforcing the same level of a behavior consistently often does not result in learning or increasing that behavior. Shaping calls for raising the standards of performance and behavior by systematically attempting to get more and better behavior per reinforcer. For example, if Johnny sits down when told, but immediately gets up and runs around again, withhold his reinforcer until he sits for 30 seconds, and then, over time, for one minute, three minutes, five minutes, and so on. In this manner reinforce closer and still closer approximations of the ultimately desired response, while thinning his schedule of rewards for sitting when told to.

Stimulus Generalization: Responding in a similar manner to stimuli different but similar to the training stimulus.

Target Behavior: The established behavioral goal(s) expressed in specific, measurable and observable terms.

Thinning and Scheduling Reinforcement: Continuous reinforcement (attempts to reward a behavior each time it occurs) is used only when establishing a new or absent behavior. When the new behavior appears well established, "thin out" the schedule of reinforcement, rewarding less and less often and unpredictably. Finally, the new behavior is praised only about once a week or so, just to maintain it. If thinning goes too fast, go back to a richer, more frequent schedule of reinforcement. If thinning goes too slowly, the client does not grow, and remains dependent on the reinforcer. This is never the goal. Heavy reinforcing is used only to teach new skills and behaviors; the rich schedules of reinforcement are constantly reduced, and older, established behaviors are maintained with thin schedules.

Time-out from Positive Reinforcement: A category of procedures used to decrease the occurrence of inappropriate behavior. Such procedures as exclusion time-out, seclusion time-out, and contingent observation are placed in this category. The time-out area is a place with very few reinforcers in it (and ideally, none), where patients go for very brief periods of time (usually 30 to 120 seconds) when their behavior is not controllable by extinction or positive reinforcement of other or incompatible behaviors (such as refusals, hitting, throwing things, etc.). Overcome accidental or natural reinforcement of these behaviors immediately after they occur by placing the patient in the time-out area where there are few or no reinforcers. Time-out is a form of "signalled extinction," in that it immediately follows an inappropriate behavior with a short stay where there are few or no reinforcers. This procedure works better when the place they leave (e.g., the classroom) is chock full of reinforcers to which the patient wants to return. Otherwise, the patient may prefer the time-out room to the classroom, and behave in a manner calculated to get there.

Typically, a patient will refuse to do as told, or will use aggressive or other inappropriate behavior. Immediately take the patient by the hand, lead him to the time-out area with the words, softly spoken, "Sammy, you hit Mary. You need a rest." The patient may cry, protest, or promise better behavior as he is being placed in time-out. This is ignored, lest crying or "giving in" to verbal behavior be reinforced. After placing the patient in the room, record the occurrence (the name, behavior, time in, time out, etc.), and stay close by, unobtrusively observing the patient, to be sure there is no self-abuse (hitting or biting himself). When the patient is quiet, usually within one minute, the patient is returned to the activity, without scolding, nagging, or further comment. Shortly afterwards, but not immediately, "catch the patient being good" and reinforce his appropriate behavior.

Behaviors that do not call for time-out include (1) those for which the reinforcers are known and can be otherwise controlled by extinction, (2) withdrawn or fearful behaviors, (3) incorrect rather than inappropriate responses (i.e., honest wrong answers or responses to questions).

Families may question the effects time-out may have on a patient. For example, a common concern is that the patient may be traumatized by being in a small room and come to fear small enclosures (claustrophobia). This is highly unlikely because of the reinforcing aspect of the total program and the extremely small amount of time actually spent in the room. Research has revealed that time-out, when properly used, has virtually never caused nor made claustrophobia worse.

Token: A previously neutral object with no reinforcing value that becomes a secondary reinforcer when that object is exchanged for other reinforcers.

Token Program Response Cost: The removal of a token or prespecified number of tokens immediately following a previously defined inappropriate behavior.

REFERENCE

1. Jackson G: Behavior Management with the Elderly. Tampa, Fla., Gerontology Program, Florida Mental Health Institute, 1979

Subject Index